THE EVOLUTION OF

POLITICAL THOUGHT

Also by C. Northcote Parkinson

PARKINSON'S LAW
AND OTHER STUDIES IN ADMINISTRATION

The

Evolution of

Political Thought

by
C. Northcote Parkinson
RAFFLES PROFESSOR OF HISTORY
UNIVERSITY OF MALAYA

THE VIKING PRESS · NEW YORK

CONTENTS

6 CONTENTS

Part III
DEMOCRACY

Part IV
DICTATORSHIP

PREFACE

MOST universities offer courses of lectures in what is called the History of Political Thought. The nature of these courses is fairly reflected in the books compiled on this subject; books written or edited by the lecturers and recommended without hesitation to their pupils. While the titles catalogued are numerous and varied, the books themselves are not dissimilar in content. Fluttering the pages of any volume, chosen at random, the reader will not fail to glimpse successively the names of Plato, Aristotle, Dante, Machiavelli, Bacon, Hobbes, Locke, Bentham and Mill. On adjacent shelves he will find editions of the works from which the compiler has drawn— More's *Utopia*, Machiavelli's *Prince*, Bacon in person and Halifax himself. A study of these books, both texts and commentary, is held to constitute a sufficient grounding in political theory, useful to the student of history and of interest indeed to anyone.

While the value of these works (or, at any rate, of some of them) is beyond question, their general tendency is not without its dangers. The reader is left with fallacies as well as facts. These fallacies are neither stated nor upheld nor even perhaps deliberately implied. They arise indeed less from the study of any given work than, as a general impression, from all. They are none the less fallacious for that and their refutation is more than overdue.

First of these implicit fallacies is the idea that political thought is confined to authors and denied to everyone else. By this reasoning we must learn the ideas of Plato and Laski and can safely ignore those of Pericles and Churchill. This is surely to give an absurd weight to the accident of authorship. The idea expressed verbally or in action may be at least as novel and potent as the idea expressed with pen and ink. Closely connected with this fallacy is the idea that political theory has its origin in ancient Greece. The classically-educated historian has rarely thought it necessary to go either further back or further afield. He may have been misled by the derivation of the words in use; and yet the absurdity of this would seem obvious enough. To deny that there were politics before the Greeks invented the word is no more reasonable than to assume that the Greeks were uncivilised until the Romans had taught them Latin.

If it is wrong to conclude that all political theory began with Plato, it is at least equally wrong to suppose that all political thinking has been done in Europe and America. Of nearly every basic political

7

concept it is true to say that the Greeks had a word for it and often the word that is still in use. That is not to say, however, that there is no Chinese word with a similar meaning. Still less need we assume that the Chinese and Indians have had no ideas of their own. There are books purporting to summarise the history of political thought of which it can truly be said that they do nothing of the kind. Candid at least are the book titles in which 'Western' political thought is specified and more candid still those which define their even narrower scope 'From Bacon to Halifax'. But while there is reason to commend the honesty of those who profess to do no more than they have done, there is less to be said for their originality and courage. Too many have followed each other along the same well-trodden track. Too few have seen that a history of political thought must be world-wide if it is not to be fallacious.

Another impression which the reader may gain from reading the current books on political thought is that the development of political institutions has progressed steadily from the days of Lycurgus or Solon down to the present day; the ultimate achievement being British Parliamentary Democracy or else perhaps the American Way of Life. There are here two separate fallacies involved. The first lies in the assumption that all history illustrates a story of betterment or progress with ourselves as the final product. The second lies in the assumption that such progress as there has been is a western achievement in which no oriental can claim even the smallest share. History records no such monopoly and no such unbroken progression. What the historian does find, however, is a recurrence of the belief that perfection has been reached and that a given constitution (like that of the United States) represents finality. There is, in fact, no historical reason for supposing that our present systems of governance are other than quite temporary expedients. To demonstrate, therefore, that all progress leads upwards to these pinnacles of wisdom is peculiarly needless. In such an attempt one ignores half the work that has already been done and all the work that is still to do.

The belief that the present or else some other recommended constitution can represent finality is as old or older than Plato. It runs through many of the texts which the student is required to read. It forms even now the basis for heated discussions as to what form of rule is best. It is essentially pre-Darwinian, however, as a mode of thought. No believer in evolution would expect to find that sort of finality. He would rather regard society as a growing tree than as a building nearing its completion. He would hope to trace a pattern of growth and decay. He would question, on principle, whether any society could be static. He would see in finality nothing more nor less than death. In practice, however, it is easier for the student of to-day to appreciate how institutions have evolved than to grasp that their evolution must and should continue. Even when the likelihood of further development is recognised, it is usually seen as a perfecting of what exists; as the process, for example, by which representative democracy can be made more representative still. But history shows us no previous example of institutions thus perfected. It reveals rather a sequence in which one form of rule replaces another, each in turn achieving not perfection but decay. The fallacy of the Utopians is to suppose that finality can and should be attained. To the believer in evolution nothing could seem less probable.

One other error implied in the existing text-books is that the published works of political theorists have had a vast influence on actual events. The student is all too apt to visualise each leader as one likely to refer to a book before deciding upon a policy. But Robespierre no more slept with *Le Contrat Social* under his pillow than did Louis XVI refer to the *Leviathan*. No actual politician is greatly influenced by a book of political theory although many have been influenced by a book of religion. The politician who reads at all will have read not only the text which the historian thinks significant but forty-nine other forgotten works of which the historian has never even heard. And if one book appears to have been his favourite it will be because the author recommends what he, the ruler, has already decided to do; or what indeed he has already done. Historically, the book comes afterwards to defend the deed. This is not to say that the book is always *written* after the revolution it seems to justify. It may be written beforehand, gaining its wide circulation only after the event. The books, by contrast, which supported the losing cause have been forgotten, overlooked, destroyed—or else never published. There is thus a natural selection among books, giving to some the popularity and survival which rewards what is relevant to the mood of an age, and ensuring for others the oblivion reserved for all that seems eccentric and out of tune. In ancient China (as in modern China) the books out of accord with the party line were deliberately burnt. In England or America the books thus out of step will remain unpublished for lack of expected sales. It is not books which influence political events. It is the events which decide which book is to be pulped and which made compulsory reading in the schools.

The significance then of the political theorist is not that he guided the ruler but that he provided the ruler with a rational explanation of what he, the ruler, had already done. His works to that extent throw light upon the age in which he lived—or at any rate upon the age in which his works were widely read. But to interpret policy throughout the ages in terms of its literary justification is open to certain objections, of which the chief is that politics are far older than political theory. To begin the story where it is usually made to begin (in Athens of the 5th century B.C.) is to omit the essential background to all human affairs; the background studied by the anthropologist. It would be untrue to say that all authors on the history of political theory have ignored this background. It is with reference to it, however, that they prove least convincing. They are apt to perpetuate by quotation the mistakes made (perhaps unavoidably) by the earlier political thinkers. These philosophers were apt to picture a happy community of primitive men suddenly deciding to organise themselves and elect a ruler.

> 'I assume' writes Rousseau,[1] 'that men have reached a point at which the obstacles that endanger their preservation in the state of nature overcome by their resistance the forces which each individual can exert with a view to maintaining himself in that state. Then this primitive condition can no longer subsist, and the human race would perish unless it changed its mode of existence. . . .'
> [The problem is] 'To find a form of association which may defend and protect with the whole force of the community the person and property of every associate, and by means of which each, coalescing with all, may nevertheless obey only himself and remain as free as before'. [To this problem the Social Contract furnishes the solution.]
> 'The clauses of this contract are so determined . . . that, although they have never perhaps been formally enunciated, they are everywhere the same, everywhere tacitly admitted and recognised'.

There might be no great harm in reading this piece of eighteenth century rhetoric provided that the antidote were to follow. The student who is advised to read drivel should at least be warned that it is drivel he is being asked to read. Wild guesses about primitive man are needless, for primitive man has survived for our study. And even the slightest acquaintance with the aborigines of Australia, Malaya or Borneo will convince the student that no human beings have ever come together with an open mind to discuss the basis of their social organisation. Nor is there any reason to suppose that our primitive ancestors in Europe or indeed in ancient Britain were in this respect very different from the peoples whose culture has remained primitive. There has never been a clean page upon which to write a constitution. Man had, from the start, physical, biological and mental characteristics; and many of these he still retains. It is by these inherited characteristics, dating back for thousands of years, that his political institutions have been influenced. Books which fail to make this clear are as misleading as they are tedious, as dangerous as they are wrong.

It is no wonder that the social anthropologist turns with disgust

[1] *Social Contract.* J. J. Rousseau. Chapter VI.

from works of political theory. In a recent and important work on the political structure of African tribes,[1] the editors explain how unhelpful they found these works to be.

> We have not found that the theories of political philosophers have helped us to understand the societies we have studied and we consider them of little scientific value; for their conclusions are seldom formulated in terms of observed behaviour or capable of being tested by this criterion. Political philosophy has chiefly concerned itself with how men *ought* to live and what form of government they *ought* to have, rather than with what *are* their political habits and institutions.
>
> In so far as political philosophers have attempted to understand existing institutions instead of trying to justify or undermine them, they have done so in terms of popular psychology or of history. They have generally had recourse to hypotheses about earlier stages of human society presumed to be devoid of political institutions. . . .

The editors, in this instance, find some excuse for the political theorist in that 'little anthropological research has been conducted into primitive political systems' and even less effort made to correlate what little has been done. While it is thus true to say that the subject remains largely unexplored, it is also manifest (even from such knowledge as there is) that the theories of 'original contract' are baseless suppositions. The anthropologist may not be ready to explain how political institutions first came into being but he is at least prepared to describe theories as 'unscientific' which are supported neither by evidence nor probability.

From a study of the existing text-books in political theory some would conclude that the whole subject were better taken from the historian and handed to the social anthropologist. Rather than leave this subject to historians whose works reflect an ignorance of anthropology, an ignorance of real politics and an ignorance of anything outside Europe and America, some would prefer to set up schools of political science. For this plan there is much to be said. The difficulty about it, as applied to political ideas current in historical times, is that every political theorist has an historical background. He thinks within the framework of the world he knows. Eliminate the historian and you lose all trace of the political thinker's background and motives. Apart from this danger, it is a question whether the historian should remain ignorant of social anthropology. It might be better to include pre-history in the syllabus which the future historian must study. Whatever is done, however, there will remain fields of investigation which the historian and social anthropologist may have to share. No great harm should result if their

[1] *African Political Systems*. M. Fortes and E. E. Evans-Pritchard. Oxford, 1940. See 4th Impression (1950), pp. 4 and 5.

activities should overlap. More harm results, as at present, in fields which each has left to the other. So far from overlapping, their present activities do not even meet.

While it would be absurd to follow previous writers in assuming that political thought begins with the Greeks, it is to them that we owe many of the political terms commonly in use. As these are not always used in exactly the same sense, it may be as well at this point to define the terms used in this book. As the Greeks perceived, there are, broadly speaking, three alternatives in government; rule by one, rule by a few and rule by many. Rule by one person can take the form of Monarchy, Despotism or Dictatorship. Monarchy is the rule by a King or Queen, depending upon religion, descent, election or established custom. Despotism is the rule by a King or Queen, established and maintained by force or cunning. Dictatorship is rule by a person who is neither King nor Queen whose authority derives from a particular emergency and whose office is widely regarded as a temporary expedient. Rule by a few can take the form of Feudalism, Aristocracy or Oligarchy. Feudalism is rule by nobles, each with control of some province or locality and many almost independent of any centralised authority. Aristocracy is rule by persons enjoying a special and often inherited respect, acting mainly through a central government under their own control. (Theocracy, or rule by a priesthood, is one form of Aristocracy). Oligarchy is rule by a few persons with no special claim to respect other than for their wealth, ability or vigour. (Bureaucracy, or rule by officials, is one form of Oligarchy). Rule by many can take the form of Democracy, Representative Democracy or Anarchy. Democracy is rule by all or by a majority of the voters, by direct expression of their will. Representative Democracy is rule by all or a majority of the voters but through elected representatives. Anarchy, if it can be termed a form of rule, means the refusal of a large number to be ruled at all.

Although the basic forms of government are only three, it would obviously be wrong to expect any government to conform exactly to any one of them. In practice, forms of rule are often mixed. Thus, a pure monarchy or despotism is difficult to maintain for long except over a relatively small area. A single ruler soon needs help and, in seeking it, becomes a little less absolute. Despotism or even Dictatorship may become monarchy by virtue of time and habit. A Democracy may still retain elements of earlier forms of rule. When, therefore, a State is here described as, say, an Aristocracy, it must be taken to mean the preponderance of Aristocratic rule, not the exclusion of any other form.

If we owe some of our terminology to Plato, it is from both Plato and Aristotle that we take the idea of sequence. As a scientist and the son of a physician, Aristotle perceived that forms of rule decay and so give place to others. He did not prescribe a single type of constitution as best for every State. The laws towards which he was feeling his way were not *The Laws* of Plato but the laws of change. With his aid we can readily perceive at least a tendency for Monarchy to turn into Aristocracy or Feudalism, for Aristocracy to become Democracy (perhaps via Oligarchy), for Democracy to turn into chaos and for order to be restored by a Despotism or Dictatorship. When the Dictatorship gives place to Monarchy the wheel has turned full circle and the process may begin again. It would, of course, be a gross exaggeration to represent this tendency as an invariable rule. The sequence is subject to many variations and exceptions. It can be disrupted as a result of war. And different lands within the same civilisation develop at different speeds so that, existing side by side, they represent different stages of the same sequence. Thus a historian of the remote future might remark that the countries of Europe mostly passed from Democracy to Dictatorship during the first half of the Twentieth Century. This would be true, broadly speaking, but he would have to note certain exceptions and explain that the various transitions were not simultaneous and that the countries affected were not necessarily adjacent to each other. We to-day can generalise about the past in much the same way, again noting the exceptions. And one factor which we can observe as regulating the speed of change is the area and physical nature of the country to be governed. It is almost impossible to govern a vast and diverse area except by loyally upholding a more or less divine Monarch. While the sequence of the forms of rule may be roughly followed, the tendency is to hurry through the forms that are obviously unworkable and return with relief to the form which offers most stability. It is perhaps this factor more than any other which prevents much valid generalisation about any given period. If the Athenians were democrats when the Persians were not, it was basically because they had a different problem to solve.

In a study, therefore, of political institutions and the ideas to which they give rise, there is reason to abandon chronology and concentrate on the successive forms of governance. In this book the plan followed is to take each form in turn and show its origin, its nature, its relative success, its theoretical justification, its decline and its decay. For this purpose the historical examples will be taken, for purposes of illustration, from any period and from any land. This must involve drawing upon the political experience of different civilisations. This is a useful process although difficult in a book of this size. But the reader who is thus encouraged to take a world-wide view should remember that the political approach is only one of several. During the life of a given civilisation the lands affected by it may undergo different forms of rule, and perhaps in a more or less logical sequence, but the civilisation has a life cycle of its own and one perhaps uninfluenced by political ideas. The rise and fall of civilisations might best be studied in terms of climate, food supply, soil-erosion, reproduction and disease. As compared with factors such as these, the forms of rule are a superficial matter. It is true that certain forms of government are often associated with a civilisation's early development. It would be far more difficult and controversial to show what type of government prevailed at its zenith or during its decay. There is, to begin with, a difficulty in agreeing as to when the zenith was reached and almost as great a difficulty in fixing a period for a civilisation's end.

If we see the sequence of political institutions as falling within the life-cycle of the different civilisations, it is relevant to ask how long a civilisation may be expected to last. The Graeco-Roman civilisation might be said to have had a life of 900-1,000 years (say, from 500 B.C. or rather earlier, to about A.D. 400). The civilisation of Sumeria and Babylon may have lasted about 1,000 years, too. If we regard the Chou, Ch'in, and Sui Dynasties of China as representing different civilisations, they might be credited with durations of 750, 800 and 770 years respectively. From A.D. 321 to 1525 India had a civilisation which thus lasted about 1,200 years. The civilisation of Inca Peru lasted 1,100 years and that of Aztec Mexico about 850. Apart from the doubtful examples of Egypt and Japan, we might be tempted to conclude that civilisations have an average life of about a thousand years. Any such conclusion would be rash but there would be some justification for denying that many civilisations have lasted very much longer. It has been argued, indeed, that the periods of high civilisation have all been relatively brief:—

> The acme of Greek civilization is confined to the fifth and fourth centuries B.C., Hellenistic civilization to the third and second centuries B.C. Rome was certainly not a really cultured country before the first century B.C., and her creative period ended with the second century of the Christian era. We may reckon the Byzantine civilization at best from the sixth to the tenth Century, the Arab civilization from the eighth to the twelfth. . . . The periods of high civilization are always short—a few centuries, sometimes hardly one century.[1]

The difficulty is one of definition. It might not, however, be wildly amiss to think of a civilisation as lasting up to about a thousand years, with its greatest achievements confined to a middle period of two or three centuries. Any sequence (or repeated sequences) in the forms of rule must usually fall within that space of time. But to associate the

[1] *The Passing of the European Age.* Eric Fischer. Cambridge, 1948, p. 191.

highest achievements with any one form of rule would be difficult, if only from a lack of agreement as to what the highest achievements are.

The plan of this book, it will be seen, is analytical. It is not to the purpose to predict the future or recommend some particular form of rule. There is included, however, an epilogue which concerns the present. This is not designed as a remedy for present ills but merely as a plea for studying them in a more scientific way.

The author's thanks are due to his pupils at the University of Malaya, with many of whom these problems have been discussed; to his secretary, Mrs. Y. J. G. Lawton, without whose tireless help the book would still be no more than a mass of illegible notes; and to Ann, who has had to be very, very patient.

C. NORTHCOTE PARKINSON

University of Malaya
Singapore

INTRODUCTION

Primitive Man

IN the Introduction to a recent work on social anthropology, already mentioned in the Preface,[1] the editors state that 'We do not consider that the origins of primitive institutions can be discovered and, therefore, we do not think it worth while seeking for them'. This may be true. It need not, however, prevent us from noting what appear to be the basic characteristics of man, considered from a political point of view. It is hardly in question, for example, that men have always (since being recognisable as men) lived in groups of some kind, family groups or tribes. Man is thus a social animal, although less so perhaps than some other creatures, especially certain insects. Man is also carnivorous, able to live on either a meat or a vegetable diet but equipped with teeth different from those of a grass-eating animal. Some at least of his food has always been trapped or pursued, fished or shot. Then again, the young of the human family (born singly, for the most part, not in a litter) are helpless for an exceptionally long period, needing protection and care for many years and maturing very slowly indeed.

These physical facts have their political implications. Among carnivorous creatures with slowly-maturing young there must be a fairly sharp differentiation between the sexes. With the young to be fed, nursed and protected, the more active pursuits must be left to the male. In hunting and kindred activities men have therefore felt superior to women. As against that, women and children must be kept out of danger if the family group is to survive. If men are killed in hunting, the survivors may still be enough for breeding purposes. The same is not true of women, upon whose number the natural increase must depend. Add to this differentiation of the sexes the prolonged differentiation between the adult and the young. Human children must be taught (and therefore controlled) for so long that their subordination becomes habitual. And this obedience to those older and more skilled may survive after the child has become an adult. In the social group a certain authority is thus vested in the older members.

The authority of age merges into the parental authority. Although

[1] *African Political Systems*. Ed. by M. Fortes and E. E. Evans-Pritchard. Oxford, 1940, 4th Impression, 1950.

primitive people often fail to recognise paternity, developing communities have all come to see in it a heightening of the authority of age in the special relationship between father and child.[1] It is this relationship which provides us with our basic notions of authority and discipline. Nearly all our common terms of respect are derived from it. We have thus the words 'Sir' (Sire), 'Monsieur', 'Little Father' (in Russian), 'Father' as addressed to a priest or 'Holy 'Father' as addressed to the Pope. Psychologists break up the idea of respect into the three elements of wonder, affection and fear. The child thus feels for his father some wonder at the ability of an older person to do what the child cannot; some affection for an older person whose intention is at least to ensure the child's survival; and some fear of an older person who may punish the child by smacking its head.

If physical characteristics have a bearing on political development, so no doubt have mental characteristics. It has thus been observed that man has taken about 500,000 years to evolve, of which period 490,000 years passed before any sort of settled existence began and 495,000 before writing was invented.[2] So that all *inherited* characteristics are pre-civilised in origin. This is obviously true of the basic instincts of hunger, fear, hatred and sex; for these are shared with other animals. But man would seem to have, in addition, such tendencies as Animism, Taboo, Fear of the Unknown and Revenge. Animism is the ascribing to animals, mountains, wind and thunder the individual character man perceives in himself. The schoolboy, having named his bicycle, will soon endow it with a personality. Animistic objects invade the undergraduate's essay, all sorts of actions being ascribed to 'The Spirit of the Reformation' or 'The Soul of India'. A whole nation becomes personified in its king or its flag. Taboo represents a confusion of mind over ethical, moral or sacred matters. It takes the form of odd distinctions between what is 'pure' and 'impure'. It surrounds the crime of incest and befogs the question of whether a man should marry his deceased wife's sister. Fear of the unknown, the novel, the foreign, is a deeply implanted emotion from which few men are wholly free. And the primitive idea of revenge lurks behind our criminal law, our prisons and our gallows. These and other instincts inform the political ideas of mankind.

The physical characteristics of man would seem obvious enough. They have often, however, been overlooked, as for example in the American Declaration of Independence, which reads: 'We hold these truths to be self-evident, that men are born equal. . . .' Whatever else

---

[1] Matriarchy appears to be an earlier institution but the term is misleading as applied, for example, to certain districts of Malaya. Matriarchy there means primarily the inheritance of property through women and dates presumably from a period when descent through the male line could not be traced.

[2] *The Mind in the Making*. J. H. Robinson. New York, 1939, p. 65.

that first truth may be it is not self-evident. It might perhaps be defended in terms of Christian or Islamic theology. Taken, however, from its religious context, it becomes difficult to sustain. Are 'men', in this sense, to include women? If so, their equality is doubtful now and was firmly denied in eighteenth century America. Are 'men' to include persons of the age of twenty or less? For these are not, and never have been, politically or even legally equal to adults. Are younger brothers equal, for that matter, to elder brothers? They were certainly not so in English or American law. Lastly, are 'men' in this sense, to include negroes? The Americans of Washington's generation had a prompt answer to *that*. But what becomes of the grand generalisation when the exceptions to it include the majority of mankind? A Christian will assert that all souls are equally valuable in the sight of God: but that equality is lost when one child is baptised and another not. Nearest perhaps to the truth was the Indian thinker Asvaghosa, who asserted that human beings are 'in respect of joy and sorrow, love, insight, manners and ways, death, fear and life all equal'.[1] But this philosopher, while attacking caste, says nothing of the other basic inequalities; the differentiation between male and female functions, the subordination of child to parent, the subordination of the young to any elder person and the subordination of the younger child to the elder. One might find a further inequality based upon the size of family, for the child who is one of fourteen is less valuable to its parents than the child who is one of two or the only one of its sex.

Our knowledge about the political ideas of primitive man goes little beyond our awareness of the basic characteristics which we still possess. What knowledge we have has been confused, moreover, by the persistent and widespread legend of the Golden Age. This legend, known to the Greeks, was also believed among the Indians and Chinese and can be paralleled by the Jewish story of the Garden of Eden and the Fall. The Hindu version of this legend is thus described by Beni Prasad:—

> In a passage of poetic brilliance the Vanaparva records how in very ancient days men lived a pure godly life. They were, in fact, equal to gods. They could ascend to heaven and return to earth at will. The wishes of all were fulfilled. Sufferings were few and real trouble or fear was none. Perfect virtue and happiness reigned. The span of life extended over thousands of years. But all this was changed after a long while. The Santi-parva, too, has it that there was at first a sort of Golden Age wherein existed neither sovereignty nor king, neither chastisement nor chastiser. All men used to protect one another righteously. But after a while their hearts were assailed by error.

[1] *Theory of Government in Ancient India.* Beni Prasad. Allahabad, 1927. See p. 219.

> Their faculties of perception were clouded; their virtue declined; greed and avarice set in. The downward course continued. . . .[1]

He refers to the same legend elsewhere, stating that:

> The Buhaddharma Purana, an Upapriâna, gives its political theory in the form of a narration of the ancient history of the human race. The world began with the golden age called Satya Yuga which was free from all sorrow and sin, disease and disputes. It was a heaven of perfect virtue and happiness. . . .[2]

The anthropologist of to-day is less prone to enthusiasm about such equality as exists among primitive peoples. Even Darwin observed that the equality observable among the Fuegian tribes 'must for a long time retard their civilisation'.[3] More recently, Landtman has pointed out[4] that such equality as exists among the Papuans, Bushmen, Hottentots, Nagas, Andamanese and other peoples is directly associated with their low degree of culture. The emergence of the idea of rank is connected with 'a somewhat higher degree of evolution'.

The Chinese Golden Age was described by Kwang-Tze, follower of Lao-Tze (604-532 B.C.) in a passage which has been rendered thus:—

> In the age of perfect virtue, men attached no value to wisdom. . . . They were upright and correct, without knowing that to be so was Righteousness: they loved one another, without knowing that to do so was Benevolence: they were honest and loyal-hearted, without knowing that it was Loyalty; they fulfilled their engagements without knowing that to do so was Good Faith. . . .[5]

This legend found ready acceptance in the eighteenth century, when talk about the 'Noble Savage' was not uncommon among literary men who had read Captain Cook's description of the South Sea Islanders. More recently, moreover, it has been defended by W. J. Perry and G. Elliot Smith, who attributed great virtues to primitive peoples, asserting that 'savages', whose merits were less obvious, had once been civilised and are thus degenerate rather than primitive. Of this theory it may suffice to say that while some primitive people might be shown to have been honest, inoffensive, contented and mild, they can also be shown to have been thin, small, hungry, dirty and diseased, and their life 'poore, nasty, brutish and short'.[6]

The modern anthropologist is less inclined to draw distinctions between primitive people and savages. He is more hesitant in fact

[1] *Ibid.*, p. 27.
[2] *Theory of Government in Ancient India.* Beni Prasad. p. 193.
[3] *Journal of Researches.* C. Darwin, Chapter X.
[4] *The Origin of the Inequality of the Social Classes.* G. Landtman. London, 1938, p. 3
[5] *Human History.* G. Elliot Smith. p. 182.
[6] *Leviathan.* T. Hobbes. Part I. Chap. XIII.

about generalising in any context. To early political institutions, moreover, he has given perhaps less attention than to anything else. The following passage, however, quoted from a standard work, may typify the views that are currently held:—

> Among simpler primitives there are above all two principles which form the foundation of government: first, the territorial principle— that is, the geographically limited area belonging to a number of people; second, the community which exceeds the single family, be it local group, clan, tribe or people. On these two pillars repose the governmentlike institutions of primitive cultures. . . .
>
> . . . In Australia and among some other food-gathering tribes the executive agencies of public opinion were the old men who, seasoned in life and in the tribal laws, not only informed the younger ones concerning the boundaries of the clan territory, but also instructed them in the laws of marriage, the rites of initiation, the distribution of food—all those norms existing from time immemorial.
>
> Our sources report unanimously that chieftainship was slightly developed or absent. . . .[1]

Whether or not food-gathering peoples lived (or still live) in a Golden Age, it seems generally agreed that their main political institution was merely the authority of the older men. Nor is this difficult to understand, for family groups which are to live on wild fruit, berries, roots, game and fish cannot grow to beyond a certain size. With a larger number than about twenty the food would be insufficient near any one camp in the recognised hunting-ground. And among as small a number as they were likely to muster the problems of government need hardly arise. Typical of food-gatherers are the Semang (or Negritos) of Malaya, about which people a great deal has been written. In 1926, it is true, Mr. R. J. Wilkinson remarked that 'with all this mass of literature we know next to nothing about the aborigines . . . books are big when facts are few'[2] but more detailed work was afterwards done by Ivor H. N. Evans.[3] He wrote of them that:

> . . . The groups seem to be but little organised, but in every camp will be found an acknowledged headman and often, too, a 'medicineman' who is also an important personage in the life of the people. . . .

The Semang can be readily contrasted with the rather more advanced aboriginal tribes, inaccurately termed the Sakai. These have a rather more settled existence, with a little agriculture, and with them the chief and the medicine-man are more firmly established. Of them Wilkinson wrote:—

> . . . we find that the smallest political unit among the central Sakai is

[1] *General Anthropology*. Ed. by Franz Boas. New York, 1938. Chap. X. *Government* by Julius E. Lips. See pp. 487-527.
[2] *Papers on Malay Subjects: the Aboriginal Tribes*. R. J. Wilkinson. 1926. p. 10.
[3] *The Negritos of Malaya*. Ivor H. N. Evans. Cambridge, 1937.

the family-group. Every family—by which is meant a living patriarch and all his descendants and not a mere menage of husband and wife—keeps together and keeps to itself: it does not unite with others for mutual protection and social intercourse. Exogamy means marrying into another family, not into another tribe. A number of these family-units living within a definite area and recognising a common hereditary chief make up the Sakai State—if such a term is permissible in the case of so small a community. . . . [The Chief] settles disputes between one family and another, and keeps peace generally in his tribe. . . .

Within the family-group property was held in common; and the unsuccessful hunter . . . [received his share of the food].

. . . Communistic ideas are strong among the Sakai. At the same time, their Communism does not imply liberty, equality and fraternity. There is a vast amount of ceremonious family etiquette and a host of technicalities regulating the mode of address of one member of the family to another. It is a serious offence for a young . . . [Sakai] to address an elder by his personal name. . . .[1]

If a state is recognisable by 'the maintenance of political order within fixed territorial limits' the Sakai may be said to have formed states. These states remain, however, in a very rudimentary form.

Mention has already been made of the 'medicineman', the sooth-sayer, wizard or magician, who figures in some of the most primitive societies and rather gains in importance as their culture becomes more advanced. His functions arise perhaps mainly from two innate characteristics of man; the tendency to fear such natural phenomena as thunder and lightning, and the tendency to dream at night. Of the Semang Wilkinson writes,[2] 'He fears lightning and thunder to such an extent that observers have credited him with the possession of a thunder-god'. If thunder thus gives rise to the idea of a god of wrath, dreams as naturally promote ideas of ghosts and immortality. The 'spirit' is thus the real self, the something which is absent when a person is asleep. Where is it? That it is free to wander is shown by the sleeper dreaming of being somewhere else and proved again when someone else has dreamt of him. On death, the same spirit is again missing and can still appear in another's dream—proof sufficient that it still exists. Here are good grounds for belief in an after-life. Evans is able to devote twelve chapters of his book to Negrito religion, chapters which cover the deities, a theory of the world's origin and theories of death, burial and the life to come. The Negritos have elaborate stories also to account for thunder, lightning, storms and eclipses. They have, too, a fairly long list of things that they must not say, do, eat or touch; and the penalties for a breach of etiquette illustrate their principal fears—illness, being crushed under a falling

[1] Wilkinson, op. cit. p. 48.
[2] Papers on Malay Subjects: the Aboriginal Tribes. R. J. Wilkinson. 1926. p. 1.

tree or being killed by a tiger. The Sakai are more superstitious still, believing not only in the Sun God and Moon Goddess but also in demons, ghosts, vampires, dragons, man-eating monkeys, giant birds and were-tigers. The communal wizard, known at least among the Semang, is a key man among the Sakai.

The soothsayer found, as he gained influence, that there were two policies open to him. In the first place, while emphasising the danger of demons and ghosts, he could offer various charms and incantations which defeat the evil spirits by their own power; many comparable devices still linger (for example, mascots, crossing the fingers, throwing salt over the shoulder). In the second place, he could assert that the benevolent Sun or Moon God was more powerful than the demons and would protect those who approached him in the right way, by personal appeal and with suitable gifts. The magician who followed the first policy was the forerunner of the scientist, the physician and the psychologist. The soothsayer who preferred the second policy was the forerunner of the priest. Generally speaking, the priest has been more honest, and (until recently) more successful.

The classic work by Sir James Frazer[1] is a study in the relationship between magic and religion, between both and kingship. In it he shows that all or most peoples have believed at one time in magic and that most of these have gradually transferred their belief to religion, often for long periods believing in both. He remarks that the sorcerer came to practise for the whole community as well as privately.

> Whenever ceremonies of this sort are observed for the common good, it is obvious that the magician ceases to be merely a private practitioner and becomes to some extent a public functionary. The development of such a class of functionaries is of great importance for the political as well as the religious evolution of society. For when the welfare of the tribe is supposed to depend on the performance of these magical rites, the magician rises into a position of much influence and repute, and may readily acquire the rank and authority of a chief or king. The profession accordingly draws into its ranks some of the ablest and most ambitious men of the tribe. . . .

This may well have been so. It is important, however, to realise, that the really primitive tribe had little to offer its magician. The Chiefship to which he might aspire (and very occasionally with success, as in Kedah) carried with it no very despotic power. The rising importance of the medicine-man depended, in fact, on a change in the habits of the tribe. While the people remained in small family groups of food-gatherers, the potentialities of both chief and magician

[1] *The Golden Bough: a study in magic and religion.* Sir James George Frazer. See Chapter IV.

were, of necessity, undeveloped. The story would be simpler if all food-gathering peoples had developed in the same way from the point at which they abandoned their primitive existence. In fact, however, they could progress in two different ways, if indeed they were to progress at all. Some concentrated on the domestication of animals and became nomadic herdsmen. Others, given different opportunities, became cultivators of the soil. In either event, the change of habits brought with it important political consequences, but these were not identical as between cultivators and pastoralists. To some extent they diverged and it is upon this divergence that some writers have laid the greatest stress. The divergence itself is fitly symbolised in the biblical story of Cain and Abel which rightly follows after the story of a primeval innocence. The danger here is to over-simplify both the divergence and its results. For while conflict between pastoralists and cultivators tended to follow, the latter being usually vanquished, it would be wrong to maintain that this was invariable. Professor Franz Oppenheimer maintained[1] that all states known to history are thus characterised by the domination of one class by another for the purpose of economic exploitation. And Professor R. H. Lowie agreed at least that the subjection of one people to another had its origin in conquest.[2] More has since been discovered, however, about the development of societies in both America and Africa and it is now clear that there are exceptions to every rule.[3]

Important among recent studies is that made of African Political Systems under the editorship of M. Fortes and E. E. Evans-Pritchard.[4] This study summarises what is known about the political institutions of eight African peoples. Three of these, the Bantu Kavirondo, the Tallensi and the Nuer, developed no government save by elders within the separate tribes. The other five, the Zulu, Ngwato, Bemba, Ankole and Kede, developed quite advanced forms of government but not in such a way as to justify any very general conclusions. While it is true that some of these peoples are cultivators, and others herdsmen—with at least one example of pastoralists (Bahima) dominant over agriculturalists (Bairu)—it is also evident that they present no sharp distinction between each other in political structure. This would seem to suggest that generalisations hitherto made about the political tendencies of pastoral peoples are not applicable to herdsmen as such but to nomadic horsemen. To find the equivalent in Africa of the Semitic nomads we should perhaps turn rather to the Fulbe who founded the Sokoto empire in the early nineteenth century.

[1] *Der Staat* (1907) quoted in *The Origin of the State*. R. H. Lowie. New York, 1927.
[2] *The Origin of the State*. R. H. Lowie. New York, 1927. p. 42.
[3] *General Anthropology. op. cit.* p. 526.
[4] *African Political Systems*. Oxford, 1940. 4th Impression, 1950.

Sir Henry Maine drew a contrast between the blood tie typical of nomadic people and the territorial tie found among agriculturalists,[1] and in general his ideas are still agreed.

> *Herdsmen and related societies.*
> . . . The individual and the patriarchal family group are the outstanding feature. The older collectivist element is replaced by individualism. The social unit is the patriarchal family group (brothers, nephews, sons, grandsons) which also claims to political independence. The tribe is headed by a chief who has been elected or whose office is hereditary. . . . Typical among the herdsmen is, above all, the development of private ownership and the accumulation of wealth in the form of stock. This at the same time presented the opportunity of developing class distinctions and of a vertical stratification of society, a differentiation of rich and poor. These beginnings of a hierarchic system among the herdsmen did not flourish until they came in contact with the agricultural societies. The law of inheritance in most of these tribes is marked by primogeniture.
> The societies of herdsmen of the Old World brought about a political revolution by the creation of large empires in Asia as well as in Africa.[2]

This last statement is, no doubt, true. But was the revolution due to their being herdsmen or to their having horses? The point is an interesting one for it is rather questionable whether the preceding remarks, applicable to Central Asia, Siberia, Arabia and Mesopotamia, are in fact equally true of Africa. Of the eight African peoples to which we have referred the Zulu come nearest, perhaps, to being purely pastoral. But of them it is stated by Max Gluckman that 'The clans had disappeared as units', and 'members of a single clan might be found in many political groups'.[3] He also remarks that 'there were few ways in which a commoner could acquire wealth'[4] and that the wealth of a chief did not give him 'opportunity to live at a higher level than his inferiors'.[5] He explains, further, that 'there was no class snobbery among the Zulu' and that 'all had the same education and lived in the same way'. If the Africans turn out to be poor examples of 'herdsmen', the factor which links the other 'herdsmen' may be found to be, not cattle but horses, and there are reasons for supposing that this might well be so. In the following pages where 'pastoral peoples' are mentioned they must be taken to mean nomadic horsemen, and not merely the owners of cattle.

To summarise the conclusions so far reached, primitive men are found to base their political institutions, such as they are, upon the

---

[1] See *Ancient Law.* Chapter IV.
[2] *General Anthropology. op. cit.* p. 515 *et sea.*
[3] *African Political Systems. op. cit.* pp. 28-29.
[4] *Ibid.* p. 45.
[5] *Ibid.* p. 44.

authority of age. They are essentially social and tend to develop family groups which are migrant within a recognised territory. If there is a larger tribal organisation the chief of it rarely has more than a vague power of arbitration. They have basic instincts common to other animals but these do not necessarily make them warlike; and many of them are essentially peaceful. They have a strong belief in the supernatural, a belief which tends to strengthen as their culture becomes more advanced. Thus, the soothsayer or magician, not unknown among the most primitive of them, becomes more important among those who have progressed. This progress, if and when it takes place, may be in one of two general directions; towards the domestication of animals or towards the growing of crops, the choice being governed by climatic and other conditions. And the further political development of each group is influenced by the change in its way of life, the pastoralists diverging most sharply from the cultivators as from the time when they become accustomed to using horses. Even from as brief a summary as this it is manifest that many later institutions are not the result of individual inspiration but are deeply rooted in the social character of mankind. At no time did primitive men attempt to frame a constitution for their body politic. They had their basic institutions from the beginning, moulded by their physical and mental characteristics and observable among the most primitive of them. Their further ideas were bounded and guided by a framework which was already there.

PART I
Monarchy

CHAPTER I

Monarchy among Agricultural Peoples

AGRICULTURE is traditionally thought to have originated in Egypt about 5000 B.C.[1] the local legend about it being thus rendered by Plutarch:

> When Osiris came to his kingdom . . . [he found] . . . the Egyptians living a life such as animals lead. He taught them the art of agriculture, gave them laws, and instructed them in the worship of the gods [of which he was to become one of the chief].

It is unlikely that one genius taught the Egyptians everything, but there is significance in the sequence of progress as here defined: agriculture, laws, religion. For agriculture indeed came first and with vast and immediate implications. Elliot Smith supposes that barley grew wild on the Nile banks, being developed through periodic floods and then spread by irrigation. He points out, moreover, following Professor Cherry, that the Nile is unique, not only in flowing from the tropics into a temperate zone but in having a double water-supply. Thus the equatorial sources maintain a steady flow while the floods in August and September come from the Blue Nile, at other times nearly dry. The inundation in September immediately precedes the cool part of the year, which begins in October. These conditions, he argues, ideally suited for the cultivation of millet and barley, are found in no other part of the world. Be that as it may, agriculture spread from Egypt, and perhaps from other centres, and transformed the lives of people everywhere. Nor would it affect the present argument if it were shown that agriculture was developed independently in more regions than one.

The political implications of an agricultural life are bound up, to begin with, in the settlement of communities in a given place and not merely within a given area. Agriculture necessitated the formation of villages—sited in the Nile Valley, it is believed, on the higher contours above flood level. Villages dependent upon agriculture could be far

[1] There is no certainty that it did not originate also in Mesopotamia, nor indeed that it did not originate in Syria, spreading thence to both Egypt and Mesopotamia. It has been pointed out that a form of wheat grows wild on the slopes of Mount Herman and elsewhere between southern Syria and Moab. *Early Man, his origin, development and culture*. G. Elliot Smith and others. London, 1931. See especially Lecture V by H. J. E. Peake. p. 122.

more populous than any encampment previously formed—there would be food for a greater number. Then, cultivation of the land soon necessitates fences and boundaries, primarily to keep animals out of the crops but leading naturally to a new idea of property and hence of law. As agriculture develops the need arises for the carpenter and metal-worker (to make and mend the implements), the builder (to construct the granary), the watchman (to guard it) and the lawyer (to settle boundary disputes). A new need arises for a calendar, by which to judge when to plant, and a new and intense interest is shown in sun and water. The weather becomes that absorbing topic of conversation that it has ever since remained.

Another result of a people turning to agriculture is that religion tends to become more important than magic. The primitive man food-gathering in the jungle is concerned with his personal or family luck. He may find fruit or edible roots. He may come across a sitting target for his arrow. But he may equally meet a tiger, a cobra, a ghost or a demon. The cultivator, by contrast, has helped to clear an area of land, perhaps pushing back the jungle. He works thenceforward in fields well known to him. The risk of meeting something unpleasant is greatly reduced and so likewise is the chance of an unexpected windfall. He has planted seed and chiefly wants a good crop. And the good or bad weather which affects one group will probably affect other groups as well. The cultivator is less concerned with the tiresome spirits which haunt trees, hills, wells and cemeteries and proportionately more interested in the beneficent gods who govern the sowing, the growth and the harvest. The task of persuading the Sun God to ripen the grain is not the individual's or family's responsibility, for all alike are involved. It is a communal matter, best handled by an expert interceding on behalf of the village. The soothsayer entrusted with this task is inevitably more priest than magician, a public officer and one of growing importance. Magic lingers in the hills and forests and among wandering folk like gypsies. It lingers too in the normal human mind. But religion became predominant as from the period when men turned to agriculture.

There can be little doubt that the change which favoured the priest also favoured the chief. The agricultural unit, the village, was larger than the family group and offered more scope to a ruler. And it offered him still wider scope when it developed into a town and, later, into a city. Apart from that, however, the agriculture which depended upon irrigation more than upon local rainfall brought many villages into close association. In some respects their interests might be the same. In other respects their interest were more likely to conflict. The economic unit, for purposes of irrigation, would ideally comprise the whole river system. It could certainly be nothing as small as a village. A more extended political power would go to the man with a calendar or else to the man who first discovered the principles of irrigation. Kingship might have grown from that alone, but in Egypt the powers of the priest were added to those of the chief. Either the priest secured the office of ruler or else it was the ruler who assumed priesthood. In Egypt, at any rate, Kingship was the result of combining the two functions in one. It is clear, however, that the religious function was regarded as the more important. The King-Priest's first duty was to intercede with the Sun God. He might incidentally rule the country but that was, by comparison, a trivial duty. Why should the Sun God listen to him? For the same reason that a human chief or patriarch will listen to a request—because it is made by his *son*. It follows that the King is the son of the god. One can readily imagine an astute ruler explaining this theory to his subjects. In fact, however, it is still more likely that it was they who explained it to him.

The Sun God cult is believed to have originated at Heliopolis, together with the solar calendar.

> . . . The man who had made himself the artificer of the new order also made himself king. When he foretold the future behaviour of the river and measured the year, his subjects believed that he was something more than a prophet: he was the cause of the changes he had accurately predicted. People believed that the king controlled the forces of Nature. He not only caused the river to rise, and then made the dry land, but by so doing this, they imagined, he created the earth, and conferred upon the waters their life-giving powers.[1]

It has been questioned indeed whether any people carried this cult as far as did the Egyptians.

> The Egyptians of the Fifth Dynasty thus had thorough-going ideals of the divine nature of their kings, and it is doubtful whether the identity between royalty and divinity was carried so far in any other state. 'The Egyptians dare not look at their king. The king could bring on rain, make sunshine . . . he was master of thunder . . . he brandishes his sceptre like a thunderbolt. As king of the harvest he turns over the earth and presides over the sowing. Sickle in hand he cuts the grain'. From him therefore could be expected the same benefits as from the gods themselves.[2]

The Egyptians may have originated kingship and carried the cult furthest, but all ancient monarchies, almost without exception, were ruled by Children of the Sun. Perry traces the idea to India, to Indonesia (including Timor, Celebes and Bali), to the Philippines, to Polynesia, to Hawaii, New Zealand, Samoa and the New World. It is

[1] *Human History*. G. Elliot Smith. London, 1930. p. 277
[2] *The Children of the Sun*. W. J. Perry. 2nd ed. London, 1927.

implicit in the Chinese conception of Heaven, to which only the Emperor could sacrifice. As for the Japanese, they have retained the cult almost to this day. A celebrated Japanese wrote of his country:—

> Great Yamato is a divine country. It is only our land whose foundations were first laid by the divine ancestor. It alone has been transmitted by the sun goddess to a long line of her descendants. There is nothing of this kind in foreign countries.[1]

Here the author is mistaken. All dynasties used to trace their pedigree to a divine ancestor. It is also important to realise that what is outmoded now in the cult was once a brilliant innovation and the very thing that distinguished a civilised people from those less advanced. As a modern author has well expressed it:—

> The ancient Near East considered kingship the very basis of civilization. Only savages could live without a king. Security, peace and justice could not prevail without a ruler to champion them. If ever a political institution functioned with the assent of the governed, it was the monarchy which built the pyramids with forced labor. . . .[2]

While it might be safe to assume that monarchy was usually the result of the chief assuming the functions of priest, the deified monarchy of Egypt seems to date from the period during which a high-priest of the Sun God made himself the ruler. Userkaf, who founded the fifth dynasty in about 2750 B.C., had been high-priest at Heliopolis. He is believed to have been the first Pharaoh to claim divine descent.[3] Previous rulers were divine, no doubt, but not until after death. The combining of the priestly and secular powers had been known also in the Sumerian cities but due to the opposite process. 'The Sumerian patesi was a magistrate who performed sacred or priestly functions; the kings of the fifth dynasty were priests who had usurped royal powers'.[4]

In Egypt the Chief and the Priest had thus become united in the person of the King and there can be no doubt that the strongest monarchies were those founded in this way. But there were from the beginning the monarchies in which the priestly power was vested separately. This was so in India and at least one story of how monarchy originated there would make its purpose more strictly utilitarian.

> . . . Another theory of the origin of the state which Mahâbhârata has preserved brings us a little nearer Hobbes. It paints the state of nature not as a Golden Age of righteousness but as a period of terrible anarchy. . . . So they lived for a while but, after some time, they felt

[1] *The Pageant of Japanese History*. M. M. Dilts. New York, 1938.
[2] *Kingship and the Gods*. Henri Frankfort. Chicago, 1945.
[3] See *Priests and Kings* by Harold Peake and H. J. Fleure. Oxford, 1927.
[4] *Priests and Kings, op cit.* pp. 177-178.

acutely the need of a king. They assembled and approached the Grand-sire, saying, 'Without a king, O Divine Lord, we are going to destruc-tion. Appoint some one as our king! All of us shall worship him and he shall protect us'. The Grandsire nominated Manu to be king but Manu replied 'I fear all sinful acts. To govern a kingdom is exceedingly difficult, especially among men who are always false and deceitful in their behaviour'. [But he was persuaded into it and given the following encouragement:—] 'Like the sun scorching everything with his rays, go out for winning victories, crush the pride of foes and let righteous-ness always triumph'.[1]

There is much that is of interest in this account and much that can be paralleled by the Old Testament story of how the Jewish kingship was founded. To begin with, a divine Grandsire was there already when the clamour began. Symbolically at least this would seem to be correct. It was from the patriarch that the king took his idea of authority, claiming afterwards to be 'the father of his people'. Apart from this, the proposal to appoint a king (if ever such a proposal was made) could come only from a people to whom the idea of monarchy was familiar. This would mean virtually copying from another and adjacent people: a procedure the more understandable if the people in question were thought to be hostile. The Jews, for example, are described as asking Samuel to choose a king for them. On his ex-pressing reluctance, they said 'Nay; but we will have a king over us; *that we also may be like all the nations*; and that our king may judge us, and go out before us, and fight our battles. . . .'[2] The words italicised suggest how readily the institution of monarchy might spread by imitation.

India provides the best, though not perhaps the only example of monarchy kept distinct from priesthood. There is much in the relationship which the Indians themselves are unable to explain.

The professional priesthood is seen practically from the very begin-ning of the Rig Veda period. Its position is entirely separate from that of monarchy. The fact is somewhat puzzling in conception. A study of the earliest organization of the other branches of the Aryan family reveals the fact that the original leader was the king, the priest and the head of the fighting host; and there is nothing to suppose that the particular branch that came to India began with a special polity or stepped lightly over some of the stages while retaining fully the wisdom derived from the experience of each. The latter fact is clear from the subsequent history of the race during which, in spite of the predominant influence of the priests (the Brahmanas), there was no attempt on their part to become king *de jure*, although they wielded, through their influence on the ruler, all the powers of the king. Any

[1] *The Theory of Government in Ancient India*. Beni Prasad. Allahabad, 1927. p. 29.
[2] *Samuel*, 8, verses 4-20.

explanation, however, of the early separation of priesthood from kingship in India must be conjectural; there is no record previous to the Rig Veda, and in the Rig Veda it is recognized as an established institution. . . .[1]

So in India the king was less than a god and less, in some ways, than the Brahmans. Elsewhere, however, the king was godlike, but in an age when the gods retained some very human characteristics and failings. The idea of the king's sanctity still, for that matter, survives.

But if ideas survive, men do not, and early history is full of the efforts made to explain the death of a supposedly immortal Sun King. In point of fact, the king often died before his time owing to a drought or excess of rainfall which he might have averted but did not. His office was not without its occupational risks. As recently, moreover, as 1890, a Malayan Annual Report contains the statement that a series of bad harvest had been attributed locally to the evil influence of the British Resident. One way or another, then, the king eventually died. The situation could be met in several ways. It was possible, first of all, to preserve his body and maintain firmly that he was still alive. Next, it could be argued that he had become a god—that he had been a god all along, in fact—and that he had returned to the home of the gods. Lastly, it could be claimed that he had been reincarnated in his successor, who was in fact the same man but now provided with a younger body.

Exactly how the Egyptians reasoned, who favoured the first of these alternatives, may not be known. We know, however, that they buried their kings with great care, producing the earliest joiners and brickmakers for that special purpose. And they provided each dead king with his food, weapons, furniture and toilet articles. Efforts of this kind also included the elaborate methods of embalming by which mummies were preserved and the even more elaborate masonry built over the grave, initially, to prevent the treasure from being stolen. With the Dynastic Egyptians monumental masonry became the chief national industry. Something of the same treatment has been accorded in many lands to the dead, and not only to the dead of royal birth. Primitive peoples have funeral rites based clearly on the belief that the spirit survives death. The Scandinavians gave their dead leaders a Viking's funeral and the Chinese still burn at funerals the pasteboard replicas of things—including motor-cars—which may be needed in the next world. The custom is understandable and especially so where royalty is concerned. The Incas of Peru were also preserved

[1] *Indo-Aryan Polity, being a study of the economic and political condition of India as depicted in the Rig Veda.* P. Basu. London, 1925. It is rash, however, to generalise too confidently. See, for example, *A History of Hindu Political Theories.* V. Ghoshal. Oxford, 1923. p. 228.

after death and periodically exhibited, and something of the same practice lingers, it is said, in University College, London. The deceased monarch is not really allowed to die.

The second theory, by no means inconsistent with the first, made the king a god and not merely a descendant of the gods. The Egyptian Osiris was thus a Deified King and the position was inherited by his Roman successors, Julius Caesar and Augustus, who were deified when they died and thereafter worshipped. Nor have other kings been without supernatural powers; the Emperor of Japan, for example, being something more than a man. The theory that deifies a king on his death inevitably makes him superhuman even while he is alive. In many lands this attempt to invest the living king with a godlike quality has made the monarch a sort of idol, seen immobile on state occasions or possibly not seen at all. A sufficiently rigid etiquette may make it almost immaterial whether the idol is actually alive or dead.

The third alternative has been fully described in *The Golden Bough*[1] and is again not inconsistent with the other two. The Egyptians portrayed their kings with a minimum of individuality, their sculptures depicting each as an impersonal image of kingship.

> . . . There is a mystic communion between father and son at the moment of succession, a unity and continuity of divine power which suggests a stream in which the individual rulers come and go like waves.[2]

The whole process hinges on the moment of succession for which some smooth organisation seems essential. It is vital to know beforehand who the successor is to be and as vital to ensure that he is actually present. The easiest way to provide for this is to fix the date in advance, putting the old king to death at an agreed moment, with his successor at hand. (Why should the old king object? His soul is merely being transferred). This custom is closely connected with a popular interest in the king's virility. It was always doubted whether an old or ailing king could fulfil his main function of making the crops grow. Better, surely, to kill him in good time. Kings were thus despatched in Cambodia, Ethiopia, on the Congo and in other parts of Africa. One way was to wait until his powers failed, as was done at Shilluk on the White Nile. In Uganda, too, the King of Ankole was never allowed to die of illness or age. 'As soon as his wives and followers observed signs of weakness, the Mugabe was given a poison which brought about his death'.[3] Another way was to allow him a

---

[1] *The Golden Bough*. Sir James Frazer. Chapter XXIV. p. 264 *et seq.* in the one-volume edition.
[2] *Kingship and the Gods.* p. 35.
[3] *African Political Systems.* p. 156.

fixed term of office—twelve years in Calicut, nine years in Sweden, eight years in Sparta and five years in Malabar. Yet another was for the people to take action when they saw fit, as at Passier on the north coast of Sumatra. The king's spirit then passed to his successor, who might have to be present to catch his last breath. The successor might be his eldest son or possibly the man (probably a relative) who killed him. The succession, in any case, was instantaneous; as in England, for example, it still is. Some kings eventually found means to die by deputy. It was a policy which kings themselves may have been the first to propose. In Siam the king thus died (by deputy) each year at the end of April. In other instances the king would sacrifice a son as his deputy; obviously a better equivalent. There are traces of this custom in the Bible. It may have been a younger son who first suggested that an animal would do instead. Originally, however, such parodies of a godly custom would have been unacceptable. It has been pointed out that the Egyptian mode of address to their kings was not 'Majesty' but 'Embodiment' or 'Incarnation'.

> . . . They are not merely respectful phrases but phrases which emphasise that the earthly ruler incorporates an immortal god. The names of the individual kings serve only to distinguish the successive incarnations.[1]

It cannot be sufficiently emphasised at this point that the primary functions of kingship, more especially in agricultural communities, were essentially religious. The temptation is to rationalise the story and explain that a king's leadership was necessary in war, or necessary indeed for many other practical purposes. Bernard Shaw said that rulers are so necessary

> . . . that any body of ordinary persons left without what they call superiors, will immediately elect them. A crew of pirates, subject to no laws except the laws of nature, will elect a boatswain to order them about and a captain to lead them and navigate the ship, though the one may be the most insufferable bully and the other the most tyrannical scoundrel on board. . . .[2]

Of modern society this may be true, but of primitive people it is certainly wrong. Peoples like the Nuer of the Southern Sudan have never appointed rulers. Nor have they, for any practical purpose, felt the need of them.

On the other hand, the king, once provided for religious purposes, was often found useful in other ways. Leadership in war was not necessarily one of them. Kingship is almost certainly older than war. Nor, for that matter, has command been invariably vested in the king

[1] *Kingship and the Gods.* p. 45.
[2] *The Intelligent Woman's Guide to Socialism, etc.* G. B. Shaw. p. 335.

even were he available and qualified. Thus we learn from the Old
Testament that when David proposed to lead his armies in person,
he was promptly overruled and told to stay at home.[1] His first
practical functions were as Judge and Lawgiver, derived in true
succession from the patriarchal chief. At the root of all legal institutions is the basic discovery that a verdict (whether right or wrong)
is better than an endless quarrel. A common primitive method of
settling a dispute was by augur or ordeal, with much the same effect
as tossing a coin. The King's verdict might or might not be just but it
had at least the merit of being final. It was the voice of God. There
were kings, too, like Solomon, with as much reputation for justice
as for finality.

Kings were also lawgivers. Laws were many of them, originally,
generalisations based on legal judgments in particular cases. Osiris
taught the Egyptians agriculture, gave them laws, and instructed
them in the worship of the gods. One of the earliest legal codes known
dates from Babylon (2123-2081 B.C.) and is the work of a king and
god, Hammurabi, who expresses in it the determination to 'uphold
justice in the land', as befitted one who was 'High of purpose, great
King, a very sun in Babylon'.[2] The functions of lawgiver and judge
were similarly identical in Egypt. 'During the period of the Old
Kingdom Egypt was governed by a strictly absolute monarchy. The
king was the sole legislator'.[3] And the laws, once issued, were the laws
of God.

In one other respect the king was extremely useful and that was in
representing the unity of the area he governed. This was particularly
important in Egypt, for example, where the Pharoah was always
separately King of Upper and Lower Egypt. It was, in fact, a dual
monarchy of which Horus and Seth were supposed to have been
rulers.[4] There were two separate administrations and two treasuries.
The Empire of the Incas was similarly called 'The-Four-in-One'. It
has been the function of many later monarchies to unite their territories in this way. Apart from that, the king, standing above the local
or patriarchal chiefs, symbolises his people as a whole. They express
their own unity in terms of their allegiance to him.

Of the fictions designed to explain the king's death, the third and
the most important implied the presence of an heir apparent. It was
natural, if only for that reason, that the king should be expected to
marry. This initially created a problem, for how could a common
person marry a god? The Egyptians overcame this difficulty by

[1] *II Samuel*, 18, verses 2-4.
[2] *Babylonian and Assyrian Laws and Contracts*. (ed.) C. W. H. Johns. Edinburgh, 1904.
Quoted in *Western Political Thought*. John Bowle. London, 1947. pp. 30-31.
[3] *The Legacy of Egypt*. Ed. S. R. K. Glanville. Oxford, 1942.
[4] *Priests and Kings*. H. Peake and H. J. Fleure. Oxford, 1927. p. 171.

making their king marry his sister, a goddess in her own right. Exactly the same solution was found by the Incas in South America. Among them, the Emperor, descended from the Sun God, married his eldest sister and designated as his successor the ablest son by that first and principal wife.[1] In other parts of the world the problem was simplified by the existence of other and adjacent kingdoms, allowing the divinely descended king to marry the daughter of another king, regarded for this purpose only as of almost equally divine descent. So Solomon, we learn 'made affinity with Pharaoh king of Egypt, and took Pharaoh's daughter and brought her into the city of David'[2]—where, she was presumably annoyed to find, the palace was not even finished. Such a practice brought with it the opportunity, on occasion, of marrying the only child of another king and so ending as ruler of two kingdoms instead of one. As against this interesting possibility, marriage alliances might complicate foreign affairs in a manner neither expected nor desired.

The marriage consummated, whether with a sister or a foreign royalty, children might be expected to result, not merely the son destined to succeed but other sons and daughters as well. These too will marry, some of them inevitably with commoners, producing children of partly royal descent. These are obvious candidates for official office, for persons of semi-divine descent cannot be allowed to starve or even to mingle on equal terms with the common people. As time goes on, to be descended from the gods becomes necessarily a characteristic of a wide and (widening) circle of relations. With a king like Solomon on the throne (with seven hundred wives and three hundred concubines) the process is likely to be accelerated. Should it become necessary, moreover, to promote some able commoner to a position higher than a minor royalty, he must be given a more than equivalent rank—perhaps with that fictitious cousinship which an English peerage still implies. The inference is that a monarchy by its very nature must create a nobility.

> The officials seem to have been originally relations of the royal house. They stand apart as a class—the Royal Kinsmen. In other words, those to whom power was delegated shared in some degree the mysterious essence which differentiated the king from all men. . . .
> As one of her main titles in the Old Kingdom the goddess of writing, Sethat, had 'Mistress of the Archives of the Royal Kinsmen', which would have been a kind of register of nobility, for no other hereditary nobility existed. . . . There were no classes or castes in Egypt. All were

[1] *Handbook of South American Indians.* Ed. Julian H. Steward. Vol. 2. The Andean Civilisation. Washington, 1946. (Smithsonian Institute). See also *The Origin and History of Politics.* W. C. MacLeod, New York, 1931. Chapter VI, pp. 213-220. These royal brother-sister marriages were found elsewhere in the Andes from Darien to the south of Peru.

[2] I *Kings,* verse 3.

commoners before the throne, except those in whose veins flowed some trace of the royal blood, however diluted. . . . The Royal Kinsmen would have formed a considerable class.

. . . It need not astonish us, therefore, to find Royal Kinsmen even in minor posts in the provincial administration.[1]

Exactly the same thing happened in Peru except for the existence there of other nobles. The result was a nobility of two grades, the superior of which could trace their ancestry to a previous sovereign. As the Peruvian kings were polygamous and quite capable of begetting up to two hundred children, the number of upper-grade nobles was far from negligible. Much the same thing happened even in societies far less advanced like that of the Zulu, in which the king was

. . . head by descent of the powerful aristocratic Zulu lineage which was looked up to by all Zulu, and his position in the national organization was strengthened, since tribes scattered through Zululand were ruled by his close relatives, who were bound to him by strong kinship ties of mutual assistance and by their common membership of the royal lineage.[2]

In short, given a monarchy, a nobility is almost certain to follow.

However divinely sanctioned, the Sun King could not rule a larger kingdom than the state of communications would allow. In an age of undeveloped roads, the ideal kingdom lay along the banks of a navigable river. The size of the kingdom depended essentially on the length of the river. The kingdoms of Egypt, Mesopotamia and India owed much of their importance to this. To develop a kingdom much beyond these original limits was something of a technical achievement, requiring perhaps (among other things) the art of writing. In the meanwhile the river kingdom was almost certain to develop a capital and this would bring with it a whole series of political needs, arising not from religious belief but from practical necessity. Without agriculture, however, no city, no civilisation, no village even, would have been possible.

---

[1] *Kingship and the Gods.* H. Frankfort. pp. 52-53. See also *Social Evolution.* V. Gordon Childe. London, 1951. p. 61, on the difference between the tombs of pharaohs and nobles as contrasted with those of commoners.
[2] *African Political Systems.* p. 35.

CHAPTER II

Monarchy among Pastoral Peoples

SOME people became herdsmen just as others became cultivators. There are vast stretches of Arabia, Palestine and Central Asia which afford grazing at one time of the year but offer little or no scope for agriculture. Peoples, therefore, who had domesticated cattle, sheep, goats, camels and horses specialised in moving between summer and winter pastures and in covering long distances where the grass is scanty. In their way of life they differed sharply from the cultivators, mainly in having no one settled home. Whereas the agriculturalist lived in one place and prayed for the rain to come at the proper time, the herdsman could go in search of it. His prayers and his religion were not, therefore, identical with those of the cultivator. Politically too he was to develop on rather different lines.

We have seen that the tendency of the cultivator was to transfer his loyalty from the family or kinship group to the unit of neighbourliness, the village. The revolutionary nature of this change must not be exaggerated. For one thing, the sense of neighbourhood must always have been there in some degree. For another, the sense of kinship still remained. Professor Lowie has pointed out that the two principles existed in sixth century Athens and that Solon had merely to strengthen the local tie as being politically more convenient.

> . . . The basic problem of the state is thus not that of explaining the somersault by which ancient peoples achieved the step from a government by personal relations to one by territorial contiguity only. The question is rather to show what processes strengthened the local tie which must be recognised as not less ancient than the rival principle.[1]

While some would disagree with this, holding that the tie of kinship is certainly the more ancient, it is at least true that the two principles of association co-existed for a long time, and indeed co-exist to-day. A Highland Scotsman's sense of loyalty to Clan Campbell or Macdonald might even now conceivably outweigh his local patriotism as a municipal voter of Croydon. And while a village life may tend to weaken the sense of kinship, a nomadic life must equally tend to strengthen it.

Social anthropologists distinguish two forms of family relation-

[1] *The Origin of the State.* R. H. Lowie. New York, 1927.

ship; the transient bilateral family, which they term the kinship system; and the grouping of persons by unilateral descent, which they term the lineage system. Only the latter, they say, establishes corporate units with a political function.[1] The Clan, that is to say, does not include relatives on the mother's side. It comprises only persons with a male ancestor in common. Among nomadic peoples it is the clan in this sense which attracts the loyalty felt by the cultivator for his village.[2] And the tribe, the political unit, is a group of clans, bound to each other by blood and often divided from other clans by blood-feuds. The Old Testament is essentially a tribal history and although the New Testament depicts the Jews as settled agriculturalists, their tribal organization is still in existence and the descent of each tribesman (as of Christ himself) is known.

The nomad has other characteristics besides his sense of kinship and lineage. He measures wealth in terms of cattle or other stock and wants few possessions unable to move on four legs. He is as unlikely to collect *objets d'art* as is a modern traveller by air. His life includes hardship but is one of relative leisure as compared with the life of the peasant. His property is of a kind subject to natural increase and also liable to a sudden diminution, creating a wide divergence in wealth between those more and less fortunate. The owner of flourishing and multiplying herds will need underlings to tend them. These he may well recruit from among other nomads whose herds have perished from disease or drought. The nomad's property may also be increased or diminished by theft. He has reason, from time to time, to covet some of the products of agriculture. He is, in general, an opponent of civilisation.

> As a settled life is favourable to civilization, so a nomadic life is the reverse. . . . By the very nature of their lives they are enemies of building, which is the first step in civilization.[3]

Among pastoral peoples, kingship is likely to take a special form. What is demanded of their king is leadership—the direction needed by a people on the move.[4] An agricultural people cannot be led, for they are static; but pastoral folk will call their king 'The Good Shepherd', a title later adapted to Christian theology. It is hardly possible for a king of this sort to become the almost invisible deity behind palace doors. He has no palace. Leading in person, he must be known to all, a man like other men but with greater knowledge and wisdom. One way, incidentally, in which his knowledge and wisdom might appear is in his greater wealth. The nomad who has gained

[1] See *African Political Systems*. p. 6.
[2] *Primitive Society*. R. H. Lowie. London, 1921. 3rd ed. 1949. p. 377.
[3] *Politics*. Aristotle, (I). p. 1319.
[4] See *Habitat, Economy and Society, a Geographical Introduction to Ethnology*. C. Daryll Forde. London, 1934. p. 408.

some wealth by luck in breeding and raising stock will turn readily
to trade as a means of becoming wealthier still. But to be known as a
good judge of cattle and horses with a flair for finding the best route to
the best pasture at the right time is a very different thing from being a
deity. In general, the men who cross the desert and sleep beneath the
stars have an intense belief in their tribal god, as the Jews had in
Yahweh, but they are not much inclined to deify a man who sleeps
in the next tent.

The herdsmen whose migrations from one pasture to another are
all within a very limited area differ less from the cultivators than do
the herdsmen who have further to go. Indeed, there are pastoral
peoples who are largely settled in one place, only the shepherds being
truly migrant. Of those with great distances to cover, a majority lay
some sort of claim to specific pastures.

> . . . The steppe-dwellers know how to make the best use of their
> pastures . . . all migrations are within the territory of the tribe, clan, or
> family group, as the case may be, various parts of which are occupied
> at different times and usually only for a short period. Even in the best
> districts a move of five to ten miles must be made every few weeks.
> The wanderings are never aimless. The pastoralists know where there
> is water, and they often visit certain pastures at a particular season.
> Many of the herders of Central Asia spend their winter in the val-
> leys. . . . Their possession of horses has given them greater mobility
> than many herders, and some of them wander several hundred miles
> during a year.[1]

The greater distances travelled are essentially due to the domestication of camels and horses. Camels were known in Babylonia from
about 3000 B.C. but were not numerous until a century later. From
the beginning, camels were bred with a view to improving their
special qualities of endurance and speed. It has been pointed out that
'many a dromedary can boast a genealogy far longer than the
descendants of the Darley Arabian'.[2] The horse appears in Babylonian records at about the same period as the camel but may have
been known in Mesopotamia before that. Horses may first have been
tamed and ridden in Turkestan, their use spreading thence to the
Iranian plateau and so to Babylon. They again were carefully bred,
their pedigrees being remembered, and their qualities developed. The
introduction of camels and horses produced not only a greater distinction between herdsmen and cultivators but also some differences
among the herdsmen themselves. Some were mounted and some were
not. In the desert, for example, the true nomad divides the human
race into two main categories, the *Hayar*, those who live in permanent

---

[1] *From Hunter to Husbandman.* J. W. Page. London, 1939. p. 99.
[2] *In the Sahara.* Canon Tristram. Quoted in *From Hunter to Husbandman.* p. 104.

houses and the *Arab* who dwell in black tents. The arabs are further divided into the *Shwayar*, who live on the edge of the desert with their flocks, and the *Bedouins* who breed camels and live for ten months of the year in the desert.[1]

It has been observed that, in partly nomadic tribes, the nomads are the more vigorous and independent of the members. 'The foremost Shaikhs of the Abaidat, Hasa . . . etc., etc. . . . are all to be found during the rains farther away in the steppe than most of their fellow-tribesmen'.[2]

The differences here described are not merely divergencies in occupation. They represent, and have presumably always represented, a series of social gradations. The tent-dweller despises the husband-man. The Bedouin despises the mere Arab. And among the Bedouin it soon appears that some tribes are superior to others. Thus we find, in the Old Testament, that Saul, when chosen as king, protests 'Am I not a Benjamite, of the smallest of the tribes of Israel? And my family the least of all the families of the tribe of Benjamin?'[3] The relative status of the different tribes and families must have been perfectly well known and scarcely a matter of dispute. Within each tribe, moreover, there are strangers and fellow-travellers, regarded as inferior to the tribesmen themselves. There must be a blacksmith, for example, but he is more or less 'untouchable'. There are other menials, camp-followers and slaves, of seven or more categories but all socially beyond the pale. As against that, at the other extreme, the office of chief is hereditary, most likely, in the senior line but subject to a necessary standard of ability, thus giving the elders of the tribe a certain latitude in choosing one of those eligible by birth. It should be observed, incidentally, that people interested in the pedigrees of horses are likely to show a similar interest in the pedigrees of men.

The inequalities so far described as characteristic of nomadic peoples are partly the result of good or bad fortune but more the result of varying degrees of courage. The nomad who remains on the fringe of the desert is withheld by timidity from claiming the higher status that would accompany a greater spirit of enterprise. His lower status is thus voluntarily assumed, at least in part, just as, among seafaring peoples, the deep-sea mariner may look down upon the fisherman who in turn despises the landsman; each being neverthe-less content to remain what he is. Among nomad riders of the horse or camel there arise, in addition, all the inequalities resulting from mounts being worse or better and riders being more or less skilled and daring.

[1] *A Reader in General Anthropology.* Carleton S. Coon. London, 1950. pp. 380-407.
[2] *The Sanusi of Cyrenaica.* E. E. Evans-Pritchard. Oxford, 1949. See Chapter II. The Bedouin.
[3] I *Samuel* 9, verse 21.

That there is a limit to the size of a pastoral group is manifest. However nomadic in character, the group, clan or tribe has a well-defined territory, the pastures in which will support no more than a certain number of cattle, sheep or draught animals. When the pastures are over-grazed, the herdsmen must either divide into smaller groups or invade the pastures of another tribe. Disputes are likely to result from either policy, and the Old Testament contains one careful explanation of how one such quarrel arose:—

> ... And Abram was very rich in cattle ... and Lot also, which went with Abram, had flocks, and herds, and tents. And the land was not able to bear them, that they might dwell together: for their substance was great.... And there was a strife between the herdmen of Abram's cattle and the herdmen of Lot's cattle. . . .[1]

The immediate solution in this instance was for Abram and Lot to separate, Abram going to Canaan and Lot to the plain of Jordan; but not every dispute would end as amicably, nor was that agreement free from the risk that each of the two groups might become embroiled with another tribe.

There can be little doubt that it was the pastoral peoples who proved most quarrelsome.

> ... The grain-grower is usually too much absorbed in cultivating his land to have any interests outside it, and such fights as he indulges in are not of his seeking. Though the most peaceful and long-suffering of men, they resent ravages on their fields, and even in quite early days seem to have come to blows with the pastoral tribes on their borders, whose beasts invaded and devoured their growing crops. We have a hint of one such episode in the story of Cain and Abel, told by the partisans of the latter, so that in the story as it has reached us no mention is made of the damage done by Abel's sheep among the crops of Cain. . . .[2]

It is probably an exaggeration to assert that agricultural peoples are invariably peace-loving, but it is clear that pastoral peoples have more occasion for dispute, both among themselves and also with their more settled neighbours. There might be competition for the earliest grass in spring or the latest grass in autumn. There might be strife over a spring or a well. There might, finally, be a season of drought during which the crops of the cultivator would become a standing temptation.

> It is not pastoralism and cultivation as such that face each other in hostility, but mobility with poverty as against sessile and vulnerable wealth. . . .

[1] *Genesis* 13, verse 2.
[2] *Early Steps in Human Progress.* Harold Peake. London, 1933. p. 229.

The essential point, so far as relations with cultivators are concerned, is that a pastoral people, especially if equipped with riding animals, has a superior mobility which, although it may at a given time be latent, is always there as an asset when there is opportunity for gain, and equally when there is need for retreat. . . .[1]

It was most probably among the pastoral peoples that conflict first began on such a scale as to merit the name of war. And war, when it came, had a great influence on the institution of Monarchy.

[1] *Habitat, Economy and Society, a Geographical Introduction to Ethnology.* C. Daryll Forde. London, 1934. pp. 405-407.

CHAPTER III

The Implications of War

THERE are reasons, as we have seen, for supposing that war originated among the nomads. Probabilities apart, moreover, it was commonly believed in ancient times that this was so. Aristotle points out that 'A pastoral people is the best trained for war, sturdy in physique and used to camping out'.[1] Even more to the point, an Arab historian writes as follows:—

> Since conquests are achieved only by dash and daring, a people accustomed to the nomadic life and the rough manners engendered by the desert can readily conquer a more civilized people, even though the latter be more numerous and equally strong in communal spirit. . . . Having no country where they live in the enjoyment of plenty, they have no tie to bind them to their birthplace. All lands alike seem good to them. Not content with lordship among their own folk and over their neighbours, they overpass the bounds of their country to invade distant lands and subdue their inhabitants. . . .[2]

All this is true enough; and if we go further and ask what are the special qualities of a good soldier we shall find that the qualities of the nomad are much the same. We would instance physical toughness, physical courage, laziness (with a capacity for energy when needed), the ruthlessness which comes, somehow, from a life of movement in the open air,[3] no tendency to be homesick, a certain cunning but no excess of brains, a great care for horses but none for standing crops or buildings, a robust common sense, a singleness of purpose and a strictly limited imagination—all these are the qualities of the nomad. If there were no other evidence shedding light on the origins of war, we could still say that the nomadic peoples had the character, the means and the motive.

War, as opposed to inter-tribal bickering, depends upon transport facilities. The peoples of Babylon and Sumeria had the camel, the ass and the wheeled vehicle by some period round about 3000 B.C. Although Sargon of Agade's conquest of Sumeria (perhaps round about 2750 B.C.) is the first large-scale war of which we have record,

---

[1] *Politics.* I. p. 1319.
[2] *In Quest of Civilization.* Ronald Latham. London, 1946.
[3] As Kinglake remarks in *Eothen.* See *Kinglake's Eothen.* Ed. by D. G. Hogarth. London, 1925. p. 28.

it is probable that there were previous wars among the Semitic tribes of Syria and Arabia.[1] But while an army of nomad or partly nomad origin, with driven herds of cattle, sheep and goats, and with vehicles drawn by oxen or asses, has sufficient mobility for war, its speed remains pedestrian. The acceleration of war begins with the introduction of the horse.

The horse in earliest use was the tarpan, a small animal of the Shetland pony type, found wild in the steppe country between the Dnieper and the Altai.[2] These had been domesticated and saddled by 2500 B.C. and were in use from the Caucasus to the Indus Valley. They gave an added mobility in war but were too small to mount a heavily equipped rider. They began to prove their real value when they replaced the ass in drawing the war-chariot. By means of the chariot, four horses (or more) could be made to carry two men, one of them heavily armed. The dreaded war-chariot (of which the first description dates from 2000 B.C.) spread as a standard weapon of war from the steppe country to Mesopotamia, Assyria, Persia, India, Tibet, China and Europe. The Babylonians learnt to respect the 'wild ass of the mountains' and the pastoral Amorites, who centred their empire on Babylon, used their war chariots to invade and conquer Egypt in about 2100 B.C., setting up there a new dynasty of the Hyksos or 'shepherd kings'. What impressed the Egyptians (to whom the horse was a novelty) was the speed with which the campaign ended.

> God was adverse to us, and there came out of the East in an extra-
> ordinary manner men of ignoble race, who had the temerity to invade
> our country, and easily subdued it by force without a battle.
> (Manetho).[3]

Once the Egyptians had learnt how to use horse-drawn war-chariots, they regained their freedom in about 1600 B.C.

The next stage in the development of the horse was apparently the crossing of the tarpan with another breed of horse, perhaps native to Libya or Persia.[4] A type of horse was eventually produced which could be ridden to battle (though not at first *into* battle) by a single archer. For centuries, meanwhile, both chariots and horsemen were to be seen on the battlefield. The earliest known detailed account of a battle relates to that of Megiddo in about 1479 B.C. The conflict was between Thothmes III of Egypt and a group of Asian princes gathered in Palestine. We have the account of a council of war, an advance by

---

[1] Wars of Sumer and Akkad are supposed to have taken place in about 2961 B.C. *See Priests and Kings.* H. Peake and H. J. Fleure. Oxford, 1927. p. 48.
[2] *Communication has been established.* A. J. H. Goodwin. London, 1937. See Chapter 3, esp. pp. 47-48.
[3] *Ancient History of the Near East.* p. 214.
[4] See *Empire and Communications.* Prof. H. A. Innis. Oxford, 1950.

the obvious and therefore unexpected route, a deployment before battle, the engagement and victory, the pursuit and the capture of Megiddo itself. Before the battle the King overruled his captains and led the army in person, his troops following 'horse behind horse'. When the battle was joined the King fought 'in a chariot of electron, arrayed with his weapons of war, like Horus, the Smiter, lord of power'.[1] The enemy (not unnaturally) fled 'abandoning their horses and their chariots of gold and silver'. When the walled town of Megiddo fell as a consequence of the victory, the loot included 924 chariots, 200 suits of armour, flocks and herds, and the reaping of the local harvest. From this narrative it is apparent that fighting strength was counted in chariots, that the leaders at least had elaborate armour, that the king might command in person and that the God Horus had become a God of War.

The Old Testament account of Pharaoh's pursuit of the Israelites dates from a rather later period but presents a similar picture. Pharaoh had horsemen in addition to his 600 chariots but the Israelites had neither.[2] They evidently fought at this period under a considerable disadvantage, being told to make the best of it. 'When thou goest out to battle against thine enemies, and seest horses and chariots, and a people more than thou, be not afraid of them . . . .'[3] This sort of exhortation remained familiar to them during the time of Saul and David—the Philistines being able to muster 30,000 chariots and 6,000 horsemen[4]—and it was not until the time of Solomon (c. 960 B.C.) that the Israelites were similarly equipped with horses purchased in Egypt. They could then muster 1,400 chariots and 12,000 horsemen.[5] At the end of the captivity in Babylon the Jewish tribesmen numbered over 42,000 but could muster only 736 horses and 435 camels as against nearly 7,000 asses and mules. Horses were evidently reserved for war. The Assyrian army included mounted archers in 800 B.C. but each of these needed a groom to hold the horse's bridle while the bow was drawn—a loss both of mobility and man-power. No horseman used a weapon other than a bow; nor, without a stirrup, would this have been possible.

The technique of chariot warfare seems to have been much the same everywhere. One man fought and the other managed the horses.

> And a certain man drew a bow at a venture, and smote the King of Israel between the joints of the harness; wherefore he said unto the

[1] Ancient History of the Near East. pp. 236-239.
[2] Exodus. 14.
[3] Deuteronomy, 20, which comprises the Jewish Field Service Regulations of the period.
[4] To quote the war correspondents of the defeated side.
[5] I Kings. 10. David had a hundred chariots only. See II Samuel 8, verse 4.

driver of his chariot, Turn thine hand, and carry me out of the host; for I am wounded. . . .[1]

In India, according to one authority, the king drove the chariot himself, but this was apparently to make room for his principal religious adviser whose prayers had to accompany every process from harnessing the horses to shooting off his arrows.[2] We learn that some chariots of later design carried a crew of three, which would certainly be advisable so long as a chief Brahman had to be one of them. Chariots are mentioned frequently in the *Iliad*. They were used for war in places as distant from each other as China and Britain. Before they could be replaced by real cavalry, two further steps in progress were necessary. First of these was the breeding of larger horses. Second of these was the invention of the stirrup.

The breed of horses was improved mainly by the Arabs but the stirrup was apparently invented in China. It was the people of Ch'in or Ts'in, living in the mountains of the upper Hoang-Ho, who first acquired horses to ride and iron weapons instead of bronze. They conquered the rest of China without much difficulty between 350 and 220 B.C. and established an empire in which good roads and fast horses played an important part. It was not, however, until long afterwards, in the sixth century A.D. that the use of the stirrup spread from China to the Middle East, transforming all warfare and making cavalry supreme on the battlefield for many centuries to come.[3] Given stirrups, the horseman could fight without dismounting, taking the shock of battle, wielding the sword and then the lance. Behind the whole epic of the Crusades there lies a story of horse-breeding and horsemanship. From it there emerges the idea of chivalry. Europeans have tended to assume that the Saracens learnt the etiquette of war from the Crusaders. This is the reverse of the truth. The custom of sparing the disarmed, the wounded, the unhorsed, the women and children comes essentially from the desert peoples of the Arab type.

> There are peoples who after a fight spare their defeated adversaries without enslaving them. The different tribes of the Arab stock have the reputation of showing their enemies remarkable clemency after a victorious fight. Regarding the Bedouins of the Euphrates it is said to be the property of the enemy and not his person which is the object of the fighting. The person of the enemy is sacred when disarmed or dismounted; and prisoners are neither enslaved nor held to other ransom than their mares.[4] This purpose is attained by merely dis-

[1] *I Kings*, 22.
[2] *The Vedic Age*. Ed. by R. C. Majumdar. London, 1951. p. 484.
[3] *Communication has been established.* A. J. H. Goodwin. London, 1937. p. 48 et. seq.
[4] Among the steppe tribes, the leaders used to ride geldings but the custom in the Middle East was different, the warrior riding a mare, his followers having geldings, mules or asses. See p. 50. *Communication has been established.* A. J. H. Goodwin. London, 1937.

mounting or wounding the enemy. The latter's arms and mare become the property of the victor, and he himself is then let go. . . . It is contrary to the Arab conscience to extinguish a kabîla (tribe). . . .[1]

The customs of the Ruala Bedouins were not necessarily those of all Arabs nor were they displayed, of necessity, towards those not of Arab stock. Thus Jeremiah wrote of the nomads 'They lay hold on bow and spear; they are cruel and have no mercy; their voice roareth like the sea and they ride upon horses'.[2] It was strictly towards other horsemen that their clemency was shown and chivalry is strictly the right word for it. But chivalry, in the sense of sparing opponents, is clearly a desert attitude of mind, closely connected with desert laws of hospitality. The main enemy (as well as friend) is the desert itself, as against which, in its more dangerous aspect, all are allied. The host who shares his provisions with a stranger may soon afterwards be himself the guest. And where all tribesmen are running similar risks there is a fellow feeling for others whose predicament is the same and an equally shared contempt for those who are running no risk at all. Similar customs are found among sailors and mountaineers. The rescue of survivors at sea has always extended, in some degree, to rivals or opponents; and even a hostile seaman deserves more respect than the mere landlubber. In similar fashion, the cavalry élite of an army which includes a despised infantry (not to mention mere camp-followers) has much in common with the cavalry on the other side.[3] The fighting may be real enough but will tend to fall short of total warfare. Neither group will fight to the point of mutual extermination for all are agreed that a future battle, without cavalry, would be no better than a vulgar brawl.

With these origins and aspects of war clearly in mind we shall find that the political implications of war are not far to seek. To begin with, war demands leadership. Among pastoral peoples the leadership is already there. In an agricultural land, ruled by a king of mainly religious and ceremonial importance, the leader must be found. Either the king must descend from his pedestal and assume a different kind of power (losing his godlike aloofness in the process) or else another leader must be appointed, assuming an authority which a king might view with some alarm. There are instances of either policy being preferred but seldom has the need for a single leader been seriously questioned. In war, as people realised from the beginning, it is usually better to decide *something*, even mistakenly, than to argue

---

[1] *The Origin of the Inequality of the Social Classes.* G. Landtman. London, 1938. p. 3.
[2] *Jeremiah*, 6, verse 23.
[3] The Indians, in estimating the strength of an army counted one chariot as equal to one elephant, three cavalry-men or five infantry. The Indian rules of warfare also enjoined the soldier to spare the timid, the intoxicated, the insane, the negligent, the unprepared, the aged, women, children and Brahmans. To this list Gautama is said to have added ambassadors and cows.

for long as to what is best. So the first effect of war is to transform the character of kingship. The king who leads his army in person becomes something less than a god but gains enormously in actual authority; provided always that the war is, or can be made to appear, victorious. The king who, like David 'stood by the gate side, and all the people came out by hundreds and by thousands',[1] might the better survive defeat but would lose much executive power in the course of the war. After victory he might well have to listen to his subjects cheering someone else.

The next implication of war concerns rather the people themselves. For they gain in war a sense of unity, born of common fears and hatreds, strengthened by common privations, efforts, disasters and triumphs. The king is made the symbol of that unity but, in his absence, (and he could not be everywhere) the sense of unity finds expression in his flag or standard. At the same time the fortification of cities strengthens a local sense of unity. And walled cities, being more compact and defined, become more urban in character; further removed from the rural and more self-consciously civilised.

With this new emphasis, however, on group loyalties, tribal or local, comes the growth of class distinctions. Monarchy creates a nobility in any case but it is war that adds to its numbers, prestige and influence. An army must be officered and not solely by the king's relatives. There will grow up, during a war, a class of nobles whose authority is based not upon religion, magic, seniority or birth but upon experience, ability, determination and courage. These nobles are to be distinguished from the common people by their superior arms and armour, by their chariots and, at a later date, by their horses. The fact of being mounted makes a revolution in outlook both in the rider and in his inferiors. The horseman is higher from the ground, sees farther, travels faster. The change in outlook might almost be compared with that brought about when man first stood on his hind legs. The horseman is *literally* looked up to. He in turn *literally* looks down upon other folk, and over them towards things more remote. He feels more than his unmounted self and, even when he is on foot, his boots, breeches and spurs have about them a lingering hint of authority, daring and privilege. He enjoys more respect than envy for even in time of peace he takes more risks than humbler folk are always ready to incur. Hence, in many languages, the word for horseman has much the same significance as 'gentleman'. The Roman Equestrian had a certain rank in society. Since then we have Knight, Knecht, Cavalier, Chevalier, Caballero and other such titles. Even in the British army, riding boots, leggings and spurs lingered for a time after horses had become scarce. Even in

[1] II *Samuel*, 18, verse 4.

India jodhpurs are worn by statesmen and diplomatists whose duties are, in fact, sedentary. And if modern drivers of tanks still insist upon their theoretical status as cavalrymen, the riding boot played a still greater part among the non-riding adherents of Mussolini and Hitler.

From war is derived the epic, the saga, the tale of heroism. While it was the King (beyond question) who terrified the enemy and won the battle, other men sometimes distinguished themselves; occasionally, even, when the king was not there. They behaved, it became clear, in a godlike manner. So they must, it seems, be gods or descendants of the gods. Thus there developed a new source of nobility. These god-descended heroes—whose deeds, recorded in song and verse, lost nothing in the telling—these men who had slain lions, tigers, dragons and giants—were not to be confused henceforth with the common herd. And if they were descended from the gods, other people were descended from *them*. While some men's reputations might suffer during a war, others rose to the status of the god-descended, the equestrian, the noble.

Other political implications of war include the subordination of women and efforts to ensure their chastity in the absence of warrior husbands and in the presence of other warriors whose administrative duties have kept them out of the actual fighting. Nor must we forget that the capture of prisoners creates or extends the institution of slavery. War also induces people to copy each other, and more especially the enemy, whose uniform and equipment is always superior. From war, finally, we inherit a grisly legacy of taxation. Horses, chariots and arms have to be paid for. Taxes bring with them all the attendant horrors of arithmetic, estimates, assessments and accounts. War is thus accompanied by and largely responsible for a vastly more complicated administration. Maps must be drawn and distances estimated. Someone must calculate what provision to make for so many men and horses over a given number of days. Someone must discover how many men are sick and how many still on parade. People must be taught something of elementary hygiene, invented probably by Moses. War, if successful, will imply the conquest of new territory with consequent problems of distance, communications, fortification, military government and taxes. And the wider the area conquered the more complex its administration will become.

In administration the basic need is for writing. The first cuneiform writing was apparently the invention of the Sumerians in about 3500 B.C. The Egyptian hieroglyphic existed, however, before 3000 B.C. Chinese writing may date from 2000 B.C. or thereabouts and is the only pictorial writing still used. There are obvious limitations to the value of any ideographic script and the great step forward (after that of writing itself) was the invention of the phonetic alphabet of twenty-two letters, at first without the vowels. This was the North Semitic alphabet, probably invented in Syria between 2000 and 1500 B.C.; the script from which, via the Phoenicians, the Greek and Roman alphabets derived. The later and more effective method of writing dates from the period during which wars became fashionable and from the area in which some of the earliest recorded campaigns took place. This may be coincidence. It is worth recalling, however, that administration, writing and bureaucracy are all closely connected with each other and that the earlier (and more difficult) writing tends to remain the accomplishment of a priestly class to which administrative work might often fall. If one result of war might be to establish or strengthen a nobility of the sword, another result might well be to establish a second nobility—of the pen.

CHAPTER IV

Monarchy and Nationalism

W E have traced authority in human affairs to the elder person, the parent, the patriarch of a family group, the chief of a tribe. We have seen that the authority of the chief is sometimes paralleled by the authority of the magician or priest. There is reason, we have found, to suspect that kingship arises, in agrarian states, from one person managing to combine the powers of chief and magician. In pastoral societies we have noted a different conception of kingship, based upon the powers of a chief who is essentially a leader of men, not aloof and godlike but active, skilful, well-mounted and rich. War arises and leads, not infrequently, to the less warlike peasants being attacked by the nomads. A nomad conquest of an agrarian people is a fairly common event, the result being to impose pastoral rulers upon an agricultural society. Egypt provides perhaps the classic example of this; and there, as elsewhere, the views (on monarchy) of the conquered proved more important, in the long run, than the views of the conquerors. Like the Roman Emperors who later assumed the same office, the Shepherd Kings found themselves stiffening into the hieratic attitude apparently expected of them. Something like mummification set in even while the king lived. And it was Egypt that provided a pattern of monarchy for the rest of the world.

Monarchy, as thus established and spread afterwards by conquest or imitation, comprised four distinct elements. The king had, basically, the paternal authority of the tribal or district chief; he was the arbitrator in cases of dispute, the father of his people. To this he had added the authority of the priest, the god-descended immortal, the embodiment of god and (finally) the god on earth. But if the king himself came of a pastoral and nomadic people, he would also be the active leader, administrator and judge. If, finally, his power had been established and maintained by war, he would be the supreme commander in the field, experienced, skilful, daring and, above all, victorious. It is fairly clear that monarchy reaches its purest form when a king contrives to accumulate and retain all these different powers, paternal, religious, active and warlike. It is at least equally clear that these different functions are partly inconsistent with each other. The active leader in matters of policy is not the ideal arbitrator in matters

53

of dispute. The enthroned king, immovable under the weight of crown and robes, high above his prostrate court, would seem incongruous in the tented field. The war leader, on the other hand, can scarcely exact a religious veneration from comrades who know him to be a man like themselves. Kings who have striven for the maximum authority have sought to strike a balance between their several roles, the predominant role being decided in part by personality but more perhaps by the nature of the problem they had to solve.

Vital to this problem is the factor of distance. When an empire is vast and varied, it was literally impossible (before the era of television) for the king to make himself personally known, as judge and leader, to any considerable number of his subjects. Even if he did, he would return from his travels to find that actual power had fallen (perhaps irrevocably) into the hands of a minister, secretary or brother. To maintain personal rule over a large empire the king would have to be everywhere at once. As this was impracticable for a man, the king had to make himself a god, present in spirit wherever his altar might be set up. Perhaps the most long-lived of monarchies have been of this type, gaining in permanence for what they may have lost in vitality. The tendency is, however, for such a monarchy to lose all but nominal power, especially during a king's minority, and turn gradually into an elaborate pageant behind which the actual government is done by others. A king who sees the danger of this may choose rather the role of military leader, keeping the substance of power and resigning something of the shadow. By the end of a life spent on the threatened frontiers, he too will find that the central administration has been taken over by someone else. The final experiments in monarchy tend to show that a large and diverse empire requires a more or less deified king, and that the kings most successful in retaining real authority have ruled over smaller and more compact areas; the sort of territories exemplified in the modern national state.

Perhaps the best example of a successful monarchy established over a wide area and yet wielding considerable powers can be taken from the history of China. Here the process was assisted by a measure of geographical unity and isolation, without which stability might have been more difficult to maintain. China, at any rate, affords the spectacle of a semi-deified monarchy wielding effective power over diverse peoples and for considerable periods of time. Chinese civilisation had developed in a China of conflicting states, no one of which mastered the rest until about 200 B.C. The Ch'in or Ts'in people, who first learnt to ride and use iron weapons, were reorganised as a centralised monarchy as from about 350 B.C. and found no other state capable of prolonged rivalry. 'To a steel tool of extreme precision was opposed a corrupt mass of crumbling states torn by internecine strife'.[1] Shih Huang-Ti made himself emperor, assumed a divine title, abolished the feudal states, reorganised China into thirty-six Provinces (to which four more were added later), standardised calligraphy, weights and measures, constructed a system of imperial roads and burnt all books that were not officially approved. The Ts'in Dynasty was actually shortlived but its central organisation was taken over by Wu Ti and eventually, after a period of disorder, by the T'ang Dynasty (A.D. 618-906) and the Ming Dynasty (A.D. 1368-1644). Despite internal troubles and the 'Dark Ages' of A.D. 220-589, China has tended to be a centralised empire under a single king. From the third century B.C. until 1912 the sacred monarch had theoretically absolute sovereignty, unlimited by law. In practice there were considerable changes but in form the government was very stable and highly organised. Successive monarchs had evolved a personal absolutism designed to guard against usurpation by a relative, a servant or eunuch, a noble or a provincial governor. Supreme religious, executive, judicial and military powers were all vested in the emperor himself. All the influences of literature, education, inspection and doctrine were organised in support of the imperial throne. And yet further stability was achieved by a deliberate abstention from foreign affairs or military conquest. The Great Wall of China symbolises a consistent policy of seeking unity and permanence within a defined and limited area. The price paid for stability was in terms of mental stagnation— such a stagnation as probably characterised the monarchy of Egypt.

It would be wrong, however, to conclude from this that the Chinese have made no contribution to political thought or practice. It is true that their ministerial and provincial administration was similar to that of other empires, although more efficient than most, but they also invented selection of officials by competitive examination together with a system of inspection and of ascertaining the views of the public. Strictly subordinating military to civilian officers, they chose both on the basis of written examinations. Boys began their education at the age of five or six, spent four or five years in practising calligraphy and memorising a dozen classic works. The more apt for study were allowed to enter for a district examination. In this the candidates (perhaps about 2,000 in each district) would spend a night and a day in composing two essays and a poem. Perhaps about twenty out of the 2,000 would be awarded the first degree. These privileged few, now exempt from taxes or corporal punishment and indeed from the magistrate's authority, spent three years in the district academy before attempting the provincial examination, held every

[1] *A Short History of Chinese Civilization.* Richard Wilhelm. London, 1929. p. 157.

third year and lasting three sessions of three days each. Theoretically the candidates might have numbered 50,000 but not all stayed the course.

> In the first session he was required to produce three essays; one on a subject from the Analects, one from the Chang Yung (Doctrine of the Mean), and one from the Ming Tzu (Works of Mencius). He must also compose a poem of eight couplets. In the second session the candidate wrote five essays, one from each of the Five Classics; and in the third session, five essays on the art of government, supporting his statements with reference to great historic ideas. His originality was shown in his application of these ideas to the problems given.[1]

It was not an examination in which originality, beyond a certain point, was likely to pay. Of those competing (17,000 to 3,000, according to the population of the province) from 184 to 52 were awarded the second degree. These worked for one more year and then took the third and highest examination at the imperial capital. This was of one session, during which the candidate wrote an essay on a current political problem - irrigation, currency, education or the like. Some 300 candidates were then awarded the third and highest degree, the top three in merit having special honours and the best of all being noted as a likely future Minister. Of the 300 'chin-shih' or achieved scholars, a third were given academic posts, two thirds admitted to the civil service.

From the Emperor's point of view, this system of recruitment had great advantages. Worked fairly, it excluded nepotism, favouritism and influence. It allowed no unfair preponderance to any one province nor even to any one class of society. It was strictly an examination in a literature which the Emperor approved. Even, however, on general principles, the system had much to commend it. It excluded the mediocre and stupid. It excluded, above all, those who lacked the stamina to go on. It has been claimed, and with justice, that these examinations afforded a moral as well as an intellectual test.[2] Their value was recognised and the principle copied successively by the East India Company (in 1832), the English· Civil Service (1853) and the Indian Civil Service (1855).[3] One might add that the later improvements on the competitive system have been manifestly less efficient.

At the same time, the limitations of the Chinese system are obvious. To arrive at an absolute order of merit, all candidates must take the same examination. This in itself excluded from public life all whose

---

[1] *China*. Ed. by H. F. MacNair. California, 1946. See also *Government and Politics of China*. Ch'ien Tuang Sheng. Harvard, 1950. pp. 22-23.
[2] See *Hsüntze, the Moulder of Confucianism*. H. H. Dubs. London, 1927. p. 11.
[3] *China, op. cit.* Chap. XXX by Têng Ssu-Yii. p. 449.

abilities were other than literary; the lawyer, the mathematician, the scientist, the merchant, the explorer, the seaman and the soldier. Only classical learning was considered and the student was invited to memorise, elucidate, comment upon and versify round the accepted ideas comprised in a fairly narrow reading. He was not encouraged to think for himself. His final accomplishment, moreover (for all practical purposes) was in reading and writing, versifying and quoting from the classics. It is the point at which higher education should begin rather than finish. One might add, finally, that the system of taking the clever boy from a poor family and giving him high office as a result of his examination marks, was not without its dangers in a society where family loyalties were so deeply-rooted. The official could hardly be illiterate but he might easily prove dishonest.

As against corruption, however, the Chinese had another device. This was the Board of Censors, established under the T'ang Dynasty and comprising two Censors-General and two Deputies; with subordinates both in the imperial capital and in the Provinces.[1] Members of this Board served a dual purpose. They were to act as a check on officialdom. They were also to ascertain the trend of public opinion and remonstrate with the Emperor on the subject of any act or policy they considered either unwise or unpopular. They were generally more successful in exposing corruption than in remonstrating with an infallible Emperor. They represent, nevertheless, an important Chinese contribution to political practice. The Chinese monarchy owed much of its stability to the system of examinations and as much again perhaps to this official inspectorate.

For much of the history of China the Emperor did in fact rule. But examples are fairly common of monarchs, similarly empowered, being gradually relegated to purely religious and ceremonial duties. Of these examples one of the best is afforded by Japan. Here, in Yamato, as it was then called, a group of tribes came successively under the influence of China, *circa* A.D. 214, and of Buddhism, A.D. 500-600. There followed, in A.D. 645, a revolution called 'The Great Change' in the course of which two reformers—Naka, a prince of the Imperial Clan, and Kamatari, a noble—reorganised Japan on Chinese lines; weakening the nobles, disarming the populace and strengthening the central government. Tribal chiefs were deprived of their lands and then reinstated as salaried officials. Examinations were introduced with a new hierarchy of rank, a different system of taxation, and an improved system of communications. A new capital was founded at Nara and the country's name changed to Nippon.

---

[1] *The Government and Politics of China.* Ch'ien Tuan-Sheng. Harvard, 1950. pp. 38, 39.

But while the powers of tribal chieftains had been, in general, curtailed, one clan had gained considerably in power and that was Kamatari's clan, the people who had brought the revolution about. Kamatari was granted estates called Fujiwara and this name was now given to a family destined to retain political power, behind a nominal Emperor, for many generations to come. For a moment it seemed that the Emperor might lose even his religious position under Buddhist domination but the Fujiwara resisted this movement (in its political aspect) and moved their Emperor to a new capital at Kyoto, away from the monastic influences at Nara. Thenceforward, until the nineteenth century, the functions of the Sacred Emperor were almost entirely ceremonial. The Fujiwara technique was to marry their daughters to the Emperors, rule while the Emperor was young and compel him to abdicate and enter a monastery if he showed signs of initiative, replacing him by another youngster, probably married to another daughter.

Perhaps the most interesting feature of this nominal Monarchy was the system by which the nobles, dispossessed of their local powers, were consoled by official sinecures and salaries. In the ninth century there were eight Ministries of State, each with anything up to eighteen departments, employing over 6,000 officials in the capital alone.[1] The departments included 'Bureau of Divination', 'Office of Imperial Mausolea', 'The Palace Women's Office' and the 'Utensils and Crockery Office'. As these and many others had to be staffed by people of good family, one cannot but see in them a Fujiwara device for keeping other people (the Emperor included) out of mischief. It succeeded, apparently, for about four hundred and fifty years.

As contrasted with monarchies which originally had (and in some instances retained) all the elements of both secular and religious power, India presents an example of monarchies in which the elements were never fully combined. For the institution of Caste in India, whatever its origin, seems to antedate the idea of monarchy. When the king came to power, the Brahman was already there and able to deny him religious supremacy. More than that, society had a structure which the king was powerless to modify, religions over which he had little control, laws which he did not originate and customs by which he might even be bound. Of early Indian history remarkably little is known, but it left the kingdoms of the Indus and the Ganges with Caste, with the Vedic cult, and with a nobility deriving their descent from previous invaders. There is evidence of earlier political experiments but, in historical times, it was evidently assumed that a society as diversified as that of India required mon-

[1] *The Pageant of Japanese History.* M. M. Dilts. New York, 1938. New ed. 1947.

archical power to give it any coherence at all. Nor was a king likely to find the task an easy one.

Caste was the division of society into five main hereditary groups: the Brahman or priestly and literate Caste, the Warrior Caste, the Farmer and Trader Caste, the Working Caste and the Slaves or Untouchables.

The superiority of the Brahman caste is a basic tenet of Hindu religion.

> Ancient India, so far as the Brahman caste presents it in its own literature, is a theocracy, in which no human power can rightfully counterbalance the authority of those living gods, the Brahmans. Nothing has been left undone by orthodoxy to provide an immovable foundation for the pre-eminence of the priesthood which holds the Vedic cult in its hands over the whole of Indian society.
>
> This traditional point of view expresses a theory rather than the actual reality of things. . . .[1]

That Brahmin pre-eminence is more apparent in Brahmin literature than in the history of India as drawn from other sources must be strictly true. Nevertheless, the Brahmins, if not always as powerful as they would have liked to be, were in a position to deny the king a part of that authority to which he might otherwise have aspired. The king was of the Warrior Caste and, although no doubt descended from the gods, found his power limited in more directions than one. 'Who will not obey the command of the person that quickly does, sees, hears, knows, causes to shine and protects everything, since he is born out of the essence of all deities?' (Brihatparasara).[2] The question, although rhetorical, might nevertheless be answered with the words 'A Brahman, who considers himself of a higher caste'. As against that, caste also made monarchy more secure.

Based originally upon a desire to avoid racial contamination (a prejudice which the British learnt in India at a later stage) the caste system effectively prevented the concentration of power in any one hand. But this handicap, limiting the king's authority, applied still more to everyone else. As Beni Prasad observes:

> . . . caste distributed the brain power, the fighting power and the wealth of the community among different sections, and prevented that combination of intellectual, martial and economic strength which led to aristocratic regime in ancient Greece. Apart from the monarch, a Hindu ruling class could wield influence rather than power.[3]

[1] *Ancient India and Indian Civilization.* Paul Masson-Oursel and others. London, 1934. p. 85.
[2] *A History of Hindu Political Theories.* V. Ghoshal. Oxford, 1923. p. 103.
[3] *Theory of Government in Ancient India.* Beni Prasad. Allahabad, 1927. pp. 66-67.

Still more important, the Brahman's ambition was limited by his own religious beliefs. Hindus have a strong belief in an after-life—stronger than is characteristic of Europeans or Chinese—which rather militates against ambition as also against the desire for reform. Writes V. R. Ramachandra Dikshitar:[1]

> 'If the Brahmans had been really avaricious or ambitious they could have easily aspired to the imperial and royal offices. If they had only wished they could have easily adorned the thrones of many a state. But instead they sought voluntarily a hard and strenuous life of fasting and penance.

The Brahman is holy from birth. He is taught the ceremonial rules, hymns and legends. He alone can perform the ritual correctly and effectually. And the ancient laws, while insisting upon the Brahman's superiority, also provide him with strict rules of life. According to these, he should spend a quarter of his life in study under a teacher; a quarter in public and private affairs as householder and husband (during which phase he should bring up a son to succeed him); a quarter as a recluse, to be spent in contemplation; and the last quarter as an ascetic, without possessions, without society and even without religious rites. During this last phase the old Brahman lives on charity, purges his heart of all desire and seeks to merge himself in Brahma—the supreme deity. Concerning this last phase the injunction is:

> Let him not desire to die; let him not desire to live; let him wait for his time as a servant for the payment of his wages. Let him patiently bear hard words. . . . Against an angry man let him not in return show anger; let him bless when he is cursed.

He is not to injure any living creature; he is to meditate, give up all attachments. The world is all *illusion*—a confused and troubled dream, to be regarded without interest.

> The wise man should regard a world which he knows to be illusion, with indifference; it can do nothing for him, he can do nothing for it; it affects him only with an ineradicable regret that it exists at all, and with a longing for its disappearance. . . .

Brahmanism is the religion of a few. It is clearly, however, an excellent belief for a Minister who may wish to restrain royal power without superseding it. A recluse who has come to regard the business of state as something akin to the pointless and slightly irritating buzzing of blue-bottles on a window pane makes a poor conspirator. The Brahmans were men with no reason to argue about their pension

[1] *Hindu Administrative Institutions.* Madras, 1929. p. 122.

rights; and their ambitions, if they had them, were not limitless. Nor were they hopeful material for the revolutionary idealist, for the Brahman could view social inequalities without much concern. The slave deserves his slavery because of his misdoings during some previous and sinful existence. The Brahman has earned his relative ease in an earlier life and will be punished in a future life if he misuses his privileges in this. Justice is a long-term process and not apparent during any one phase of existence. It is not the less real, however, for that; and there is certainly no cause to interfere with its progress, even were interference possible.

Royal power in India was thus rather limited than threatened by the power of the Brahmans. The king himself was head of the Warrior caste and might also meet opposition among its members. But the warriors lacked the wealth and education to form a real aristocracy, while the merchants lacked both education and prowess. The result was that kingship was little threatened during long periods of Indian history. It was thought to be essential (as it probably was) to hold the state together. And Indian political thought is not directed towards discussing alternative forms of rule but rather towards considering how to make monarchy effective. If monarchy is thus assumed, the problems that remain are three; how to choose the right king; how to educate the future king in youth; and how to ensure that the reigning king has the best possible advice. These themes underlie most of the political thought of ancient India and more especially of the Maurya period, in the early days of Chandragupta (c. 305 B.C.), from which much of our information is derived.

As regards choice of a future king, it was strictly limited, of course, to the royal family. The king had, after all, to be a descendant of the gods. But it was not essential for the eldest son to succeed. The present king and his ministers could exercise a choice. This custom was transmitted to Malaya, where the setting aside of unacceptable princes has always been known. But while a choice might be made, it was obviously convenient to make the choice as soon as possible so that the future ruler might be trained for the work he would have to do. We read that a future king's education should begin at the age of three, with the alphabet and mathematics, and should continue from the age of eleven in logic, economics and politics. Passing on to higher studies in military science and history, he was to complete his formal education at sixteen. Then he was to marry and become a subordinate in a department of state. Finally he would be promoted to a higher post as General or Governor of a Province, probably being consecrated as heir-apparent at about the same time.[1] The Malay custom by which the future ruler is supposed to pass through

[1] *The Theory of Government in Ancient India.* Beni Prasad. Allahabad, 1927. p. 218.

other offices before reaching the highest is derived from this Hindu system and is open, incidentally, to similar objections.

There are other sources from which we may gain a more detailed, if less systematic, account of the curriculum of study thought desirable for an heir-apparent. In a work called Sûtrâlankâra[1] a learned author lays down a syllabus on these lines:—

> The Veda, archery, medicine, sacrifices, astronomy, grammar, the origin of writing, the performance of sacrifices, eloquence, rhetoric, the art of love, interest, purity of families, the ten names, computations, chess, dice, the study of origins, music and song, the art of playing on the conch, dancing and laughter, the art of prestidigitation, education, the making of garlands of flowers, massage, the science of precious stones and valuable materials for clothing, silk, sealing, weaving, wax work, strategy, sewing, sculpture, painting, arrangement of garlands, interpretation of dreams, interpretation of the flight of birds, horoscopes of boys and girls, the training of elephants, the art of playing on the tambourine, the rules of battle array, the domesticating of horses, the carrying of the lance, jumping, running and fording a river.

To the modern educationalist, interested in 'comprehensive' schools and eager to discourage premature specialisation, there is much in this syllabus worthy of careful study. To the student of political thought it suggests that the prince was at least kept out of mischief, with 'free activity' reduced to a minimum.

Once the chosen prince succeeded to the throne, following his years of education and administrative experience, the Indian thinkers were intent on seeing that he worked methodically, perhaps mainly so that his official advisers could have regular access to the presence. Two suggested time-tables for the day seem worth quoting in full. Neither is an account, one may assume, of what an actual king did. Each is rather a philosopher's idea of what the ideal king ought to do.

6.00 to 7.30 a.m.	Supervising receipts and expenditure.
7.30 to 9.00 a.m.	Affairs of citizens and people.
9.00 to 10.30 a.m.	Bathing, Vedic chanting and eating.
10.30 to noon a.m.	Affairs of the officers of state.
12.00 to 1.30 p.m.	Council with ministers.
1.30 to 3.00 p.m.	Rest and amusement.
3.00 to 4.30 p.m.	Supervising the army.
4.30 to 6.00 p.m.	Regarding enemies and military operations.
6.00 to 7.30 p.m.	Receiving intelligence officers and others.
7.30 to 9.00 p.m.	Bathing, eating and prayers.
9.00 to 1.30 a.m.	Music and sleep.

[1] Ibid.

1.30 to 3.00 a.m.   Again music and thoughts of the morrow.
3.00 to 4.30 a.m.   Other state business pondered over.
4.30 to 6.00 a.m.   Morning greetings by Ministers.[1]

A relatively undisciplined European ruler, after only four and a
half hours sleep, might have been tempted, in these circumstances to
return the ministers' greetings with derision. For him the alternative
programme might have seemed slightly preferable:—[2]

3.00 to 4.00 a.m.   Supervising accounts.
4.30 to 7.30 a.m.   Bath and prayers, physical exercises.
7.30 to 11.15 a.m.   Official business.
11.15 to 12.45 p.m. Dinner, rest and reading.
12.45 to 2.15 p.m. Justice and Council.
2.15 to 3.45 p.m.   Hunting.
3.45 to 4.30 p.m.   Parade and army muster.
4.30 to 6.00 p.m.   Evening prayer and meal.
6.00 to 7.30 p.m.   Report of Spies.
7.30 to 3.00 a.m.   Rest and sleep.

The picture of kingship thus presented in Indian literature differs
sharply from other conceptions of that office. The king is not to be
the hieratic figure upon which religious ritual centred in Egypt or
Japan. He was not to be an active soldier, normally absent on the
frontiers or in the field. He was not to be a tyrant, doing what he
chose. He was expected to be a patient administrator, dealing with
routine business at the proper time, auditing accounts, conferring
with departmental chiefs, inspecting troops and reading reports.
No doubt kings would often fall short of this ideal pattern (and as
often perhaps go beyond it) but there is reason at least to suppose
that the Indians, or at any rate the Brahmans, pictured their king as
an actual ruler with real powers and definite duties. They never,
however, thought of him as ruling without advice.

The guidance of ministers was essential to the Indian theory of
kingship and much thought was given to the problems involved; the
choice of ministers, their number, their duties and their procedure in
council. First of the ministers was the Purohita, the chief Brahman,
a man distinguished, it was supposed, by learning and character.
Kautalya advises:

. . . that he may be appointed or selected as the purohita who belongs
to a distinguished and good family, highly learned, versed in all the

[1] *Hindu Administrative Institutions.* V. R. Ramachandra Dikshitar. Madras, 1929.
[2] Even though the time allocated to hunting would seem to offer a rather restricted
scope.

sacred lore, as well as the science of astronomy, and the theory of polity, skilled in propitiating gods by the various rites prescribed in the Athava Veda, to ward off calamities providential or otherwise occurring in the kingdom. Him the king should follow as a student his teacher, a son his father, and a servant his master. . . .[1]

The Purohita's duties were basically religious and ceremonial but it was also generally agreed that the king could do nothing without him. 'It is only a kingdom under the guiding hand of a Brahman that will last long'. According to another (and Brahman) source, ' A king without a purohita is like an elephant without the mahout'. Whereas elsewhere the king might be the chief priest himself, in India he was an administrator but with a priest at his elbow of almost equal (and sometimes perhaps superior) power. The Purohita, whose salary was enormous, accompanied the king in battle, uttering prayers, encouraging the troops, threatening the cowardly and seeing to it that the army was drawn up 'in the formation invented by Aditya or by Usanas'—which would seem to show that religious influence went quite far enough.

The purohita usually formed one of an Inner Cabinet of four; the other three being the Mantrin or Chief Adviser, the Commander-in-Chief and the Heir apparent. These dealt with matters of the greatest secrecy. But they were also members of the full Mantra or Council, which numbered eight, ten or possibly twelve, with probably a majority of the Warrior Caste. Some arguments were put forward by a tenth century thinker[2] for limiting the council to three, five or seven. The numbers in fact varied, those included being normally perhaps the Treasurer, Foreign Minister, Chief Justice, Minister of the Interior, Minister of Works, Minister of Revenue and Agriculture; with sometimes, in addition, the Chamberlain and the Commander of the Household Troops. There was also a larger Council of thirty-seven representative members, including four Brahmans, eight of the Warrior Caste, twenty-one of the wealthier Farmers and Merchants, three picked Sudras and one very carefully chosen Suta. We read of other ministers in charge of prisons, forests, frontiers and forts. When council meetings were held, considerable care was taken to ensure secrecy. A special detached building was used for the purpose, to prevent eavesdropping, and no living creature allowed within earshot; a rule which applied not only to human beings but to dogs, deer and (more reasonably) to parrots.

Procedure was carefully laid down. It seems to have been understood, in the first place, that the king could make no major decision without consulting his ministers. On the other hand, the decision,

[1] See The Vedic Age. Ed. by R. C. Majumdar. London, 1951. p. 484.
[2] Theory of Government in Ancient India. Beni Prasad. Allahabad, 1927. See pp. 235-236, etc.

when made, was his. He was not bound by a majority vote and might obviously pay more attention to some advisers than to others. Somadeva Suri, a tenth century thinker, thus urges the king to ignore the advice of soldiers when deciding between war and peace.

> There is another precaution necessary in deliberation of state. Military officers are not to be consulted in the determination of policy. They are only too ready to clutch at war. Strife is the law of their being. They are not to have a hand in the formation of policy lest they involve the state in needless wars. Besides, if they are placed in control of civil policy, they may grow dangerously proud and powerful. So, according to Somadeva, the policy of the state is never to be governed by the army.
>
> In conducting negotiations, the king and councillors alike should observe gravity and courtesy. Politeness enables one to achieve the deadliest objects. The peacock, endowed with a sweet voice, makes short work of snakes. It is, again, mere folly to speak too much, or disclose too much. Above all, one should not lose one's temper or presence of mind. Fortitude in adversity constitutes real greatness. A yet greater danger to the state is popular indignation which should never be roused.[1]

There is sound advice here. The theme of deadly politeness is touched upon, incidentally, by other authors.

> 'The king, we are told, should be humble in speech alone, but sharp at heart like a razor. He should carry his foe on his shoulders as long as the time is unfavourable, and when the opportunity arrives he should dash his enemy to pieces like an earthen pot on a piece of rock'. The king who desires prosperity should slay the individual who thwarts his purposes, be this person even his son, brother, father or friend. . . . When wishing to smite, he should speak gently. After smiting, he should speak gentlier still; after striking off the head with the sword, he should grieve and shed tears. . . .[2]

To propose too many amendments to resolutions moved from the chair might possibly prove unwise. And yet it was evidently the aim to reach an agreed solution to the problems debated. A unanimous decision was the ideal. Once it was reached or the matter at least decided, the verdict was placed on record, the minute being signed not merely by the king but by all the ministers present.

The procedure is described as follows:—

> Without a written document no business of state was done. A matter was endorsed first by the home minister, the lord chief justice, the minister of law, the minister of diplomacy, with the fixed style 'This is not opposed by us', i.e. their departments had no objection. The Minister of Revenue and Agriculture endorsed with the remark

---

[1] *Theory of Government in Ancient India.* Beni Prasad. Allahabad, 1927. pp. 235-6.
[2] *A History of Hindu Political Theories.* V. Ghoshal. Oxford, 1923. p. 103.

'The note is all right'. The minister of finance: 'Well considered'; then the president of the Council inscribed in his own hand 'Really proper'. Next the *pratinidhi* wrote: 'Fit to be accepted': the *yuvaraja* following with 'Should be accepted', in his own hand. The ecclesiastical minister endorsed 'This is agreeable to me'. Every minister affixed his seal at the end of his note. Finally the king wrote 'Accepted', and set his seal. He was supposed to be unable to go through the document carefully and the Yuvaraja or someone else was to make this endorsement for him, which was shown him. After this first stage was over the minute was signed by all the ministers as the Council. Finally it was once more presented to the king who 'without delay' wrote 'Seen' as he had not the 'capacity' to criticize it.[1]

Some of this reads as if the earlier kings, (Chandragupta, perhaps) had been unable to read, or unable perhaps to read Sanskrit.

It would of course be wrong to base a general conception of Hindu government upon isolated texts spread over hundreds of years. It would be at least equally wrong to conclude that the principles of cabinet government were discovered in India and spread thence to other lands. We should probably be justified, however, in concluding that councils and cabinets are influenced everywhere by similar conditions. The ideal committee for *secrecy* is three (as one Indian pointed out). The ideal committee for reaching a sensible decision fairly quickly is five or seven. As numbers increase beyond that point, discussion becomes difficult and people begin making speeches. This is sufficiently known. Other members are added, nevertheless, and for two good reasons. In the first place, expert knowledge is needed on more than six topics. In the second place, the persons included cannot oppose while those left out can and probably will. Expanding on these principles, the numbers in council rise inexorably to ten, twelve or fifteen. By the time the number twenty is reached, the five most important members will be meeting beforehand to make previous decisions in secret conclave. Thenceforward the business of the larger council becomes increasingly formal and some of its members are demanding admission to the Inner Cabinet. As it proves impossible to exclude them, the business of the Inner Cabinet itself becomes more formal . . . and so the process continues. It is evident that the Indians knew all about it in the Maurya period and are rediscovering now anything they had forgotten since.

Theoretically, the system of a chosen king, educated for his office and advised by ministers of experience and probity is a good one. In practice it falls short of the theoretical ideal. The fashion is to point out that the king may be weak, wicked or even insane. But there would still be difficulties even if all the kings were strong, virtuous and

[1] *Hindu Administrative Institutions.* V. R. Ramachandra Dikshitar. Madras, 1929. p. 141. The 'yuvaraja' was the heir apparent, the ecclesiastical minister, the Purohita.

sensible. For they would still be human beings and liable to the accident of birth and death, disease and mishap. The theory of how the heir apparent should be trained breaks down if the king outlives his son, and perhaps his grandson as well. The system is weakened if a king succeeds prematurely, at the age of three or five, with all the problems of regency. Apart from that, a king can be ill for long periods, crippled by an accident or left childless as the result of an epidemic. A theoretically stately procession of monarchs is interrupted, in practice, by periods during which the ruler is too young, too old, too sick or too deaf. Worse still are the periods of doubt during which uncertainty prevails as to who the next king is to be. So far as India was concerned, what would in any case have been a defect in monarchy was made far worse by the institution of polygamy. In a regime lacking any precise rule governing the succession the Harem was perhaps the chief menace. It produced a horde of rival princes, each backed by a jealous mother. For the king the problem was ever present. Should he send his younger brothers to govern remote provinces? That would make it easy for them to rebel. Should he then keep them at court, under his own eye? Why, then they would poison him.

There was no real answer to the problem. Kautalya suggests that the Harem should be isolated, walled, moated and approached by a single well-guarded door. The guards should be females, eunuchs or old men.[1] In fact, a Hindu palace seems to have been organised as much to ensure safety as comfort.

> Everything bespeaks precaution. The structure of the palace itself includes mazes, secret and underground passages, hollow pillars, hidden staircases, collapsible floors. Against fire, poisonous animals, and other poisons there is diverse provision, including trees which snakes avoid, parrots and carika birds which cry out on seeing a serpent, other birds which are variously affected by the sight of poison. Everyone has his own apartment, and none of the interior officials are allowed to communicate with the outside. . . . Material objects, as they pass in and out, are placed on record and under seal. According to Megasthenes (XXVII, 15) the king changes his apartment *every night*. The kitchen is a secret place and there is a multitude of tasters. . . .[2]

As this passage suggests, the Civil Service was large. Nor was it confined to the royal residence. We learn of a revenue system drawing its funds from an excise on liquor, gambling, salt and prostitution. We have salary lists showing that the Purohita and Crown Prince were paid on the same scale and twice as highly as anyone else. We find the physician placed on a salary scale level with the chariot-

---

[1] *The Theory of Government in Ancient India*. Beni Prasad. Allahabad, 1927. p. 122
[2] *Cambridge Modern History*. Vol. I. p. 493. By F. W. Thomas.

driver, horsetrainer and carpenter, receiving half the income paid to a captain of infantry. We find much of the apparatus of modern government, with procedures similar to those of governments which still exist. What we do not find is any suggested alternative to monarchy. For the result of any palace plot or assassination could only be to replace one king by another. It involved no threat to monarchy itself.

To find an example of a king who managed to retain all the combined authority of patriarch, priest, ruler and war-leader, we must turn to Europe and to that period in history when monarchy was at its height. For it was in Europe that the idea of nationalism gave to kingship that additional splendour which only a united people could give. The king with merely paternal power could be no more than the senior among others of almost equal authority. The king too closely identified with God might tend (as in Egypt or Japan) to become the stuffed dummy of religious veneration and practical impotence. The king entirely occupied in the business of government may be caught in the wheels of his own routine (as happened, no doubt, to many Indian kings). The king, finally, who is primarily a leader in war (like a seventeenth century Prince of Orange) will be unpopular if the war goes badly and redundant when it is over. Greatest in power was the king who avoided each of these pitfalls. Greatest, in fact, was Louis XIV. He lacked the absolute power of a modern dictator; to which no king could possibly have aspired. But within the religious and traditional framework of monarchy he had perhaps as great an authority as one man has ever borne; not so much from any unique quality in him as from the wave of nationalist feeling upon which he rode.

Nationalism was the sentiment which grew up in the later Middle Ages in such kingdoms as were then unified (or in process of unification) within strategic and defined frontiers which enclosed people who were coming to speak a single language. Medieval kingdoms had often been scattered territories—part in France, for example, and part in England or Spain—comprising peoples differing from each other in customs and speech. Formidable were the first consolidated states, of which England was among the earliest. Rival kings endeavoured to follow suit, creating national realms, each from fear of the other. France arose from fear of England, Great Britain was formed from fear of Spain, Germany from fear of France, Austria-Hungary from fear of Germany and Italy from fear of Austria. Nationalism was the unifying force and the Holy Roman Empire and Italy were for long weakened by the lack of it. Nationalism was expressed in monarchy and sad was the fate of Poland which had only an elective crown. The two biggest exceptions to the rule of kingship in seventeenth century Europe were the Netherlands and England, and these reverted to monarchy under the pressure of war, and indeed under the pressure of war with each other. They ended their conflict not only both monarchies but both, momentarily, under the same monarch. By the last half of the seventeenth century, nationalist monarchy had become the fashion and Louis XIV of France was the model of what a national monarch should be.

Louis had and retained all the basic elements of power but heightened by the love of his subjects for the France they saw embodied in him, a France to be defined by the Alps, the Pyrenees and the Rhine. 'The King's authority was very nearly the same as that exercised by the head of a family', writes Paul Viollet,[1] and Louis himself told his expected successor to 'Think of them as your children' and 'Set your subjects an example that a Christian father sets his family'. This tradition of royal fatherhood was strong and had been especially maintained by Henri IV who once told his Parlement 'You see me in my private room . . . like the head of a family [come] to speak frankly to my children'. With it went the king's special responsibilities in receiving petitions and settling disputes. But the King also had his share of divinity. Louis was convinced, for one, that his authority was delegated to him by God, and indeed conferred at his coronation. It was, he admitted, a secular authority, for he conceded the Pope a measure of control in his own proper sphere. Suger had described Louis VI as 'the Vicar of God Whose living image he bears in himself'[2] and the idea had lost nothing of its force when Louis XIV ruled in his turn. In his *Memoirs* (assuming them to be genuine) he clearly explains the view he took of his own sacred office:

> . . . occupying, so to speak, the place of God, we seem to be sharers of His knowledge, as well as of His authority.
>
> Exercising as we do the Divine function here below. . . .
>
> Kings, whom God appoints the sole guardians of the public weal. . . .[3]

Pictures of his coronation show that even Catholic ritual could afford him a position as God's representative on earth. But that was not all, for there was an added pagan feeling about Versailles, where the motif of the Sun or of Apollo pervaded the architecture, the sculpture and the painting. In the background, behind the Christian theology, the King's magical and life-giving powers remained; a legacy from Rome and Egypt. But his belief in his divine mission

[1] *The Old Regime in France.* Frantz Funck-Brentano. 1926. Trans. by H. Wilson. London, 1929. p. 145.
[2] Funck-Brentano, *op. cit.* p. 149.
[3] Quoted in *The Splendid Century.* W. H. Lewis. p. 41.

stopped short of the absurd. If he was something of a public idol at Versailles, he could relax at Marly and be a man again.

He ran less risk of becoming an idol than he did of being caught in the wheels of administration. As St. Simon remarked, 'Give me an almanac and a watch and . . . I will tell you what the King is doing'. His daily routine was not invariable but it is reminiscent, at least, of the time-table prepared for Indian kings by Indian philosophers (see pp. 62-63). It seems to have followed some such plan as this:—[1]

8.00 a.m.	The King is called
8.15 a.m.	Greetings by Ministers and Court
9.00 a.m.	Prayers
10.00 a.m.	Council
12.30 p.m.	Chapel Royal for Mass
1.00 p.m.	Visits the Ladies
2.00 p.m.	Dinner
3.30 p.m.	Exercise
5.00 p.m.	Council
7.00 p.m.	Reception, with music
10.00 p.m.	Supper
11.00 p.m.	Visits the Ladies
11.30 p.m.	Receives Ministers and Court
12.00 p.m.	Sleep

Louis considered it his duty to know everything (especially his own country), to work eight or nine hours a day, to do justice and show mercy and to put the good of the State before every other consideration. He considered himself responsible for his work to God, and to God alone. He had given serious thought to the nature of monarchy and pointed out that, in lands where there was no king 'Instead of having one sovereign power as they should, nations are subject to the whims of a thousand tyrants'.[2] That he assumed the entire responsibility for day-to-day administration is shown from his own *Memoirs* in which he writes:—

> It is always worse for the public to control the government than to support even a bad government which is directed by Kings whom God alone can judge. . . . Those acts of Kings that are in seeming violation of the rights of their subjects are based upon reasons of State—the most fundamental of all motives, as everyone will admit, but one often misunderstood by those who do not rule.[3]

[1] Based on Funck-Brentano and W. H. Lewis, *op. cit.* Some of the hours given are only approximate and some, in fact, varied. Supper, e.g. might be as late as 11.30.
[2] *Louis XIV.* Louis Bertrand. Trans. C. B. Chase. New York, 1928. p. 312
[3] *Ibid.* See p. 313. See also *A King's lessons in statecraft.* Ed. by J. Longnon. London, 1924.

Reasons of State are thus comprehended only by the King and those who assist him. Nor, it is obvious from Louis XIV's practice, was his power—derived both from God and from Reasons of State—to be shared with others. He did not rule through his nobles but through middle-class officials like Colbert and Louvois. There were Councils of State, of Despatches, of Finance, of Commerce and of Conscience, together with a Privy Council. The Secretaries of State held key positions but with authority directly derived from the King. They merely gave advice when it was required and then carried out decisions which the king had made.

The nobles, whose birth, property and privilege might have given them a measure of independent authority, more especially in the provinces, were rendered impotent, partly by their own Caste system and partly by deliberate royal policy. Caste in France had the same political result as in India. It prevented any other man combining (as the king did) the powers of the divine, the intellectual, the financier and the soldier. The Nobility of the Sword, itself split into jealous categories, was forbidden to engage in trade—forbidden by a sixteenth century decree enacted at the instance of the merchants themselves.[1] The Nobility of the Robe had a monopoly of official and legal offices but were practically excluded from high rank in the army, which was reserved for Nobles of Ancestry or anyway of Birth. The Financier or Banker might purchase a title of nobility but would remain, socially, non-existent. Bishops and Abbots, of noble birth, had something like a monopoly of education but were kept from political power and vowed to celibacy.[2]

What caste had begun the king took care to finish. The experiences of his youth had taught him to deprive the nobles of political office and experience (save in diplomacy). This left them idle and potentially mischievous. Louis wanted to have them, therefore, under his own eye, and adopted, therefore, a policy such as had long been familiar at the Imperial Court of Japan. He gave many of the highest nobles a sinecure position in his own household, one involving ceremonial duties and a constant attendance at court. Others attended to angle for such sinecures, others to avoid the royal displeasure which their absence would attract, and others again (the lesser fry) attached themselves to the greater. By the end of Louis XIV's long reign, the nobles' lives had come to centre on the king, on the routine and ceremonial of monarchy. Their lives had come to centre, in fact, on Versailles.

Versailles was built, largely, between 1669 and 1710, although much

---

[1] This law was not repealed until 1756.
[2] See *The European Nobility in the Eighteenth Century*. Ed. by A. Goodwin. London, 1953. See pp. 22-42.

of what now exists is of later date. The lesser palaces of Trianon and Marly were built after 1688. They do not represent a personal extravagance.

> The cost of Versailles was not undertaken for a man, it was undertaken for a nation; the man and the nation were indistinguishable. Its gigantic size is the crowd surrounding monarchy. Its continual level lines are the timelessness of monarchy: the claim to be enduring.[1]

Versailles was certainly a shrine of nationalism as symbolised by kingship. But it was also the place where an entire upper nobility was absorbed in entertainment, clothes, retinue, building, ritual and gambling. Life at court was exhausting, splendid, tedious, dazzling, comfortless and costly. Before utterly condemning all this frivolity, however, let us remember that Louis was actually governing the country from Versailles.

The king, we have seen, combined powers which were paternal, divine and administrative. He was also the leader in war. Kingship represented nationalism and the first thing to be nationalised was war. It was the seventeenth century which saw the organization of national armies on lines we still follow, invented by Maurice of Nassau and Gustavus Adolphus. It is from the seventeenth century that we derive the Regiment, Battalion, Squadron, Company and Troop; the Colonel, Lieutenant-Colonel, Major, Captain, Lieutenant, Sergeant and Corporal. And the holders of these ranks drew no authority from their own titles of nobility but solely from the king's commission or appointment. War was thus nationalised and only battles 'royal' would henceforth be allowed. Nor would the king himself be absent. He was present at battles—or, to be more precise, at sieges—and shared a life under canvas with his generals. He could be quite accurately depicted in contemporary art as astride his charger. Between the legs of his horse could be seen the smoke drifting lazily over the threatened bastion, while (nearer the eye) the pioneers might be glimpsed pressing forward from the second parallel to the third. And while his generals may sometimes have prayed for his departure, his presence may well at times have been effective, more especially in convincing the other side that they would have to capitulate in the end. So Louis could be fairly regarded as a war leader and one who was, in fact, almost constantly at war. His prestige stood high so long as he could be represented as victorious.

Nationalism was the force that lifted Louis to such an unexampled height of power. To the authority of paternity, religion, government and war leadership he could add the growing sentiment which made him the symbol of France itself. He could represent a growing unity

[1] *Monarchy. A Study of Louis XIV*. Hilaire Belloc. London, 1938. pp. 327-328.

within a defensible frontier. He could typify French resistance to the Habsburgs and the old idea of the Empire. His was not the power of the modern dictator, who can crush all opposition by force. His was rather the greater prestige of one with whom his subjects can identify themselves. His magnificence was theirs, his palace was theirs, his fame was that of France and so theirs again. There is little reason for supposing that the French peasants grudged the cost of Versailles. There is more reason to suppose that they gloried in it.

CHAPTER V

Monarchy justified by Divine Right

WE must not expect to find arguments set forth to justify monarchy in countries or during periods which offered no possible alternative. Monarchy is perhaps the more established when it is not justified but merely assumed. This was not true of medieval Europe. From as early, however, as the fifth century A.D., monarchy was one alternative among other forms of rule. There were propagandists, moreover, who upheld the royal authority. One of these, quoted by Jonas of Orleans and Hincmar of Rheims, adjured the king:

> to prevent theft; to punish adultery; not to exalt the wicked to power; not to nourish unchaste persons and actors; to destroy the wicked from the face of the earth . . . to defend churches . . . not to give ear to the superstitions of magicians, soothsayers and pythonesses; to put away anger . . . to hold the Catholic faith in God . . . etc.[1]

The duties, which are stated, indicate the powers, which are implied. But better arguments for monarchy come, as might be expected, from England, where a national monarchy was first extablished. The earlier of two notable propagandists was the anonymous author of several treatises written between 1080 and 1104. He may have been from that date in the household of the Archbishop of York.[2] This author would make the King God's Representative, with bishops and clergy his subordinates. The King, he says, is 'Vicar of God' as from his coronation and the Pope is only Bishop of Rome. The later and more moderate advocate of kingship is John of Salisbury, author of *Policraticus* or *The Statesman's Book* (of 1159) and a friend of Pope Adrian IV. He wrote as follows:—

> For myself I am satisfied and persuaded that loyal shoulders should uphold the power of the ruler; and not only do I submit to his power patiently, but with pleasure, so long as it is exercised in subjection to God and follows His ordinances. But on the other hand if it resists and opposes the divine commandments and wishes to make me share

[1] *The Statesman's Book of John of Salisbury.* Trans. by John Dickinson. New York, 1927. Introduction, p. liii.
[2] *Authority and Reason in the Early Middle Ages.* A. J. Macdonald. Oxford, 1933. p. 115.

in its war against God; then with unrestrained voice I answer back that God must be preferred before any man on earth. Therefore inferiors should cleave and cohere to their superiors, and all the limbs should be in subjection to the head; but always and only on condition that religion is kept inviolate. . . .

. . . whatsoever is attempted foully and with malice against the head, or corporate community, of the members, is a crime of the greatest gravity and nearest to sacrilege; for as the latter is an attempt against God, so the former is an attack upon the prince, who is admitted to be as it were the likeness of deity upon earth.[1]

In fact, a principal medieval argument for kingship was based on the belief that Heaven is a Monarchy and that Earth should be the same. All earthly lordship, as Gierke writes, was 'a limited representation of the divine Lordship of the world'.[2] The analogy of head and members was also a favourite medieval metaphor; and there are University Heads of Departments even now.

An even greater medieval political thinker was St. Thomas Aquinas himself (1227-1274) who in his *De Regimine Principum* analysed forms of government very much as Aristotle had done but with this difference that he regarded the State as serving the individual and not the other way about. He too defends monarchy (preferably elective) provided that its claims do not conflict with those of the Church. His argument runs thus:—

. . . That is best which most nearly approaches a natural process, since nature always works in the best way. Among members of the body there is one which moves all the rest, namely the heart: in the soul there is one faculty which is pre-eminent, namely, reason. The bees have one king, and in the whole universe there is one God, Creator and Lord of all . . . it follows of necessity that the best form of government in human society is that which is exercised by one person.[3]

But St. Thomas's monarch has the support of the Church only while subordinate to it. For the object of the people in forming a society is to live virtuously and 'come to the enjoyment of God'. The lay ruler cannot lead them to this and 'under Christ's Law, kings must be subject to priests'.[4] So it happened that the lay rulers of Rome came, by divine providence, to be the subjects of the Pope. How could the Kingdom of God be otherwise ruled?

. . . The administration of this Kingdom has been committed, not to the kings of this world, but to priests, in order that the spiritual should

The Statesman's Book of John of Salisbury. Trans. by John Dickinson. New York, 1927. Chap. XXV. pp. 258-259.
[2] *Legacy of the Middle Ages.* p. 518.
[3] *Aquinas. Selected political writings.* Ed. A. P. D'Entreves. Trans. J. G. Dawson. Oxford, 1948. pp. 12-13.
[4] *Aquinas, op. cit.* pp. 12-13.

be distinct from the temporal; and above all to the Sovereign Roman Pontiff, the Successor of Peter, the Vicar of Christ, to whom all the kings of Christian people should be subject as to our Lord Jesus Christ Himself.[1]

There are, he argued, two orders of kingship, but the spiritual is supreme over the temporal and the Pope has the power to deprive a sovereign, by excommunication, of the right to rule. On this subject, where St. Thomas was moderate, other Papal supporters were violent. Some, like Manegold of Lautenbach argued that King and Emperor could alike be removed by the people themselves for misconduct.

> If one should engage a man for a fair wage to tend swine, and he find means not to tend but to steal or slay them, would not one remove him from his charge?[2]

Others, and Innocent III among them, were intent to show that Charlemagne was given his Empire by the Pope and that the Empire, whenever vacant, reverted to the Pope again. It was Augustin Trionfo (in the reign of John XXII) who went further than this, maintaining[3] that the Pope is supreme and that from his will there is no appeal, not even to God. The Pope, by his theory, could depose any Emperor and choose another. Ptolemy of Lucca (who completed St. Thomas's book) maintains that the Pope *is* Emperor by right and merely delegates his authority to laymen.[4] The claims on this score of Boniface VIII, who triumphed over the Emperor, went even beyond those of Innocent III.

These extreme views of Papal authority became more difficult to sustain after 1305, when there was a rival French Pope set up at Avignon. Pierre du Bois, writing at that time (*c.* 1307), wanted to destroy the temporal power of Church and Pope. He wished, in effect, to make the King of France the ruler of Christendom, or perhaps even Emperor. He desired to confiscate church property and set up a League of Nations and International Courts of Law. His *De Recuperatione Terrae Sanctae* is a remarkably prophetic book. Pierre du Bois looks to the future while his contemporary, Dante Alighieri, looks only to the past. But Dante's *De Monarchia* (*c.* 1309), written as it was in a lost cause, is interesting as a reflection of what Imperial protagonists had been no doubt arguing long before. Writes Dante:

> Now it is admitted that the whole human race is ordained for a

[1] *The Social and Political Ideas of some great Medieval Thinkers.* Ed. by F. J. C. Hearnshaw. London, 1923. p. 101.
[2] *Illustrations of the History of Medieval Thought and Learning.* Reginald Lane Poole. London, 1932. p. 203.
[3] Poole, *op. cit.* pp. 222-223.
[4] *Cambridge Medieval History.* Vol. VI. p. 632.

single end, as was set forth before. Therefore there must be one guiding
or ruling power. And this is what we mean by monarch or emperor.
Thus it appears that for the well-being of the world there must be a
monarchy or empire.[1]

But this argument from necessity is the least part of his case. He
shows that the Roman Empire 'in subjecting the world to itself, did
so by right';[2] a right proved above all by the fact of Christ choosing
to be born under Roman rule and at a moment chosen 'in order that
the Son of God, made man, might be enrolled as a man in that
unique register of the human race' that Augustus had ordered.
'Christ, then, gave assurance by deed that the edict of Augustus . . .
was just',—and hence that the Romans ruled with God's consent.
Nor is the Pope an intermediary. The Emperor's authority comes
directly to him from God—'descends upon him without any mean
from the fountain of universal authority'.[3]

Rather later than Dante (in 1324) came Marsiglio with his
'*Defensor Pacis*'[4] which does not stop at merely defending elective
monarchy as a necessary expedient or a thing approved by God. He
attacks Papal pretensions to rule at all, maintaining that 'the power
of the clergy is . . . not only restricted to spiritual affairs: it can only
be given effect to by spiritual means'. There is nothing coercive about
the Gospel and all texts which may seem to authorise the temporal
power or jurisdiction of the clergy are flatly contradicted by the text
'My kingdom is not of this world'. Marsiglio was propagandist for
the Emperor against John XXII but his arguments are practically
those of the Reformation.

Medieval political thinkers were relatively few and it would be
rash, no doubt, to base too many theories on the few of their works
that have survived. It would seem, however, that they could find good
cause to support monarchy but differed from each other as to the
proper relations which should exist between King and Church.
While the more nationally minded in England, and later in France,
were eager to invest the King with religious powers, it is clear that
actual kings were always controlled, in some measure, by the Church,
and often handicapped by their own lack of knowledge.[5] John of
Salisbury urges that a prince should always be able to read. 'If,
nevertheless, out of consideration for other distinguished virtues, it

[1] *A Translation of the Latin Works of Dante Alighieri.* Temple Classics. 1934. De
Monarchia. p. 141.
[2] Dante, *op. cit.* p. 195.
[3] Dante, *op. cit.* p. 279.
[4] Lane Poole. *op. cit.* p. 230 *et seq.* See also *Legacy of the Middle Ages.* p. 520.
The *Defensor Pacis* was written by Marsiglio of Padua and John of Jandun, 'two pupils
of damnation'.
[5] But the king was not exactly a layman either. See *Kingship and Law in the Middle
Ages.* F. Kern. Trans. by S. B. Chrimes. Oxford, 1948. p. 38.

should chance that the prince is illiterate, it is needful that he take counsel of men of letters if his affairs are to prosper rightly'.[1] And where would he find men of letters, save in the Church? But if the king were thus limited in power, the consensus of opinion was in favour of monarchy as such. The most fervent advocates of Papal power and clerical privilege were far, as a rule, from demanding the abolition of kingship. In proclaiming that kings should be subordinate they implied at least that kings should exist.

Last of the medieval thinkers we should notice is Nicolo Machiavelli who was born in 1469 and was therefore about 25 when Italy was invaded by the French, the Italian towns and castles falling before a relatively novel use of artillery. Machiavelli held public office in Florence from 1494 to 1512, and was then sent into exile. First fruit of his leisure was his book *The Prince*, completed in 1513. It contains maxims of statecraft based on the tortuous byways of Italian politics and is interesting in that it illustrates how completely dead were Medieval ideals in Italy before anything new was invented to replace them. Obsessed by the contrast between the glories of ancient Rome and the futile impotence of the Italian States he knew, Machiavelli demanded a restoration of everything ancient. Apart from that, he completely mistook the causes of the Italian failure in war and diplomacy. Nor do his subtle maxims foreshadow the behaviour of the new kings of the newly consolidated nation states. These kings were feeling their way towards a new conception of monarchy, and it was before this new reality that all the Italian subtleties would be blown away like cobwebs.

The Reformation had much to do with it. The kings who denied Papal authority and confiscated Church lands added the powers of Pope to the powers of King and used both to stamp out feudalism. But the Papacy was so weakened by this defection that the Catholic Kings gained an almost equal independence as the reward for their loyalty. Nationalism, in this religious aspect, was not a movement inspired by kings for their own benefit. It was a genuine movement among people who willingly invested their national king with the powers of Emperor, Pope, Church and Peerage. So far from being the unscrupulous and futile Prince of Machiavelli's imagining, the sixteenth century king became far more than a man. He was to embody in himself the whole territory he ruled, focussing its divergent provinces, centralising its language and moulding its peoples into one. Shakespeare illustrates this process in Henry V, showing not merely the sixteenth century glory of kingship but the almost intolerable burden of responsibility which the king had now assumed.

[1] *The Statesman's Book of John of Salisbury*. Trans. by John Dickenson. New York, 1927.

Upon the king! let us our lives, our souls
Our debts, our careful wives
Our children, and our sins lay on the king!
We must bear all. O hard condition!
Twin-born with greatness, subject to the breath
Of every fool, whose sense no more can feel
But his own wringing. What infinite heart's ease
Must kings neglect that private men enjoy!
And what have kings that privates have not too
Save ceremony, save general ceremony? . . . .
'Tis not the balm, the sceptre and the ball,
The sword, the mace, the crown imperial. . . .

Note the expressions used 'our souls' (hitherto the affair of the Church), 'the balm' (of Coronation), and 'the crown imperial'. Shakespeare was watching the birth of a new idea; that of sovereignty on the national scale; the unchecked sovereignty of the king.

It did not at first seem inevitable that nationalism would produce a kingship of this kind. Sir Thomas More, born in 1478, almost alone among political thinkers in having a practical knowledge of government, makes his *Utopia* a national state but with a ruler elected merely for life. His returned traveller thinks that 'the kingdom of France alone is almost greater than that it may well be governed by one man' and that a French King would be foolish to seek more territory elsewhere. He assumes that France, like Utopia, should be a national state. Luther firmly supported any prince against any rebellion and, after 1531, held that it was for the ruler to put down false doctrine. Erasmus, by contrast, pleaded for a limited monarchy but did so before a dwindling audience.[1] The age of Divine Right had already dawned.

In the published works of James I of England we find the theory of Divine Right explained by one who professed to inherit it. Beginning his theorising in 1598, he explained that the King is God's minister and lieutenant and monarchy the form of government nearest to that of heaven.[2] The hereditary king is responsible to God, not to his people, nor to the Laws. Resistance to a lawful monarch is against Holy Scripture, even should he rule wickedly. As time went on and as he met opposition, James put his claims in an even more extreme form. 'The state of monarchy', he declared in 1609, 'is the supremest thing on earth'. Kings are justly called gods, for their powers are a replica of the Divine omnipotence. Like God they may 'make and unmake their subjects . . . they have power of raising and casting

[1] *Erasmus and the Northern Renaissance.* M. M. Phillips. London, 1949. Chap. 4. p. 123 *et seq.*
[2] *The Social and Political Ideas of some great Thinkers of the 16th and 17th Centuries.* Ed. by F. J. C. Hearnshaw. London, 1926. Chapter V. pp. 105-129.

downe; of life and of death. . . . They have power to exalt low things and abase high things, and make of their subjects like men at the chesse. . . .' James carried this doctrine to its limit as only a Protestant might. 'It is atheisme and blasphemic to dispute what God can doe, so it is presumption and high contempt in a subject, to dispute what a King can doe. . . .'

It is too commonly assumed that claims such as these were universally resented from the first. They were not alien, however, to the author of *Henry V*, nor presumably to the audience for which his plays were produced. The divinity attaching to the monarch seems to have been welcome, in fact, so long as there was another and foreign monarch to oppose. Divine Right was always acceptable if it were the right to claim God's help against the alien. Erasmus was quick to notice how ardent were the clergy in preaching:

> . . . a just, a religious, or a holy war. And which is yet more wonderful, they make it to be God's Cause on both sides. God fights for us, is the cry of the French pulpits; and what have they to fear that have the Lord of Hosts for their Protector?—Acquit yourselves like men, say the English and the Spaniard, and the victory is certain; for this is God's cause, not Caesar's. . . .[1]

As against the divinely guided Philip II of Spain, Elizabeth could not be invested with too much divine authority. Once this had been done, however, it was not easy (at least in logic) to deny the same divinity to a duly anointed successor—and even to one at peace with Spain. The English clergy in 1640 agreed that

> 'The most high and sacred order of kings is of Divine Right, being the ordinance of God Himself, founded in the prime laws of nature, and clearly established by express texts both of the Old and New Testaments'.[2]

As late as 1681 we find the University of Cambridge conceding to Charles II, in a public address, exactly the authority claimed by James I.

> We still believe and maintain that our kings derive not their title from the people but from God; that it belongs not to subjects, either to create or censure but to honour and obey their sovereign, who comes to be so by a fundamental hereditary right of succession, which no religion, no law, no fault or forfeiture can alter or diminish.[3]

Nor should it be assumed that responsibility towards God was, in the seventeenth century, a mere form of words. It was not a way of

[1] *Social and Political Ideas of the Renaissance and Reformation*. Ed. F. J. C. Hearnshaw. p. 168.
[2] *The Divine Right of Kings*. J. N. Figgis. Cambridge, 1922. p. 142.
[3] *The Seventeenth Century*. G. N. Clark. p. 224.

saying that the King was not responsible at all. His responsibility was heavy and the average king was well aware of it. He might be allowed a divine sanction coupled with an absolute power but that divine sanction in itself set bounds to the way in which the power might be used. His power was limited not so much by any political opposition as by the very nature of his office. Although, as we shall see, there were practical arguments used in favour of kingship, there can be no doubt that it was the appeal to Holy Writ which carried more weight among the people at large. Nationalism and Divine Right were basically the same idea, the latter always acceptable when the former was in danger.

CHAPTER VI

Monarchy justified by Expedience

IT was not until republicanism appeared in religious guise that
arguments, other than religious, were needed to justify kingship.
Calvin's arrival in Switzerland in 1534 heralded the setting up there of
a Calvinist Republic at Geneva. Calvin converted what was already
an oligarchy of merchants into a protestant theocracy. The Genevan
magistrates were to see to it that God was obeyed, defaulters punished
and heretics killed. Henceforth it might well be insufficient, at least in
protestant circles, to show that monarchy was approved by God. It
could not even be shown that monarchy was approved by all godly
persons, for this was no longer true. It became increasingly necessary
to find other arguments by which godly believers in Monarchy might
convince equally godly republicans. There had to be an appeal to
reason and the number gradually increased (in the later seventeenth
century) of those to whose reason an appeal could be hopefully
addressed. A few of those who had fought over monarchy in youth
were willing to discuss its merits and defects in middle age.

First of these pure theorists was Jean Bodin, born in 1529, whose
Six books of the Republic[1] date from 1576. Bodin was a law teacher
and advocate who held a position at one time in the household of the
Duc d'Alençon. He may have been a protestant at one period but
later became a freethinker. He wrote in defence of the French
Monarchy, which was hardly then established. His ideas are somewhat confused but he argues, first and foremost, that there must be
a sovereign power in the State and that this power must be vested in
the King. A group, he maintains, cannot have a will.

> In a democracy sovereignty is vested in a majority: and a majority
> is not only, at best, an ignorant, foolish and emotional mob, but shifts
> continually and alters from year to year.[2]

He thus dismisses the idea of democracy, pointing out that men are
unequal and that there is less real liberty in a democracy than under
any other form of rule. 'True popular liberty consists in nothing else
than ability to enjoy one's goods in peace, fearing not at all for one's

[1] *The Social and Political Ideas of some great Thinkers of the 16th and 17th Centuries.*
Ed. by F. J. C. Hearnshaw. London, 1926. See pp. 42-62.
[2] *A History of Political Thought in the Sixteenth Century.* J. W. Allen. London, 1951.
pp. 437, 483.

life and honour or that of one's wife and family'. Nor is he more inclined to favour an aristocratic State which he thinks will certainly be ruined by the feuds and jealousies of its members. Only a monarch can ensure order and none but a monarch can create any sense of unity. So Bodin bases his plea for monarchy, not on God but on the nature of things; one of the things being private property. Arguments such as these were still more or less heretical and Thomas Hobbes, using similar reasoning at a far later date, was promptly dubbed an atheist. As mathematical tutor to Charles II, he was once free to expound his ideas before a fairly attentive audience. Charles's subsequent views were more akin to those of Hobbes than to those of James I.

Hobbes begins his argument in *Leviathan* (1651) by supposing that men were once in 'a state of nature'. Complete liberty for all then makes peace impossible. Men thus live in chaos, war and fear.

> In such condition, there is no place for Industry; because the fruit thereof is uncertain; and consequently no Culture of the Earth, no Navigation, nor use of the commodities that may be imported by Sea; no commodious Building; no instruments of moving, and removing such things as require much force; no knowledge of the face of the Earth; no account of time; no arts; no Letters; no Society; and which is worst of all, continuall feare, and danger of violent death. . . .[1]

To escape from this misery, men agree (as reason suggests) to laws. It is found, however, that the self-interest of individuals leads to the laws being broken. Men cannot be bound by words. Laws, to be useful, must be enforced. They need, therefore, a Common Power for defence against foreigners and against each other. Such a power can result only from each individual surrendering a part of his natural rights, to be vested in one man or one assembly, to which all must then submit their will and their judgment.

> This is more than Consent or Concord; it is a real Unity of them all, in one and the same Person, made by Covenant of every man with every man, in such a manner as if every man should say to every man, I authorise and give my Right of Governing myselfe, to this Man, or to this Assembly of Men, on this condition, that thou give up thy right to him, and authorise all his Actions in like manner. This done, the Multitude so united in one Person is called a Common-Wealth. . . . This is the Generation of that great LEVIATHAN, or rather (to speak more reverently) of that Mortal God, to which we owe under the Immortal God, our peace and defence. . . . And he that carrieth this Person is called SOVERAIGN and said to have Soveraign Power; and every one besides, his SUBJECT.[2]

Hobbes is careful to explain that the Sovereign himself (or itself) is

[1] *Leviathan*. Thomas Hobbes. Everyman Edition, 1937. pp. 64-65.
[2] *Leviathan*. p. 91.

no party to the contract. The subjects have made an agreement with each other, not with him. He cannot break the contract for he has made none. He could make no agreement with the multitude as a contracting body for it did not exist as such until the contract was made. He could make no agreement with the individuals singly which would not be void as a result of their subsequent agreement among themselves. His rule, therefore, is absolute and he has promised nothing. As against that, the subject has surrendered only political rights, retaining his essential freedom:

> . . . such as is the Liberty to buy and sell, and otherwise contract with one another, to choose their own aboad, their own diet, their own trade of life, and institute their children as they themselves think fit.

While thus enumerating almost the exact rights which the modern citizen has so largely lost, he reserves to the Sovereign the control of religion, reminding us of one of the few freedoms which the modern citizen has retained.

Hobbes' Leviathan *could* be an assembly but he usually assumes that it will be a King. He does not regard the contract or covenant between subjects as an historical fact so much as an implied agreement. Whatever may be thought of this theory, Hobbes puts the case for sovereignty and shows that, with religion nationalised, there can be no legal limit to the powers of the Sovereign. He shows that, whatever the tyranny of the ruler, it is preferable to the tyranny of men over each other in a state of anarchy. He thus provides a reasoned basis for monarchy, claiming too that reason in political matters should prevail.

> The skill of making and maintaining Commonwealths, consisteth in certain Rules, as doth arithmetique and Geometry; not (as Tennis-play) on Practise onely: which Rules, neither poor men have the leisure, nor men that have the leisure, have hitherto had the curiosity, or the method to find out.[1]

It is a mathematician's approach and not acceptable even now. At the time, the arguments of a reputed atheist would carry little weight. His reasoning was far less acceptable than the awful logic of James I's teaching; that logic which led his son to execution.

Although Sir Robert Filmer lived from 1588 to 1653, his chief work, *Patriarcha*, was not published until 1680, when it was used to justify the personal rule of Charles II.[2] The doctrine of Divine Right had suffered under the Commonwealth, and the Restoration of

---

[1] *Leviathan.* Thomas Hobbes. Everyman Edition, 1937. p. 110.
[2] *Patriarcha and other Political Works.* Sir Robert Filmer. Ed. by Peter Laslett. Oxford, 1949.

Charles II had been brought about by those whose belief in monarchy was of a severely practical kind. Filmer's arguments suited the Tory mood of the moment and were untainted by atheism. Filmer had written primarily to deny Bellarmine's thesis that 'Secular or civil power is instituted by men; it is in the people unless they bestow it on a Prince'. This Filmer refuted by writing:

> I see not then how the children of Adam, or of any man else, can be free from subjection to their parents. And this subordination of children is the fountain of all regal authority, by the ordination of God himself. From whence it follows that civil power, not only in general is by Divine institution, but even the assigning of it specifically to the eldest parent. Which quite takes away that new and common distinction which refers only power universal or absolute to God, but power respective in regard of the special form of government to the choice of the people. Nor leaves it any place for such imaginary pactions between Kings and their people as many dream of.[1]

Here Filmer is on firm ground. For whatever weight we may give (or not give) to the Bible as the word of God, we must concede it some authority as anthropology. That paternal rule is a fact is as clear as that the theory of contract is only a theory. We need not follow Filmer, however, in tracing the ancestry of Kings by the elder line to Adam. Nor need we conclude, as he does, that to deny the rights of elder sons is to land oneself in 'the desperate inconveniences' of communism.

Filmer then goes on[2] to show from history the imperfections of Democracy as compared with Monarchy:—

> Indeed, the world for a long time knew no other sort of government but only monarchy. The best order, the greatest strength, the most stability and easiest government are to be found in monarchy, and in no other form of government. The new platform of common-weals were first hatched in a corner of the world, amongst a few cities of Greece, which have been imitated by very few other places. Those very cities were first for many years governed by Kings, until wantonness, ambition or faction made them attempt new kinds of regiment. All which mutations proved most bloody and miserable to the authors of them, happy in nothing but that they continued but a small time.

He goes on to consider the history of Rome, denying that it was a Republic for more than 480 years, at most, and showing that the great achievements of Rome date in fact from the time of the Emperors— 'For no democracy can extend further than to one city'. When it does extend further:

> As it is begot by sedition, so it is nourished by arms: it can never

[1] *Patriarcha.* Sir Robert Filmer. p. 57.
[2] *Ibid.* pp. 86-93.

stand without wars, either with an enemy abroad, or with friends at home. The only means to preserve it is to have some powerful enemy near, who may serve instead of a King to govern it, that so, though they have not a King among them, yet they may have as good as a King over them, for the common danger of an enemy keeps them in better unity than the laws they make themselves.

Events of the seventeenth century went some way towards proving Filmer's general thesis *Popular Government more Bloody than a Tyranny'*. Experience seemed to show that monarchy was best. Neither would Filmer have the king other than sovereign. In his pamphlet *The Anarchy of a limited or mixed Monarchy* he denies that the king can either share his power or submit to the laws—which are, after all, of the king's making. If the king's power is to be restricted by law, who is to enforce the law? Whatever the answer, sovereignty must lie in the enforcing power, not the king, and so the State in that event is not a monarchy at all. He takes the instance of Poland and concludes that it is a kind of republic.

The example of Poland, added to the example of the Commonwealth in England, had a powerful effect on later seventeenth century and eighteenth century Europe; a far greater effect, certainly, than any arguments Filmer could take from Aristotle or the Bible. During the eighteenth century, more especially, the arguments for monarchy were based more and more upon its practical convenience, less and less upon its divine origin and sanction. And when we reach the later half of that century, the age of the enlightened despots, we find that the kings themselves claimed rather to be efficient than divinely inspired. Chief of the enlightened monarchs was Frederick the Great, who despised Christianity; and next to him came Catherine of Russia, a usurper. Both were admirers of Voltaire and of reason, and their contemporaries Charles of Naples, Charles III of Spain, Joseph of Portugal and George III of England and Hanover, could all claim to be enlightened rulers in their different ways.

Spokesman for enlightened monarchy was Frederick of Prussia, from whose successive works, beginning with the *Antimachiavel* of 1740, we gain a clear idea of how he viewed his own office. Having dismissed Christianity with these words:

> An old metaphysical romance, filled with marvels, contradictions and absurdity, born in the ardent imagination of Orientals, has spread into our Europe. Enthusiasts have purveyed it, careerists have pretended to accept it, imbeciles have believed it. (*Second Political Testament*, 1768).[1]

—he bases his monarchy on the assertion that hereditary rule is the

[1] *Frederick the Great, the Ruler, the Writer, the Man.* G. P. Gooch. London, 1947. See Chapter XII.

easiest system to work and that republics soon collapse. The king is no more than a man and, in being the first judge, the first general and the first financier, is at the same time essentially the first servant. Clearest statement of all comes in the *Political Testament* of 1752:—

> A well conducted government must have a system as coherent as a system of philosophy, so that finance, policy and the army are co-ordinated to the same end, namely, the consolidation of the state and the increase of its power. Such a system can only emanate from a single brain, that of the sovereign.[1]

Frederick and his contemporaries mostly took their ideas from France and, in particular, largely from Voltaire. The works of Voltaire are copious but he wrote no single volume upon politics. It is easier, in general, to discover what he disliked than what he approved. But while his attitude towards Frederick was not always cordial, his support of enlightened monarchy was fairly consistent. One would search in vain in his books for praise directed towards any other form of rule. 'Democracy' he writes 'seems suitable only to a very little country'.[2]

As for Equality:

> . . . it is as impossible for men to be equal as it is impossible for . . . two professors in theology not to be jealous of each other.[3]

He continues, moreover:—

> The human race, such as it is, cannot subsist unless there is an infinity of useful men who possess nothing at all. . . .[4]

Nor does he show complete faith in any sort of parliament:

> One distinguishes between the tyranny of one man and that of many. . . .
> Under which tyranny would you like to live? Under neither; but if I had to choose, I should detest the tyranny of one man less than that of many. A despot always has his good moments; an assembly of despots never.[5]

That Voltaire was not isolated in this preference is apparent from the works of François Quesnay and the Physiocrats, who also, in the main, wanted to see power concentrated in the hands of a single enlightened ruler.

In England, George III did not lack a measure of support among men of intellect. If Voltaire had perhaps the best brain in France,

[1] *Ibid.* p. 282.
[2] *Voltaire's Philosophical Dictionary.* Selected and translated by H. I. Wolfe. London 1929.
[3] *Ibid.* p. 116.
[4] *Ibid.* p. 117.
[5] *Ibid.* p. 308.

Samuel Johnson had clearly one of the best brains in England. While differing from Voltaire in nearly everything else, Johnson had as little use for republics or for democracy.

> 'So far is it from being true that men are naturally equal, that no two people can be half an hour together, but one shall acquire an evident superiority over the other'.[1]

On another occasion he said:—

> 'Sir, you are to consider, that in our constitution, according to its true principles, the King is the head; he is supreme; he is above everything, and there is no power by which he can be tried'.[2]

And again,

> 'The mode of government by one may be ill adapted to a small society, but is best for a great nation'.[3]

And, finally,

> '. . . a prince of ability . . . might and should be the directing soul and spirit of his own administration. . . .'[4]

Living in a country which had been itself a Republic, and surrounded by friends professing a wide variety of political opinions, Johnson could never be made to see that the world would be much improved by constitutional reforms. Said Boswell, on one occasion:

> 'So, Sir, you laugh at schemes of political improvement.'

And Johnson replied:

> 'Why, Sir, most schemes of political improvement are very laughable things.'[5]

Much work remains to be done on the political theory of enlightened monarchy. Historians have been too hypnotised by the approach of the French Revolution to allow much importance to authors who cannot be included in the select list of its causes. But while there is much to do, we cannot expect further research to reveal a strength in enlightened monarchy which it did not and could not possess. For it is evident that the king who preached enlightenment had never a fraction of the prestige of the king who derived his authority from God. More than that, his authority derived more from the old doctrine than the new. His subjects still believed in divine right even when the king himself was exchanging letters with

---

[1] *Boswell's Life of Johnson.* Ed. by G. B. Hill. Revised by L. F. Powell. Six volumes. Oxford, 1934. Vol. II. p. 13.
[2] *Ibid.* Vol. I. p. 423.
[3] *Ibid.* Vol. III. p. 46.
[4] *Ibid.* Vol. II. p. 117.
[5] *Ibid.* Vol. II. p. 102.

Voltaire. Once this capital sum of divinity had been expended, all that was left was the king's claim to be more efficient than any alternative form of government. But this was an insecure foundation for any permanent form of monarchy. The argument would be weakened as soon as a successful alternative appeared. The argument would be demolished as soon as the efficient king was succeeded by a less efficient heir. This danger was apparent to Frederick the Great himself who wondered, shortly before his death, whether his heir was fit to succeed at all. Should his nephew prove soft, idle, extravagant and uninspiring, he foretold that neither Prussia nor the house of Brandenburg would last a decade. 'I frame a thousand prayers' he wrote, 'that my forecast may be wrong, that my successors may do their duty like sensible beings, and that Fortune may avert the major part of the catastrophes by which we are threatened'.[1] It is not clear to whom he was praying, but we may be justly critical, in any case, of a system of rule in which Fortune plays so large a part. No system will last for ever and here is one which cannot last for long.

[1] *Frederick the Great, the Ruler, the Writer, the Man.* G. P. Gooch. London, 1947. p. 294.

PART II

Oligarchy

CHAPTER VII

Feudalism

IN creating a nobility, kings prepare the way for their own downfall. Nor is the process avoidable. Their own children and grand-children form the basis of the nobility, their own generals and advisers form its successive accretions, their own conquests accelerate its growth. With a nobility thus brought into existence, the king is faced with potential rivals for power. If he disperses them among distant provinces they will seek to gain independence. If he keeps them at hand, they will plot against him when not actually quarrelling with each other. Inevitably, the line of kings will be broken at some point by the succession of a child, a saint or an imbecile. When that moment comes, the nobles will try to seize power. If they fail to do so collectively, at the centre, the result is feudalism.

While it would be wrong to describe this process as invariable, examples of it are at least fairly common. China, for instance, became a Feudal State towards the end of the Chou Dynasty (before 500 B.C.) and was ruled until about 250 B.C. by hereditary nobles with ranks corresponding to those of Duke, Marquis, Count and Baron. These in turn had their own vassals, their own advisers and officials, their own special training. This was the age, as it has been called, of the Warring States. Some shadow of the central government remained but its territory had fallen apart into so many almost independent fragments. According to one authority, these numbered at one time five or six thousand. A similar process is evident in Japanese history when a cultured and sophisticated court lost control of the provinces and saw them fall into the hands of local gentry, whose rivalries soon destroyed any semblance of unity or order. In England the king was for nearly a century, from 1399 to 1485, but the chief among the Dukes and Earls, having little more than-precedence among the Nevilles and Talbots, the Beauchamps and Stanleys.

Although we could find examples of Feudalism in India, China and Japan, Medieval Europe affords the classic background for chivalry. Granted that the priests of the period have told us their case, using a learning based on classic or holy writ, they have not distracted our attention entirely from the facts. The chief political fact was the armoured horseman, the tank of the period, on his own ground invincible. The second political fact was the stone-built, fortified castle. It was within a strategic framework of castles that the medieval kings, bishops and knights played their game of chess. And they played it according to rules evolved during the Crusades and largely copied from the other side. The effect of the Crusades was to bring European fighting men into close contact with the Arab world of horsemanship. They eventually came home with new horses and new ideas. The medieval world of Christendom was shaped by Oriental influences, copied from forms developed in Syria, derived from experience gained by Princes of Antioch and Counts of Tripolis, steeped in the legends of Ascalon, Tiberias, Trebizond and the Horns of Hattin. The Christian knights had learnt their chivalry in the desert.

The medieval contributions to politics must be disassociated, surely, from Empire and Papacy and the struggle for the prize that was not there. The political interest of the Middle Ages must centre rather on what is more typical: chivalry, monasticism, the cities and the universities. These are the political equivalent of Gothic architecture. They represent ideas that were new then, unknown before and weakened since. They also represent, at bottom, the same political idea; the idea of an organisation which is not local (like a City State), nor all-embracing (like an Empire), but which exists in different and scattered places, comprising members who are bound together by a common loyalty and a common training.

Chivalry, or Chevalerie, derived from the Arabs, is the basic conception and it means essentially a code of conduct among *horsemen*. The medieval armoured cavalryman was a man-and-horse, both carefully and expensively bred, trained and equipped. Descent mattered, both in the horse and in the man. Each needed a pedigree. Training mattered, too, and that of the knight covered his upbringing from the age of seven to the age of twenty-one; a training in how to ride, jump, wrestle, swim, hunt, hawk, joust and endure fatigue. But the knight's effectiveness in battle depended not only upon himself but upon a team of assistants—squire, page, grooms, armourer, spare horses and packhorses. There were five or six non-combatants for every man who fought. But the knight could not operate under certain conditions—in mountains, woods, marsh, night or fog. He was, like a modern tank, rather blind and rather dependent on auxiliaries. He needed *time* to arm and so could be surprised in camp unless guarded by infantry. Although relatively invulnerable in battle, he might quite easily find himself taken prisoner. He was too highly trained to know any occupations other than fighting, hunting and acting as judge. And even the hunting was not purely for sport. As Machiavelli pointed out:

He must follow the chase, by which he accustoms his body to hardship, and learns something of the nature of localities, and gets to find out how the mountains rise, how the valleys open out, how the plains lie, and to understand the nature of rivers and marshes, and in all this to take the greatest care.[1]

The art was, in fact, to learn from hunting what the modern soldier learns from the map. A final characteristic of the knight lay in his attitude towards women. Removed from his mother and sisters at the age of seven, he was brought up in another household and there taught to attend the ladies with respect. His actual education was purely among men and his later way of life took him away from his womenfolk for considerable periods. He tended, perhaps for this reason, to idealise them; although not necessarily the one he had married. During his absence, on a Crusade, for example, his family might be almost unprotected.

From these and other factors, some of them religious, a pattern of conduct emerges. To begin with, all knights in Christendom, (whatever their quarrels with each other) were agreed on the necessity of maintaining their own order and making the peasants supply them and their servants with food and drink. In warfare among themselves they killed individuals but rarely slaughtered families of noble birth. They spared women, clergy and children by mutual agreement, partly to protect their own and avoid retaliation. They usually spared each other's squires, pages and grooms, as non-combatants. And the idea of sparing the unarmed leads at once to the indignation felt on finding others less scrupulous. This leads in turn to the idea of protecting the weak; an idea implicit in the vows of knighthood. They usually fought, almost by agreement, on a chosen field and in daylight, without attempting any ruse, stratagem or surprise. They were quite used to being taken prisoner (which was not disgraceful) and treated their prisoners—if of equal rank—with just such consideration as they hoped to receive. They had, in fact, a code of etiquette. It still lingers, contrasting with the ideas of the Japanese, for example, whose etiquette is different. They had a science of heraldry, partly to identify friend and foe, superior and junior, on the battlefield; and partly to trace descent. They had heralds, who could safely approach the enemy. They abided, in general, by the rules of war.

What are the political implications of chivalry? It involves, first of all, the idea of a politically privileged class, enjoying a particular power and prestige but earning it by such a training as many might fear to undergo and by such a continued and arduous service as others might well prefer to avoid. In assessing the knight's special prestige, inherited directly from nomadic traditions, we must distinguish sharply between respect and envy. We feel envy, perhaps,

[1] *The Prince.* Trans. by W. K. Marriott. Everyman Edition. London, 1906.

for those who are wealthy and surrounded by luxury but reserve our respect for those whose achievements are beyond us. The respect we may feel for the climbers who conquered Everest is not unconnected with the dismay we should most of us have felt if suddenly offered a place in the team. The knight's code of honour contained no promise of comfort but involved him in some risk of death. Of those who stood aside when he passed, many would have firmly refused to change places with him.

Chivalry next implies an idea of equality as between adult and trained members of a particular order or society; a group as wide as Christendom with a sort of language of its own. It was and is a peculiar sort of equality, allowing of all the ranks of office like Constable and Marshal, allowing of all the grades of nobility from Duke, Marquis, Count and Baron down to plain Knight or Esquire, and yet ensuring, for certain purposes, that all are on one footing as gentlemen. The idea survives to this day in an Officers' Mess. It survived until recently in the duel, a custom which used to expose all gentlemen in an equal degree to a certain kind of risk. In Japan during its feudal period the Samurai—distinguished from other folk, as were European gentlemen, by the wearing of the sword—had something of the same equality, but not merely in fighting. They also shared in common the obligation to commit suicide rather than suffer dishonour. As no similar obligation lay on humbler people, this is a parallel instance of an equality not of comfort but of danger.

Chivalry implies, lastly, a kind of sportsmanship which makes it possible to reconcile conflict (nowadays verbal conflict, as for example in Parliament) with courtesy, and even friendship, between opponents; a necessary aspect of political debate. The medieval knight going to the aid of a wounded opponent was not only perpetuating an old Arab custom but also furnishing the precedent according to which an officer to-day may salute a prisoner of war who is senior to him in rank. It is the tradition of a warfare confined by general consent to certain people, certain places and even to certain times of year. It was the better aspect of Feudalism that its tendency was to keep warfare within bounds. The removal of these restrictions has brought with it no very obvious advantage.

Chivalry was one aspect of Feudalism: Monasticism was another. And indeed knighthood and monasticism have something in common and actually overlapped in the military orders. But the Orders of Knighthood were not as strict as the Rule of St. Benedict, which was contemporary with the work of Justinian, based upon civil and canon law, and upheld to this day as a monument of common sense; the common sense expressed in the feeling that men who live without women must not live without rules. The Rule of St. Benedict sets a standard of monastic conduct, not too hard to be enforced nor 'too easy-going to be a means of perfection',[1] and provided for the monk the same sort of training and test that knighthood did for the soldier. The Abbot or Prior, the Abbess or Prioress, the Monk or Nun had gained a certain place in the Feudal structure, a certain authority or privilege in the world, partly by birth and partly by education but at a price which was known to everybody. They were to be respected rather than envied. And the world was thus provided with a set of administrators, scholars and clerks who were unlikely to have personal ambitions of a certain kind, whose integrity was in some measure established, and in whose relationship with each other there was an element of equality as between members of an exclusive society.

Politically, the monastic heritage is extremely important. The Rule of St. Benedict and its later variants provided the models for a written constitution. The procedure in Chapter provided a model for the orderly conduct of business. The system of Visitation gave precedent for any regular system of inspection. And, finally, the sending of delegates to the annual Conferences or Chapters of the Order (more especially the Dominican) was a thirteenth century experiment in representative democracy.[2] There is something more than symbolism in the fact that the English Parliament meets and has always met in what used to be monastic precincts. It must, however, be remembered that the monks of Christendom professed an Oriental religion and had still earlier models of monasticism in the East; models older than Christianity itself. Although the Buddhist monastery had no higher organisation than the single (and often large) community, its internal organisation was highly developed politically as well as culturally. Control lay in a full meeting of the members, provided there was a quorum and provided that the decisions made were not opposed to Buddhist scripture.[3] Something of this practice may well have passed from Buddhist to Christian monasteries.

Like monasteries, medieval cities also had their place in the feudal system; and these offered a governmental pattern of their own. The Ancient World had known both City States and Empires in which City States were included. The City State was both a City and the territory about it and such States were known in the Middle Ages, Venice, for example, being one. There were City States ruled by a Bishop, like Durham, the diocese and territory being one. But there were also, in the Middle Ages, many rulers who lived in their castles or moved round their estates, leaving cities to govern themselves.

[1] *Saint Benedict and the Sixth Century.* Dom John Chapman. London, 1929. p. 203.
[2] *A History of Political Theory.* G. H. Sabine. London, 1952. p. 268.
[3] See *Theory of Government in Ancient India.* B. Prasad. Allahabad, 1927. pp. 321-330.

Many cities thus owed allegiance to a distant King or Emperor, but to no one else, and yet had no territory outside their quite limited boundaries. They were self-governing in a new way and gave a new meaning to the word 'citizen'. For the Athenian or Roman voter was originally a farmer, seen in the city only on market days. But the citizen of Paris, Augsburg or London was almost certainly a crafts-man or merchant and quite probably nothing else.[1] Walled Cities were packed tight with people and were too small—as a result of economies in length of fortification—to develop much district feeling within the walls. Their corporate loyalty was strong but the citizens developed secondary loyalties to their Craft, Mystery or Guild. Within each Guild, membership was graded, with apprentices, journeymen, masters, aldermen and presiding Master. And the actual government of the City was apt to be entrusted, in practice, to the heads of Guilds in rotation. But these Guilds were not purely local. Membership of a Mystery in one City carried with it at least an honorary membership of the equivalent Mystery in the cities adjacent or most nearly connected by trade. Guild membership was a super-national organisation, in fact, very much like Monasticism or Chivalry.

To complete the picture, there were the Universities. These offered the same sort of privileged position, to be gained by much the same laborious means. The scholar served the same sort of apprenticeship as the Squire or Draper. He spent five or six years in mastering his basic subjects—grammar, rhetoric and logic; arithmetic, geometry, music and astronomy—before graduating in Arts. Only then could he enter one of the higher Faculties of Theology, Law or Medicine. In Theology a further six years might be spent in becoming Bachelor of Divinity, and twelve or thirteen years altogether in achieving the Doctorate. Once earned, the doctorate gave the right to lecture at *any* university in Christendom, not merely at the University in which the degree was obtained. Similarly, a Doctor of the Civil Law had a high social status and was eligible for public office. Full membership of a higher Faculty carried its privileges, in fact, but they had to be earned before they could be enjoyed. In university life, again, there was a measure of equality. It was, however, equality among people similarly qualified who had gained a certain position by years of effort. The typical medieval institutions are all thus characterised. In all there are the same elements: membership of an international society; apprenticeship; the passing of a test; an oath of loyalty; the recognition of a code of professional conduct; and the award of a definite place in a respected hierarchy.

Although the merits of European Feudalism are worthy of note,

[1] See *Cambridge Medieval History*. Vol. VI. pp. 473-503.

they do not characterise feudalism wherever it appears. Elsewhere and in general, the merits of feudalism are less tangible. The obvious advantage of multiplying centres of semi-independent rule is that the arts flourish in proportion to the potential number of patrons. Whether we are to count the Buddhist temples in Japan, the palaces in Italy or the Court Orchestras in eighteenth century Germany, we are bound to recognise that the fragmentation of an Empire gives great scope to the artist. And Confucius learnt more at different courts than he would ever have learnt at one. As against that, feudalism brings endless if petty warfare which, harmless as it may be when compared with conflict on the national scale, creates a demand for the restoration of order. Monarchy is hailed with relief by those who have lived for long under a militant feudalism.

If we seek for a literature intended to justify feudalism as against the arguments for a centralised efficiency, we shall find it less in political treatises than in ballads, legends, chronicles and songs. The praise of feudalism is implicit in the Song of Roland, the Japanese legend of the Forty Ronin, the Border Ballads and the Chronicles of Froissart. To reasonings about improved administration the Feudalists reply most effectively by trumpet calls, fluttering banners, the names of heroes and a rousing chorus. These arguments are unanswerable. It would be wrong, however, to conclude that there were no arguments of a different kind. The Barons who drew up the clauses of Magna Carta had a point of view. That they expressed it in legal rather than philosophic terms is itself significant, for they clearly regarded their relationship to the king as one to be defined by law. In a later age, theorists were to speak of a social contract, real or implied, between ruler and people. The Barons at Runnymede, at once more powerful and more practical, drew up an actual contract and made the king seal it. As a modern historian has emphasised:

> The rule of law was the most clearly realized political principle of the feudal age, governing the conduct of lord and vassal alike. . . .[1]

It follows that the political theories of feudalism are mostly in legal form. Many, moreover, date from a period before any very articulate peerage had emerged. It was only at a later date, when national monarchies were already being established, that feudal theories were occasionally invoked by those opposed to royal absolutism. It is only in the sixteenth century and from rather isolated sources that we learn what the case for feudalism had been. It appears, for example, in a *Defence of Liberty against Tyrants*[2] written in 1579,

---

[1] *The Constitutional History of Medieval England.* J. E. A. Jolliffe. London, 1937. p. 157.
[2] *A Defence of Liberty against Tyrants.* Ed., with introduction, by H. J. Laski from the English edition of 1689. London, 1924.

probably by Duplessis-Mornay, adviser to Henry of Navarre.

What does the case for feudalism amount to? It is based on the need to restrain royal power by law and contract. Nobles were of a privileged class, having gained their special rights by birth and training. Other classes—the bishops and clergy, abbots and monks, university doctors and masters, master-craftsmen and burgesses—also had special privileges which were secured by law and custom, parchment and seal. As these privileges had been earned and usually paid for, it was of the essence of the bargain that the law should be binding on the king as well as on the subject. The law was therefore of higher authority than the king; and the law had to be enforced. By whom? Not by any individual noble but by any large group of nobles who conceived that their 'liberties' had been infringed. And their liberties included the powers they enjoyed over other people—even royal powers as exercised, within their lordships, by the lords of the Welsh Marches. As against a royal tyranny, exceeding the bounds of law, the greater lords could oppose a military power greater than the king's. If primarily guarding their own interests, it could be shown that they were incidentally guarding the interests of others. They did so, moreover, by virtue of the very feudal obligations by which they were themselves bound. Vassalage was a contract binding on both parties and not merely on the vassal. And the king, besides, was vassal to God.

> Briefly, even as those rebellious vassals who endeavour to possess themselves of the kingdom, do commit felony by the testimony of all laws, and deserve to be extirpated . . . now for that we see that God invests kings into their kingdoms, almost in the same manner that vassals are invested into their fees by their sovereign, we must needs conclude that kings are the vassals of God, and deserve to be deprived of the benefit they receive from their lord if they commit felony . . . if God hold the place of sovereign Lord, and the king as vassal, who dare deny but that we must rather obey the sovereign than the vassal?[1]

Here is a useful doctrine for a restive nobility. But the author goes further and remarks that the King of France makes his coronation oath before twelve peers who represent the people as a whole, 'which shows that these twelve peers are above the king'.[2] This is not an argument that would have appealed, at first sight, to Louis XIV. But the author of *A Defence of Liberty* is on firm ground in preferring an actual coronation oath to an imaginary social contract. He goes on to explain that an oath of this kind is almost universal.

> For neither the emperor, the king of France, nor the kings of Spain, England, Polander, Hungary, and all the other lawful princes; as the

---

[1] *A Defence of Liberty, op. cit.* p. 79.
[2] *Ibid.* p. 131.

archdukes of Austria, dukes of Brabante, earls of Flanders, and Holland, nor other princes, are not admitted to the government of their estates, before they have promised to the electors, peers, palatines, lords, barons, and governors, that they will render to every one right according to the laws of the country, yea, so strictly that they cannot alter or innovate anything contrary to the privileges of the countries, without the consent of the towns and provinces; if they do it, they are no less guilty of rebellion against the laws than the people are in their kind, if they refuse obedience when they command according to law.[1]

The author later draws a sharp contrast between a lawful king and a mere tyrant. The former is distinguished by his willingness to share power with his relatives and peers.

The tyrant advances above and in opposition to the ancient and worthy nobility, mean and unworthy persons; to the end that these base fellows, being absolutely his creatures, might applaud and apply themselves to the fulfilling of all his loose and unruly desires. The king maintains every man in his rank, honours and respects the grandees as the kingdom's friends, desiring their good as well as his own.[2]

The advocate of Feudalism can thus show that a nobility is needed to keep the king in check and that only a tyrant will use any but his hereditary advisers. He could also have shown (had the point interested him) that the noble who resists illegal demands—conveyed perhaps by 'mean and unworthy persons'—is the indirect means of saving others from oppression. Perhaps the most eloquent defence of feudalism ever uttered came from Edmund Burke as he saw its last remnants destroyed in France. He laments the plight of Marie Antoinette in a famous passage which concludes:—

. . . little did I dream that I should have lived to see such disasters fallen upon her in a nation of gallant men, in a nation of men of honour, and of cavaliers. I thought ten thousand swords must have leaped from their scabbards to avenge even a look that threatened her with insult. But the age of chivalry is gone. That of sophisters, economists, and calculators, has succeeded; and the glory of Europe is extinguished for ever. Never, never more shall we behold that generous loyalty to rank and sex, that proud submission, that dignified obedience, that subordination of the heart, which kept alive, even in servitude itself, the spirit of an exalted freedom. The unbought grace of life, the cheap defence of nations, the nurse of manly sentiment and heroic enterprise, is gone! It is gone, that sensibility of principle, that chastity of honour, which felt a stain like a wound, which inspired courage whilst it mitigated ferocity, which ennobled whatever it touched, and under which vice itself lost half its evil, by losing all its grossness.[3]

[1] *Ibid.* p. 149.
[2] *A Defence of Liberty*, op. cit. p. 185.
[3] *Reflections on the Revolution in France.* Edmund Burke. Everyman, 1935. p. 73.

That there was a case for Feudalism in its strict sense, and for the other institutions connected with it—chivalry, monasticism, cities and universities—is sufficiently clear. That there was a case against it is clearer still. For Feudalism, at its worst, could destroy the Kingdom. It could do so especially through the rebellious lord seeking help from beyond the nearest frontier. It could do so in a different way if feudal lords tried to replace the king by a committee of themselves, lacking as they would any real trust in each other. It could do so, finally, in the event of a disputed succession with different parties supporting different candidates for the throne. Considered in isolation, feudalism was more dangerous than useful. It must, however, be remembered that European aristocracy, a more hopeful form of government, was rooted in feudal traditions. The aristocrats who sought and obtained control of the central government had still a measure of feudal interest in the provinces. More than that, they inherited from the feudal lord that determination to protect the rights of the individual as against the State. The individual was always essentially the feudal lord himself but the freedom he sought for his own family was extended gradually to other families as well. The defence of liberties merged imperceptibly into the struggle for freedom.

CHAPTER VIII

Aristocracy

ARISTOCRACY, the rule of the respected few, is normally the sequel to monarchy. It is easier for an aristocracy to establish its power within a state already formed, inside boundaries already defined and through institutions already in existence. Nor is it necessary for the monarchy to disappear. The Egyptian monarchy, the earliest of which the history is known, was largely overshadowed by the nobility during the fifth dynasty (2750-2250 B.C.) and still more during the sixth, but the monarchy, in form, remained. The same was roughly true of China under the Han Dynasty. At Sparta, a predominantly aristocratic state, the dual kingship survived and with a share of influence. At Athens the monarchy gave place quietly to aristocracy during the eighth century. At Rome, by contrast, the kings were dethroned, about 509 B.C., by the nobles, and the kingship lingered on only in the form of the Rex Sacrorum, a sacrificial office of minor importance. Rome provides perhaps the best early example of aristocracy in its republican form.

Rome is first known to us as a City State of an almost Greek pattern but with a marked geographical difference. Rome is placed neither in a mountain valley nor on an island. It is not even on the coast.[1] It lies halfway up the Italian peninsula, at the lowest point at which the Tiber could be bridged, and in the middle of a not very defensible plain. This plain, in turn, forms a part of a geographical area sharply defined by the Alps and the sea. The Romans had a strong motive to enlarge their territory to its natural limits and they quite soon controlled an area larger than, say, Attica. They were neither traders nor seamen[2] and so extended their territory not by colonisation but by adding one adjacent area to another. In 294 B.C. the male citizens of military age numbered 262,321. By 169 B.C. they numbered 312,885. By the middle of the third century there must have been a million people other than aliens and slaves. Politically, their problem resembled neither that of the Athenians nor that of the Hindoos. Rome was a monarchy when its territorial expansion began

---

[1] *Geographic Background of Greek and Roman History.* M. Cary. Oxford, 1949. pp. 130-133.
[2] See *An Economic History of Rome.* T. Frank. London, 1927. p. 118.

but with a nobility comprising the leaders or elders of the original tribes of Latium. These were the Patricians, members of 'gentes' or known families, alone able at first to bear office. Beneath them, a wider class of Equites included those able to provide themselves with a horse for service in war. The respective words, the one suggesting fatherhood and the other the cavalryman's prestige, are significant. It was the Patricians who rid themselves of the Monarchy and divided the royal power between two officers, the Consuls, each elected for one year.

The problem, for an aristocracy, is one of preventing (on the one hand) a revival of kingship and (on the other) a revolt of the people. The two Consuls represented a Patrician device to serve the former purpose. Each had civil, military and judicial powers, but the one was a check on the other and their period of office was short. The Republic lasted, in fact, for about 250 years, guarded by a complex but unwritten constitution. It would hardly have lasted so long if the Patricians had not yielded to the pressure of wealthy men of Plebeian birth. They yielded to a growing pressure between 471 and 367 B.C., finally allowing one of the two Consuls to be a Plebeian. The poorer Plebs played a part in the struggle and gained some elective functions. The wealthier Plebs were virtually admitted to an aristocracy which they considerably strengthened. Rome acquired, as a result, a mixed constitution, predominantly aristocratic but with elements of democracy and monarchy.[1]

This constitution was never planned as a whole. It embodied the political gains of various groups and so represented a balance of forces. Such a balance can be maintained in two ways; either by the continued pull of the same forces, each as weighty as at first, or else by a legal stabilisation of the positions gained. It was by law, written or unwritten, that the position was stabilised; and law, in Rome, became extremely important. The leading Romans were mostly to combine in themselves the character of lawyer and soldier—the two professions which most promote a sense of reality. Starting with a complex political structure, they hammered out something workable and did this without resorting to any theorist. Cato claimed, according to Cicero, that the Roman Republic was not framed by any one genius but by the work of generations. This was true and it was the cause of the multiplicity of public offices and assemblies which seems, in retrospect, so confusing. Besides the two Consuls were six Consular Tribunes, a number of Praetors (eventually, sixteen), two Censors, five (and ultimately ten) Tribunes, four Aediles, four (and finally forty) Quaestors, twenty-six police magistrates (the XXVI viri) and a number of Military Tribunes. All above the rank of Military

[1] *Roman Political Institutions*. L. P. Homo. London, 1929.

Tribune had a mixture of administrative, legal, financial and judicial duties. All without exception were elected for a limited term of office.

Election is quite compatible with aristocracy provided that the same people, or the same sort of people, are always chosen. This was ensured in Rome by two devices; the 'cursus honorum' and the distribution of votes. The 'cursus honorum' was the accepted rule by which no one was eligible for election to a higher office until he had served in a lower. The man with political ambitions had to enter, at about the age of eighteen, a series of alternating military and civil offices which might lead him to election, finally, as Consul. The periods of office and periods of ineligibility were such as to prevent anyone becoming Consul before the age of 43. As a political career thus admitted of no other activity, and as the offices were mostly unpaid, the 'cursus honorum' was open only to those already wealthy at the age of eighteen and with an assured income for life.

The distribution of votes was most carefully planned in the Comitia Centuriata, to which all Roman citizens belonged. This mass meeting voted by Centuries, the citizens being organised on military lines, and each century recorded one vote, that of its own majority. This might have been a democratic system had the Centuries each numbered one hundred voters. In fact, however, while each Equestrian Century numbered one hundred (and there were eighteen of these) the other Centuries, graded on a property qualification, varied in strength from 142-200 in the Pedites of the First Class and 320 in Classes 2 to 5, down to 130,000 in the Proletarian Century. The Centuries numbered 193 in all, so that the Equites and the Pedites 1st Class had by themselves, if they agreed, a bare majority of 98 votes. If there was disagreement the twenty Centuries of the 2nd Class voted until 97 votes had been recorded. Then the voting stopped and the result was announced. The third, fourth, fifth and unclassified Centuries rarely had occasion to vote at all. Within each Century voting was secret, voters collecting in an enclosure and each recording his vote as he left by ballots marked U.R. (uti rogas) or A (antiquo), by writing the name of the candidate on a 'tabella', or (on cases of criminal appeal) by ballots marked L (libero) and D (damno). The functions of this important assembly included the declaring of war, the passing of legal enactments on the recommendation of Senate, and the election of Consuls, Censors and Praetors.

More democratic was the Concilium Plebis, which comprised in theory 250,000 or 300,000 voters and met on market days. No considerable proportion of them could in fact be collected. Had it been possible, moreover, the difficulty would have been to explain to them the point at issue. Tribunes and Plebeian Aediles were elected by this Assembly, which may sometimes have tested the relative popularity of the candidates—or their popularity, at any rate, among a chance collection of the unemployed. In practice, however, those eligible to stand for election had to have served previously as Legatus Legionis (or some other army rank), as Quaestor before that, and previously as military Tribune and police magistrate. To these earlier offices they had been appointed without troubling the Concilium Plebis and, if of Patrician birth, they need not seek election there at all. The Concilium Plebis was essentially a safety valve by which popular discontent could, in the last resort, make itself felt.[1] So far as election went, the voters merely had to chose between men of the same sort, all of rank and property, all with legal and military training, all members of a definite class with its own social customs and standards of conduct. They could not have suddenly elected one of themselves and there is little evidence that they would have chosen to do so even if given the chance.

We have seen that the institutions which were democratic in form were aristocratic in practice. But the whole structure centred upon an institution, the Senate, which was not democratic even in theory. This body, with important functions in foreign policy, finance and legislation, comprised at first 300 (later 600) members, all of whom held or (as in most cases) had previously held, high magisterial office. They were not elected but passed automatically into Senate on completion of their period of office. Senate had thus about twenty new members each year, roughly replacing its losses by death. It was summoned and presided over by a Consul or, in his absence, by the Praetor Urbanus, who introduced the business to be discussed. Having done so, he asked the opinion of each Senator in turn until the sense of the house had become apparent. Each Senator could speak for as long as he liked—and not necessarily to the motion—and could even, by continuing until sunset, talk the motion out. The president brought the discussion to an end when he saw fit and put the matter—although this was rarely necessary—to the vote. Magistrates in office did not vote. The rest moved to one side or other of the house. The motion carried might be vetoed as unconstitutional but would otherwise become a 'senatus consultum' with legal effect, recorded and announced. In legislative matters the 'senatus consultum' did not become a law (lex) until passed in turn by an assembly. There were no organised parties and little use was made of committees. No minutes were kept and the proceedings were comparatively brief. The Roman of Republican days was a man of few words and the more senior seem, in practice, to have swayed the rest by their reputation more than by their eloquence.[2]

[1] See *Roman Political Institutions*. F. F. Abbott. Boston, 1911. Chapter X, pp. 220-243. See also *Roman Public Life*. A. H. J. Greenidge. London, 1930.
[2] *Roman Public Life*. A. H. J. Greenidge. London, 1930. Chapter VI. pp. 261-272.

Viewed as a structure or mechanism, the Roman constitution seems complex, confused and unworkable. It had, to all appearance, too many legislatures, too many independent officials, too many elections and too many rules. No distinction was ever made between legislative, executive and judicial functions, nor even between military and civil. It worked, nevertheless, to some purpose. Rome was governed, in effect, by a class of men of similar birth, similar training, similar experience and (one might add) similar limitations. They all understood each other very well and probably reached agreement privately before Senate even met. The magistrates could have nullified the powers of Senate. But why should they? They were magistrates only for a time and thereafter Senators for life. The Senators might have obstructed the work of those in office. But why should they? They had all been in office themselves. Senate might have become dangerously divorced from the people at large. But it was not altogether closed to talent, nor entirely insensitive to upper middle-class opinion. The people, finally, might have found means to demand a share in government. But the Roman ruling class was a true aristocracy. Its members were respected for their courage and ability, not merely envied for their wealth. Of the aristocrats, every one had served in the field without disgrace, every one had a legal and administrative training, every one had served as executive and judge. They affected, moreover, a Spartan simplicity in dress and manner, resting their influence merely on birth, reputation and known achievement They were able, between them, to conquer the known world.

There have been other ruling aristocracies besides that of Rome. Nor are these confined to the West. The Chinese aristocracy, ruling at certain periods through Imperial machinery of government, was unlike the Roman in being more cultured and better educated, with a sharp distinction drawn between civil and military functions. The same would be true of the Japanese aristocrats of the Fujiwara period but with this difference that they also produced a class of educated women, whose diaries and novels were to form a valuable part of the literature of Japan. In a complete study of the subject, such as cannot be attempted here, a variety of evidence could be compiled. It may, however, be doubted whether any modern example of aristocracy can be as interesting or complete as that afforded by seventeenth-nineteenth century England. It is all the more interesting in that the adjacent countries, showing the same tendencies, failed to achieve the same result. They failed, moreover, for reasons which throw considerable light on the nature of effective aristocratic rule. The Monarchy which rested on Divine Right in the sixteenth-seventeenth centuries weakened during the eighteenth century and tended, throughout Europe, to turn either into aristocracy or into Monarchy self-justified in terms of enlightenment. But the success of the aristocracies in supplanting monarchy varied with the way in which the aristocracies were formed. In some important respects, the English aristocracy resembled no other.

To realise the difference between the English and most other aristocracies we must observe, first of all, that the English language has no equivalent of the French 'de', the German 'von' or the Dutch 'van'. English Barons and Baronets are 'of' a named locality but not to the extinction of their original surname. And, as between surnames, there has never been a clear distinction between what is noble and what is not. We must next observe that the English law of primogeniture, in confining technical nobility to the eldest son, throws emphasis on an actual title, within the power of the Crown to bestow, and disregards the prestige of birth, which the younger sons must equally share. With these basic peculiarities, the English nobility was further modified in its membership by the salient events in English history. Most of the great medieval houses had become extinct, through battle and attainder, during the Wars of the Roses. The Dukedoms of Cornwall and Lancaster had been absorbed by the Royal House. A new nobility, recruited from the landed gentry and merchants, had grown up as a result of the Dissolution of the Monasteries. But this in turn was involved in the Civil Wars of the seventeenth century, many of the older families being ruined by fines and confiscations. By 1660 most of the English estates had changed hands repeatedly. Of the surviving nobility hardly one could claim what the French would have described as ancestry. Families of the 'Ancienne chevalerie' in France claimed to have been noble since 1360. More than that, however, they needed to establish (before obtaining a commission in the army) their noble descent on *both* sides. They had to show sixteen quarterings in their coat-of-arms. It is to be doubted whether any English family could have shown that—let alone the thirty-two quarterings which were boasted in some fantastic and crumbling chateaux. Queen Elizabeth could not have done so, one of her ancestors having been Lord Mayor of London. As for the noble houses, they had been constantly marrying, to their advantage, into the families of lawyers, wine-merchants, shipowners and adventurers. Nor were their younger sons averse to trade. As Voltaire pointed out, at the time when Sir Robert Walpole governed Great Britain, his younger brother was no more than a Factor at Aleppo. It was this absence of caste which facilitated the concentration of political, military, religious and financial powers among the same people. The English aristocracy of the eighteenth century was, in fact, a body of very mixed origin, constantly recruited from below, with highly developed instincts in law and business. By French standards, noble birth in England simply did not exist.

The aristocrat, in the English sense, first appears in the reign of Elizabeth. He was a man of respectable family, who at least knew who his grandfather was. He was a landowner of considerable wealth and made up in education for what he lacked in ancestry. He was something of a scholar and often a musician or poet. He was an athlete, a horseman and soldier and sometimes a seaman as well. By the early seventeenth century his training had been standardised. From the village school or a private tutor, he went to the grammar or public school. Then he entered the University and completed his groundwork in Latin, Mathematics, Divinity and perhaps Greek. Leaving Oxford or Cambridge, very probably without graduating, he next attended the Inns of Court and obtained at least a smattering of law. Then he set off on the Grand Tour to France, Germany and Italy, spending a year or more in learning French and Italian. There followed a campaign or two in the Low Countries. After that he was fit for duty as Justice of the Peace, fit to appear at Court and fit before long to take a seat in Parliament. How developed even before then were the traditions of Parliament may be learnt from a treatise of 1562-6, published in 1583.

> ... In the disputing is a mervelous good order used in the lower house. He that standeth uppe bareheaded is understanded that he will speake to the bill. If more stande up, who that first is judged to arise, is first harde, though the one doe prayse the law, the other diswade it, yet there is no altercation. For everie man speaketh as to the speaker, not as one to an other, for that is against the order of the house. It is also taken against the order to name him whom ye doe confute, but by circumlocution, as he that speaketh with the bill, or he that spake against the bill and gave this and this reason. And so with perpetuall Oration not with altercation, he goeth through till he do make an end. He that once hath spoken on a bill though he be confuted straight, that day may not replie, no though he would channge his opinion. So that to one bill in one day one may not in that house speake twise, for else one or two with altercation woulde spende all the time.[1]

Such rules of debate as these were the work of gentlemen, lawyers, merchants and soldiers; men of great experience. There was little of democracy about it but there was evidence of a close alliance between aristocracy and middle class. It provided a good school of statesmanship even when the House of Lords was more important. By the late seventeenth century moreover the English aristocrat rarely made a mistake over architecture, gardens, portraits, trees, horses or dogs. He was rightly trained for his main political task, which was to

---

[1] *De Republica Anglorum:* A Discourse on the Commonwealth of England. By Sir Thomas Smith. Ed. by L. Alston. p. 34.

establish aristocratic government under the guise of monarchy.

The fall of James II and the crowning of William and Mary brought in a weakened monarchy, dependent on the party which had brought about the revolution of 1688; a party which might turn at any time to intrigue with the fallen king. What is remarkable is the speed and certainty with which the English aristocrats set up a government of their own, retaining a diminished kingship but effectively concentrating the power in their own hands. By the middle of the eighteenth century the Government, the Parliament, the Church, the Army and the Universities were all so many different aspects of aristocracy. And all Europe watched to see what the result would be in terms of strength or weakness. The answer came in the Seven Years War of 1756-63 and the total defeat of France. Henceforth the upholders of monarchy could say, if they wished, that an aristocratic form of rule was impious, unprecedented and wrong. But they could not regard it as unworkable, and they could not deny its success.

To what was this success due? It was due, no doubt, in part, to causes unconnected with the form of government as established. But, such causes apart, aristocracy revealed a certain strength of its own. It combined scope for individual enterprise with a certain consistency in public effort. Sea power, trade and colonisation formed an intricate pattern in which war was used to capture trade and trade increased to pay for war. Only an aristocracy of that peculiar kind could have achieved its purpose in that peculiar way. It was the close connection between statesmen, admirals, shipowners, planters, underwriters, gentry, soldiers and bankers that made success possible. More than that, the structure of society provided initiative where it was wanted (on the fringes of a growing empire) and consistency where that was wanted (at the centre). The policies of kings proved, for the purposes of naval war, at once too interfering and too variable. Where so much depends upon a single man, policy may waver when he falls sick or grows old. Policy may be reversed when he dies. But the solid commercial interests of a governing class are fairly permanent in their nature. Behind the brilliance or eccentricity of the individual lurks the abiding purpose of a class.

CHAPTER IX

Aristocracy justified in Theory

THE essence of aristocracy lies in the respect accorded to the aristocrat by others; a respect to be enhanced more by deeds than words. Respect, moreover, is rarely accorded to those who demand it. In a well established and effective aristocracy the member of the ruling class assumes, but does not explain, his superiority. Should he be compelled to justify his power, it will be proof that his position is crumbling. The order obeyed without question comes normally from someone to whom the possibility of disobedience does not even occur. It is natural, therefore, that books written avowedly to justify aristocracy are rare. And aristocracy is apt to masquerade as something else; as monarchy sometimes or even as democracy. The true aristocrat is respected for his virtues; and modesty is one of them.

The only superiority a man can claim without some loss of dignity is that of descent. For one thing, the claim can be silent; the display of a name, a title, a coat-of-arms. For another, the superiority claimed is not one of personal merit but of ancestry. It is permissible to claim for an ancestor what one cannot claim for oneself. As against this, the most effective aristocracy is one in which noble birth plays only a minor part. In such an aristocracy, continually recruited from below and always sensitive to the opinion of the people (or, anyway, the people who matter), to boast of ancestry may give actual offence to others. Among the ruling class of eighteenth-nineteenth century England there were men without birth, fortune or even any very obvious ability; people who were 'in society' through being thought amusing, good-looking, well-dressed or somehow useful. It was and had always been impossible to say who exactly the aristocrats were, or why. So that English defenders of aristocracy appeared, in general, to be defending something else; usually, the constitution. The theorists of Republican Rome had no easier task and our earliest justifications of aristocracy are no more candid about it than are the most recent.

The Romans were not themselves given to theorising about politics and they left it to a Greek, Polybius, to explain their institutions to posterity. He had at least the merit of knowing his subject, being held in Italy as a hostage of the Achaean League for sixteen years, from 167 to 151 B.C. His main intention was to write a history of the

Republic and it was only incidentally that he paused to study the principles of Roman government.[1] He follows Aristotle in assuming a sequence in the forms of rule, postulating a periodic return to barbarism as the result of pestilence, famine and flood. He suggests that the sequence in the forms of rule can be arrested only by combining them in a constitution wherein the subversive tendencies of each are counteracted by the rest. He finds such a system in that planned for Sparta by Lycurgus and thinks that the Romans have reached the same goal by a less theoretical route. He explains how the Consul is held in check by the Senate and the Senate in turn by the Assemblies, the members of which will come, as soldiers, under the absolute power of the Consul. Cicero (who should have known better) follows this theory in his *Republic* and concludes, in effect, that everything has been so wisely arranged by the Romans' ancestors that there is little or no reason to alter anything. At the time he wrote it was in fact altering itself fairly rapidly and heading, indeed, for a state of anarchy which could end only in dictatorship. What he describes is, in effect, the Republic he would have liked to preserve. And he regards it, as Polybius did, as a balanced regime, not as an example of aristocracy in decline. That it was a declining aristocracy is apparent, nevertheless, from all that followed.

From the time of the Roman Republic down to the end of the seventeenth century A.D. there are few examples of aristocracy in Europe, and such as there are seem to be limited in scale. Venice was ruled by an aristocracy of merchants but so, in a sense, were many other medieval towns. The Venetian example, interesting as it is, rises hardly above the level (in scale) of the City State. Where, however, as in the Netherlands, a federation of City States comes into existence, the opportunity occurs for aristocracy on a rather larger scale. The opportunity was there but the Dutch inclined rather more towards democracy and served, with England, to discredit that form of rule. One of the greatest of Dutchmen, Hugo Grotius (1583-1645), who first defined the word 'State' for the purposes of International Law,[2] gave his decided preference for Monarchy. It remained for England to demonstrate the merits of aristocratic rule, doing so in conscious imitation of Rome. The seventeenth century had witnessed a struggle in England between monarchy and aristocracy; a struggle only possible because the aristocrats disagreed with each other about religion. The momentary result was an experiment in democracy

[1] *A History of Political Theories, Ancient and Medieval.* W. A. Dunning. New York, 1927. pp. 113-114.

[2] A community of Western and Christian civilisation, with an organised government capable of making and observing treaties, with a fixed territory within which its sovereignty is complete, and a stability which seems likely to offer permanence. See *Western Political Thought. An Historical Introduction from the Origins to Rousseau.* John Bowle. London. 1947. Chapters IV and VII.

which ended promptly in military dictatorship. This brief experience convinced the English that monarchy was preferable to either and the restoration of Charles II in 1660 might have, just conceivably, resulted in a monarchy of the fashion set by France. But the astute Charles II was succeeded by a Roman Catholic. This sufficed to unite the two religious parties for just long enough to dethrone James II and instal William of Orange in his place. From 1688 the belief of the English aristocracy was that monarchy was necessary, as had already been proved, but that the real power must be vested in themselves. To explain what they had done, and what they intended, they needed their own political prophet. In John Locke they found him.

John Locke (1632-1704) was a scholar patronised by the Earl of Shaftesbury who came to England, from exile, in 1689, and published his two *Treatises of Government* in 1690. His first object was to demolish the *Patriarcha* of Sir Robert Filmer, in vogue since 1680; his second, to justify the Revolution of 1688 by proving that sovereignty lies in the community, not in the king. It is needless to follow Locke all the way in his refutation of Filmer, for the discussion is one which must seem to us rather futile. Filmer had rightly insisted that paternity is, in some sense, the origin of political power. But his attempt to show that the Stuart kings had their sovereignty by a right of descent or right of conveyance going back to Adam is not particularly helpful. Locke writes eleven chapters to show that this claim is baseless and finally summarises his argument in a more compact form, as follows:—[1]

> *Firstly*. That Adam had not, either by natural right of fatherhood or by positive donation from God, any such authority over his children, nor dominion over the world, as is pretended.
>
> *Secondly*. That if he had, his heirs yet had no right to it.
>
> *Thirdly*. That if his heirs had . . . the right of succession . . . could not have been certainly determined.
>
> *Fourthly*. That if even that had been determined, yet the knowledge of which is the eldest line . . . [is] . . . utterly lost.

With this reasoning we may agree, turning however with some relief to his more constructive work in Book II. Locke begins his own theory of government by firmly stating that men are born equal when in a state of nature.

> This equality of men by Nature, the judicious Hooker looks upon as so evident in itself and beyond all question, that he makes it the foundation of that obligation to mutual love amongst men on which he builds the duties they owe one another and from whence he derives the great maxims of justice and charity.[2]

[1] *Of Civil Government*. John Locke. Everyman edition. London, 1943. p. 117.
[2] *Ibid*. p. 119.

Actually, Hooker is not quite as definite as that. He merely asserts that:

> Every independent multitude, before any certain form of regiment established, hath, under God's supreme authority, full dominion over itself, even as a man not tied with the bond of subjection as yet unto any other, hath over himself the like power.[1]

Locke nevertheless assumes agreement and goes on to maintain that men are also born free except in that the Law of Nature enjoins each 'that being all equal and independent, no one ought to harm another in his life, health, liberty or possessions'. The duty of enforcing this law is vested in all alike. The right of property derives from the value of work put into it. Children are born in a subordination to parents but outgrow it and thereafter need merely honour their parents. He admits that parental authority tends, in practice, to linger. 'Thus the natural fathers of families, by an insensible change, became the politic monarchs of them too' and sometimes left able and worthy heirs. But this, he insists, does not create Civil Government, the characteristic of which is law and its impartial enforcement. Political Society derives not from fatherhood but from agreement.

> Men being, as has been said, by nature all free, equal and independent, no one can be put out of this estate and subjected to the political power of another without his own consent, which is done by agreeing with other men, to join and unite into a community for their comfortable, safe, and peaceable living, one amongst another, in a secure enjoyment of their properties, and a greater security against any that are not of it. . . . When any number of men have so consented to make one community or government, they are thereby presently incorporated, and make one body politic, wherein the majority have a right to act and conclude the rest.

Locke here postulates a society formed *before* the nature of its government has been agreed. He meets the objection that no account exists of men so forming a political society by explaining that 'Government is everywhere antecedent to records . . . [so that] . . . it is with commonwealths as with particular persons, they are commonly ignorant of their own births and infancies. . . .' He goes on, however,

> I will not deny that if we look back as far as history will direct us, towards the original of commonwealths, we shall generally find them under the government and administration of one man.[2]

He even admits that in small family societies, 'government commonly began in the father'. But when different families came to live together, and when a father died 'it is not to be doubted, but they

---

[1] *The Political Ideas of Richard Hooker*. E. T. Davies. London, 1946. p. 65. Hooker asserts the 'Contract' theory as did, later, Bishop Hoadly.
[2] Locke, *op. cit.* p. 168.

used their natural freedom to set up him whom they judged the ablest. . . .'

Conceding that the earliest governments of which we have record were monarchical, he asks why people 'generally pitched upon this form'. He refers to the example of paternal rule, to men's initial inexperience of tyranny and to the need for leadership in war, and concludes that men would naturally 'choose the wisest and bravest man to conduct them in their wars . . . and in this chiefly be their ruler'. He points out, however, that forms of government vary. The important thing is that men voluntarily enter it by agreement. They do this in order to preserve their property, obtain an impartial judge and ensure that his judgments are enforced. In thus forming a society they give up to it their original equality, liberty and executive power. But the power of the society must be for the common good and must achieve the three basic purposes for which it was formed, and thus ensure 'the peace, safety and public good of the people'. This can be done through democracy, oligarchy or monarchy, or any compromise between them.[1] But, whatever the form of government, the supreme power must be the legislative.

The legislative power, though supreme, is not limitless. It can be no greater than the power originally entrusted to it by individuals. And they cannot give to it what they do not possess. As no one has the right to destroy or enslave either himself or anyone else, that right cannot have been transferred to the legislative. That body, therefore, 'can never have a right to destroy, enslave or designedly to impoverish the subjects'. By similar reasoning, the fact that no man can be judge in his own cause prevents the individual from conferring any such rights on the legislative. The judicial power must be separate. Government must be by declared laws, enforced by authorised judges.

> These are the bounds which the trust that is put in them by the society and the law of God and Nature have set to the legislative power of every Commonwealth, in all forms of government. First: They are to govern by promulgated established laws, not to be varied in particular cases, but to have one rule for rich and poor, for the favourite at Court and the countryman at plough. Secondly: These laws also ought to be designed for no other end ultimately but the good of the people. Thirdly: They must not raise taxes on the property of the people without the consent of the people given by themselves or their deputies. And this properly concerns only such governments where the legislative is always in being, or at least where the people have not reserved any part of the legislative to deputies, to be from time to time chosen by themselves. Fourthly: Legislative neither must nor can transfer the power of making laws to anybody else or place it anywhere but where the people have.[2]

[1] Locke, *op. cit.* p. 189.
[2] Locke, *op. cit.* pp. 182-183.

Locke argues that the supreme power cannot take any man's property without his consent.

> ... For the preservation of property being the end of government, and that for which men enter into society, it necessarily supposes and requires that the people should have property, without which they must be supposed to lose that by entering into society which was the end for which they entered into it; too gross an absurdity for any man to own.

True, there must be taxation but only by the consent of the majority, given by themselves or by their representatives.

Locke maintains that there must be, in addition to the legislative body, 'a power always in being which should see to the execution of the laws' and a power to deal with 'war and peace, leagues and alliances'. These two powers must, in practice, be the same and with the additional duty, most likely, of convening the legislative body. But the legislative, which Locke conceives as only periodically in session, remains superior to the executive power, normally entrusted to a single man.

> Where the legislative and executive power are in distinct hands, as they are in all moderated monarchies and well-framed governments, there the good of the society requires that several things should be left to the discretion of him that has the executive power.[1]

He considers that the ruler must have a certain discretion, if only to prevent injustice by a too strict observance of the law. This is prerogative, an equity which may come in time to be embodied in the law, such being no encroachment on prerogative.

> Those who say otherwise speak as if the prince had a distinct and separate interest from the good of the community, and was not made for it; the root and source from which spring almost all those evils and disorders which happen in kingly governments.

But Locke is careful to explain that the prerogative of a king should be something far short of despotism, which is no less than

> ... an absolute arbitrary power one man has over another, to take away his life whenever he pleases; and this is a power which neither Nature gives, for it has made no such distinction between one man and another, nor compact can convey. For man, not having such an arbitrary power over his own life, cannot give another man power over it, but it is the effect only of forfeiture which the aggressor makes of his own life when he puts himself into the state of war with another. ... And thus captives, taken in a just and lawful war, and such only, are subject to a despotical power.[2]

[1] *Ibid.* p. 199.
[2] Locke, *op. cit.* p. 205.

Locke quotes James I as stating that he was bound by 'the fundamental laws of his kingdom', both tacitly and by coronation oath,
and but for that would be a mere tyrant. He explains, however, that it
is not only monarchies that may be tyrannical. 'Wherever law ends,
tyranny begins'. And the resistance to an unlawful tyranny may lead
to the dissolution of government.

This last subject is discussed in Chapter XIX.[1] Governments are
overturned, he explains, in two ways; by foreign conquest, or by internal dissension. Foreign conquest destroys society itself and needs
no further comment. Internal dissension may cause the legislative to
break up or dissolve, as for instance when the prince 'sets up his own
arbitrary will in place of the laws' or 'hinders the legislative from
assembling . . . or from acting freely'. The prince can produce the
same result by tampering with the electoral system, by betraying the
State to a foreign power, or (finally) by so neglecting and abandoning
his office that the laws are no longer enforced. The government can
be as readily overturned through the legislative or the prince making
themselves 'masters or arbitrary disposers of the lives, liberties or
fortunes of the people'. For as the reason 'why men enter into society
is the preservation of their property', a failure to preserve it destroys
government and justifies revolt. Even the legislative can become
corrupt.

> The end of government is the good of mankind; and which is best
> for mankind, that the people should be always exposed to the bound-
> less will of tyranny, or that the rulers should be sometimes liable to be
> opposed when they grow exorbitant in the use of their power, and
> employ it for the destruction, and not the preservation, of the proper-
> ties of their people?[2]

Locke's general argument, of which the above is more or less the
conclusion, can be summarised thus:—Men are born equal, with
equal rights under the Law of Nature. They agree with each other to
form a society, mainly to preserve property and secure justice.
Justice can derive only from law; so the supreme power in society
must be the legislative. But even the legislative is limited in power by
the original agreement; nor may it encroach on the powers of the
judiciary. There must also be an executive, probably a single ruler,
but he too must be restrained by law. Finally, when the legislative is
overturned, the society is dissolved and men are free to rebel and
start afresh with another mutual agreement.

As an argument this may not seem particularly impressive. The
basic assumptions are far less convincing than those of Sir Robert

---

[1] Locke, *op. cit.* p. 224.
[2] Locke, *op. cit.* p. 233.

Filmer, and the theory of the formation of society by agreement is quite unhistorical. If the agreement does not exist, the proper limitations in the power of legislative and executive are not established; and the right of rebellion remains as doubtful as ever. The argument need convince no one. But Locke's treatises are significant in that they embody four vital political ideas, arising not from academic theories but from the political experience of his generation. These reiterated ideas are Property, Law, the Separation of Legislative, Executive and Judicial powers, and the Limits set to the powers of government as such. These have proved potent ideas, especially in America. But it might not seem, at first sight, that Locke had produced exactly the arguments needed to support an aristocracy in power following the Revolution of .1688. This talk of original equality might not be greeted with any deafening applause in the House of Lords. But all that was merely theoretical stuff which few politicians would bother to read. His essential, positive doctrines—property, law, the separation of powers and the limits set to government—all add up to one thing, and that is Freedom; or the freedom, anyway, of the property owner. And while the Peers of 1688 intended to keep power for themselves (as against the king), the gentry at large cared more for freedom than for a share in government. Locke says nothing directly to justify aristocracy. How could he? In England aristocracy could never be justified for it could not even be defined. It did not mean birth; it never meant title; it did not always mean wealth; it seldom meant even dress, fashion or accent, and rarely could be equated with education. Its most stable feature was personal freedom and property in land, to be defended by law against the interference of government. And this defence of property and freedom rested with a legislature representative of property and a judiciary which government could not control.

The English aristocracy, like their feudal predecessors at Runnymede, involuntarily secured for others what they were intent only to gain for themselves. To have secured freedom for the peerage would, in England, have left all their younger brothers in bondage. To have limited privileges to men with a coat-of-arms dating from before 1500 would have excluded half the people who were obviously important. To have confined privileges to men with a coat of arms dating from before 1360 would have excluded practically everyone. Explanations of what constituted an 'esquire' or 'gentleman' were never more than partly successful, including as they did a fair number of those it was intended to keep out and excluding a few of those who had obviously to come in. As no exact definition was possible, as in France, of the word 'gentleman', the freedom of the aristocrat came to be conferred inadvertently on the merchant and farmer.

As regards immediate effect, we must remember that Locke wrote to justify an event which had taken place. His reasoning all leads up to a description of the constitution of 1688 and a defence of the changes which had brought it into being. His work was not at first accepted with much enthusiasm by the Whigs (perhaps because he proved too much) and it was naturally resented by the Tories as directly contradicting their doctrine of Divine Right.[1] Locke was rewarded by two offers of an embassy (which he refused) and by the offer of a minor government post (which he accepted) in 1696. It was not until after his death in 1704 that his doctrines began to gain influence and he had a definite vogue throughout the eighteenth century.

The two political treatises were not Locke's only works and we must note at least one other, *An Essay concerning Toleration* (written in 1667). In this he asserts that the ruler's functions are confined to 'securing the civil peace and property of his subjects'. He divides religious beliefs into three categories: those 'purely speculative' such as 'the belief of the Trinity, purgatory, transubstantiation, antipodes'; those which affect conduct 'in matters of indifferency' such as marriage, divorce, polygamy, wills, holidays, food and abstinence; and lastly, those 'moral virtues and vices' which 'concern society and are also good or bad in their own nature'. As regards the first, Locke holds that there should be complete freedom. As regards the second, the government may command or forbid actions which affect 'the peace, safety and security' of the people. As for the third, Locke firmly asserts that 'the law-maker hath nothing to do with moral virtues and vices . . . any otherwise than barely as they are subservient to the good and preservation of mankind under government'. Locke expressed these views again in his *Letter concerning Toleration* (1689), by which year the principle of toleration had, in England, been more or less agreed. Locke had incidentally had some part in drawing up the Constitution of the American State of Carolina in 1669, in which the freedom of the colonists to worship as they chose was expressly laid down. This was the beginning of the not inconsiderable influence his ideas were to have in America. His doctrine of the separation of powers is embodied even in the United States constitution. As against that, it might well be argued that Locke's plea for toleration, and the limits he sets to the functions of the State (both being aspects of freedom) are his most valuable, if not wholly original, contributions to political thought. It would be untrue to assert that Locke's dream of a 'secular' State (without moral purpose) was the reality of eighteenth century England. But it came more nearly true than it did anywhere else or indeed than it has in England since. As for his

[1] *John Locke's Political Philosophy*. J. W. Gough. Oxford, 1950. pp. 120-135.

main principle of freedom, that was stoutly maintained and was still being upheld when the century drew to its close.

It was indeed towards the end of the eighteenth century that the whole spirit of the English system was summarised by Edmund Burke (1730-1797). Burke was a pupil, in some measure, of Montesquieu, having, like everyone else, read and admired his book *Esprit des Lois* (1748). This work was based in part on a study of English institutions and in part on a reading of Locke. He naturally recommended a constitutional monarchy. His approach was, nevertheless, for the period, extremely scientific, revealing some idea of ethnology and criminology. His book ran through some twenty-two editions in eighteen months and had influence on Catherine II, Frederick the Great and Louis XVI. Burke was among his readers but learnt still more from Montesquieu's own source of inspiration, English institutions as they actually existed. Burke lays down as his first principle that Society is not a machine but an organism—like a tree or an animal. His second principle is Prudence—deliberation, sobriety and moderation. His third principle is the necessity for the long view, backward and forward. He utterly rejects the idea of majority rule and the will of the people. He argues that our forefathers and descendants, who can have no vote, are also involved and that a present majority has no right to undo the work of those who are dead or blight the future of those still to be born. Society is a family, not a collection of individuals, and the family includes old and young, ancestors and descendants. His fourth principle is that the wisdom of our ancestors is not lightly to be set aside, and for this reason; that their institutions, unlike those proposed by innovators, are known to be workable. His fifth principle is liberty, but only as connected with honesty, justice and wisdom. His sixth principle is Balance. Government, he insists, should display a just balance between Monarchy, Aristocracy, the Church and the Commons. Monarchy should be given power but held in check by Aristocracy as representing stability and permanence. The Commons should represent a minority of the people, those of adult age, fair education and sufficient leisure. But the representatives are never merely to reflect the views of the electorate. Once elected, they should be guided by their own wisdom and experience.

Burke was, in all this, no theorist. He describes and actively defends the institutions he knew and respected and the principles generally approved among his colleagues and friends. He follows Polybius in praising a constitution in which monarchy, aristocracy and democracy are blended. He follows Cicero in regarding as so blended a constitution in which aristocracy in fact predominated, and which he wanted to preserve. He does not, however, praise aristocracy as such.

He commends rather the principles upon which it is based and the
chief merit for which an aristocratic rule is distinguished. The
principles he values are those of moderation, proportion, foresight
and respect for the past. The merit he finds in an aristocracy is
Freedom.

CHAPTER X

Theocracy

THE Empires of the Ancient World were normally ruled by a king who was also a god. Given a priesthood to support his divinity, we have thus an element of theocracy in the oldest kingdoms. But theocracy, rule by a priest or priests, is only one form of monarchy or aristocracy and not, in itself, of great political importance. It would hardly be possible to distinguish between the religious and political functions of the ancient monarchies; and in the instances (as among the Jews) where the priests had taken the place of the kings, then political and religious powers were at least co-extensive. The people were all of the one religion and they showed no particular desire to extend its benefits to anyone else. The political interest of an actively religious rule begins at the point when it is applied to people who are not of the same religion. Nor is such a rule applied to others except in the name of a missionary religion; a religion which enjoins the believer to make converts among the heathen. Although, therefore, the earliest monarchies were, in some measure, theocratic, the political interest of theocracy must centre mainly on the missionary and the persecuting religions. And of these the first was Buddhism.

Contemporary with the Jewish prophet Isaiah, contemporary with Heraclitus, contemporary with Confucius, lived in India Gautama, known to history as the Buddha. He was a prince who lived round about 500 B.C., not far from Benares. At the age of twenty-nine he began to study under Brahman teachers. Having reached a state of enlightenment (Buddha means the Enlightened) he preached at Benares, as did the other mendicant monks, his followers. His doctrine was based on the 'four noble truths'; that life is pain; that the pain is due to a craving for life; that the solution is to discipline that craving; and that the secret of that discipline is to escape from the wheel of life. The way of deliverance includes avoiding the three vices; ignorance, lust and hatred. Most of this was perfectly consistent with Brahman doctrines. He differed mainly from the Brahmans, perhaps, in failing to accept their ideas of caste. He was original, moreover, in giving up fasting and penance and in denying, in effect, the existence of a personal god or an individual existence after death. His Nirvana or ultimate good was a cessation, merely, of life and pain. Doctrines such as these were too subtle and metaphysical even for his own disciples. They were resisted by the Brahmans and appealed only to a few.

After Gautama's death (c. 482-472 B.C.) his followers created a new religion round his reputation and memory. By 300 B.C. they were wrangling about doctrine and by that time Buddha (the unbeliever) had become a god. This new religion made no great progress in India but, absorbing certain Indian ideas, became a doctrine of deliverance with Buddha himself in the role of Messiah. In this form it was spread by active missionaries (not by force) in Burma, Siam, Malaya, China and Japan. It absorbed many local gods and legends, becoming, for the simpler devotees, a religion of magic and wonder; remaining, for others, an austere philosophy. In India Buddhism reached its peak under the Emperor Asoka, who temporarily converted Ceylon to that faith in 251 B.C. It now forms two main branches; the one in Ceylon, Burma and Siam; the other in China, Japan, Java, Sumatra and Tibet. Buddhism brought with it everywhere its own kind of learning and philosophy, its own humanitarianism and ethics, its own ritual and art. More than that, the Buddhist priests were educated men whose knowledge extended to medicine, textiles, architecture, bell-founding, engraving and sculpture. Buddhist temples were and are places of great beauty. Buddhist monasteries were and are centres of learning, charity and refuge. Buddhism was once almost established as a form of rule in Japan.

In only one country has a Buddhist government been set up as a theocracy, and that is Tibet; a country in which ritual and prayer occupy the energies of quite half its three million inhabitants. Rule centres on the Dalai Lama, reincarnation of his predecessors and Vice-Regent for the Buddha. He is assisted by a Council of Ministers and a Parliament, and all the nobles are made (or were made) to accept public office. Real power rests, however, in the 400,000 monks who are or were collected in 5,000 monasteries; and more especially in the four largest, all near Lhasa. Celibacy on this scale is hardly compatible, one would think, with racial survival. As a form of government, nevertheless, Buddhism can claim (as can the Papacy) the merit of having proved exceptionally stable.

Although Buddhism is an example, and perhaps the first example, of a missionary religion, it has not been generally associated with religious persecution. To this rule, however, there is one big exception. When the Emperor Asoka, third of the Mauryan dynasty, succeeded to the throne in about 268 B.C., he proclaimed himself a Buddhist and Buddhism the state religion. More than that, he used the machinery of government to disseminate its teachings. For practical purposes, these teachings, in so far as they affected the subject, were summarised in what is called the Second Minor Rock Edict, which reads as follows:—

Thus saith His Majesty:

> Father and mother must be obeyed; similarly, respect for living creatures must be enforced; truth must be spoken. These are the virtues of the Law of Piety which must be practised. Similarly, the teacher must be reverenced by the pupil, and proper courtesy must be shown to relations.
>
> This is the ancient standard of piety—this leads to length of days, and according to this men must act.[1]

As these precepts were acceptable, for the most part, to Asoka's subjects and as he avowed a general toleration in other respects, this Edict might seem a harmless injunction to observe what were in fact established customs. But 'respect for living creatures' meant a partial enforcement of vegetarianism as from 243 B.C.

> . . . Many kinds of animals were absolutely protected from slaughter in any circumstances; and the slaying of animals commonly used for food by the flesh-eating population, although not totally prohibited, was hedged round by severe restrictions. On fifty-six specified days in the year, killing under any pretext was categorically forbidden; and in many ways the liberty of the subject was very seriously contracted. While Asoka lived, these regulations were, no doubt, strictly enforced by the special officers appointed for the purpose; and it is not unlikely that deliberate breach of the more important regulations was visited with the capital penalty, as it was later in the days of Harsha.[2]
> . . . Sacrifices involving the death of a victim, which are absolutely indispensable for the correct worship of some of the gods, were categorically prohibited, at least at the capital, from an early period in the reign. . . . Men might believe what they liked, but must do as they were told.[3]

A respect for life so fanatical as to involve capital punishment would seem somewhat remote from the philosophical ideas of Gautama himself. But the transformation of a Founder's ethical teaching into an elaborate and rigid ritual is the normal way in which religions develop. In this instance Asoka, who conquered Kalinga with (it is said) enormous bloodshed, used his powers to the utmost in support of Buddhism.

> . . . But the millenium had not arrived and human nature was not changed by the affirmation of great spiritual truths. The miracle which Asoka expected by his proclamations of the Dharma did not come to pass; and the spiritual insight which he so earnestly desired to give to

[1] *The early History of India from 600 B.C. to the Muhammadan Conquest*. Vincent A. Smith. 3rd ed. Oxford, 1914. p. 178.
[2] Vincent A. Smith. *op. cit.* p. 177.
[3] *Ibid.* p. 179.

all his subjects is less evident in early Buddhist records than extravagant faith in the wonder-working powers of the bodily relics of the Saints who taught the Good Law.[1]

If Asoka's ideas were remote from those of Gautama, the ideas of the common folk in India were still more remote from those of Asoka.

The development of the theocracy of Byzantium and Rome can be traced back not merely to the teachings of Christ but to the organization of the Roman Empire. Politically, the story is simple in outline. The Roman Republic had a military success with which its political organization was quite unable to cope. The Roman constitution was basically that of a Greek colony. To use it for governing Italy was to stretch the system to breaking point. To use it for governing the known world was impossible. Republican Rome had no executive body smaller than the Senate, no permanent officials, no specialists in diplomacy or finance. In so far as the existence of democratic assemblies meant inviting the unemployed of Rome to advise on the governance of an Empire, the system was merely absurd. For the most successful general to make himself ruler was more or less inevitable. Julius Caesar, the first Commander-in-Chief to assume political control, annexed Egypt and made it part of the Empire. His successor, Augustus, (warned by Julius Caesar's fate), moved cautiously, assuming only Consular powers and the title of 'Princeps' or first citizen. He avoided anything like royalty. But, whereas Augustus was only 'Princeps' in Rome and 'Imperator' in the Provinces, he was Pharaoh in Egypt, successor to the Hellenistic monarchy of the Ptolemies and seated upon the world's most ancient throne. In Egyptian monuments the Roman Emperors were to appear with inscriptions reading 'the Everliving, the Beloved of Isis, the Beloved of Phtha'.[2]

The tremendous inheritance of Egypt brought the Roman Emperors not only deity but an example of efficient administration based upon a strict separation of the military and civil powers. It was not until the reign of Domitian that the living Emperor was called 'Deus'. It was Aurelian, however, who proclaimed himself the representative of the Sun God, to resist whom henceforth would be impious as well as criminal. The imperial bureaucracy grew up under Claudius (A.D. 41-54) and the Senate lost to it the last of its powers in 271. Before that, under Hadrian (A.D. 117-138) there had been established the imperial council of state, the imperial secretariat and the imperial system of postal communication. What is most significant however, about his reign is that he spent half his time away from Rome—

[1] *The History of Aryan Rule in India*. E. B. Havell. London, 1918. p. 102.
[2] *The Age of Constantine the Great*. Jacob Burckhardt. Trans. by M. Hadas. London, 1949.

in Spain, Syria, Britain and Africa—being away for five or six years
at a stretch. This shows that the imperial administration could run,
and did run for years, in the Emperor's absence. It was latterly
copied less from Egypt than from the Sassanian administration in
Persia; a ministerial system of the typically Oriental type. The Empire
was governed by what came to be called the Sacred Consistory,
comprising the heads of departments and the Chief Secretary of
State. Beneath it, the Imperial Secretariat included six main
branches. The other departments were those of the Interior,
Finance, Crown Property, the Imperial Household, Justice, War,
Transport and Police. With the Secretariat, the total is nine, the
exact number of the ministries under the Ts'in Dynasty in China. The
ministries are also practically the same but with the one major
difference that the Chinese had no police, the Prefect of the City's
place being taken, with them, by a Minister for Economic Affairs.[1]

The Roman fusion of Soldier, Administrator and Lawyer had
broken up. And if it is true that the soldier, in becoming more purely
a soldier, became far less of a statesman, it is also true that the
administrator became more efficient in becoming more specialised. It
is even truer that the lawyer became more efficient when relieved of all
but legal duties. The great Roman jurists applied to the Empire the
customs of many different peoples, compared with each other in the
light of Stoic philosophy, expounded with Greek intellectual subtlety
and enforced with Roman strictness. It was the beginning of scientific
jurisprudence, marked by the Perpetual Edict of Hadrian and crowned
long afterwards by the Institutes of Justinian. The result of this new
emphasis on law would eventually be the doctrine that the Emperor
himself was subject to law. This, however, was long after the Emperor
Constantine shifted his capital to the new city he had built on the
Bosphorus, on the site of the older Greek Colony of Byzantium.
The court so transplanted became more openly oriental and the
change in itself foreshadowed the division of the Empire on the death
of Theodosius in 395. The western Empire collapsed in 410 but that
in the East survived and offers us another example of a State influenced and impelled by a missionary religion. This religion was
Christianity.

So far as we know, Christ himself had no political ideas at all
except in so far as he explicitly accepted Roman rule and would take
no part in any movement for its overthrow. He preached a doctrine
not wholly unlike that of Buddhism but among a people and in a
setting of a totally different kind. His was the semitic world of the
Middle East.

[1] See *Roman Political Institutions*. L. P. Homo. p. 269. *Legacy of the Ancient World*.
W. G. de Burgh. London, 1947. p. 253 and *Cambridge Ancient History*. Vol. XI. p. 432.

> Semites had no half tones in their register of vision. They were a people of primary colours, or rather of black and white, who saw the world always in contrast . . . their thoughts were at ease only in extremes. They inhabited superlatives by choice . . . their convictions were by instinct, their activities intuitional. Their largest manufacture was of creeds; almost they were monopolists of revealed religions. Three of these efforts . . . endured. These were Semitic successes. Their failures they kept to themselves. The fringes of the desert were strewn with broken faiths. The common base of all the Semitic creeds, winners or losers, was the ever-present idea of world worthlessness. . . . The Semites hovered between lust and self-denial. They were incorrigible children of the idea, feckless and colour blind, to whom body and spirit were for ever and inevitably opposed.[1]

If the ideas of Christ himself were, like those of Gautama, ethical and abstract, his followers had much the same background as earlier believers in Judaism and later believers in Islam. Of the revealed religions the three of most permanent political effect came from the fringes of the same desert and were doomed to mutual hostility not because they are so different but because they are so alike. Christ's followers, like Gautama's, interpreted his teachings in the light of their own preconceived ideas. They had the mental outlook, when outside Palestine, of an unpopular minority which founded its unity on a book. From that sacred scripture they derived an idea of kingship but with divine sanction conferred by anointment at the hands of a prophet. They were God's Chosen People and, convinced that the divine plan would include their redemption and satisfy their hatred. Beneath a veneer of Hellenistic culture, they had all the Semitic intolerance. But the early Christians were also influenced by the destruction of Jerusalem, temple and all, in A.D. 70, which strengthened in them that hatred of the Romans which is expressed in Revelation. They were later influenced by intermittent persecution, both by the Jews and by the Romans; the former regarding them as deviationists and the latter as abstainers from formal Emperorworship.

The essentials of Christian teaching, from the political point of view, are to be found in the doctrines concerning the fatherhood of God and the future life. A belief that God is father of all makes all human beings brothers and sisters and therefore (more or less) equal in value at least to God. Logically pursued, the doctrine abolishes all inherited rank or inherited slavery. Emphasis on the future life was not wholly new in itself but was new at least to many Christian converts. It involves the belief that the present life is merely a training (and elimination) of candidates for heaven. By Christian teaching the poorest and worst-treated have quite possibly the best chance of

[1] *The Seven Pillars of Wisdom.* T. E. Lawrence. London, 1937. pp. 40-42.

redemption, so that present inequalities may be made good hereafter. One might add that the Christian ethical teaching, with its insistence upon a high moral standard in honesty, kindness, abstinence and self-sacrifice, might mean that a Christian State (were one established) would have a moral purpose going far beyond the functions of any previous State. In the meanwhile, there was nothing in Christianity to justify armed revolt against even a pagan ruler; still less against a ruler even nominally a Christian. It was, however, found possible to justify resistance to heresy; to doctrines, that is to say, which would imperil the souls of those induced to believe in them. In Christianity the priesthood had been important from the beginning, having special power to convey the forgiveness of sins. As Christ had never married and as his closest followers had followed his example in this, all sexual relationships were regarded as more or less sinful and a concession, at best, to human weakness. So the Church's officers, at least, had to be celibate and there was, from the beginning, a definite place in the Church for those who forsook all human relationships and possessions, devoting themselves to contemplation and prayer. A final Christian characteristic was the desire to convert others for their own good and to save them from destruction or eternal torment. Although wholly benevolent in origin, this could lead in the end to persecution. It was something hitherto almost unknown.

Jewish opposition led the Christians to seek for converts outside their own racial group, and their missionary efforts had a great measure of success. Romans of the more conservative type attributed the decline of their Empire to subversive Christian propaganda. It was in fact the other way about. In an age of growing uncertainty and confusion people turned to a revealed religion, showing a new interest in the next world as they came to expect less in this. Nor was Christianity the only religion to benefit from this growing insecurity. No other group, however, held such a typically Indian belief with such Arab intensity. Christians were peculiarly non-political believing as they did in an early end of the world with the second coming of Christ; an expectation which lingered, in fact, until A.D. 1001. In the meanwhile, however, their world, in the west, did end. The sack of Rome by Alaric in 410 had a stunning effect upon all to whom the Empire had seemed eternal. The catastrophe—repeated in 455—was almost unthinkable. The western Empire crumbled and the Bishop of Rome, remaining at his post after the collapse, found himself the heir to its prestige and to some indeed of its political power and territory. Rome was to be the centre, henceforth, of a new theocracy which still exists. We have seen already (pp. 75-76) some of the arguments used to maintain its supremacy against any revival of the secular power.

In the Eastern Empire, centred on Constantinople, the story was entirely different. Rome here survived but in an orientalised form. Gibbon describes with eloquence how oriental, how Persian, it had in fact become.

> The manly pride of the Romans, content with substantial power, had left to the vanity of the east the forms and ceremonies of ostentatious greatness. But when they lost even the semblance of those virtues which were derived from their ancient freedom, the simplicity of Roman manners was insensibly corrupted by the stately affectation of the courts of Asia. The distinctions of personal merit and influence, so conspicuous in a republic, so feeble and obscure under a monarchy, were abolished by the despotism of the emperors, who substituted in their room a severe subordination of rank and office, from the titled slaves who were seated on the steps of the throne to the meanest instruments of arbitrary power. The multitude of abject dependants was interested in the support of the actual government, from the dread of a revolution, which might at once confound their hopes, and intercept the reward of their services. In this divine hierarchy (for such it is frequently styled), every rank was marked with the most scrupulous exactness, and its dignity was displayed in a variety of trifling and solemn ceremonies, which it was a study to learn, and a sacrilege to neglect. The purity of the Latin language was debased, by adopting, in the intercourse of pride and flattery, a profusion of epithets, which Tully would have scarcely understood, and which Augustus would have rejected with indignation. The principal officers of the empire were saluted, even by the sovereign himself, by the deceitful titles of your Sincerity, your Gravity, your Excellency, your Eminency, your sublime and wonderful Magnitude, your illustrious and magnificent Highness.[1]

However nauseating this ceremony might be to a good republican, the Byzantine Empire had at least the merit of success. And there can be no doubt that the stability of the Eastern Empire was largely due to its alliance with Christianity. It was Constantine who recognised in this widespread religion a stabilising force which he could use for political ends. He used Christianity even before he professed it.[2] It was he who, at the Council of Nicaea, managed, as chairman, to induce the bishops to agree on the Nicene Creed. At this period Constantine retained all the prestige of the God-Emperor. He was approached with a ritual of prostration and it was a privilege to approach him at all.[3] It was only on his deathbed in 337 that Constantine was actually baptised. And his successors, Christian in their turn, lost little of his sanctified authority.

[1] *The History of the Decline and Fall of the Roman Empire.* Edward Gibbon. London, 1888. Vol. II. pp. 197-9.
[2] *Western Political Thought.* John Bowle. London, 1947. p. 125. See also *Byzantine Civilisation.* Steven Runciman. London, 1933. p. 79.
[3] *Byzantium, an Introduction to East Roman Civilization.* Norman H. Baynes and H. Baynes and H. St. L. B. Moss (editors). Oxford, 1948.

It might be thought that the Eastern Empire presented, at this period, a typical monarchy of the type familiar in Egypt, Persia or China. But there was this significant difference that Christianity is a missionary religion and that Byzantine religion, as now established, was intolerant in a new way. The tradition of Roman Law was maintained to a large extent but the aim of government was no longer secular. The State was responsible for morals, conduct, teaching and belief. The administration in later Byzantium was paternal in the extreme and affected daily life to a degree hardly equalled or exceeded until the present day. We hear of the tenth century Prefect of Constantinople fixing prices, wages and hours and licensing the opening of new shops. Migration and travel was discouraged, and travellers had to have passports. Work had to be found for the unemployed. The sabbath had to be duly observed and the good citizen had to be orthodox. As already discovered in Buddhist India of Asoka's time, the government which adopts or absorbs the doctrines of a missionary religion must assume functions far in excess of those ordinarily assumed. The essence of religious persecution lies in government swayed by religious beliefs which not all those governed may share. Under a theocracy religious persecution is all but inevitable.

Like Christianity, Islam derives from the Semitic peoples of the desert. Like Christianity again, it has been modified by the peoples and civilisations which its adherents have conquered or absorbed. It sprang up among the nomad tribes of Arabia, living midway between a declining Roman Empire and a declining empire of Persia. These desert people have made periodic invasions of the Fertile Crescent, as it has been called, which lies temptingly to the northward of their poor, barren land. The rise of Islam represents just such another invasion but informed with a different purpose. Until the time of Muhammad, who was born about A.D. 570, each Arab tribe had possessed its own tribal god (the Jews' Jahweh was one of them) with a worship involving sacrifice, prayer, omens, images and 'Jinns' or demons. Mecca was a place of pilgrimage because of its 'caaba' or black stone and 'Allah' or 'Lord' was the title any Arab would give to any god.[1] Being influenced by more civilised peoples near them, the Arabs knew something of Judaism and Christianity.

Muhammad was born at Mecca, married at the age of 25 and began, some years later, to see visions and hear voices. An angel appeared to him when he was aged forty and again two or three years later. Then he had repeated revelations and some people thought him mad. He preached the need for submission (Islam) to the one god (Allah), together with prayer, abstinence and alms-giving. Persecuted for his views, he fled with his followers to Medina in 622 (the Hegira)

[1] *The Arabs in History*. Bernard Lewis. London, 1950. Chap. I.

and there became all-powerful. He captured Mecca in A.D. 630 and made it the capital of Islam. Soon afterwards, in 632, he died, leaving the Koran for his followers' guidance. As the Western Roman Empire had virtually ceased to exist in 476, and as Heraclius defeated the Persians at Nineveh in 627, there was a political vacuum to the east and west of Arabia. On the other hand, Byzantium remained strong. The Arab invasion split, as it were, on the rock of Constantinople and flowed eastwards and westwards, its furthest tide reaching China in one direction and France in the other. The Arabs could have achieved nothing on this scale without a powerful creed. For Muhammad, remember, with his personality and his gifts as a ruler, was dead before this great movement had even begun. It was his ideas that went so far and so fast, sometimes even outstripping his followers themselves, well mounted as they were.

Islam is summarised in one basic profession of faith. 'There is no God but Allah and Muhammad is the prophet of Allah'. There is no room here for tolerance. The followers of the prophet belonged to a brotherhood of the faithful, superseding all blood-ties. They were to be distinguished by the pious observances of prayer (facing Mecca), by attendance at the Mosque, by keeping Friday as the 'Sabbath', by complete abstinence from wine, by fasting during Ramadan and by the pilgrimage to Mecca. They were allowed to be polygamous, with up to four wives at a time—the women to go veiled. Followers of the prophet were also bound to fight the infidel and make Islam prevail everywhere, the fallen in this war being sure of paradise and the non-combatants bound at least to help by contributing towards the cost of the war. Muslims revealed, in particular, a growing hostility against Judaism and Christianity; the former because the Jews had been opponents of the prophet, the latter because the doctrine of the Trinity was not strictly monotheistic.

Of the people of Islam it has been said:—

> This community is different from any other: it is the chosen, the holy people, to whom is entrusted the furtherance of good and the repression of evil; it is the only seat of justice and faith upon earth, the sole witness for God among the nations, just as the Prophet had been God's witness among the Arabs.[1]

The doctrine, therefore, of human equality has no support from the orthodox Muslim. As against that, Muslims claim to be politically equal among themselves.

> As to the Muslim theory of government, it is embodied in two verses of the Quran 'Consult with your companions in conduct of affairs' (3 ; 159) 'The way of the Companions of the Prophet to govern

[1] *The Legacy of Islam.* Ed. by Sir Thomas Arnold. Oxford, 1931. p. 284.

their affairs is by counsel' (42 : 38). These verses lay down for all time the guiding principle of government. . . .

As to the political ideal of Islam, one could quote instances from Islamic history to show the absolute equality of all men in Islam, the head of the State, the Caliph, not excepted. This conception of justice which differentiates between the subject and the ruler is repugnant to the Muslim. To the Quran both the servant and the master, the slave and the king, have equal legal status. . . .[1]

Failing more explicit guidance from the Koran, the Muslim must turn for political advice to Islamic history and tradition. This would be more helpful if the Arabs had recorded their history more promptly.[2] Traditions they have, nevertheless, in plenty, and these emphasise the duty of obedience to the ruler.

'The Apostle of God said: after me will come rulers; render them your obedience . . . if they are righteous and rule you well, they shall have their reward; but if they do evil and rule you ill, then punishment will fall upon them and you will be quit of it. . . .'[3]

We have, therefore, in Islam, two somewhat conflicting ideas; the Arab concept of equality in brotherhood and an added idea of obedience to a ruler; and indeed to *any* ruler. Equality was difficult to sustain, in any case, because Muhammad left a widow, daughters and uncles, all of whom were bound to be privileged; and he also left friends who were in the best position to know what he thought or what, in given circumstances, he might have done. As for the authority of the ruler, that was bound to grow among an aggressive people, faced with problems of war, conquest, empire and administration. And Muhammad had left them, in lieu of advice, his own example; and his powers seem to have been pretty absolute. What he failed to leave was an appointed successor, an heir, or any directions as to how his successor should be appointed; if indeed there was to be a successor at all.

When Muhammad died there were four parties of Muslims: the Early Believers (who had taken part in the Hegira); the Believers of Medina (who had invited him there); the converts of Mecca (converted by force after the capture), headed by the aristocratic family of the Umayyad; and a party of mixed origin which expected God to appoint the Prophet's successor.[4] After much disagreement, Abu Bakr (the Prophet's father-in-law) was elected, to be followed by

---

[1] *Muhammad 'A Mercy to all the Nations'*. Al. Haji Qassim Ali Jairazbhoy. London, 1934. p. 239.
[2] *The Law of War and Peace in Islam. A Study in Muslim International Law*. Majid Khadduri. London, 1940.
[3] *The Caliphate*. Sir Thomas W. Arnold. Oxford, 1924. pp. 48-50.
[4] *Development of Muslim Theology, Jurisprudence and Constitutional Theory*. Duncan B. Macdonald. London, 1903. (Chapters I and II).

Umar in 634. Both these belonged to the party of the Early Believers, but when Umar died in 644, the Umayya clan secured the election of Uthman (son-in-law of the Prophet), who was assassinated in 655 by a son of Abu Bakr. The fourth or legitimist party then gained the choice of Ali, another son-in-law of the Prophet. He was supplanted by the Umayyads, who ruled, more or less, until 750; one branch, indeed, in Spain, surviving until 929 or later. In Arabia itself the Khalifate virtually ended with the Mongol conquest of 656 when the Abbasids fell. The Ottoman Sultans claimed to be Khalifa as from 1538 but with little real authority over any other Muslim rulers. Orthodoxy has been upheld not so much by the Sultans as by the Sharif families of Mecca.

Muslim orthodoxy is largely a matter of Muslim law. Muhammad had ruled Medina and, later, Mecca, acting as judge, using local customary law when he thought good, using his own judgment (or revelation) when that seemed to him better. In place, therefore, of a legal code, he left his decisions in the accidental sequence of their delivery. Decisions made to settle squabbles among the Medina townsfolk are found to cover subjects as various as prayer, ritual ablution, poor-rates, fasting, pilgrimage, business transactions, inheritance, marriage, divorce, intoxicants, the holy war, hunting, racing, vows and slavery. The result is an elaborate but unsystematic system of conduct.

> How, indeed, can we meet a legal code which knows no destinction of personal or public, of civil or criminal law; which prescribes and describes the use of the toothpick and decides when a wedding invitation may be declined, which enters into the minutest and most unsavoury details of family life and lays down rules of religious retreat! Is it by some subtle connection of thought that the chapter on oaths and vows follows immediately that on horse-racing, and a section on the building line on a street is inserted in a chapter on bankruptcy and composition? One thing, at least, is abundantly clear. Muslim law, in the most absolute sense, fits the old definition, and is the science of all things, human and divine. . . . It takes all duty for its portion and defines all action in terms of duty. Nothing can escape the narrow meshes of its net. One of the greatest legists of Islam never ate a watermelon because he could not find that the usage of the Prophet had laid down and sanctioned a canonical method of doing so.[1]

The Caliphate in its original form, provided with the prophet's detailed guidance, was no ordinary monarchy or priesthood. It might, in different circumstances, have become a theocracy comparable to that of Rome. It did not, however, last long enough for that.

[1] *The Development of Muslim Theology, Jurisprudence and Constitutional Theory.* D. B. Macdonald. London, 1903. pp. 66-67 and Appendix I, pp. 351-357.

In point of fact, the caliphate as it is fondly imagined by jurists never had a real existence . . . hardly had the first Muslim generation died away when the practical needs of a great polity, and the unruly temper of the Arabs, combined to transform the caliphate first into a personal rule under the Umayyads; then, under the Abbasids, into a monarchy on the Persian pattern, whose apparent orthodoxy but ill-concealed the despotism, the violence, and the administrative mismanagement which were pushing the empire to its ruin.[1]

But if the Muslim Empire was short-lived it survived at least long enough to demonstrate its religious intolerance in Persia, Syria, Egypt and Spain. And it differed from Christian intolerance in the one important respect, that conversion was not its object. In conquered territories the unbelievers were left in possession of their lands but specially taxed. They were destined for hell-fire as infidels but extensive conversion to the true faith would have been financially undesirable. The Muslim imposed social and legal disabilities and then left the subject population to its own devices.[2] It would be true, therefore, to say that while the Arab Muslims imposed a rigid code of conduct on themselves, they rarely attempted to enforce the same rules on others. On the other hand, their avowed policy of conquest, the Holy War, brought them into continual conflict with Christians who were, if anything, less tolerant than they. After the fall of the Caliphate, the Arabs added little that was new to the practice or theory of politics. The Muslim ruler was much like any other oriental king but with a special responsibility towards his co-religionists and a sense of equality with them for purposes of religion. This ideal is well expressed in a letter from the Caliph Omar to the Governor of Basra:—

> . . . Strike terror into wrongdoers and make heaps of mutilated limbs out of them. Visit the sick among Moslems, attend their funerals, open your gate to them and give heed in person to their affairs, for you are but a man amongst them except that God has allotted you the heaviest burden.[3]

For the rest, the functions of a Muslim ruler have been defined as judgment, taxation, the Friday worship and the Holy War. He is accorded no legislative power, God being the only law-giver and his laws already known. He does not normally even interpret the law, that being the work of experts in jurisprudence. His duties were simple and so remained as long as government was centred in Arabia. In conquered territories the Muslim ruler usually inherited the more

---

[1] *The Legacy of Islam.* Ed. by Sir Thomas Arnold. Oxford, 1931. p. 301.
[2] *The Arabs in History.* Bernard Lewis. London, 1950. p. 140.
[3] *An Introduction to the Sociology of Islam.* R. Levy. 2 vols. London, n.d. Vol. I. p. 284.

complex administration of a more settled people. While the arabs retained the position of an alien aristocracy, ruling in the name of God and his prophet, they found themselves compelled to employ advisers, financial experts, architects, engineers, physicians, teachers and artists. And these tended more and more to be Christians, Persians and Jews. The administration soon altered radically in character, much to the resentment of fanatical Muslims.[1] At Baghdad, Damascus, in Tunis and Andalusia, Muslim rule became less and less distinguishable from that of any oriental monarchy. Perhaps the most distinctive feature was the way in which men of wealth were encouraged to gain religious merit by founding mosques and hospitals, building bridges and rest-houses (for pilgrims) and constructing reservoirs and aqueducts.[2] The greatest arab achievements were intellectual and resulted from combining the ideas of the various peoples they had conquered. But this arab bridging of the gap between East and West, vitally important as it was in matters of pure science,[3] was perhaps least fruitful in political development.

The most interesting example of a Muslim State being super-imposed upon a people with a different religion is that of Mogul India. Historically, this happens quite late, for the Mogul Empire in India was not founded by Babar until 1505 nor completed until the time of Akbar (1556-1605). These Moguls were of Mongol descent but came more immediately from Turkestan. They were Muslims and brought a Muslim army into the Delhi kingdom of Hindostan; until then divided between five Muslim and two Hindu rulers.[4] It is interesting to see how Muslim rule developed, more especially in the reign of Akbar and Aurangzib.

> The duties of a Muslim king in an Islamic state . . . require him to rule in accordance with the Quranic law . . . it may be noted that Islamic law divides the subjects under a Muslim king into two sections, believers and non-believers, and imposes a duty upon the king to see that believers live as true Muslims, and non-believers remain in the position allotted to them as Zimonis, a position which denies them equal status with Muslim subjects, but guarantees security of life and property and the continuance of their religion and religious practices under certain defined conditions.
>
> Thus a Muslim king, besides performing the ordinary duties connected with his office, has also to uphold the dignity of his religion through defined channels and to rule according to Islamic law.
>
> The impossibility of ruling India on these lines was felt as early as the thirteenth century. . . .[5]

[1] *A Short History of the Middle East*. G. E. Kirk. London, 1948. p. 24.
[2] *Muslim Institutions*. Maurice Gaudefroy-Demombynes. London, 1950. p. 114.
[3] *Muhammad 'A Mercy to all Nations'*. Al-Haji Qassim Ali Jairazbhoy. London, 1934. p. 222.
[4] *The Agrarian System of Moslem India*. W. H. Moreland. Cambridge, 1929. p. 21
[5] *The Central Structure of the Mughal Empire*. Ibn Hasan. Oxford, 1936. p. 306.

The impossibility appears from what Jalal-ud-din is said to have remarked to his chief adviser. 'Every day Hindus, who are the deadliest enemies of Islam, pass by my palace beating drums and trumpets and go out to the Jamna and practise idolatry openly . . . and we call ourselves Muslims. . . .'[1] This is a confession of failure. But the fact is that a King by Hindu ideas was more sacred and more important than Muslim law would quite allow him to be. A Hindu king was less restrained by law. The Hindus had no theory of equality before God. So that the process by which a Muslim monarchy succumbed to the prevailing Hindu atmosphere of India had its consolations for the monarch himself.

Something of this process may appear from the style of address used respectively at the Courts of Babur and Humayan. Babur was officially described as:

> . . . King of the four quarters, and of the seven heavens; celestial sovereign; diadem of the sublime throne; great of genius and greatness-conferring; fortune-increaser; of excellent horoscope; heaven in comprehensiveness; earth in stability; lionhearted; clime-capturer; lofty in splendour; of active brain; searcher after knowledge; rank-breaking lion rampant; exalter of dominion; ocean-hearted; of illustrious origin; a saintly sovereign; enthroned in the kingdom of reality and spirituality.[2]

This cold and laconic description would not suffice for Humayan, who was:

> . . . Theatre of great gifts; source of lofty inspirations; exalter of the throne of the *Khilifat* of greatness; planter of the standard of sublime rule; Kingdom-bestowing conqueror of Countries; Auspicious sitter upon the throne; founder of the Canons of justice and equity; arranger of the demonstrations of greatness and sovereignty; spring of the fountains of glory and beneficence; water-gate for the rivers of learning; brimming rain-cloud of choiceness and purity; billowy sea of liberality and loyalty; choosing the right, recognising the truth; sole foundation of many laws; both a King of dervish race and a dervish with a King's title; parterre-adorning arranging of realm and religion; garland-twiner of spiritual and temporal blossoms; throne of the sphere of eternal mysteries; *alidad* of the astrolabe of theory and practice; in austerities of asceticism and spiritual transports, a Grecian Plato; in executive energy and the paths of energy, a second Alexander; pearl of the seven oceans and glory of the four elements, ascension-point of suns and dawn of Jupiter; phoenix (*huma*) towering to the heights of heaven.[3]

This not unfavourable prospectus, whether accurate or not in all

[1] *Ibid.* p. 307.
[2] *The Akbarnama of Abu-l-Faal.* Trans. by H. Beveridge. Vol. I.
[3] *The Commercial Policy of the Moguls.* D. Pant. Bombay, 1930. p. 30.

particulars—and some parts of it seem at least open to argument—is not especially Muslim. Indeed, the words 'sole foundation of many laws' are in virtual contradiction of Islamic doctrine. On the other hand, these titles of respect (verging perhaps on flattery) suggest how completely the Muslim practice had been assimilated by the Hindu tradition. It involved as exacting a routine for Jahangir as it had for Chandragupta. Akbar worked even more continually and Aurangzeb, if he worked less, prayed more; so that he slept, it is said, only three hours in the twenty-four. The Moghul system of government was equally in accordance with Hindu precedent, and the list of Ministers originally much the same. But the effect of adding a Muslim intolerance to a Hindu administration was to add considerably to the government's tendency to interfere in every aspect of life. This is indicated by Akbar's creation of new departments of agriculture, pensions, price-control, inheritance, minerals and forests.[1] Humayan is said to have grouped the departments into four categories, dealing respectively with Fire, Air, Water and Earth; logically satisfying, perhaps, as a plan and yet not without an element of mystery, too.[2] Ministers were paid either by the Treasury or by the allocation of revenue from a certain area, but any fortune they accumulated reverted when they died to the Emperor.[3] Revenue derived mainly from land, the one-sixth of the produce collected under Hindu rule rising to between a third and a half in Muslim India. There were, in addition, customs duties, inheritance taxes, a poll-tax claimed from Christians and Jews, a tax on salt and state monopolies established in saltpetre, indigo and lead. State interference extended to religion and Akbar made a spirited but unsuccessful attempt to unite Islam and Hinduism in a new state religion with himself (an agnostic) as Pope.

While the Moghuls thus tried to unify Hindustan and abolish Muslim dominance, their rule was nevertheless far from secular.[4] Their administration was penetrated with the idea that the State must promote morality and punish irreligion and vice. Thus, the 'kotwal' of the Moghul period fairly carried out the duties of the Nagaraka or Town Prefect of Mauryan days.

> For the *Kotwal* kept a register of houses and roads; divided the town into quarters, and placed an assistant in direct charge of each quarter, who had to report daily arrivals and departures; he kept a small army of spies or detectives . . . he enforced a curfew-order; kept an eye on the currency; fixed local prices and examined dealers' weights and measures; kept inventories of the property of persons dying

[1] *Cambridge History of India*. Vol. IV. Mughul Period. Cambridge 1937. p. 133.
[2] *The Commercial Policy of the Moguls*. D. Pant. Bombay, 1930. p. 30.
[3] *Mughal Rule in India*. S. M. Edwards and H. L. O. Garrett. Oxford, 1930.
[4] *A History of the Great Moghuls*. (1605-1739) Pringle Kennedy. Calcutta, 1911.

intestate; set apart wells and ferries for the use of women; stopped women riding on horseback; prevented cattle slaughter; kept a check on slavery; expelled religious enthusiasts, calendars, and dishonest tradesmen, from the urban area; allotted separate quarters to butchers, sweepers and hunters; set apart land for burial-grounds; and arranged for the illumination of the town on the occasion of festivals and holidays. This by no means exhausts the tale of the kotwal's duties. He was expected to know everything about everybody; to visit condign punishment upon any one who demeaned himself by consorting and drinking with a public executioner; to prevent *sati*, if the woman was disinclined to sacrifice herself; to put a stop to circumcision before the age of twelve; to prevent the slaughter of oxen, buffaloes, horses and camels; and during the reign of Akbar, to enforce also the observance of the *Ilahi* calendar and of the special festivals and ritual prescribed by the Emperor.[1]

To quote another source:

The *Kotwal* must appoint one or more brokers, to transact the various kinds of commercial business; and, after taking security from them must station such in the market place that they may afford information regarding such things as are bought and sold. He must also make it a rule that every person buying or selling, without the advice of the above-mentioned brokers, will be deemed in fault; that both the name of the buyer and seller must be written in the register of daily transactions.[2]

While we may feel a certain sympathy for the *kotwal*, whose leisure would seem to have been strictly limited, we must also note the wide variety of actions (not obviously harmful in themselves) which might involve punishment. These range from using the wrong calendar to setting a woman on horseback; from drinking with the hangman to selling a chicken without the advice of the official broker. Nor did government interference end there, for a characteristic of Moghul policy was the discouragement of the use of intoxicants. The maker, the seller, and the drinker of wine could all be punished. For excess in drinking the penalties were still more severe, even under Akbar (who drank wine himself). During his reign, wine was obtainable only on medical advice and from an official wine shop. 'Persons who wished to purchase wine, as a remedy for sickness, could do so by having their name, and that of their father and grandfather, written down by the clerk'.[3] The ways of officialdom do not change, it seems.

If Akbar was half-hearted as a moralist, Aurangzib (1658-1681) more than made up for it.[4] A strict Muslim, he appointed a censor

[1] *Mughal Rule in India*, op cit. pp. 185-186.
[2] *The Commercial Policy of the Moguls*. D. Pant. Bombay, 1930. p. 44.
[3] *Ibid*. p. 45.
[4] He even ordered the destruction of Hindu schools and temples, while continuing to encourage, as Akbar had done, the Muslim schools devoted to the study of Urdu and Persian.

(*Muhtasib*) in every large city 'to enforce the prophet's laws and put down forbidden practices, such as drinking, gambling and the illicit commerce of the sexes'.[1] The same officer was to punish heresy, blasphemy, omission of the five daily prayers and failure to observe Ramayan. Later in life Aurangzib became still more puritanical and forbade music at court.

> But this attempt to elevate mankind by one stroke of the official pen failed, as Akbar's social reforms had failed before. Aurangzib's government made itself ridiculous by violently enforcing for a time, then relaxing, and finally abandoning a code of puritanical morals opposed to the feelings of the entire population, without first trying to educate them to a higher level of thought. As Manucci observed, there were few who did not drink secretly, and even the ministers and qazīs loved to get drunk at home. Gambling continued to be practised in his camp, and his order to all the courtesans and dancing girls to marry or leave the realm remained a dead letter.[2]

On this last point Akbar had been less drastic, contenting himself with the formation of a prostitutes' quarter outside each town, with a superviser and clerk appointed 'to register the names of those who resorted to them. No one could take a dancing girl to his house without permission'.[3] These rules, while indicating disapproval, also suggest a desire to share in the profits. As Aurangzib pointed out, 'Kingship means the protector of the realm and the guardianship of the people . . . a king is merely God's elected custodian and the trustee of His money for the benefit of the subjects'.[1]

As an early experiment in Socialism, Moghul India was less complete than the Chinese experiment of A.D. 9 to 25. Akbar could hardly rival Wang Mang with his nationalisation of land, timber, iron and copper. On the other hand, the Moghuls fully demonstrated just how over-centralised a State could become. What was the result? It was ruin. It was ruin, moreover, of a peculiar kind.

> . . . in the India of our period the working of the administration was, next to the rainfall, the most important factor in the economic life of the country. It acted directly on the distribution of the national income to an extent which is now difficult to realise, for in practice the various governments disposed of somewhere about one half of the entire gross produce of the land, and they disposed of it in such a way that the producers were left with a bare subsistence or very little more, while the energies of the unproductive classes were spent in the struggle to secure the largest possible share. The reaction on production was inevitably unfavourable; producers were deprived of the natural

[1] *The Cambridge History of India*. Vol. IV. p. 230.
[2] *Ibid.* p. 230.
[3] *The Commercial Policy of the Moghuls*. D. Pant. pp. 45-46.

incentive to energy, because they could not hope to retain any material proportion of an increase in their income; men of ability or talent were discouraged from producing . . . it was better to be a peon than a peasant; and critics who express surprise at the tendency of Indian brains and energy to seek employment in the service of the State will find ample explanation in the history of the centuries during which no other career was possible.[1]

What W. H. Moreland and his readers may have found difficult to visualise in 1923, we are now perhaps in a better position to focus. It needs nowadays no such effort of imagination to picture a State in which productive and creative energy has been brought to a standstill by excess of administration. It is even easier for us to foresee the national bankruptcy which is likely to result. The process, in Moghul India, was relatively swift. By the reign of Aurangzib a policy of over-taxation had produced a scarcity of peasants and a tendency for land to go out of cultivation. François Bernier, who spent eight years as physician at the Moghul Court, remarked upon this, pointing out that

> . . . many of the peasantry, driven to despair by so execrable a tyranny, abandon the country, and seek a more tolerable mode of existence, either in the towns or camps; as bearers of burdens, carriers of water, or servants to horsemen. Sometimes they fly to the territories of a Raja, because there they find less oppression. . . .[2]

In fact, by the reign of Aurangzib, government was defeating its own end. All interest was concentrated upon the division of the annual produce and no attention was paid to any plan for increasing it. The system was bound to collapse, and collapse, in effect, it did. But the interest, for our present purpose, of this experiment is not in its economic aspect but in the moral purpose which impels a theocracy into thus attempting to control every human activity from the cradle to the grave.

Theocracy has not, of course, been confined to Oriental kingdoms. Contemporary with the Moghuls, for instance, lived John Calvin, who inspired the setting up of a theocratic Republic at Geneva. Calvin's doctrines centre upon predestination. He taught

> . . . . that God, by his eternal and immutable Counsel, determined once and for all those whom it was his pleasure to admit to salvation, and those whom, on the other hand, it was his pleasure to doom to destruction: we maintain that this counsel, as regards his Elect, is founded on his free mercy, without any respect of human merit. While those whom he dooms to destruction are excluded from access to life

[1] *From Akbar to Aurangzib, a study in Indian Economic History.* W. H. Moreland. London, 1923. p. 233.
[2] *The Agrarian System of Moslem India.* W. H. Moreland. Cambridge, 1929. p. 147.

by a just and blameless but at the same time incomprehensible decree. In regard to his Elect, we regard calling as the evidence of election and Justification as another symbol of its manifestation.[1]

Geneva was ruled by an oligarchy of merchants and it was these that Calvin converted, making them all eager to appear (and manifestly) as of the Elect. The result was an identification of the objects of Church and State. The magistrates were to see that God was obeyed, backsliders punished and heretics killed. What this Calvinist discipline meant is apparent from the Registers of the Genevan Council from 1545 to 1547.

> A man who swore by the 'body and blood of Christ' was condemned to sit in the public square in the stocks, and to be fined.
> Another, hearing an ass bray, and saying jestingly, 'Il chante un beau psaume', was sentenced to temporary banishment from the city. . . .
> . . . A young girl, in Church, singing the words of a song to the tune of the psalm, was ordered to be whipt by her parents.
> Drunkenness and debauchery were visited with more severe penalties; adultery more than once with death. Prostitutes who ventured back to Geneva were mercilessly thrown into the Rhone. Cards were altogether prohibited. Rope-dancers and conjurers were forbidden to exhibit. . . .[2]

But while Calvin and Aurangzib had thus so much in common, the former's rule was far the more effective as extending over only a small area. For a time at least, Geneva was very godly indeed. But it was no part of Calvinist doctrine to make men forswear their business and seek a life of contemplation. They were to continue their normal work, showing their membership of the Elect by their conduct. This would mean strict morality, sobriety, plain dress and no ritual. But how could they show that God approved of them? One way was by worldly success, known as 'making good'. So that morality soon came to include the virtues likely to promote success: hard work, abstinence, punctuality, exact accounts, tidiness and a strict control over the young and the poor. Ensuring that employees did their work had the double merit of making money and preventing the idleness which would lead to mischief. Here was the ideal religion for merchants and industrialists, tending to favour wealth but discourage luxury. A typical hatred of the Calvinist was for the theatre, as combining colour, music, beauty, worldliness, frivolity, sex, sin, waste of money and waste of time. The calvinist wanted a republic ruled by people like himself, necessarily a small minority. Mankind being mostly

[1] *Institutes.* John Calvin. Bk. III, XXI, 5-7. See *Western Political Thought.* John Bowle. London, 1947. pp. 277-283.
[2] *The Political Consequences of the Reformation.* R. H. Murray. London, 1926. p. 91.

damned 'except in so far as Grace rescues some, not many, who would otherwise perish', the Elect were of necessity few. If they were power-less, Calvin told them to be patient and accept the trial of their faith; but later Calvinists, like Knox and Buchanan, were more inclined to preach resistance to Catholic tyranny. When weak, they talked of Natural Law and the limits of State interference. When strong, they talked of the need for a godly discipline. In denying themselves many pleasures which others would think harmless, they could still take pleasure in power and cruelty. Their final authority was God; that is, holy scripture as interpreted by themselves.

CHAPTER XI

Theocracy justified in Theory

THEOCRATIC government, if based upon a revealed religion, rests upon an assumption which is, to the believer, manifestly true. Simplest of these is the Muslim creed 'There is no God but Allah and Muhammad is the prophet of Allah'. Once that is agreed, the rest follows logically. Government should follow Muhammad's precept and example. If it is agreed, similarly, that 'Jesus is the Son of God', it remains only to discover and follow his ideas and practice. The Buddhist's argument had been much the same and was framed at an earlier date. It need not astonish us, therefore, to discover that the more fervent believers in the revealed religions have left us few works of political theory. On the one hand, they have many of them regarded this world as too transitory to be worth amending. On the other hand, such reform as is worth while must be in accordance with God's will. And, granted the assumption that God's will is known, the idea of accepting any lesser authority is manifestly absurd. The theoretical explanations of Theocracy are not, therefore, concerned for the most part with the abstract question of what is best. They are concerned more with interpreting God's will and applying it to the problem in hand.

Among the first of these religious thinkers was St. Augustine (A.D. 354-430) the Bishop of Hippo, his diocese being now known as Bona, in Algeria. More of a philosopher than St. Ambrose, he wrote his *De Civitate Dei* after the sack of Rome in 410, not completing it however until 426. His first object was to prove (as he easily might) that Rome's fall was not due, as some alleged, to the weakening influence of Christianity. He goes on, however, from there to show that the world is divided into two societies, those who dwell in the invisible City of God, and those who dwell in sin. The worldly society must be absorbed by the City of God, for 'the hell of secular society unredeemed by Christianity is not even capable of improvement'. He infers, therefore, that Christianity can improve the State. More than that, he would have the State closely bound up with the Church. He does not, however, in so many words, make the lay ruler subordinate. A modern writer has expressed Augustine's position thus:

> The Christian ruler needs the Church for guidance in the spiritual

life: the bishops need the help of the secular law to deal with secular affairs; in theory they ought to work together in harmony, but the moment they cease to do so the spiritual authority will be invoked. St. Augustine has stated the fundamental axiom that the secular state was spiritually dead unless it made a close alliance with the Church, and human life only intelligible and significant in the light of the doctrine of the Fall and the Redemption.[1]

That is St. Augustine's basic assumption but he argues, further, that God has prescribed (and was bound to prescribe) how even the secular State should be ruled. In an eloquent passage he asks, in effect, how it could be otherwise:

Wherefore the great and mighty God with His Word and His Holy Spirit (which three are one), God only omnipotent, Maker and Creator of every soul, and of every body, in participation of whom, all such are happy that follow His truth and reject vanities: He that made man a reasonable creature of soul and body, and He that did neither let him pass unpunished for his sin, nor yet excluded him from mercy: He that gave both unto good and bad essence with the stones, power of production with the trees, senses with the beasts of the field, and understanding with the angels: He, from whom is all being, beauty, form and order, number, weight and measure: He, from whom all nature, mean and excellent, all seeds of form, all forms of seed, all motion, both of forms and seeds derive and have being: He that gave flesh the original beauty, strength, propagation, form and shape, health and symmetry: He that gave the unreasonable soul, sense, memory and appetite, the reasonable besides these phantasy, understanding, and will: He (I say) having left neither heaven, nor earth, nor angel, nor man, no nor the most base and contemptible creature, neither the bird's feather, nor the herb's flower, nor the tree's leaf, without the true harmony of their parts, and peaceful concord of composition; it is no way credible, that He would leave the kingdoms of men, and their bondages and freedoms loose and uncomprised in the laws of His eternal providence.[2]

St. Augustine's argument proceeds from this point. The secular State has a right order of its own and, rightly ordered, can be useful to those who dwell in the City of God. It has a relative value, based upon and adjusted to sinful human nature. Thus, such institutions as government, property and slavery have a value where sin has made an absolute righteousness impossible. When the secular State is absorbed by the City of God they will disappear. In the meanwhile, they are better than disorder and are instituted accordingly by God. But St. Augustine is careful to emphasise that the supreme good cannot be attained by any earthly means, whatever pagan philosophy

[1] *Western Political Thought*. John Bowle. London, 1947. p. 138.
[2] *The City of God*. St. Augustine. Translated by John Healey. 1610. Reprinted, London, 1931. (Chapter II).

may have taught. Thus the pagan virtues of temperance, prudence, justice and fortitude do not lead (without God) to happiness; and fortitude by itself leads only to suicide. The supreme good is eternal peace, peace of the soul, which comes only from God. It should be attained successively in the home, the city, the state, the world and the universe. Until this happens, a relative peace may be enjoyed in any society based on love where:

> They who exercise authority are in the service of those over whom they appear to exercise authority; and they exercise their authority not from a desire for domination but by virtue of a duty to give counsel and aid.[1]

While, however, agreeing that a wise and virtuous rule may exist, he emphasises that the rule is ordained by God and that a bad rule is intended as a punishment.

> . . . This one God . . . whilst it was His pleasure, let Rome have sovereignty: so did He with Assyria and Persia who (as their books say) worshipped only two gods.
> . . . And so for the men: He that gave Marius rule, gave Caesar rule: He that gave Augustus it, gave Nero it. . . . He that gave it to Constantine the Christian, gave it also to Julian the Apostate, whose worthy towardness was wholly blinded by sacrilegious curiosity. . . .[2]

So far from advising revolt against a bad ruler St. Augustine doubts even whether it matters sufficiently.

> For what skills it in respect of this short and transitory life, under whose dominion a mortal man doth live, so he be not compelled to acts of impiety or injustice. . . . [He argues that the States conquered by Rome might just as well have given in by agreement.] For what does conquering, or being conquered, hurt or profit men's lives, manners, or dignities either? I see no good it does, but only adds unto their intolerable vainglory, who aim at such matters, and war for them, and lastly receive them as their labour's reward. . . . Take away vainglory and what are men but men?[3]

He remarks elsewhere on the futility of war, observing that one State will attack another 'and if it conquer, it extols itself and so becomes its own destruction . . . thus is the victory deadly; for it cannot keep a sovereignty for ever where it got a victory for once'. He points out that men desire an earthly peace and seek it through war, but even if they gain it (while still neglecting the City of God and eternal victory) 'misery must needs follow'. He returns to this theme in Chapter XII, Book XV.

[1] St. Augustine. *op. cit.* Introduction. p.xliii.
[2] *Ibid.* Chap. VIII. Book V.
[3] *Ibid.*

> ... joy and peace are desired alike of all men. The warrior would but conquer: war's aim is nothing but glorious peace: what is victory but a suppression of resistants, which being done, peace follows? So that peace is war's purpose, the scope of all military discipline, and the limit at which all just contentions level. All men seek peace by war, but none seek war by peace. For they that perturb the peace they live in, do it not for hate of it, but to shew their power in alteration of it. They would not disannul it, but they would have it as they like; and though they break into seditions from the rest, yet must they hold a peaceful force with their fellows that are engaged with them, or else they shall never effect what they intend. Even the thieves themselves that molest all the world besides them, are at peace amongst themselves.

If peace is thus desired by all, how much better is the universal peace which comes from God.

St. Augustine has thus little encouragement to offer to the intending rebel. Nor has he more than spiritual consolation to offer to the slave. He supposes that slavery may be a punishment for sin but argues that there are worse fates than slavery.

> ... it is a happier servitude to serve man than lust: for lust (to omit all the other passions) practises extreme tyranny upon the hearts of those that serve it, be it lust after sovereignty or fleshly lust. But in the peaceful orders of states, wherein one man is under another, as humility does benefit the servant, so does pride endamage the superior. But take a man as God created him at first, and so he is neither slave to man nor to sin. But penal servitude had the institution from that law which commands the conservation, and forbids the disturbance of nature's order: for if that law had not first been transgressed, penal servitude had never been enjoined.

> Therefore the apostle warns servants to obey their masters and to serve them with cheerfulness, and good will: to the end that if they cannot be made free by their masters, they make their servitude a freedom to themselves, by serving them not in deceitful fear, but in faithful love, until iniquity be overpassed, and all men's power and principality dis-annulled and God only be all in all.

Speaking thus as member of a formerly (and still potentially) persecuted minority, St. Augustine thus preaches a doctrine of non-resistance. The persecution is by God's will and for the benefit of those afflicted, whose compensation shall be in the life hereafter and whose immediate consolation may be in the thought that the persecutor is doing more harm to himself than to those he oppresses. But there is to this doctrine an important exception. It does not matter under whose rule a person may live 'so he be not compelled to acts of impiety or injustice'. But what if he *is*? St. Augustine does not expressly enjoin resistance but the doctrinal loophole is there. For, granted that the believer should suffer death rather than commit an act of impiety, must he also resign himself to having his children brought up as pagans and so lost to salvation? The inference is that he may ultimately have to resist oppression in the name of Christ.

But a far greater importance attaches to St. Augustine's advice to. the Christian who finds himself in power, with the force, the numbers and the law on his side. How is he to use his authority? First of all, he is (as we have seen) to serve those over whom he appears to rule. His responsibility is to be a burden rather than a privilege, more especially if he is Emperor.

> For we Christians do not say, that Christian emperors are happy, because they have a long reign, or die leaving their sons in quiet possession of their empires, or have been ever victorious, or powerful against all their opposers. These are but gifts and solaces of this laborious, joyless life; idolators, and such as belong not to God (as these emperors do) may enjoy them. . . . But happy they are (say we) if they reign justly, free from being puffed up with the glossing exalta-tions of their attendance, or the cringes of their subjects, if they know themselves to be but men . . . if their lusts be the lesser because they have the larger licence . . . if they do all things, not for glory, but for charity, and with all, and before all, give God the due sacrifice of prayer, for their imperfections; such Christian emperors we call happy, here in hope, and hereafter, when the time we look for comes indeed. . . .[1]

Here we have a sketch of the ruler's character, his essential humility, but no suggested policy. A hint of what he is to do is contained, how-ever, in another passage, devoted to the example of the Christian martyrs, which concludes:—

> . . . the kings whose edicts afflicted the Church came humbly to be warriors under that banner which they cruelly before had sought utterly to abolish: beginning now to persecute the false gods, for whom before they had persecuted the servants of the true God.[2]

This is an historical statement and one we need not question. But St. Augustine does not blame the later persecution as he blames, or seems to blame, the first. 'Warriors' we may take in a metaphorical sense if we choose. But it is doubtful whether St. Augustine could consistently deplore any political pressure which would lead to conversions and to the baptism of those otherwise damned to all eternity.

On the vital question of how the Christian ruler is to treat pagan or heretical subjects St. Augustine is not explicit. He is, on the other hand, emphatic on the question of how a Christian master should treat his

[1] St. Augustine, *op. cit.* Chap. XV. Book V.
[2] St. Augustine, *op. cit.* Chap. XXXIX. Book XIV

children and servants. Dealing with what he calls 'the just law of sovereignty', he explains[1] that 'our righteous forefathers' did not treat their servants and their children alike in all respects, *save in matters of religion.* For religious purposes they were fathers of their households, servants and all.

> ... But such as merit that name truly, do care that all their families should continue in the service of God, as if they were all their own children, desiring that they should all be placed in the household of heaven, where command is wholly unnecessary, because then they are past their charge, having attained immortality, which until they be installed in, the masters are to endure more labour in their government, than the servants in their service. If any be disobedient and offend this just peace, he is forthwith to be corrected, with strokes, or some other convenient punishment, whereby he may be re-engraffed into the peaceful stock from whence his disobedience has torn him. For as it is no good turn to help a man unto a smaller good by the loss of a greater: no more is it the part of innocence by pardoning a small offence, to let it grow unto a fouler. It is the duty of an innocent to hurt no man, but, withal, to curb sin in all he can, and to correct sin in whom he can, that the sinner's correction may be profitable to himself, and his example a terror unto others. Every family then being part of the city, every beginning having some relation unto some end, and every part tending to the integrity of the whole, it follows apparently, that the family's peace adheres unto the city's, that is the orderly command and obedience in the family has real reference to the orderly rule and subjection in the city. So that 'the father of the family' may fetch his instruction from the city's government, whereby he may proportionate the peace of his private estate, by that of the common.

If we accept St. Augustine's comparison between family and state (or city), we may fairly assume that the relationship is not that of a one-sided imitation. If the father of a household is to copy the impartial sway of the town council, is not the ruler to regard himself as the father of his people? Should he not treat his subjects as the father is to treat his children? St. Augustine's ideal ruler is to regard his responsibility as a heavy burden, assumed reluctantly. This was no novelty as an idea—Indian Brahmans had the same conception and had it long before. But the Christian ruler, if he regards his subjects as his children, may, and in fact must, curb and correct sin in such fashion that 'the sinner's correction may be profitable to himself and his example a terror unto others' And what is sin? Sin is and can only be the sort of action which Christ would have disapproved. The subject will fare ill, therefore, who differs from his bishop or ruler in his interpretation of Christ's teaching. And he will certainly fare worse if he rejects it altogether.

[1] St. Augustine, *op. cit.* Chap. XVI. Book XV.

As against the gods of pagan mythology, St. Augustine can afford to be only mildly severe. He regards them as devils rather than illusions. The stage-plays connected with their cult he regards as merely obscene. As for historians who contend that the world has existed for many thousands of years, they are talking nonsense; worse, they are talking heresy. Holy scripture gives the world a past history of six thousand years at most.[1] But St. Augustine was not seriously worried about pagan beliefs, which he knew to be on the wane. The mischief was to begin when the Church should be confronted, not by a dying pagan mythology but by an active faith like Islam, as positive as Christianity in doctrine and almost as intolerant in practice. Towards such a heresy the Christian attitude is perfectly clear from the fifth century onwards. It is the argument outlined in *The City of God* and absorbed by such readers as Gregory the Great, Charlemagne, Peter Abelard and Dante. By this argument the secular State is necessary and ordained by God, even a bad ruler deserving obedience. But the Christian ruler must seek the advice of the Church in matters of doctrine and ethics; for his is only a man, and not even a priest. The Christian prince must then, on ecclesiastical advice, curb sin and correct sinners for their own good. This may not seem an attractive programme to the reader of to-day. But it is the logical consequence of all that St. Augustine believed. Granted his original premise that all unbelievers are destined for eternal torment, it scarcely matters what means are used to save them. A little violence may surely be used to prevent a blind man going over a precipice. It is cruelty to spare the child punishment. It is worse cruelty to allow the heretic to corrupt others. Better, far better, is the chastisement which helps the sinner to repent.

It would be possible to trace this central theme of theocratic government through the whole history of Medieval Europe. We could quote extensively from the trial of St. Joan to illustrate the inexorable logic of this doctrine. It is conveniently summed up, however, in the sentence pronounced by the judges, the Bishop and the Inquisitor; and again in the report sent afterwards to the Pope from the University of Paris. The sentence reads:

> . . . As often as the poisonous virus of heresy obstinately attaches itself to a member of the Church and transforms him into a limb of Satan, most diligent care must be taken to prevent the foul contagion of this pernicious leprosy from spreading . . . . The decrees of the holy Fathers have laid down that hardened heretics must be separated from the midst of the just, rather than permit such pernicious vipers to lodge in the bosom of Our Holy Mother Church, to the great peril of the rest. . . .

[1] St. Augustine. *op. cit.* Chap. X. Book XI.

... we denounce you as a rotten member, which, so that you shall not infect the other members of Christ, must be cast out of the unity of the Church, cut off from her body, and given over to the secular power ... [i.e. to be burnt alive].[1]

The letter agreed by the University of Paris, 'the light of all knowledge and the extirpator of errors',[2] is more significant still.

> We believe, most Holy Father, that vigilant endeavours to prevent the contamination of the Holy Church by the poison of the errors of false prophets and evil men, are the more necessary since the end of the world appears to be at hand.
>
> ... So when we see new prophets arise who boast of receiving revelations from God and the blessed of the triumphant land, when we see them announce to men the future and things passing the keenness of human thought, daring to accomplish new and unwonted acts, then it is fitting to our pastoral solicitude to set all our energies to prevent them from overwhelming the people, too eager to believe new things, by these strange doctrines, before the spirits which they claim to come from God have been confirmed. It would indeed be easy for these crafty and dangerous sowers of deceitful inventions to infect the Catholic people, if everyone, without the approbation and consent of our Holy Mother Church, were free to invent supernatural revelations at his own pleasure, and could usurp the authority of God, and His saints. Therefore, most Holy Father, the watchful diligence lately shown by the reverend father in Christ, the lord bishop of Beauvais and the vicar of the lord Inquisitor of Heretical Error, appointed by the apostolic Holy See to the kingdom of France, for the protection of the Christian religion, seems to us most commendable.
>
> [the letter describes the trial and execution].
>
> ... Wherefore it was clearly recognised by all how dangerous it was, how fearful, to give too light credence to the modern inventions which have for some time past been scattered in this most Christian kingdom, not by this woman only, but by many others also; and all the faithful of the Christian religion must be warned by such a sad example not to act so hastily after their own desires, but to listen to the teachings of the Church and the instruction of the prelates rather than the fables of superstitious women. For if we are at last through our own faults arrived at the point where witches falsely prophesying in God's name but without His authority, are better received by the frivolous people than pastors and doctors of the Church to whom Christ formerly said, 'Go ye and teach the nations', the end is come, religion will perish, faith is in decay, the Church is trampled underfoot and the iniquity of Satan dominates the whole world.

This fairly sums up the case for Theocracy; nor is it without substance. To begin with, the statement that a general tendency to listen

[1] *The Trial of Jeanne d'Arc.* Trans. and ed. by W. P. Barrett. London, 1931. pp. 328-329.
[2] Barrett. *op. cit.* p. 307.

to individual thinkers rather than to the accepted doctrine would mean the end of the Church is manifestly true. That is exactly what happened, and more especially in France. It is true again that many of the 'modern inventions' were silly or even harmful. Nor can it be denied that reported miracles are likely to be investigated more competently by theologians than by ignorant peasants. As against that, there seems to many people, and indeed to many Christians, a certain divergence between the example given by Christ and the example made by his followers in the market place of Rouen in 1431.

In concluding, as they did, that the end of the world was at hand, the doctors of the University of Paris were not far from the truth. The end of their world was indeed approaching. But it would be utterly wrong to assume that the history of European Theocracy ends with the Reformation. Religious persecution continued in its Protestant guise and indeed continues still. Its essence is still what it has always been; government in accordance with doctrines which those governed may not share. Charge III in the indictment of St. Joan read 'That this woman is apostate, for the hair which God gave her for a veil she has untimely cut off, and also, with the same design has rejected woman's dress and imitated the costume of men'. In the London of to-day it is natural for any intelligent person to wonder whether St. Joan's offence, on this particular charge, might not have been less than capital. But laws as fantastic are everywhere being enforced and supported by arguments which are just as absurd. To marry a second wife in England is as much an offence as to drink wine in Pakistan— or, at one time, in the United States. To buy a lottery ticket is perfectly proper in a Muslim state but is illegal in the British colony adjacent. A Chinese gambling game is stopped by a British police officer who then goes on to play bridge at his Club. To smoke tobacco is innocent, to smoke opium is a crime. The book that is compulsory reading in one country is promptly seized and burnt in the next. All states are still theocratic in so far as their laws are based upon a revealed religion and not upon principles of reason. The extent to which this is so is shown by the divergence of the laws themselves. In so far as they are reasonable, they are mostly alike as between one State and another. In so far as they differ completely they are based on revealed religion. For the revelations of the divine will presented to mankind by those apparently inspired, while all impressive in their own way, have shown little resemblance to each other.

CHAPTER XII

The Theocracy of Communism

IF the political characteristics of Theocracy are to include a Founder, a Mythology, a Sacred Book, a Priesthood, a place of pilgrimage and an Inquisition, Communism must be ranked among the great religions of the world. There are some who will object that a religion implies a god. There is enough,..perhaps, in this objection to justify allotting Communism a chapter to itself. There is not, clearly, reason sufficient to exclude it from the list of religions. For Buddhism was founded by a thinker who certainly believed in no god within the comprehension of his disciples. He might have believed in something akin to the Life Force as revered by George Bernard Shaw. But that did not prevent him founding a religion, with sects and heresies and biblical criticism. For lack of any god in which he believed, his followers simply made a god of him. There is therefore no reason to suppose that the deified Lenin will not be the god of Communism. For the atheist becoming a god there is ample precedent already.

While, however, Communism would seem to be a nascent or actual religion, it is not a creed of great importance in the history of political thought; and this is due, in the main, to the circumstances of its origin. Karl Marx, founder of the creed, was born at Trier in Rhenish Prussia in 1818. The son of a Jewish lawyer who turned Protestant in 1824, he studied jurisprudence, history and philosophy at Bonn, graduating in 1841 after submitting his doctoral thesis on the philosophy of Epicurus. His revolutionary and atheistic ideas prevented him from becoming a lecturer at Bonn but allowed him to marry Jenny von Westphalen, sister of the Prussian Minister of the Interior. Marx then went to Paris where he became close friends with Frederick Engels. He was deported from France in 1845 and joined the Communist League in Belgium. He was in France again during the revolution of 1848 but then returned to Germany, where he edited a newspaper until banished again in 1849. He then took refuge in London and lived there until his death in 1883. Most of his writing was done after 1850 and in the reading room of the British Museum, *Das Kapital* being unfinished when he died. He and his wife lived in two rooms in Dean Street,[1] where they had six children of whom three

[1] This was not Marx's only address. By 1881 he was living at 41, Maitland Park Road, N.W.

(all daughters) survived. He lived upon an allowance of £350 a year from Engels, a legacy of £800 and an occasional sovereign for an article in the *New York Tribune*. Marx lived at his desk, knew little of practical affairs and less of the working class he sought to befriend. After thirty years in London he still lived among German exiles, knowing nothing about England or the English. He had all the single-minded purpose of a Hebrew prophet (which is what he was) and ruthlessly sacrificed his wife and family, friends and disciples. He had an abstract pity for the poor but his capacity for hatred was more obvious than his capacity for affection.

So much biography is essential to fix the date and background of his work. Marxism may sound contemporary as a doctrine but Marx himself lived in the world of Dickens, Wellington and Queen Victoria. His was a background of top-hats, frock-coats and horse-drawn carriages. He lived long ago, making prophecies which, whether proved or disproved, are no longer predictions. Much has happened since his time, including two world wars and several industrial revolutions, the lengthening of human life by about ten years and the invention of contrivances which may well extinguish human society altogether; or, anyway, the civilisation of which Karl Marx was the rather bilious product. Much can be claimed for Marx as a thinker, a prophet, and a personality. But there is one thing which no one can claim. No one can now regard his ideas as *new*.

His ideas are older even than the dates of his career would suggest. For he was not, in his Dean Street period, trying to discover the laws of economics. He had decided in advance what he was trying to prove. His views are already outlined in the Communist Manifesto of 1847-8, which he helped to compile.[1] He began writing *Das Kapital* in 1867 but to prove theories he had accepted in 1845 or earlier. *Das Kapital* remains the text-book of communist economic thought. There are, however, few other subjects in which the student is given a text-book begun in 1867 and embodying theories dating from 1845. Nor, incidentally, does Marx quite manage to achieve a scientific im-partiality. The violence of the sedentary philosopher breaks out when he interrupts his economic argument with words like these: 'The expropriation of the immediate producers was accomplished with merciless vandalism, and under the stimulus of passions the most infamous, the most sordid, the pettiest, the most meanly odious'. Surely a consistent materialist would have seen these sordid passions as mere obedience to the economic laws by which all are governed? And if we are to use words like 'infamous' about people who are 'merciless', we must have some moral standards by which to judge

[1] *Social-Economic Movements.* H. W. Laidler. London, 1948. (International Library of Sociology and Social Reconstruction). Chapter 14. pp. 130-144.

them. But moral (that is, religious) standards are bourgeois ana-chronisms in which Marx could not possibly believe.

Das Kapital is not, therefore, comparable with any scientific textbook. It has been called 'The Bible of the Working Man', an expression which gives a clue to its nature. It should rather be com-pared with the Bible, the Koran or the Analects. It is only religious texts that never go out of date. But if it is a religion that we have to study, we shall have to distinguish between the doctrine taught by the Founder and the Theology evolved since by his admirers. Thus we have, in Marxism, the Bible of Orthodoxy which none may contra-dict. We have the priests who preach on selected passages. We have the scholars who wrangle over the interpretation. We have all the early intolerance of Christianity and all the early fanaticism of Islam. There is an Inquisition to deal with heretics just as Christians have dealt with their own deviationists in the past. After this process the Marxism practised may have only a theoretical relationship to the original doctrine. The legends, literature, customs and ritual built up round the Founder's memory must always tend to obscure what he actually taught.

Marxist doctrine, if we omit for the present what is not vital to the argument, centres upon the philosophy of dialectical materialism, the Marxist view of History and the Marxist doctrine of revolution. The materialist believes that the only world is that which we perceive with our senses and that our ideas are only a reflection of what we perceive. The idea of 'Dialectics' is borrowed from Darwin and applied by Marx to society. According to this theory nature and society are in the midst of a dynamic evolutionary development. This evolution is by a process of conflict, contradiction or struggle between two opposing forces or ideas; collision between which produces something different from either. Thus, Private Property (the Thesis) conflicts with the Proletariat (the Antithesis) to produce the Abolition of Property and Class (the Synthesis). This may not seem immediately helpful but it reminds us of one advantage that Marx had and which previous thinkers had lacked. The *Origin of Species* appeared in 1859 and Marx had read it. More than that, he grasped its implications. Whereas most theoretical writers had de-cided (like Plato) on an ideal organization of society, towards which men should strive, Marx realised that its organization could not be static. However originally fixed, it would evolve. What he was seeking to discover was not a final and frozen state of achievement but the laws which would govern the expected development. Marx was to that extent thinking on modern lines.

To come now to the Marxist interpretation of history, Marx held that all ideological and political ideas are rooted in material or economic circumstances. The current moral and ethical ideas may be honestly held (and a few individuals may even preach, ineffectually, the opposite point of view) but they are based, in fact, on economic interests. It follows that all the conflicts recorded in history—whatever their pretext—were conflicts over material wealth. In the words of the manifesto: 'The history of all known society, past and present, has been the history of class struggles'. This theory is pursued back to the Middle Ages when a dissatisfied merchant class used the idea of nationalism to lessen the power of nobility, church and Pope. The Reformation—to follow the argument—intensified the process; from which period the merchant class or bourgeoisie went on to abolish, or reduce to impotence, the monarchy as well. Politically secure, the bourgeoisie could then multiply its wealth by successive revolutions in agriculture, commerce and industry. The result is a Capitalist Society, defended by parliamentary rule. But the Capitalist Society has an inward tendency by which profits fall unless sustained by further mechanisation, by the exploitation of new markets or by a change in the scale of industry—the smaller capitalists being absorbed by the greater. So the rich become richer and fewer, the proletariat poorer and larger until the tyranny of the few becomes absurd. Revolution follows, as a result of which the proletariat seizes power. This sequence is inevitable and invariable and can end in no other way. The dictatorship of the proletariat is bound to come.

There is substance in this argument as an analysis, from one point of view, of the history which Karl Marx had studied. We should, however, beware of concluding that any one scholarly interpretation of history is truer than any other. History can be looked at from a variety of angles—the political, the religious, the medical, the legal, the scientific and the cultural (to name no others)—and the difference between the resulting books lies in their authors' approach. Thus the same object can be viewed from different directions, from near at hand or from far away. It is needless to argue about the merits of the different viewpoints. They all give us an aspect of truth. No sensible historian will maintain that his point of view is the only one that matters. He may consider, however (and he probably will) that too few people have appreciated the merits of his viewpoint. He may also believe (and invariably does) that certain other historians are cross-eyed, colour-blind and afflicted with cataract in both eyes. He will sympathise with them publicly about their ailments and disabilities but he will not argue that their standpoint is an impossible one. The truth was there for them to see but it just so happened that they were—for all practical purposes—blind. Should a scholar write a history of civilisation solely in terms of plumbing, high explosives or venereal disease, we should not seek to belittle his work on that account. He has a right to his own point of view. In exactly the same way, any sane scholar will find much that is valuable in the economic interpretation of history. But when some enthusiastic person seizes upon this one aspect and flatly denies that there is any other, the historian will regard him as an amateur; a man who has read one book and found in it the whole truth of the universe. And an amateur is exactly what Karl Marx was.

What else could he be? He spent, it is true, many years of study but during a period when there was all too little for him to read. We have seen that his major advantage, as a political thinker, lay in his knowledge of the theory of evolution. But we do not suppose that he (or Darwin for that matter) knew more than a fraction of what is known to-day. Biology, like Physics and Chemistry, has progressed rather dramatically since 1883; as most people probably realise. Fewer, perhaps, will realise that the study of History has progressed as much. Karl Marx could read Ranke, Treitschke, Guizot and Thiers, but the systematic study of history in England had hardly begun. In 1847, the date by which his main theory had been formed, Stubbs was aged 22 and Cunningham and Maitland were not yet born. Gardiner began to publish his *History of the English Revolution* in 1863, Stubbs his *Constitutional History* in 1874. The first volume of Lecky's *History of England in the 18th Century* appeared in 1878 and Cunningham's *Growth of English Industry and Commerce* in 1882. The *English Historical Review* published its first number in 1886 (after Marx had died). Marx was also dead before F. W. Maitland had the Downing Chair at Cambridge, before Freeman took the Chair at Oxford and long before the publication of the *History of English Law*. The Oxford School of History was not even separated from that of Law until 1872, nor Sir J. R. Seeley appointed Regius Professor at Cambridge until 1869.

History has progressed, in fact, since 1847 and progressed still more since the turn of the century. It has moved backwards into pre-history, forward into the events which have happened since Marx's death, outwards into Oriental and American fields hitherto uncharted and inwards into the history of science of which we have so far scarcely scratched the surface. Marx tries, in effect, to formulate a general rule from a single example. Whereas we have evidence of civilisations rising and falling over a period of some 30,000 years, Marx rests his economic theory on an analysis of about 500 years of one civilisation; and his analysis ante-dates the very beginnings of economic history as a serious field of study.

If Karl Marx based his prophecy on a too narrow range of facts, there is a fallacy implicit in the prophecy itself. This might be called the fallacy of the three Weird Sisters. They hailed Macbeth, it will be remembered, as Thane of Glamis, as Thane of Cawdor and as 'King hereafter'. This last prediction had for Macbeth the credibility attaching to a third prophesy when two have proved correct. But the first told him nothing but what he and they and everyone knew. The second told him of something which had already taken place but of which they had prior information. The third prophecy has therefore to stand alone, a mere assertion, unsupported by any previously successful forecast. Marx argues that because a merchant class or aristocracy seizes power from a nobility, monarchy and church, it will diminish in size through the operation of economic laws until it becomes vulnerable to the lower-class revolt which he regards as inevitable. But this does not follow. For one thing, the tendency for industry to concentrate may be paralleled by the tendency of an aristocracy to disperse and so widen the governing class. For another thing, Marx does not allow for the effect of his own and other similar predictions. Whereas his admirers could agree to hasten the result which Marx thought in any case certain, his opponents might take steps to avert a result which they could regard as, at any rate, possible. Apart from that, we can now better assess the prophecy of 1847 in the light of all that has occurred since. There was good reason for expecting revolutions in 1847 and one such revolution actually took place. Tension afterwards lessened and the various Socialist groups (the First International, as their organisation has since been called) made little progress. In fact, those who upheld Marx's views had far more influence in 1848 than they were to have in 1860-80, a period of less potential disorder. The revolution which Marx expected to happen in Germany seemed, in Bismark's time, extremely remote. The revolution which he would have liked to see in Britain was as improbable but for a different reason. For most of the English Socialists turned out to be Methodists and similarly pious people to whom Materialism (and therefore Marxism) was merely irreligious.

Marxism appealed mainly, in the end, to Russian revolutionaries. For these had something to work on; a discontented people, an intellectually worried and conscience-stricken aristocracy and an obsolete medieval form of government which no other European people could approve. Except in Russia, communism mostly died out, to be revived only after 1917. Russian communists mostly lived outside Russia and were widely tolerated, either because they were not taken seriously or because of the dislike felt for Tsarist Russia by all European liberals. The political principles upon which Tsarist government was founded were Autocracy, Nationality and Orthodoxy. The political methods for which Russia was noted involved the constant use of secret police, spies, informers, torture and Siberian exile. There are said to have been 3,282 executions, after trial, between 1906 and 1913. Neither these principles nor these methods appealed to Queen Victoria or Mr. Gladstone. They seemed then (they even seem now) essentially wrong.

Russian revolutionaries had, therefore, secure bases in Europe from which to organise revolt in Russia. But what sort of government was to take the place of the one they meant to overthrow? It was on this subject that their holy scripture was least helpful. Karl Marx had very little to say about politics as such. He merely asserted that the proletariat, once in power and having no other class to rule and subdue, would find politics needless and the State itself unnecessary. Meanwhile, until the State 'withers away', there must presumably be government of some kind. Marx apparently envisaged his proletarian dictatorship as centring on a Commune or Communal Council, having both legislative and executive functions and based upon a universal franchise. It is clear that his proletariat will abolish all standing military forces, all offices that are not elective and all churches—or, anyway, all religious endowments. Negatively, the Marxist programme is fairly complete. We know little of Marx's more constructive ideas on the political side. As for the State 'withering away', Marxist doctrine makes actual revolution essential to progress; and the military or semi-military leadership needed for a successful revolt seems, in practice, easier to introduce than to terminate. Apart from that, Marx had perhaps hardly understood the political implications of his own creed. For, granted that industrial combines would become larger and larger, as he said they would and as they did, the organisations built up could only be taken over (after the revolution) by the State. Marx was no machine-wrecker, no William Morris or G. K. Chesterton. He neither wanted nor expected to see the last capitalist hurled into the blazing ruins of the last factory. Granted, however, that the factories were to remain after the capitalists had all been hanged, they would obviously be nationalised. And how could a State controlling whole industries be expected to 'wither away'? And what would happen to the industries if it did?

Karl Marx was not a fool and the clue to the absurdity of his political idealism lies mainly in the period from which it dates. To a man born at Trier in 1818, graduating at Bonn in 1841, the idea of industry on the modern scale was altogether alien. His was the background of the Rhineland, the vineyards and the little German towns. It was easy for him to picture a revolution in which large capitalists—the biggest tradesmen in each town—were eliminated. It was easy for him to imagine, in his bucolic surroundings, how groups of peasants and workers could then run industries for themselves. Given the disappearance of war, foreign relations, church and king, no political functions would remain; none, at least, beyond the capacity of a socialistic town council. He hardly realised the implications of the railway; and the growth of industries as we know them did not begin until about 1870. Had he foreseen the scale of modern industry, he would not have assumed that the State could 'wither away'. He would have known that it would have economic functions even if it had no other. And he might, in that case, have paid a little more attention to the political aftermath of the revolution he wished to bring about. As it was, his political ideas scarcely progress beyond the lamp-post on which the last capitalist is to be hanged. From the moment when they overthrew the Tsar his Russian admirers had no further help from Marx. They were left to work out the problem for themselves and their solution was the simplest imaginable. They gave Russia almost exactly the same government as it had had before.

This result was partly due to the character of the Russian Marxists and partly to the nature of the problem they were left to solve. Their party had grown up in conspiratorial fashion in an atmosphere of danger, suspicion and fear of betrayal. They developed the strict party discipline that was essential for safety. They developed a fanatical adherence to the word of Karl Marx, whose writings were as important to them as was the Talmud to the exiled Jews. Many of them, incidentally, were in fact Jewish, like Marx himself. They had a tendency, Jewish again, to quarrel over the exact interpretation of biblical texts. When the Tsarist government collapsed during the First World War, the small Communist Party was disciplined enough and quick enough to seize power during the disorders which followed. Their power was consolidated by external dangers against which a party leader could appeal to nationalist sentiment. The result was that their Autocracy (of the party chief), their Nationalism (as defenders of Russia) and their Orthodoxy (as Marxists) reproduced the main principles, and encouraged them to adopt the same methods, as the government they had overturned.

This is the more comprehensible when we remember that their problem was the same. Soviet Russia comprised, even in its early days, $8\frac{1}{2}$ million square miles, nearly $\frac{1}{6}$th of the earth's surface; an area larger than the United States and China together. Distances ranged up to 5,000 miles from East to West, and almost 3,000 miles from North to South. The population was nearly 192,000,000 in 1939, comprising Russians, White Russians, Ukrainians, Armenians, Georgians, Jews, Turkemans, Mongolians, Germans and Finns, with some seventy languages spoken and taught. Most of these people were backward, illiterate, irresponsible and feckless. To govern a country so much larger than Europe or the United States is a formidable task. It could not, in any case, be governed in the same way as England or New Zealand. It must be a federation, to begin with, like the United States. But to maintain a unity among peoples so numerous, scattered, diverse and backward is the task for a god, not for a man. Such a federation can be held together only by the same means as adopted in ancient Egypt or China; by a State Religion, a Priesthood and a Deified Emperor. That was what Russia had before and it was what Russia was to have again. But even that would not suffice without bringing to bear upon the problem all the devotion of the Jesuits, all the fanaticism of Islam and all the calculated cruelty of the Tsarist police. All this too might fail without a continual foreign threat and pressure which has to be invented when it does not exist.[1]

What has been called 'the dropping of the Utopian element in Marxism'[2] would have been inevitable in any Socialist State much larger than a village. In a country like Russia the idea of the State 'withering away' could not last five minutes. So far from 'withering away' the State in Russia has become more powerful, more complex, more inescapable than in any other country in the world. The Constitution of the Union of Soviet Socialist Republics (as amended in 1947)[3] comprises 146 Articles, refers to sixteen different Republics, a Supreme Soviet with two Chambers, a Presidium with sixteen Vice-Presidents, Credentials Committees, a Council of Ministers, thirty-six all-Union Ministries, twenty-three Union-Republican Ministries, a Supreme Court, a Procurator-General, and the Soviets of territories, regions, autonomous regions, areas, districts, cities and rural localities. As the Union-Republican central Ministries are all represented again by corresponding Ministries in each of the sixteen Republics, and as there are separate Ministries of Internal Affairs, State Control, State Security and Justice, there would seem to be few signs of the 'withering away' process as yet. The mind rather reels when confronted by the mere list of executive and legislative bodies. Elections are innumerable, the citizen taking part severally as an inhabitant, a producer, a consumer and possibly as a party-member as well. The whole structure is more elaborate even than that of the United States and with full rights guaranteed for everyone—freedom of speech, freedom of the press, freedom to vote, freedom of assembly and freedom of association. The suffrage is universal, equal, direct and secret. The constitutional structure of the U.S.S.R. could not be more democratic in principle. It is perceptibly less democratic in practice.

When announcing the Constitution of 1936, Joseph Stalin is

As Karl Marx wrote in 1853: 'There is only one way to deal with a Power like Russia, and that is the fearless way.' The *Russian Menace to Europe*. Ed. by P. W. Blackstock and B. F. Hoselity. Illinois, 1952. p. 269.

[2] *The Spirit of Post-war Russia*. Rudolf Schlesinger. London, 1947. p. 180.

[3] *An Introduction to Russian History and Culture*. Ivar Spector. New York, 1949. Appendix. p. 411.

reported as saying 'I must admit the draft of a new Constitution really does leave in force the regime of the dictatorship of the working class, and also leaves unchanged the present leading position of the Communist party of the U.S.S.R.'[1] We may take his word for it. But we must also be clear in our minds about what that 'leading position' amounts to. It was created, in the first instance, by Lenin, and ante-dates all the democratic machinery of government. When Bertrand Russell met Lenin in 1920, he found it difficult at first to see him as other than commonplace.

> I think if I had met him without knowing who he was, I should not have guessed that he was a great man; he struck me as too opinionated and narrowly orthodox. His strength comes, I imagine, from his honesty, courage, and unwavering faith—religious faith in the Marxian gospel, which takes the place of the Christian martyr's hopes of Para-dise, except that it is less egotistical. He has as little love of liberty as the Christians who suffered under Diocletian, and retaliated when they acquired power. Perhaps love of liberty is incompatible with whole-hearted belief in a panacea for all human ills.[2]

Lenin's strength of character lay, no doubt, in the qualities which Bertrand Russell imagined him to possess. His political strength, however, lay in his firm refusal to take the easy way. From 1900 onwards he must have been almost overwhelmingly tempted to accept whatever recruits that came. He refused instead to have any that he could not trust. As Sidney and Beatrice Webb pointed out:

> . . . Lenin had no use, within the Party, for mere sympathisers, for partially converted disciples, for adherents who based their acts on Christianity or a general humanitarianism, or on any other theory of social life than Marxism, nor even for those whose interpretation of Marxism differed from his own. . . . For the instrument of revolution that he was forging he needed . . . a completely united, highly dis-ciplined and relatively small body of 'professional revolutionists', who should not only have a common creed and a common programme but should also undertake to give their whole lives to a single end. . . . The creation of such a body was no easy task. In interminable controversies between 1900 and 1916, we watch Lenin driving off successively all whom he could not persuade to accept his model; all whom he con-sidered compromisers or temporisers; opportunists or reformists; half-converted sympathisers who clung to one or other form of mysti-cism for which Karl Marx had found no place. . . .[3]

When the Russian Revolution took place, the party members numbered only 30,000 but these were all picked, indoctrinated,

[1] *Laidler. op. cit.* p. 423.
[2] *The Practice and Theory of Bolshevism.* Bertrand Russell. London, 1920. p. 37.
[3] *Soviet Communism: A new civilisation.* By Sidney and Beatrice Webb. 2 vols. London, 1937. Vol. I. pp. 341-342.

tested and reliable. And it was, of course, Lenin's exclusion of vaguely left-wing idealists which made Communism a religion, incompatible with any other. Membership from the beginning implied rigid orthodoxy, implicit obedience, austerity of life and willingness to face hard work, hardship and danger.

> The Communist who sincerely believes the party creed is convinced that private property is the root of all evil; he is so certain of this that he shrinks from no measures, however harsh, which seem necessary for constructing and preserving the Communist State. He spares himself as little as he spares others. He works sixteen hours a day, and foregoes his Saturday half-holiday. He volunteers for any difficult or dangerous work which needs to be done. . . . The same motives, however, which make him austere make him also ruthless. Marx has taught that Communism is fatally predestined to come about; this fits in with the Oriental traits in the Russian character, and produces a state of mind not unlike that of the early successors of Mahomet. Opposition is crushed without mercy. . . .[1]

Party membership is attractive, therefore, to the young and fanatical, to the austere and ardent, to those with a sense of mission. It does not attract everybody and of those it does attract many are rejected at the outset, rejected during probation or 'purged' at some later stage. During the period 1922-27 from 16,000 to 25,000 members were expelled each year, for slackness, dishonesty, drunkenness or similar offences.[2] Numbers, therefore, have mounted only slowly. There were fewer than half a million members in 1920 and only two and a half million in 1939. If there were four and a half million in 1942, the membership would have been just over two per cent of the population. Party members are said to have numbered 6,300,000 in 1947 but the percentage remains low and the policy has always been to keep the membership exclusive. Parallel with the official assemblies, the Party has its own organisation, with local Committees, an All-Union Congress, a Central Committee and a Political Bureau (Politburo) which has been the most important governing body in Russia. The Secretary-General of the Party was, for many years, Joseph Stalin, and this was, for most of that time, the only office he held.

The relationship between Party and State has been defined by Stalin in these words:

> . . . In the Soviet Union, in the land where the dictatorship of the proletariat is in force, no important political or organizational problem is ever decided by our soviets and other mass organizations, without directives from our Party. In this sense, we may say that the

---

[1] Bertrand Russell. *op. cit.* p. 27.
[2] Sidney and Beatrice Webb. *op. cit.* Vol. I. p. 375.

dictatorship of the proletariat is substantially the dictatorship of the Party, as the force which effectively guides the proletariat.[1]

This admission and the known fact that the vast majority of Ministers, Deputies and Officials are in fact Party members, taking their orders from the Party, justifies us in classifying this form of government as a Theocracy. It has sometimes been held that it is, rather, a Dictatorship. As against that, Sidney and Beatrice Webb concluded, after careful investigation, that it is not.

> We have given particular attention to this point, collecting all the available evidence, and noting carefully the inferences to be drawn from the experience of the past eight years (1926-1934). We do not think that the Party is governed by the will of a single person; or that Stalin is the sort of person to claim or desire such a position. He has himself very explicitly denied any such personal dictatorship in terms which, whether or not he is credited with sincerity, certainly accord with our own impression of the facts.[2]

There can be no doubt that Stalin's power was greater during the Second World War but the same would be true of Churchill or Roosevelt. Before that war, Stalin surely exercised something far short of dictatorial powers. But if we have little reason for concluding that he was a dictator, we have ample evidence for concluding that he was a god. We are told that, when Lenin died:

> . . . His remains were interred in a dark-red granite mausoleum in the Red Square of Moscow, which is backed by the Kremlin wall. Three-quarters of a million people waited in line to view his remains for an average of five hours in an arctic cold of 30 degrees below zero before they were able to take their turn in passing through the hall where he lay in state.[3]

It is with reference to this deification of Lenin that the Webbs were able to explain how Stalin in turn became a god. It was, they explained, because the party leaders deliberately exploited the traditional Russian reverence for a personal autocrat.

> . . . This was seen in the popular elevation of Lenin, notably after his death, to the status of saint or prophet, virtually canonised in the sleeping figure in the sombre mausoleum in Moscow's Red Square, where he is now, to all intents and purposes worshipped by the adoring millions of workers and peasants who daily pass before him. Lenin's works have become 'Holy Writ', which may be interpreted, but which it is impermissible to confute. After Lenin's death, it was agreed that his place could never be filled. But some new personality had to be

---

[1] *Leninism.* By J. Stalin. Vol. I. 1928. p. 33. Quoted in *Soviet Communism: a new civilisation.* By Sidney and Beatrice Webb. London, 1937. 2nd ed. Vol. I. pp. 430-431.
[2] Sidney and Beatrice Webb. *op. cit.* Vol. I. p. 432.
[3] Laidler. *op. cit.* p. 393.

produced for the hundred and sixty millions to revere. There presently ensued a tacit understanding among the junta that Stalin should be 'boosted' as the supreme leader of the proletariat, the Party, and the state. His portrait and his bust were accordingly distributed by tens of thousands, and they are now everywhere publicly displayed along with those of Marx and Lenin.[1]

As a potential god, Stalin (the atheist) had a useful qualification in the training he had received in the Theological Seminary of Tiflis. He at least must have understood what was required of him as the third person of a Trinity in which Marx was God and Lenin, Christ. And the first thing expected of him was a proper reverence for the gods senior to him.

> At the next Congress of the Soviets after Lenin's death, Stalin chanted his sacred vow in the name of the revolution: 'Departing from us, Comrade Lenin bequeathed to us the duty of preserving and strengthening the dictatorship of the proletariat. We swear to thee, Comrade Lenin, that we will not spare our energies in also fulfilling with honor this thy commandment!'[2]

Lenin had himself ridiculed and detested all religion as 'the thousand-year-old enemy of culture and progress', but Stalin now invoked his name in what amounts to a public prayer. He addressed the dead man as if he were still there in spirit. But nothing he could say about the dead Lenin could surpass what was soon being said about himself, reaching a crescendo of adulation on his seventieth birthday in 1949. And one thing apparent from all that was said is that deification actually lessens the power of the person deified. This was true of the god-kings of Egypt and it remains true to-day. The deified king is imprisoned by his own legend, restricted by the ritual of his own cult. The other thing apparent is that the king is deified by his subjects' wish, not by his own. Lenin would hardly have accepted worship in his lifetime but he was powerless to save his dead body from the adoration of the naturally religious. As for Stalin, he accepted his role with something like complacence. Deification begins with good publicity.

> . . . The same heroic pictures of Stalin appeared in Moscow, Prague, and Peiping. Always the image of the Leader was sublimely glorified. Edgar Snow says he counted Stalin's name fifty-seven times in one four-page issue of a Moscow daily even at the height of the paper shortage in World War II. In 1950, with paper more plentiful, one issue of *Pravda* mentioned Stalin 91 times on the front page alone; 35 times as Josef Vissarinovich Stalin; 33 times as Comrade Stalin; 10 times as Great Leader; 7 times as Dear and Beloved Stalin; and 6 times as Great Stalin. The Yugoslav newspaper which did this bit of research into the

[1] S. and B. Webb. *op. cit.* p. 438.
[2] *Communism, Democracy and Catholic Power.* Paul Blanshard. London, 1952. p. 70.

processes of deification also recorded the fact that Stalin is commonly described elsewhere in the Soviet press as Great Leader of Mankind; Great Chief of All Workers; Protagonist of Our Victories; and Faithful Fighter for the Cause of Peace.[1]

Stalin's fiftieth birthday in 1929 called forth a series of epithets comparable with those applied to earlier Asian kings (see p. 135). Among these may be quoted the following: The greatest military leader of all times and nations, Lenin's Perpetuator in Creating the Theory of the Construction of Socialism, The Theoretician and Leader of the Fight for Peace and Brotherhood among the Peoples, the Military Genius of our Time, Mirrored in the Literature of the Peoples of the World, Teacher and Inspired Leader of the World Proletariat, Coryphaeus of World Science, Theoretician and Initiator of the Transformation of Nature in the U.S.S.R., the People's Happiness, Brilliant thinker and scholar.

Paul Blanshard has also been at pains to collect certain other literary references to Stalin which are as significant in their own way.

Father! What could be nearer and dearer than that name?

Multiform is the all-compassing power of Stalin's genius. Not a single field of the creative endeavors of the Soviet people but has been illumined by the rays of his intellect which has pointed the way to the new summit of achievement.

The shoots of all that is new, progressive, beautiful and exalted in our life reach out to Stalin as to the sun. Stalin inspires our people and gives them wings. Stalin's words, Stalin's kindness and solicitude are a source of life-giving strength to millions.[2]

He quotes a poem written by Mikhail Isakovsky which reads, as translated:—

He has brought us strength and glory
And youth for ages to come,
The flush of a beautiful dawning
Across our heaven is flung.
So let us lift up our voices
To him who is most beloved.
A song to the sun and to justice,
A song that to Stalin is sung.[3]

Another poem reads:—

O Great Stalin, O leader of the peoples,
Thou who broughtest man to birth,
Thou who purifiest the earth,
Thou who makest bloom the spring,

[1] Blanshard. *op. cit.* p. 71.
[2] *Ibid.* p. 73.
[3] *Ibid.* p. 74.

Thou who makest vibrate the musical chords,
Thou splendor of my spring, O Thou
Sun reflected of millions of hearts.[1]

After reading or chanting such poems as these, the next and logical step for the communist was to make pilgrimage to the Kremlin and walk where Stalin has trod. 'Let us fall on our knees and kiss those holy footprints!'[2]

Hysteria apart, there is great significance in the themes which underlie these outpourings. The important words are Father, Sun, Rays, life-giving strength, spring; these and the various references to fertility. When words like these are used we are fairly back in the world of Pharaoh, Osiris and the Golden Bough.

The implications of this godhead are immediate. A certain stability has been gained but the actual king-priest is crippled and mummified. He cannot take any active part in war, partly because the people will not let him (see page 36) and partly because he dare not risk the consequences. What if a reverse follows his visit to the scene of operations? What if he is made to look like an amateur beside some general? What if he trips over some wire and falls into a shell-hole? No, the battlefield is ruled out for the Military Genius of our Time. So long as he stays at home, defeats can be blamed on the generals in the field, who have been disobedient or (more probably) treacherous. But most other activities are ruled out for the same sort of reason. He dare not mount a horse in case he should fall off. He dare not shoot in case he should miss. He dare not paint a picture in case someone else's should seem better. He dare not visit another country in case he should be made to seem less important than its ruler. He dare play no game in case he should lose. There is scarcely anything he can do except work behind closed doors, preside over councils, execute any possible rival, appear dramatically on infrequent state occasions, make oracular speeches and wait for the embalming and the glass case which is the final fate of a god. In a Theocracy, as the King becomes mummified, it is the priests who tend to rule.

It would be possible to quote from a thousand books in praise of Communism. They should be classified, however, as theology rather than as political thought. For just as St. Augustine's theory rests on the assumption that Jesus is the Son of God, from which all else follows, so Marxist theory rests on the assumption that Karl Marx is God, Lenin his prophet and the current Ruler his infallible interpreter. Granted these axioms, there is room to discuss how Lenin would have solved a particular problem, or even what Marx meant in some passage more than usually obscure. But discussion on these lines

[1] *Ibid.* p. 74.
[2] *Ibid.* p. 75.

is uninteresting to those who deny the axioms upon which all else depends. Those, however, to whom the Marxist axioms are least acceptable must consider that Communism, as a religion, has at least provided an answer to the practical problem of ruling China. There are many, no doubt, who would prefer to see Russia and China ruled on very different lines. These should recall that a Russia ruled in western democratic fashion would not be Russia. It would fall into as many fragments as did Europe when the Roman Empire collapsed. Such a disintegration would be a relief to many other peoples but we cannot expect the Russians to welcome it. They would be vulnerable to external dangers of which they have had considerable experience.

While it would be rash to assert that Russia, within its present boundaries and with its present peoples, could not be governed except theocratically, it is at least fair to say that no previous example exists of such an area being governed in any other way. Nor has the theocratic element been absent from governments with a far simpler problem to solve. The New England Puritans, a minority of 'Saints' among a greater number of 'strangers', had all the deep convictions, all the austerity, all the devotion and all the intolerance of the modern communist. They left a permanent influence on America and even upon people to whom their virtues now seem least attractive. It would surely be wrong to deny that there is anything of value in the idea of a chosen minority undergoing an arduous training, assuming special and onerous responsibilities, foregoing any material reward and devoting their lives to a chosen faith. Would it not be equally wrong to question the right of the majority to accept the leadership of these few? For there is little evidence to show that the majority in Russia is averse to being led. There are democrats who will assert the infallibility of the people but only so long as it is democracy that the people choose. There is much in this attitude of the very intolerance which the democrat is eager to condemn in others. That the Russians and Chinese will evolve in time a system of government different from the type they now regard as orthodox is tolerably certain. That it will resemble that of Britain or the United States is most improbable. It would be odd indeed if the same answer were to prove correct for problems in their nature so entirely different.

PART III

Democracy

CHAPTER XIII

The Origins of Democracy

IN commenting upon the course of history, St. Augustine is shrewd enough to suggest (as did Sallust before him) that the Athenians exceeded other people more in their publicity than in their deeds.[1] Most subsequent scholars have been more credulous, one result being a surprisingly widespread belief that the Athenians were the inventors of democracy. That they were nothing of the kind is tolerably clear. What we owe to the Athenians is not the thing itself or even its name but the earliest detailed account of how a democracy came into being, flourished and collapsed. Of the Indian democracies, which were probably older, we have all too little precise information. There is, however, a sense in which many people have had a measure of democracy in their village life. Of China it has been said:—

> The family, the clan, the guild and the unorganised gentry play the leading part in rural and urban self-government; but . . . there is an endless variety of groups and associations organised on a free and voluntary basis for an endless variety of social ends and purposes which make China a vast self-governed and law-abiding society, costing practically nothing to maintain.[2]

There was likewise a great measure of democratic activity in ancient India, considerable powers being left to families, clans, village communities and guilds. The Russians also had their *mir* or village community, their *artel* or craft guild; the former being an assembly of the peasants, the latter of workers in the towns. The Anglo-Saxon folk-moot had its parallel in Vedic India.[3] It would be difficult, therefore, to decide in what country democracy first appeared. Nor would it be much easier to find the oldest republic. The choice would lie perhaps between various states of northern India. These were presumably monarchies at an earlier period, as some were to remain, but some were republican from about 500 B.C. or even earlier. One people, the Lichchhavis, with their capital at Vaisali, were republicans before the time of Cleisthenes and perhaps

[1] *The City of God.* John Healey. Trans. Reprinted, London, 1931. Chap. II. Book XIV.

[2] *Democracies of the East.* R. Mukerjee. London, 1923.

[3] *Indian culture through the ages.* S. V. Venkateswara. London, 1932. In two vols. Vol. II. *Public Life and Political Institutions.* p. 24.

even earlier than Draco.[1] They were ruled, it is said, by an assembly numbering 7,707. These enfranchised citizens may have been only about one in twenty of the total population but the 20,000 voters of Athens were only perhaps one in eighteen. The honour and support which the Lichchhavis gave to their greatest contemporary, Gautama (or the Buddha), contrasts favourably, one might add, with the hemlock which the Athenians prescribed for Socrates. And if the Lichchhavis had their untouchables, the Athenians had their slaves. There were other republics in the Punjab and the Indus valley, especially between 500 B.C. and A.D. 400. They offered, some of them, a stout resistance to Alexander's army. There is even mention of three republics forming a federation in the vicinity of Delhi.[2] There was nothing comparable to this in southern India, it appears, but there the local government among the Tamils was more highly developed and on even more democratic lines, with a public assembly electing the village council.

While it might prove impossible to decide when and where democracy first appeared, it is somewhat easier to discover how. For such facts as are known point clearly to its being normally a development of aristocracy. We learn, for example, that all the voters of Vaisali were called 'Raja' just as all modern British taxpayers are addressed by the Board of Inland Revenue as 'Esquire'. The enfranchised Lichchhavis recognised, in fact, no class distinction among themselves 'everyone thinking that he was the Raja'.[3] It was that same equality and voting procedure which was copied by the Buddhist monasteries, and it is at least an interesting speculation to wonder whether some of the same ideas passed via western monasticism into modern democratic practice. Whatever the truth may be about that, it is evidently the tendency for an aristocracy to lose its powers by diffusion and dilution. The process is essentially biological, closely resembling the earlier process by which monarchy itself declines. If the essence of aristocracy is noble descent, all children of noble parentage are equally what the Indians would call *Kshatriyas* or warriors. They must become more numerous in each generation. Nor can they all be wealthy. In time, moreover, they cannot all even be soldiers. The *Kshatriyas*, for example, of the Indian republics 'followed trade and commerce' as well as arms.[4] Once this stage has been reached, democracy is in sight. This process is termed 'timocracy' by Plato.[5]

The process of diffusion, as noble blood becomes more common, is

[1] *Hindu Civilization.* R. K. Mookerji. Bombay 1950. pp. 203-207.
[2] *State and Government in Ancient India.* A. S. Altekar. Benares, 1949. pp. 78-79.
[3] R. K. Mookerji. *op. cit.* p. 205.
[4] Altekar. *op. cit.* p. 75.
[5] *Greek Political Theory.* Sir Ernest Barker. 4th ed. London, 1951. pp. 251-2.

matched by the simultaneous process of dilution; a process which the Indian caste system was carefully designed to prevent. In lands with a less rigid system of class distinction, it was always difficult, in practice, to exclude from the upper class a growing number of the skilled, the able or the dangerous. Knightly rank has always been won on the battlefield and can scarcely be denied to the merchant whose travels may bring him into comparable peril. And if the merchant wears the sword, the lawyer sent on embassy deserves no less. But no trader or professional man can deny a measure of respect to his customers or clients. He who sells can claim no superiority over those who buy. When in doubt, he will prefer to call the stranger 'Sir' or 'Lord'. That his customers are all 'ladies and gentlemen' is the proof in fact of his success. There is thus a tendency in most languages for the word 'gentleman' to become meaningless, being applied eventually to all above the status of peasant, or to all perhaps not actually slaves.

The assumption of 'gentle' rank by so large a number is not inconsistent with the claim by a minority to a still higher status. But the claim becomes difficult to sustain as against others whose birth, education, military prowess and wealth is not perceptibly inferior. Such a claim, if persisted in, may end in middle-class revolt. If, on the other hand, the claim is tacitly dropped, a democratic equality has been practically achieved. Historically, the tendency has been for the privileged class to split, the more snobbish provoking by their conduct a revolt with which the less snobbish are openly sympathetic (not without advantage to themselves). The French Revolution of 1789 provides us with a classic example of this process. Had none of the aristocrats believed in aristocracy the rising would never have begun. Had they all believed in aristocracy, it might have been easily suppressed. As it was, some were unpopular, more were undecided and a few were openly on the side of the unprivileged. The same situation existed in Britain during the period 1900-1920. The aristocracy was too uncertain of itself to make any spectacular stand against the quiet revolution which was taking place. Many sought to escape the unpopularity which a few had earned. There emerged the Mirabeau type, the Etonian socialist. None dared uphold the principle of aristocracy as such save in the most evasive term. The collapse of aristocracy was further hastened by two other factors which may well have been important at similar periods of transition in the past. One factor was the failure to breed, common among the politically uncertain. The other was the incidence of war casualties, falling most heavily upon the limited class from which future leaders might otherwise have been drawn. The British aristocracy went down before the revolution of 1914-18, victims of a conflict in which generals lost their reputation while subalterns lost their lives. The survivors of a war in which the dangers had been experienced by all alike could do nothing but talk about the virtues of democracy. Death duties finished what machine guns had begun.

To study in any detail the process by which aristocracy turns into democracy, we must turn first to Athens and Rome. And one feature of European democracy, as seen in classical times and as contrasting with the democracies of the East, is the emergence of the individual. The Oriental attitude to this phenomenon has been well expressed by Professor Radhakamal Mukerjee:—

> The realisation of right had been from the first a social function; but its enforcement was incumbent on the unit groups of individuals (families, clans, tribes, village communities or guilds bound together by friendship). The acquisition by the State of supreme and unlimited power and jurisdiction over society and its economic, social and cultural interests has been a gradual but inevitable development in the West; and this apotheosis of the State has given a wrong trend to civilisation. In China and India, the rules of conduct evolved by the unit groups of individuals still constitute the communal code, while the rules of morality form a second code, set above the communal law and embodying a larger aggregate of duties. The two together embrace the whole field of life; and much that falls to State or government in the West to further public welfare by means of the creation and administration of law is left to myriad local groups and assemblies in the communalistic polity. Unregulated individualism and absolute State authority go together. . . .[1]

What was novel, in fact, about the republic of Athens was not its democracy as such but its emphasis on the individual rather than on the group. Once the individual citizen becomes the unit, divorced from his clan or trade guild or village, he is immeasurably weakened in his relationship with the State. And the State is correspondingly strengthened as group loyalties disappear.

Athens was ruled at first, like other States, by a god-descended king. But whereas at Rome the king was dethroned by an aristocratic revolution, at Athens the monarchy was gradually and quietly replaced[2]. First we hear of the king's successor being chosen from among members of the royal family. Next we hear of a General and a Judge (both of royal blood) appointed to assist the king. Then the office of judge or Archon is thrown open to men of noble family (c. 725 B.C.), the period of office being reduced from ten years to one. The appearance of the Council of Nine, and the Areopogus or Council of the 'Eupatridae', marks the aristocratic control which existed during the later days of the monarchy. By 683 B.C. Athens was an aristocratic republic.

[1] *Democracies of the East*. R. Mukerjee. London, 1923. pp. 78-79.
[2] *The City-State of the Greeks and Romans*. W. Warde-Fowler. Ed. of 1931.

Thus the constitutional frame in which the city-state was built was aristocracy. With settled life personal leadership had given place to the steady influence of a class. Overseas this class was sometimes the original settlers who kept political power in their own hands. In Greece proper long-established wealth or pride of birth, displayed in the keeping of horses or the membership of aristocratic clans, had shown itself too in the service of the state. As the king had dwindled, so the old assembly of freemen disappeared or counted for little. The state was the possession of those who had the freedom to serve it. . . .[1]

But aristocracy had no very firm basis among the Greeks. It had no strong religious sanction, the Greeks not being, by Eastern standards, a very religious people. It had no monopoly of learning, for the Greeks, taking their civilisation from Asia (and being the first European people to experience it), had adopted the simple phonetic alphabet of the Phoenicians. It had no monopoly of wealth, for the Greeks were seafarers and traders, living in a rather poor land. It had no basis in luxury for the Greek tastes were simple; nor in leisure, for most Greeks seem to have had that. It had, above all, no basis in horsemanship for horses, though used, played a relatively small part in Greek life. Greece (apart from Thessaly) had neither the pasture on which horses could graze nor the terrain in which cavalry could operate. It has been pointed out, moreover, that the horses which are represented in the Parthenon frieze are little larger than ponies. No iron shoes were used before the second century B.C. and Greece is a stony land. Unshod, without saddle or stirrups, the horses of the breed represented in these carvings could have been of no use in the charge.[2] Aristotle himself remarks that the upper class in Thessaly could subdue the rabble. That this was untrue in Athens is one reason why the aristocratic phase there was relatively brief. It lasted, in fact, from about 750 B.C. until about 600 B.C. The framework of democracy, created by Solon (Archon in 594 B.C.) and perfected by Cleisthenes (c. 525 B.C.), lasted until about 338 B.C.

The essential point in the reforms of Solon and Cleisthenes was the abolition of the clans. Democracy in the Greek sense was incompatible with communal organisation or with the continued influence of the areopogus.[3] The constitution, after the citizens had been reorganised into ten new 'demes' or townships of non-tribal character, can be regarded as a bold experiment in direct and representative democracy. By the time of Pericles, sovereignty lay in the Ecclesia, the assembly of free citizens of military age, numbering perhaps 20,000 in theory, paid for their attendance, and meeting at least forty

[1] *The Cambridge Ancient History.* Vol. III. p. 700. (Chapter XXVI, Professor F. E. Adcock).
[2] *The Economics of Ancient Greece.* H. Michell. Cambridge, 1940.
[3] Its powers were mostly abolished in 462 B.C. See *The Greek City and its Institutions.* G. Glotz. London, 1950. p. 125.

times a year.[1] Executive power was delegated, however, to the Council of Five Hundred elected annually by the Ecclesia, meeting every five days and sitting fifty at a time. This Council delegated much of its power in turn to Committees. These Committees dealt with Justice, War, Finance, Education, Religion, Dockyards and Accounts. Members of the more important Committees (War, Finance etc.) were elected from the Council in office. Those serving on the less important Committees were chosen by lot. Total committee membership came to 1,200-1,400 all told, so that everyone would have his turn in office. Courts of Law were equally democratic in character, each comprising 500 members of the Ecclesia sitting as a kind of jury.[2]

The citizens with full political rights thus numbered 20,000 at most out of a total population of over 320,000. No voting rights were accorded to women, minors,[3] aliens or slaves. Nor would such a system have been even possible without slavery, to provide the citizens with leisure, or tribute (drawn from the subject cities of the Athenian League) to provide the voters with their pay. But when all these limitations have been conceded, it remains true that it was as real a democracy as has ever, perhaps, existed. It was government by the many and involved the active and direct participation of as many people as was practicable. More than that, the defects of Athenian democracy were democratic defects, arising not from the restriction of the suffrage but from its breadth. There is every reason, in fact, for concluding that a wider franchise would have made them not better but worse.

What were these defects? The first was inherent in a system which gave equal political rights to the rich and the poor. It is true that the Athenian 'poor' excluded most of those whom we should describe as the working class; for these were slaves. But there were citizens quite poor enough to envy the wealth of the others. Nor did their comparative poverty make them less politically active in a state where political service was paid. Their natural instinct was to tax or fine the rich out of existence. The reaction of the more prosperous was to form societies for mutual protection and political reform. These activities were, or could be regarded as treasonable, and the result was a series of prosecutions of the wealthy between 410 and 405 B.C. Those not actually prosecuted were blackmailed with the threat of prosecution. Many, like Euripides and Agathon, fled to Macedonia.

---

[1] Actual attendance was very much less. At the only division for which we have exact figures, 3,616 men voted. There may have been 5,000-6,000 present on more important occasions. See A. Zimmern, *The Greek Commonwealth*. Oxford. Ed. of 1952. p. 169.

[2] See *Cambridge Ancient History*. Vol. V, p. 98 et seq. (Chap. IV) and A. Zimmern, *op. cit.* p. 175.

[3] Voters had to be over 20 years of age, making their possible number about 20,000. But by the end of the Peloponnesian War it was practically impossible to collect even 5,000. See Zimmern, *op. cit.* p. 169.

Alcibiades fled to Thrace. The Athenian Courts of Law proved an ideal mechanism for pursuing these feuds as the people were sitting in judgment on what might be their own cause; the confiscation of property. The active treason of the wealthy was an important factor in the defeat of Athens in 405 B.C.

The second major defect lay in the division of the spoils. Public funds were spent in the payment of an enormous civil service, with large numbers of people thus taken from productive work. The precise statistics here are in dispute and it is a question whether a half or merely a third of the citizens were in public employment. There seem, at any rate, to have been 20,000 so employed in the fifth century B.C. This total admittedly included 6,000 soldiers and sailors; and the 6,000 paid jurors might of course be regarded as old-age pensioners or unemployed. Still, with all allowances made, the officials were fairly numerous. They included some 2,850 policemen, 700 home civil servants, perhaps 300 in the colonial service,[1] 500 members of Council and over 3,000 subordinate officials, benefactors, retired athletes and orphans. There are many, no doubt, who would regard full employment, in this sense, as a merit rather than a defect. It was essentially dependent, however, on a revenue from overseas acquired by anything but democratic means. This revenue apart, it was simply a living on capital, a fundamentally unstable process. Public servants could not, of course, be dismissed as redundant, they and their friends being voters.

The third major defect lay in external affairs. Athens could not have lasted for long in any case after the rise of Macedonia but it remains roughly true to say that the Athenians were most successful between 466 and 428 B.C. when ruled, in practice, by Pericles, and far less successful during later periods of more typically democratic rule. Thucydides is emphatic about this:

> Pericles, powerful from dignity of character as well as from wisdom, and conspicuously above the least tinge of corruption, held back the people with a free hand, and was their real leader instead of being led by them. For not being a seeker of power from unworthy sources, he did not speak with any view to present favour, but had sufficient sense of dignity to contradict them on occasion, even braving their displeasure. . . . But those who succeeded after his death, being more equal one with another, and each of them desiring pre-eminence over the rest, adopted the different course of courting the favour of the people and sacrificing to that object even important state-interests.[2]

---

[1] These were not 'career' civil servants but elected amateur officials, serving for a limited period of office. The number given does not include the slaves in public ownership who formed the more permanent element in the establishment; nor the Scythian archers who were employed to keep order.

[2] *Thucydides II*, 65 quoted in *A History of Greece* by G. Grote in ten volumes. London, 1888. Vol. V. p. 95.

What is particularly interesting is that the Athenian failures and mistakes were in precisely the fields of activity in which later democracies have also tended to fail; that is to say, in colonial policy, foreign policy and war.

There is, of course, a basic anomaly in a democratic state having colonies at all. The Athenian legend had been built up round the story of Greek resistance to Persian imperialism. The obvious and expected fate of the Greek cities was to be conquered severally by the nearest centralised monarchy of any size; and indeed this eventually happened. During their period, however, of independence, the Athenians based their reputation upon the epic stories of Marathon and Salamis. The Athenian Empire began as an alliance of free cities against the threat of imperialism. From about 472 B.C. its character began to change and in 454 B.C. the treasury of the federation was removed from Delos to Athens. Throughout the period, in fact, of aristocratic leadership from 466 to 428 B.C., the allied cities gradually became colonial territories; subject to Athens, their champion against Persia. Under aristocratic rule, the Athenians might justify their own imperialism or at least find excuses for it. The paternal authority they had accepted for themselves they might logically recommend to others. But when, from about 429 B.C., their rule became more purely democratic—a rule of the people, for the people and by the people— no possible excuse remained for denying to others the complete freedom they claimed for themselves. Of the ethics of the situation the Athenians were fully aware, but they would not forego the advantages of their imperial position. More than that, they enforced their rule with a cynical ferocity which should always be remembered in discussing the merits of the Athenian experiment.

Two examples of Athenian imperialism are particularly worthy of note, both dating from the period immediately following the death of Pericles. It was in 428 B.C. that news came to Athens of the impending desertion of the tributary city of Mitylene—the rulers of which state desired the independence which they in turn denied to Antissa, Eresus and Pyrrha. The Athenians blockaded and besieged Mitylene and finally brought about its surrender. There followed that astonishing debate in which Cleon, the leather-seller, procured a popular decision to massacre the entire Mytalenaean population of military age. Orders were sent to carry out this decree but the debate was resumed on the following day. Defending the decision taken against a plea for mercy put forward by Diodotus, Cleon called for justice:

> . . . warning the assembly that the imperial necessities of Athens essentially required the constant maintenance of a sentiment of fear in the minds of unwilling subjects, and that they must prepare to see their empire pass away if they suffered themselves to be guided either by

compassion for those who, if victors, would have no compassion on them—or by unreasonable moderation towards those who would neither feel nor requite it—or by the mere impression of seductive discourses.[1]

On this occasion the moderate party won, another ship being sent to overtake the first, bearing a cancellation of the previous decree. But even counsels of moderation involved killing over a thousand prisoners in cold blood—instead of the six thousand as at first decided upon. The cruelty involved is less striking, perhaps, than the argument of political expediency put forward to justify it.

An example made of Mytilene, the Athenians then discovered, with Cleon's help, that they could themselves avoid war-taxes simply by doubling the amount of the tribute payable under treaty by the subject cities. This increase was announced in 425, a demand being also sent to the neutral island of Melos, the inhabitants of which had never entered the Athenian Empire at all. They refused to pay but it was not until 416 B.C. that the Athenians had the forces to spare with which to coerce them. In that year an expedition was sent, bearing a demand for the arrears. The Athenian envoys are said by Thucydides to have been perfectly candid about their motives.

> We shall not trouble you with specious pretences, either of how we have a right to our Empire because we overthrew the Persians, or are now attacking you because of wrong that you have done us. You know as well as we do that right, as the world goes, is only in question between equals in power, while the strong do what they can and the weak suffer what they must.[2]

The men of Melos were not prepared to submit. They told the Athenians that the gods would favour the cause of the just. To this the men of Athens replied as candidly as before:

> When you speak of the favour of the gods we may as fairly hope for that as you, neither our pretensions nor our conduct being in any way contrary to what men believe of the gods, or practise among themselves. Of the gods we believe, and of men we know, that by a necessary law of their nature they rule wherever they can. It is not as if we were the first to make this law, or to act upon it when made. We found it in the world before us, and shall leave it in the world after us; all we do is to make use of it, knowing that you and everybody else, having the same power as we have, would do the same as we do. Thus, so far as the gods are concerned, we have no fear at all.[3]

Melos finally surrendered after a siege lasting some months. The Athenians put to death all the grown men and sold all the women

[1] Grote. *op. cit.* pp. 169-172.
[2] *The Greek Commonwealth.* A Zimmern. Oxford, 1952. p. 441.
[3] Zimmern. *op. cit.* pp. 442-443.

and children as slaves. Six months later an Athenian fleet and army was sent to conquer Sicily and failed disastrously. By 412 B.C. most of the Athenian Empire was in revolt.

In foreign policy the Athenians of this same period committed at least one outstanding crime and one outstanding blunder. At the time of the battle of Marathon the state of Athens had had as its sole ally the city of Plataea. When this was besieged by the Peloponnesians, the men of Plataea sent to Athens for help. Assistance was promised in accordance with the existing and old-standing alliance but none was sent. Plataea held out for two years but had then to surrender. What remained of the garrison amounted to 225 men, and these were all put to death.[1] Plataea was only thirty miles from Athens and could have been relieved without much difficulty. But there seemed to be no advantage to be gained by doing so. And the forces which might have saved Plataea in 427 B.C. were actually deployed against Mytilene. Athenian friendship was even more dangerous than Athenian hostility. But the betrayal of Plataea was matched in folly, though not in crime, by the rejection of the Spartan offer of peace in 425 B.C. It was made at a moment when the Athenians were in a strong position. The Spartan envoys were allowed to address the Athenian Assembly and then withdrew. Persuaded by Cleon, the people decided upon impossibly harsh terms. These were communicated to the envoys publicly. Nor were they refused. The envoys merely asked to discuss the terms with commissioners appointed to negotiate. Cleon then said that this proposal proved the dishonesty of their intentions. If they had anything to say, let it be said openly before the assembly. This was agreed with acclamation.

> The Lacedaemonians, seeing that whatever concessions they might be prepared to make in their humiliation it was impossible for them to speak before the multitude and lose credit with their allies for a negotiation in which they might after all miscarry and, on the other hand, that the Athenians would never grant what they asked for upon moderate terms, returned home from Athens with their mission unfulfilled.[2]

It should suffice to say that the Athenians were never to have as favourable an opportunity offered them again.

Lastly, there is the failure in war. Noteworthy in this connection are two events of differing importance but each significant in its own way. The first was the attempt to surprise Mitylene. The plan was to attack the city at the time of a religious festival during which the entire population would have gone to worship at the temple of Apollo Maloeis, leaving their walls deserted. But this plan had to be dis-

[1] Grote. *op. cit.* pp. 179-184. Vol. V.
[2] Zimmern. *op. cit.* pp. 438-439.

cussed in the public assembly, allowing ample time for information to reach the Mitylenaeans, who promptly cancelled the festival and prepared to defend themselves. The second event was the surprising result of the debate in which, following the dismissal of the Spartan envoys, the politician Cleon urged the vigorous prosecution of the war. In doing so he said or implied that he would have done better than the generals were doing. He was instantly challenged to take the command himself. While his political opponents joined in the cry, expecting a failure which would ruin him, his friends took up the challenge on his behalf and urged him to try his hand.

> Friends as well as enemies thus concurred to impose upon Cleon a compulsion not to be eluded. Of all the parties here concerned, those whose conduct is the most unpardonably disgraceful are Nicias and his oligarchal supporters, who force a political enemy into the supreme command against his own strenuous protest, persuaded that he will fail, so as to compromise the lives of many soldiers, and the destinies of the state on an important emergency, but satisfying themselves with the idea that they shall bring him to disgrace and ruin.[1]

In point of fact, Cleon won and returned to Athens in triumph. It was a success more fatal, however, than any defeat could have been, for it encouraged him to assume the command again when the situation was less favourable and so led to the disaster at Amphipolis, largely attributable to Cleon's inexperience and panic.

What is most significant about this affair is not the defeat of Athens but the extent to which its internal politics could jeopardise its security. When party feeling runs so high that a commander comes to be appointed through the influence of those who hope for his defeat, the prospects of the campaign are poor indeed. It is true that the decline of the Athenian Empire was due to many factors unconnected with the Athenian form of government. Neither Lycurgus nor Demetrius of Phalerum could have restored Athenian hegemony even had they tried. But the fact remains that the Athenian experiment revealed where democracy is likely to fail. It proved that the voters of an imperialist state may pay little heed to the welfare of their subject peoples. It tended to prove that the voters may prove unmindful of any obligations or alliances concluded by their predecessors but since found to be inconvenient. It also seemed to suggest that the party struggles within a democratic state may confuse its military effort. It would have been rash to conclude then as it would be to agree now that every democratic state is bound to commit exactly these mistakes. Still less should we forget that states ruled on quite opposite principles have come to grief for different reasons—or even for the same reasons. But we may be justified in thinking that these

[1] Grote. *op. cit.* Vol. V. p. 256.

are the errors to which a democracy is most exposed. They may be avoided perhaps but we need at least to know that they are there.

The Athenian experiment in democracy is the more worthy of study in that its results were confirmed, to some extent, in the histories of the other Greek City States; cities about which less is known. The process by which aristocracy turns into democracy was repeated in Corinth, Thourioi, Naxos and Cyrene.[1] The struggle, the class war, between the more and the less prosperous citizens was at least a common feature in these other cities. At Miletus in 630 B.C. there were two parties, called respectively 'The Wealthy' and 'The Handworkers'.[2] At Cyrene five hundred of the wealthy were executed in the course of the revolution of 401 B.C. Such revolutions were fairly common, although by no means invariable, and usually (not always) led to a counter-revolution at some later date. It was the resulting variety in forms of rule which afforded the Greek theorists their opportunity for comparison—a better opportunity perhaps than any thinker has had since. Nor was it wasted. The scholars of the Lyceum in Athens were able to collect and compare the constitutions of a hundred and fifty-eight cities. They had seen many democracies in their rise, their fulfilment, their decay and their collapse. They felt more ready to generalise than do modern theorists whose experience is so much less. And what do they conclude?

> A democracy then, as I imagine, arises when the poor, prevailing over the rich, kill some and banish others, and share the places in the republic and the magistracies equally among the remainder. . . .[3]

Plato goes on to describe how democracy may turn into anarchy, the magistrates losing their authority over the people and the elders losing their authority over the young.

> Just as if . . . a father should accustom himself to resemble a child and to be afraid of his sons, and the son . . . neither to revere nor to stand in awe of his parents, that so indeed he may be free. . . . The teacher in such a city fears and flatters the scholars and the scholars despise their teachers. . . . And in general the youth resemble the more advanced in years, and rival it with them both in words and deeds: and the old men sitting down with the young, are full of merriment and pleasantry, mimicking the youth, that they may not appear to be morose and despotic.

Plato continues from there to show how employers lose control of their slaves and husbands of their wives until finally even the domestic animals claim their independence.

[1] *Greek City-States.* Kathleen Freeman. London, 1950.
[2] K. Freeman. *op. cit.* p. 140.
[3] *The Republic of Plato.* Trans. by H. Spens. Everyman, 1927. (Eighth Book). p. 270.

> . . . For readily even the puppies, according to the proverb, resemble
> their mistresses; and the horses and asses are accustomed to go freely
> and gracefully, marching up against any one they meet on the road
> unless he give way. . . .[1]

Aristotle generalises as boldly from an even wider experience.
Liberty, he says, is the first principle of democracy. 'The results of
liberty are that the numerical majority is supreme, and that each man
lives as he likes.'[2] Democracy, he realises, will lead to a demand that
all should have equal possessions as well as equal rights (Book II).

> For the real difference between democracy and oligarchy is poverty
> and wealth. Wherever men rule by reason of their wealth, whether they
> be few or many, that is an oligarchy, and where the poor rule, that is a
> democracy. . . [3]

He returns to the theme in Book VI:

> . . . Every citizen, it is said, must have equality, and therefore in a
> democracy the poor have more power than the rich, because there are
> more of them, and the will of the majority is supreme.[4]

What the will of the majority is likely to be, in at least one respect,
Aristotle very well knows:

> . . . Democrats say that justice is that to which the majority agree . . . if
> justice is the will of the majority . . . they will unjustly confiscate the
> property of the wealthy minority.[5]

Some would deny that such a confiscation is unjust. But the rights
and wrongs are not to our present purpose. What is significant is that
Aristotle, having carefully collated the political experience of a wide
variety of Greek City States, is able to assure us that Athens was not
exceptional. Democracy was tried repeatedly, in different places and
for differing periods of time, and if any one conclusion can be reached
from a study of the results it is that democracy will lead, sooner or
later, to socialism.

---

[1] Plato. op. cit. p. 278.
[2] Aristotle's Politics. Trans. by Benjamin Jowett. Oxford, 1931. Analysis, p. 19.
[3] Aristotle. op. cit. Book III. p. 116.
[4] Ibid. p. 239.
[5] Ibid. p. 241.

CHAPTER XIV

Democracy at Rome

THE democratic phase in Roman history is so brief that a cursory treatment of Roman political institutions is apt to give the impression that Rome passed directly from aristocracy to Dictatorship and Empire. This is not quite true. Rome passed through the same stages as Athens had done but with a different emphasis in point of time. Rome presented a far bigger problem than Athens had ever done; bigger in area and in population. So that there could be far less pretence of collecting a representative gathering of the people. Nor, had this been done, would it have been easy for any one speaker to address them. Nevertheless, the Roman constitution was basically that of a Greek city, with democratic assemblies playing a theoretically important part. When the Roman aristocracy began to lose grip, the attempt to make Rome a democracy was facilitated by the existence of institutions and laws which had only to be revived.

The aristocratic governance of Rome rested, in its later period, upon the concrete success of the second Punic War. But the two parties, the exclusive and the excluded, were in existence and the prestige of the former tended to decline, more especially during the third Macedonian war. It could be argued that the ruling class had been corrupted by wealth.

> Opposed to the rule of such an oligarchy were many of the dispossessed, who longed for economic security; many of the plain citizens, who longed for an efficient and civil government; the more ambitious members of the rising Equestrian Order, who longed for political power; and such aristocrats as had fallen on evil times, or were for some reason or other at variance with those in power, and longed for dignitas.
>
> When their power and the title to it were challenged, the ruling oligarchy, perhaps with complacent self-praise, or in an attempt to give their social and political supremacy an air of moral superiority, were pleased to consider and call themselves Optimates. . . .[1]

Leader of the Populares, as the opposition party was called, was Tiberius Gracchus, Tribune in 133 B.C. He tried to revive the practice of bringing legislation before the popular assembly without submit-

[1] *Libertas as a political idea at Rome during the late Republic and early Principate.* Ch. Wirszubski. Cambridge, 1950. p. 39.

ting it to Senate. He succeeded for the moment by rather questionable means but was killed soon afterwards in a faction fight. The democratic party, inactive for nine years, was revived by Gaius Gracchus, a revolutionary intent on avenging his brother's death. Securing election as Tribune in 124 B.C., he relied for his power upon the populace of Rome. Perhaps his most significant piece of legislation was the Lex Frumentaria under which corn was bought by the State and sold to the citizens at less than the market price.[1] This first law of the kind fell short of the Athenian direct payment to voters but led to further and similar bids for popular favour, ending in the logical outcome of 58 B.C. when Clodius made the distribution entirely free.

Socialist measures of this kind could be financed only from two sources; taxation of the wealthy or taxation of the Empire. Gaius Gracchus chose the latter method. His brother had chosen the former, passing (or rather reviving) a law which allowed the State to confiscate land owned by individuals in excess of a fixed maximum acreage, and redistribute it among the landless. Land had been in fact confiscated, at a low compensation, under this law. Gaius now altered the system of taxation in the wealthiest of the Roman provinces, that of Asia. Hitherto the provincials had paid moderate taxes, raising them themselves.

> This system was now abolished: extensive direct and indirect taxes were imposed, and the usual method of collecting them through tax-farmers was adopted as in Sicily and Sardinia with this important distinction—instead of being put up to auction in the provinces, as was done in these two cases, so that the contracts were often undertaken by provincial companies, it was enacted that the taxes of the whole province should be leased at Rome, so that the provincials themselves were practically excluded. The general result was that Asia became the scene of most scandalous extortion. . . . [2]

The democratic movement thus included some of the main features of Athenian democracy. Nor was it altogether resisted by the aristocrats, for these had split, in normal fashion, the Optimates being opposed when most reactionary by a group of moderates—an aristocratic party which centred at one time on the younger Scipio. Weakened by disunity among themselves, the Senators watched the process by which political sovereignty was transferred from the Senate to the Comitia. Gracchus had managed to unite against the aristocracy the wealthier citizens of other than noble birth and the poor citizens now living, in part, at the public expense. While this alliance held, the democratic group could continue to rule Rome. It became the object of the Senatorial party to split the coalition, which

[1] *The Cambridge Ancient History*. Vol. IX, 1932. pp. 59, 165 and 524.
[2] *A Constitutional and Political History of Rome from the earliest times to the reign of Domitian*. T. M. Taylor. London, 1899. p. 256.

Livius Drusus did by the simple means of outbidding Gracchus in generosity at the Treasury's expense. Gracchus failed to secure re-election in 121 B.C. and was killed in the riots which were now a feature of these political contests. For a time there was an uneasy balance of power, accompanied by serious military disaster in Numidia; a capitulation due at least in part to the absence of the Consul, Spurius Albinus, in Rome at the time of the elections. Shortly afterwards a successful general of the Senatorial party was recalled as a result of democratic pressure. Worse was to follow in 105 B.C. when a costly defeat, with 80,000 casualties, was attributed to the mutual hostility of two generals, one aristocratic and the other not. The democratic party reached its peak of success in 100 B.C. when the popular leader Saturninus was in alliance with the general, Marius. It must then have seemed inevitable that Rome should become and for long remain a democracy.

If the establishment of a persistently democratic form of rule seemed probable then, it would equally seem now, in retrospect, that all the elements needed were present. The Republican aristocracy had lost all special claim to respect. The trade expansion which had followed the Punic Wars and the revenues since drawn from Sicily, Spain, Macedonia and Africa had opened a vast field for political corruption. What had been an aristocracy had become an oligarchy, with direct or indirect financial interests in tax-farming, banking and contracting. The middle class, the peasant soldiers of an earlier period, had mostly vanished; partly as a result of war casualties and partly through the ruin of soldiers exiled by war from their land. The landless citizens who flocked into Rome formed an idle and demoralised urban population of voters. In 104 B.C. the Tribune Philippus thus declared that there were not 2,000 landowners in the citizen body—which then numbered 394,000, mostly proletarians. Mixed farming had declined, land being devoted more to olives, vineyards and garden-produce. Food was mostly imported and distributed at below cost price. The populace was led by professional politicians of obscure birth and the oligarchs had been compelled to retreat from one position to another until little remained of their prestige and less of their effective power.

Why did no fairly permanent democracy result? The main obstacle to the establishment of a democratic form of government lay in the mere size of the problem. The Athenians were relatively few and could make some pretence of assembling a representative body of citizens to conduct public business on democratic lines. But the practical difficulty (and doubtful wisdom) of assembling the citizens of Rome was manifest. The eventual result could only be chaos, as the more responsible citizens could see for themselves. Even, however, if the practical problems were solved, the decisions reached would not be democratic in any real sense of the word. The vote did not extend to the rest of Italy, still less to the Roman Empire as a whole. Nor could it be extended more widely against the opposition of those already voting. The decisions made would nevertheless affect a vast and growing territory—countries which the Roman voters had never seen and could not, perhaps, have even found on the map. There was far less moral basis for a democracy in Rome than there had been for democracy in Athens. In the most careful analysis, it did not even make sense.

The only possible means of establishing anything like a real democracy would have been to extend citizenship to the empire and devise some means of representation of the provincial interests at Rome. As a result of the revolt called 'The Social War', an attempt was in fact made to extend the franchise. The Lex Julia and Lex Plantia Papiria (of about 90 B.C.) extended the franchise widely in Italy but there was little danger of the newly enrolled citizens (who brought the total to 910,000) appearing in great numbers to exercise their rights. Nor does it seem that any system of representation was ever seriously discussed. The practical difficulty then (as now) of reforming an electoral system is that those actually in power are usually well satisfied with the process which brought them into office. Those in opposition are more disposed to be critical but only so long as they are powerless. So little was done and Rome steadily progressed towards anarchy, an interesting feature of which was the debasement of the currency as a means of financing the continuance of the dole.

From about 99 B.C. there began a reaction against democracy, supported clearly by a body of moderate opinion. The political struggle fluctuated but the Consul Sulla was able, with the use of force, to restore the power of the Senate. In doing so, he had some of the democratic leaders put to death. He then strengthened the Senate by the addition of another 300 members and enacted a law under which no measure could be brought before the Comitia without the Senate's prior consent. The democratic experiment was almost at an end. It did not end completely, however, until 82 B.C. when Sulla, returning to Rome from the East, defeated the democrats at the Colline Gate—not, however, before they had massacred the leaders of the Optimates. Sulla, who was extremely able but not personally ambitious, set about the task of restoring the republic. He was appointed Dictator and was perhaps the first to hold that office by name in its modern sense.

The first chapter of Sulla's rule opened with the most awful incident in the history of Rome. In virtue of his unlimited power he outlawed all who had fought under the flag of the Democratic party, except those who had submitted to him on his return; their lives were forfeited, their property confiscated and sold, their descendants debarred from all political preferment. This general proclamation was soon replaced by a formal list of those to be despatched; it contained 4,700 names. . . .[1]

The democrats thus eliminated, at least for the time being, Sulla restored to the Senate all and more than all its previous powers.

The authority and power of the Senate were increased at the cost of the tribunes and the popular assembly. All the rights it had enjoyed before the legislation of the Gracchi were now restored to it. To Sulla it was obvious that the Senate could, and the rabble of Rome could not, govern a world-wide state. . . .[2]

What may have been obvious then is less obvious to us now. For a Senate in which all leaders, on either side, had been killed, and in which all that remained were in fear of the same fate was not, in practice, a very effective body of men. Sulla nevertheless relinquished his dictatorship in 79 B.C., apparently expecting the Republic to take on a new lease of life. It did not do that and indeed it barely survived Sulla's death in the following year.

Whatever Sulla's precept may have been, his example had mainly served to demonstrate with what ease a successful general might become dictator. Nor did Senate prove able to cope even with a revival of the democrats. As Heitland says:

The death of Sulla ushers in the final period of revolution, the period in which the Roman Republic, deprived of its master, proved that it could not do without one.[3]

The period from 78 to 59 B.C. saw the rise of new generals under the uncertain rule of the restored oligarchy. Two events of the greatest political significance were the Catilinian conspiracy and the election of Julius Caesar as Pontifex Maximus. The conspiracy of Catiline, had it succeeded, would have led to a general and virtually anarchist attack on property, accompanied by a massacre of the wealthy. It was foiled but in such a way as to reveal the government's essential weakness. The attempt to rule an Empire through the political machinery of a Greek City State was coming to an end.[4] And the election of Julius Caesar as Pontiff or Chief Priest was a hint of the sort of rule which was destined to take its place. Only a divine ruler could

[1] T. M. Taylor. *op. cit.* p. 295.
[2] *A History of the Ancient World.* M. Rostovtzeff. Vol. II. Trans. by J. D. Duff. Oxford, 1928. p. 125.
[3] *The Roman Republic.* W. E. Heitland. Cambridge, 1923. Vol. III. p. 1.
[4] See *The Roman Revolution.* R. Syme. Oxford, 1939. See also *The Roman Middle Class in the Republican Period.* H. Hill. Oxford, 1952.

effectively control the territories which the Republic had conquered. The Republic, if weakened by its occasional military failures, was essentially killed by its own military success.

That a successful general should make himself ruler, to the intense relief of all but the fanatics, was inevitable. The Roman constitution provided no executive body and no permanent officials. It provided no administration comparable with that of Egypt, Persia or China. It lacked, above all, the focus which could be given only by a deified head. And what is particularly interesting is the early date by which this last need was perceived by one who was in a posititon to supply it.

Julius Caesar belonged to a family, to begin with, of divine descent. He could and did claim Aeneas of Troy as his ancestor, and Aeneas was the son of Venus. He also claimed a descent from the Alban kings, and they in turn were descendants of Mars. 'The connection with Venus was always emphasized more than the less well authenticated descent from Mars'.[1] Public mention was made of this claim as early as 68 B.C. Then came his election as Pontiff, as heir therefore to nearly all the religious functions of the old Roman kings. Familiar as he was through his military life with Asia, Cilicia and Bithynia, he knew all about the oriental conception of monarchy. Anything he did not know about its practical application he learnt later on in Egypt. Caesar's first Consulship began in 59 B.C. By 44 B.C. he had been elected Dictator for life. What his political programme would have been had he lived long enough to fulfil it, we are not to know. What we do know is the fact of his virtual deification. It centred, first of all, on the temple of Venus Genetrix—on Venus considered as mother of the Julian house. This was built in the Forum and Caesar's statue was erected in front of it. Nor was this all. A further statue of him in the temple of Quirinus was set up in 45 B.C. with the inscription 'To the unconquered god'. In the following year he was given the title of 'parens patriae'.

> In the other honors we find Caesar not so much of the father of the Roman state as the heir of the Hellenistic kings. His birthday was made a festival on which public sacrifices should be made; it was provided that annual sacrifices for his safety should be undertaken and that each year the magistrates should swear to uphold his acts. Games to be celebrated in his honor every four years were decreed and a day in his name was added to each of the great festivals of Rome. . . . It was voted to build a temple to Concordia Nova because it was through him that men enjoyed peace and concord. The name of the month Quinctilis was changed to Julius. . . . But the final step came when the senate decreed him to be a god and commanded the erection of a temple to

[1] *The Divinity of the Roman Emperor*. L. R. Taylor. Connecticut .1931. p. 59.

him and his *Clementia*, thus formally providing for his enshrinement in state cult. . . .[1]

Caesar's death at the hands of enraged republicans led only to the eventual installation of his nephew in the place that he had come to occupy. What is more significant, perhaps, about this succession was that Augustus, relinquishing all claim to be Dictator and preferring to be called Princeps or First Citizen, was careful to uphold his uncle's divinity and later, in due course, to assert his own. It was the religious aspect of Julius Caesar's position that he chose to inherit.

It was a mere ninety years from the first assertion of democracy in Rome to the time when Julius Caesar was installed not merely as dictator but as god. Within that short space occurred all the democratic movements from that led by Tiberius Gracchus to that led by Catiline. In the process we can trace how oligarchy at Rome turned into democracy, how democracy involved class-war and socialist revolution, how class-war led to chaos and how dictatorship resulted in turn from that. The process at Rome was unusually rapid. Most rapid of all, however, was the process by which the dictator was made a deified king. The change from a republican austerity to a deified kingship was well within the space of fifteen years. Nor was it the corruption of an institution that had been good in itself. It was, rather, the only way out of a situation that had become intolerable.

[1] L. R. Taylor. *op. cit.* p. 67.

CHAPTER XV

Democracy justified by Religion

THE rule of the many means in theory that the more important issues should be decided by a majority vote of those to whom the franchise is extended. This theory implies a political equality between those voting, one vote being as good as another. We know of devices that have been used to give an unequal value to the votes cast but these we associate with states tending, like Rome, towards the rule of the few. Democratic theory rests on the assumption that the voters are, at least for political purposes, equal. The democrat, when faced with the fact that those who are politically equal are economically divided into classes which are unequal in every other way, has a choice between two lines of policy. He can either assert that it is only political equality that matters and that other distinctions, while present, are trivial. Or else he can demand the abolition of all economic inequalities so that citizens declared to be politically equal are then made as equal as possible in all other respects. In practice, the first argument is difficult to sustain. The tramp selling matches on the curb may be the political equal of the millionaire who sweeps past him in a high-powered car. Each has but one vote and both are subject to the same laws. To most people, however, (and especially to the tramp) the inequality of their circumstances would seem to be more striking than the special sense in which their privileges are the same. The democrat tends therefore to adopt the other line of argument. Citizens equal in one respect should be made equal in all. The experience at least of Greece and Rome, in so far as it is recorded, suggests that democracy leads directly to socialism—the equalising of all incomes with the possible exception of those enjoyed by the socialist thinkers themselves. Nor is it easy to see how it could possibly be otherwise. The same experience would suggest that socialism will tend to lead in turn to anarchy, bloodshed and dictatorship.

An exception, however, to this probable sequence is offered by communities in which a practical equality has existed from the first. These are the monasteries founded by the stricter adherents of a revealed religion. It is manifest that a monastery offers the perfect setting for democratic experiment. The inmates will readily concede their equality in the sight of God, to whose service they are all equally dedicated. They have no possessions. Their education will have been virtually the same. They are celibate, childless and abstemious. No one can be superior to another in wealth, marriage or posterity, and any differences which may result from birth or upbringing will tend to disappear. It is not surprising, therefore, to find that later democratic theory is rooted in revealed religion and that democratic practice derives, in part, from monastic rule.

Buddhism originates, as we have seen, in a part of India where a type of democracy was known. Whether from that origin or from the nature of monasticism itself, Buddhist monks evolved a democratic organisation within what was necessarily a theocratic framework. Rule of a Buddhist monastery was vested in a full meeting of its members. Unanimity was desired but, when this was unobtainable, a majority vote would suffice. The rules of procedure, however, were strict. There had to be a quorum, a minimum number present. Every motion had to pass two or four readings, the first being formal. Any motion might be referred to a committee, either as a form of closure or because irrelevant and pointless speeches were being made. And the vote could be taken in three ways; the open vote (by a show of hands or some similar means), the whispering vote (in which the teller was told in a whisper by each monk in turn) and the secret vote. This last method was the most scientific. Coloured wooden pins or tickets were distributed, each monk taking one secretly and showing it to no one else. When the count had been made, the result had to be accepted. But to this rule there were two exceptions. The proceedings were void if there had been an irregularity of procedure. They were void also if they could be shown to be unconstitutional—contrary, that is to say, to Buddhist scripture. If valid in every way, the decision taken was referred to as an Act.

It is of special interest to note that Buddhist procedure was far in advance of anything evolved in Athens or Rome. It was far in advance, for that matter, of British practice now. It spread to China and Japan and remains as the sovereign power in Tibet. What is difficult, however, is to establish a definite connection between the monastic democracies of Buddhism and Christianity. For the present it may suffice to point out that the same features appear in each. The monasteries of Christendom held regular 'Chapter' meetings at which members voted on matters of common business. They also held conferences of each 'Order', attended by representatives of the different monasteries, and it was perhaps at these that the idea of elected representation was first evolved. Wherever founded and in whatever faith, the monasteries provided a useful background for

[1] See *Theory of Government in Ancient India*. Beni Prasad. Allahabad, 1927 pp. 321-330.

democratic experiment. For the equality which in the world at large is a theory becomes, in a monastery, more nearly a fact.

But monastic equality is only one contribution made by the revealed religions to democratic theory. Buddhism, Christianity and Islam are at one in stressing the concept of human equality before God. The idea in its simplest form is merely that differences in strength, size and intelligence as between one human being and another can be scarcely perceptible from heaven. There is furthermore a basic equality in the facts of birth, childhood, mating, sickness, senility and death. Buddhist equality is on a long-term basis but runs counter nevertheless to the Hindu institution of Caste. Christian equality is based on the doctrine of the fatherhood of God, in the light of which the believers are equal as brethren. Muslim equality runs counter to Arab tribal differences, instituting a fictitious kinship in the faith which extends a religious equality to all followers of Islam. It cannot be said, however, that these religious concepts had initially much political effect. Buddhism has normally existed alongside ordinary types of government. Christianity in its Catholic form has always allowed of a certain inequality as between priest and layman. Nor has it proved incompatible with a variety of political institutions. As for Islam, its democratic theory has rarely tended towards democratic practice. It is important to remember, in this connection, that a strong belief in the after-life provides a poor motive for seeking equality in this.

A theoretical religious equality had little practical application in Europe until the period of the Reformation. It remained important, nevertheless, in restraining the lengths to which inequality might otherwise have gone. The Christian ruler might claim divine right but he could not claim divine descent, Christ having been childless. There were priests at hand to remind him that he was only human and mortal. He ran little risk of being deified. And the idea of human equality, based on religious doctrine, was at least latent among the peasantry. It found expression in occasional peasant revolts. During one of these, in England, the rebels chanted 'When Adam delved and Eve span, who was then the gentleman?' What is most significant about this slogan is not the political sentiment so much as the biblical context. Although subject to feudal rule, the catholic peasants attended church and were taught a faith which implied (while not stressing) a basic equality in baptism, communion and burial. In the sixteenth century this aspect of Christianity received more publicity, partly through the laity's access to holy writ and partly because the devout sometimes found themselves subject to rulers who were not of the same sect. If oppressed by a heretic, the people surely had the right —in fact, the duty—to rebel. But such a right would seem to suggest that sovereignty lay, and had always lain, in the people themselves. An acquaintance with classical literature, by then becoming less exceptional among laymen, also led to talk about the democracies of ancient Greece. Reluctant theologians were driven to defending the idea of equality, if only among their co-religionists.

So the first practical support for democracy in modern Europe came from religious minorities intent on justifying their resistance to persecution. These minorities, were Catholic or Protestant, were often composed of quite humble people. Having lost their natural leaders, whom they had to regard as heretical, they vested authority in themselves. Lainey, second General of the Society of Jesus, said something about the sovereignty of the people in 1562, at the Council of Trent. The idea was put forward by Mariana in 1598 and again in 1599 in a work dedicated to Philip III. Another writer, Rossaeus, explained 'that the people can extend, restrain, change, and, if circumstances demand it, completely suppress their government and institute another, under another form'. The Jesuit Suarez defended the people against their ruler, the poor against the rich. He was upholding the doctrine intended, however, for Catholic subjects under Protestant rulers. Less was heard of it in the France of Louis XIV, where democratic ideas were mostly confined to protestants, and protestants mostly confined to jail. In England, similarly, democratic theory first became coherent among extreme protestants who found Queen Elizabeth's Church of England not protestant enough. They could not admit the rightful power of King, Parliament, Bishops or Gentry and were driven therefore to conclude that political power should be vested in themselves, a minority of people really in touch with God. As Hobbes remarked,

> For after the Bible was translated into English every man, nay every boy and every wench that could read English, thought they spoke with God Almighty and understood what he said.[1]

The fact that the idea of human equality should spring up among persecuted Huguenots in France and dour Calvinists in Scotland may serve at least to remind us that the idea is religious. It came to the fore among the seventeenth century Puritans and went with them to America. It reached America separately from Holland and Switzerland. 'Let not Geneva be forgotten or despised' wrote John Adams, second President of the United States. It is true that Puritan equality did not extend to catholics or negroes. It did not even extend to Puritans of a different sect. We read of Fifth Monarchy Men, Baptists and Levellers, as also of Quakers, whose 'counterfeited

---

[1] *Hobbes.* G. P. Gooch. London, 1939.

simplicity renders them the more dangerous'.[1] These and the avowed communists or Diggers, the extreme party led by Winstanley, were never conspicuous for their tolerance of each other. They were agreed, however, in opposing any idea of inequality based on ancestry. To the inequalities of wealth they opposed a far less united front. They achieved, nevertheless, and transmitted to later British nonconformists a vague idea that men are equal, in some sense, at birth. They would not accept any claim to superiority based on descent, courage, manners, speech or dress. Some would even reject a claim to superiority based upon worldly success. All, however, would assert their own claim to an intimate footing with God. When democratic ideas of quite different origin reached England in the late eighteenth century, they were welcome, up to a point, among people already steeped in nonconformity. And, later, it was upon a foundation of nonconformity that the British Labour Party was built.

Puritanism found another home, as we have seen, in the American colonies. The godly colonists of New England received great encouragement when the Roundheads triumphed in the Civil War and were correspondingly estranged from England when the monarchy was restored. They were still more estranged when the English monarchy showed signs of life in the person of George III. People of republican views formed the hard core of the American resistance to England. Their success in the War of Independence (with French help) caused in Europe a wave of republican and egalitarian sentiment, derived indirectly from Republican Holland and Roundhead England. Instead of looking, as some had done, to the success of the aristocratic government of England, thinkers began to take their inspiration from the United States; as many of them still do.

Of the revealed religions Christianity is almost alone in having made a significant contribution to democratic theory and practice. But that contribution, however historically important, is extremely limited in scope. From the doctrine of the fatherhood of god has been derived the notion of the brotherhood, and therefore the equality, of man. This concept, based upon Christ's revelation, is perhaps our sole authority for the statement commonly made that men are or should be politically equal to each other. Christian doctrine has little else to offer in this field of thought and Christian custom adds nothing but some monastic techniques of debate which could as readily have derived from Buddhism. Much has been made of particular texts, like that of rendering to Caesar the things that are Caesar's. But the unreality of conclusions based on such a text is

[1] See *English democratic ideas in the Seventeenth Century.* G. P. Gooch. 2nd ed. Cambridge, 1927. See also *The Good Old Cause, the English Revolution of 1640-60.* Christopher Hill and Edmund Dell. London, 1949.

manifest. Christ was obviously not concerned with politics at all. What he had to say on the subject was not intended as political guidance and can mean very little when taken from its context. Christ having taught that men are brothers in the faith, a later theorist can explain the inference that all adult citizens should be equally entitled to vote. But that was not what Christ was talking about. That was not the message he was trying to convey. We have no means of knowing what he would have thought of a ballot-box had he been shown one, but what evidence there is would indicate no likelihood of his expressing even the most polite interest. Attempts to extract political advice from the new Testament are unscholarly, dishonest or absurd.

But there has been one religious leader to whom politics mattered rather more. This was Mahatma Gandhi. If the democracy of the future is to be based upon revealed religion, Gandhi must clearly be the prophet to whom democrats must turn. Of recent years, Gandhi is, in fact, almost alone in having anything new or useful to say about democracy. He is and will almost certainly remain the greatest democratic thinker of the twentieth century. But the ideals in which Gandhi believed were rooted in Hindu soil. He was well acquainted with Christian doctrines, some of which he could approve, but he stood apart from such democratic thought as can be traced back to ancient Greece. He was too religious a man to accept any separation of religious, social and political ideas. As Nirmal Kumar Bose puts it:

> The foundation of Mahatma Gandhi's life is formed by his firm faith in God. He looks upon God as that Universal Being which en-compasses everything and of which humanity is one small part. God is also the Law working behind all that manifests itself to us through the senses; for the Law and the Law-maker are not distinguishable from one another. . . . The highest aim of human life is to try to dis-cover the Law, and while so doing to purify every act of our life in conformity with the Law, in so far as it has been revealed to us by enquiry.[1]

With this faith, Gandhi built up a body of political ideas in which the existence and the will of God is rather assumed than proved. His knowledge of God was gained and strengthened by personal religious experience. His conception of God, although subtle and comprehen-sive, allowed him to receive direct and personal guidance. He heard 'Voices' and in this resembled both Socrates and Joan of Arc.[2] Nor was he prepared to prove the existence of God by any purely rational argument. His belief amounted to a certainty in itself. As against this, he wanted his ideal State to be secular. He would have no State

[1] *Studies in Gandhism.* Nirmal Kumar Bose. Calcutta, 2nd ed., 1947. p. 337.
[2] *The Political Philosophy of Mahatma Gandhi.* Gopinath Dhawan. Ahmedabad, 1946. p. 48.

religion even if there were doctrinal agreement among all. 'If I were a dictator, religion and State would be separate. I swear by my religion. I will die for it. But it is my personal affair. The State has nothing to do with it. . . .'[1] In this there is an apparent contradiction. He would have the State secular but calls in God to draw up the constitution. The process of reasoning by which he would justify his political ideas is an essentially religious process and unacceptable to those who would question his first axiom.

Gandhi's views cannot, however, be disposed of as quickly as that. For his conclusions are at least partly based upon a worldly experience which his critics must allow to be valid. His observation was exceptionally acute and he had a wide and practical knowledge of affairs. He was a barrister-at-law, not without practice. He had travelled in Europe and South Africa, organised an ambulance Corps, edited a Journal and made himself the leader of a political party. He might be a saint but he was certainly not a fool. And, as compared with many theorists, he knew what he was talking about. He realised, as he was bound to do, that politics are, at best, an unavoidable evil. 'If I seem to take part in politics', he said, 'it is only because politics to-day encircle us like the coils of a snake. . . .'[2]

In the ideal State, he held, like Karl Marx, politics would become needless. Until then, they are unavoidable, even for one whose main interests are religious. As he put it, 'those who say that religion has nothing to do with politics, do not know what religion means'.[3] He might have added that they do not know what politics mean either.

It would have been at least normal for Gandhi to have returned from his travels to India, convinced (as so many Indians have been convinced) that all India needed was independence and a democracy on western lines. But Gandhi wanted to be free of English ideas as well as free of English control, and the impression he gained of British democracy was that it was a dismal failure. It leads, he thought, to nothing but imperialism, exploitation, corruption, instability and war. Parliaments he thought a dreary waste of time and money. He considered the Members of Parliament hypocritical, selfish and lazy. The conclusions they reached were not even final. 'What is done to-day may be undone tomorrow'.[4] He thought the voters as fickle as Parliament, led by dishonest journalism and exploited by the ruling classes. He summarised his conclusions in 1934 in these words:—

> Western democracy is on its trial. If it has already proved a failure, may it be reserved to India to evolve the true science of democracy by

[1] Gopinath Dhawan. *op. cit.* p. 239.
[2] Gopinath Dhawan. *op. cit.* p. 42.
[3] *Ibid.*
[4] Gopinath Dhawan. *op. cit.* pp. 332-333.

giving a visible demonstration. . . . Corruption and hypocrisy ought not to be the inevitable products of democracy, as they undoubtedly are today. Nor is bulk the true test of democracy. True democracy is not inconsistent with a few persons representing the spirit, the hope and the aspiration of those whom they claim to represent. I hold that democracy cannot be evolved by forcible method. The spirit of democracy cannot be imposed from without. It has to come from within.

He expands this last thought in another context, maintaining that the right to vote in the democratic States has proved a burden to the people because it has been obtained by pressure rather than by acquiring the fitness to use it. In his view a right could only be earned by the performance of a duty. Self-government in a State could only be the sum total of the self-control shown by the citizens. He did not merely deny that the right which has not been earned is wrongly acquired. He denied that it had been acquired at all. 'The true source of rights is duty . . .' he said publicly in 1925. 'If leaving duties unperformed we run after rights, they will escape us like a will o' the wisp. The more we pursue them the further they will fly'. Gandhi was not uninfluenced by western ideas. He corresponded with Tolstoy. He had once fallen under the spell of Ruskin.[1] But for western democratic practice he had no use at all.

What he had recognised was the dilemma which the Greeks had found in their earliest experiments in democratic rule. In any naturally formed human society one effect of civilisation will be to divide people into rich and poor. Make the people sovereign and the poor will use the machinery of government to dispossess the rich. By the time they have done so the government will have become an over-centralised tyranny, probably under a dictator. The whole sequence is of a kind familiar to the Hindus, resembling their own conception of the Wheel of Life. And Gandhi saw that the only escape is to remove the desire for gain which is the motive force throughout. He thought of the wealthy and the downtrodden as both criminal and both in fact committing the same crime. The organising of large-scale industry, the source of disproportionate wealth and poverty, is itself sinful. Gopinath Dhawan thus summarises Gandhi's views on this question:—

> . . . Conscious adoption of handicrafts is an important step towards world peace in so far as mass production, which can only subsist on the control of large markets, is the mainspring of modern international rivalries, imperialistic exploitation and wars.
> In national affairs large-scale industry vitiates democracy. For it leads to concentration of economic power and this implies corres-

[1] *Gandhi, an Autobiography.* Trans. by Mahadev Desai. London, 1949. p. 248.

ponding concentration of political power and the ever present possibility of the abuse of such power.

Mass production degrades workers and deprives them of their dignity and worth. It uproots them from the purity and naturalness of domestic atmosphere in rural areas, baulks their creative urge and turns them into mere statistical units.[1]

Gandhi emphasised that it is not merely capitalism that is evil but industry itself.

Machinery has begun to desolate Europe. Ruination is knocking at the English gates. Machinery is the chief symbol of modern civilization, it represents a great sin. . . .

Industrialism is, I am afraid, going to be a curse for mankind. Industrialism depends entirely on your capacity to exploit, on foreign markets being open to you, and on the absence of competitors. . . . The fact is that this industrial civilization is a disease because it is all evil.[2]

Here he was at one with William Morris and G. K. Chesterton. Nor would he agree for a moment with those who think to mitigate the evils of industrialism by a policy of nationalisation. For that could only mean transferring to the State a power which is quite dangerous enough even in the hands of individuals.

I look upon an increase in the power of the state with the greatest fear because, although while apparently doing good by minimizing exploitation, it does the greatest harm to mankind by destroying individuality which lies at the root of all progress.

The state represents violence in a concentrated and organized form. The individual has a soul, but as the state is a soulless machine, it can never be weaned from violence to which it owes its very existence.

It is my firm conviction that if the state suppressed capitalism by violence, it will be caught in the coils of violence itself and fail to develop non-violence at any time.

What I would personally prefer would be, not a centralization of power in the hands of the state but an extension of the sense of trusteeship; as in my opinion, the violence of private ownership is less injurious than the violence of the state.[3]

Gandhi saw that democracy and spiritual unity is impossible in a State torn apart by the conflict between the rich and the poor. But the only way to bring about economic equality is by example and argument.

. . . To induce the rich to accept the ideal of economic equality and hold their wealth in trust for the poor, he would depend upon persuasion,

[1] Gopinath Dhawan. op. cit. p. 222.
[2] Studies in Gandhism. Nirmal Kumar Bose. 2nd ed. Calcutta, 1947. p. 30.
[3] Selected writings of Mahatma Gandhi. Selected and introduced by R. Duncan. London, 1951. pp. 244-245.

education, non-violent non-co-operation and other non-violent means. According to Gandhiji the theory of the trusteeship of the wealthy for their superfluous wealth lies at the root of the doctrine of equal distribution. The only alternative to trusteeship is confiscation through violence. But by resorting to violence society will be poorer 'for it will lose the gifts of a man who knows how to accumulate wealth'. Non-violent non-co-operation is the infallible means to bring about trusteeship because the rich cannot accumulate wealth without the co-operation of the poor in society.[1]

Gandhi maintained that confiscation of private wealth is a crime and one that defeats its own end. A democracy thus based on violence will not be a democracy at all.

What sort of society is to result when industry and capitalism have been abolished by non-violent means? Gandhi's ideal is taken from the Indian countryside. Society must centre on the co-operative village as a self-governing unit. Power must be decentralised to the utmost, leaving self-contained villages to manage their own affairs. Each village will be a democracy based upon individual freedom.

What higher organisation will there be? Gandhi's ideal was

. . . the classless and Stateless society, a state of self-regulated enlightened 'anarchy', in which social cohesion will be maintained by internal and non-coercive external sanctions. But as this ideal is not realizable, he has an attainable middle ideal also—the predominantly non-violent State. Retaining the State in this second best society is a concession to human imperfection. . . . The State will be a federation of decentralized democratic rural . . . communities. These communities will be based on 'voluntary simplicity, poverty and slowness'.

Gandhi left very little for the State to do, but he explained, in outline, how its affairs should be conducted. All adult and working citizens should vote for village representatives. These would vote in turn, electing district representatives. These would elect provincial representatives who would then elect a president. He held that these indirect elections would diminish excitement, bribery, corruption and violence. His ruling bodies were to have a relatively small membership: 'True democracy is not inconsistent with a few persons representing the spirit, the hope and the aspirations of those whom they claim to represent'. For government he wanted 'a few chosen servants removable at the will of the nation'.[3] For president he wanted an ascetic and saint.

This picture, in outline, of an ideal or semi-ideal State is attractive. In so far, moreover, as Gandhi was basing his argument on political failures he had seen and village communities which he knew, he

[1] Gopinath Dhawan. *op. cit.* p. 221.
[2] Gopinath Dhawan. *op. cit.* pp. 382-383.
[3] Gopinath Dhawan. *op. cit.* p. 197.

merits very careful attention. It must, however, be remembered that he derived his ideas also from divine revelation. To many, ideas so derived are acceptable. But Gandhi's inspiration, if taken as evidence, extends to matters still more doubtful. High in his list of principles came that of prohibition. Low in the same list comes that of Nature Cure, based on the idea that 'Disease is impossible where there is purity of thought'. If we are to accept Gandhi as an inspired prophet we must accept not only his political principles but also his permitted drugs, which are 'earth, sky, air, sunlight and water'.[1] If, on the other hand, we reject his literal inspiration, we are left with no logical basis upon which we can agree. To any but a Hindu his axioms may be unacceptable.

[1] See Duncan. *op. cit.* Also *Reminiscences of Gandhiji.* Ed. C. Shukle. Bombay, 1951. p. 101.

CHAPTER XVI

Democracy justified by Reason

THE doctrine of religious equality existed side by side in eighteenth century Europe with doctrines of equality based only on rational argument. The two sorts of egalitarianism meet and mingle in the American Revolution. They merge, above all, in the *Declaration of Independence*, passed by Congress on July 4th, 1776 and signed on the 19th. It was written by Thomas Jefferson, the impetus which brought it into being coming initially from North Carolina and Virginia. Ten States voted for it, three against; New York being one. The most interesting words are these:—

> We hold these truths to be self-evident, that all men are created equal, that they are endowed by their Creator with certain unalienable Rights, that among these are Life, Liberty and the pursuit of Happiness. That to secure these rights Governments are instituted among Men, deriving their just powers from the consent of the governed. That whenever any Form of Government becomes destructive of these ends, it is the Right of the People to alter or to abolish it. . . .[1]

'The document', it has been remarked 'is full of Jefferson's fervent spirit and personality, and its ideals were those to which his life was consecrated. It is the best known and the noblest of American State papers. . . .[2]

Well known and noble the words may be. But what do they mean? As for the axioms stated, they were not self-evident to Jefferson, for he took them from Locke. They were not self-evident to Locke because he took them from Hooker. And Hooker, when consulted, turns out to be less certain about it than Locke seems to have supposed. In any case, Hooker's arguments and Jefferson's alike assume a Creator of mankind (as mankind now is) and are useless to an agnostic and useless even to a believer in the theory of evolution, who must hold that man (recognisable as such) was not *created* at all but evolved from the animals.

It is of particular interest, however, to see how Jefferson's theory hovers between the religious and the rational. The existence of the

---

[1] *The American Government.* E. W. Carter and C. C. Rohlfing. New York, 1952. Appendix.
[2] *Encyclopaedia Britannica* article on Declaration of Independence. See also *Jefferson and the Rights of Man.* D. Malone. Boston, 1951.

Creator is self-evident and so are his main intentions. But it is the people, not the Creator, who have established government and their purpose in doing so is known. When their purposes are not achieved, the government may be altered or abolished. Whatever theological basis there may be for the doctrine that men are created equal, it is surely doubtful whether Christ, let alone Buddha, would have regarded the pursuit of happiness as an inalienable right. Indeed, few religious thinkers would recommend the pursuit of happiness at all. Most would perhaps agree that happiness is achieved incidentally by people who are pursuing something else. As for Jefferson's theory about the origin of government, it is wholly mistaken. The function of the earliest rulers over defined States was to make the crops grow. They were not appointed to secure liberty and it is not obvious that the builders of the pyramids ever made this their main object in life. Jefferson's theory begins with doubtful theology and ends with an historical assertion that is clearly wrong. Of this some of his colleagues may have been uneasily aware. Jefferson's noble sentiments were not, at any rate, repeated in the Constitution of the United States, as drawn up and agreed on 17th September, 1787.

This Constitution begins simply:—

> We the PEOPLE of the United States, in order to form a more perfect Union, establish Justice, insure domestic Tranquility, provide for the common Defence, promote the general Welfare, and secure the Blessings of Liberty to ourselves and our posterity, do ordain and establish this Constitution for the United States of America. . . .

—and so gets down to business by defining the relationship between the thirteen States and the Federal Government. And it may well be thought that the principal American achievement was rather in establishing a (more or less) workable Federation than in proclaiming the doctrine of human equality, concerning which the several States were far from agreement. Between October, 1787, and August, 1788 the principal architects of the Constitution—Alexander Hamilton, James Madison and John Jay—defended it in the pages of the *Federalist*[1] with the object of securing its ratification by the different States. These articles in the *Federalist* afford an early and authoritative commentary upon the United States Constitution and have served since to make American ideas more widely known and more commonly accepted.

The opposition which the *Federalist* arguments were designed to overcome came from those intent on maintaining the autonomy of the several States. Their objections were partly met by the provision in the Constitution itself of a strict separation of powers and a Supreme

[1] *The Federalist, or the New Constitution.* Alexander Hamilton and others. Ed. by Max Beloff. Oxford, 1948.

Court vested with the duty of safeguarding the Federal agreement. Their attention was also drawn to two possibilities they may have overlooked; one being that the colonies, if not united, would be vulnerable to external aggression; the other being that the colonies, if entirely independent or united in several groups, would certainly fight each other.

> . . . To presume a want of motives for such contests . . . would be to forget that men are ambitious, vindictive, and rapacious. To look for a continuation of harmony between a number of independent unconnected sovereignties, situated in the same neighbourhood, would be to disregard the uniform course of human events, and to set at defiance the accumulated experience of ages. . . .
>
> But notwithstanding the concurring testimony of experience in this particular, there are still to be found visionary, or designing men, who stand ready to advocate the paradox of perpetual peace between the states, though dismembered and alienated from each other. The genius of republics, they say, is pacific; the spirit of commerce has a tendency to soften the manners of men. . . .
>
> [But] Have republics in practice been less addicted to war than monarchies? Are not the former administered by men as well as the latter? Are there not aversions, predelictions, rivalships, and desires of unjust acquisition, that affect nations, as well as kings? Are not popular assemblies frequently subject to the impulse of rage, resentment, jealousy, avarice, and of other irregular and violent propensities?
>
> . . . Let experience, the least fallible guide of human opinions, be appealed to for an answer to these inquiries.[1]

It will be apparent that the framers of the Constitution lacked something of Jefferson's idealistic fervour. Their feet, we may agree, were on the ground. But they lived, nevertheless, in the period which led up to and included the French Revolution, and the connection between American and French ideas was close. Symbolising this connection was Tom Paine (1737-1809), the Quaker teacher, exciseman and journalist who migrated to America in 1775 and took an active political part in the War of Independence. He wrote a book called *Common Sense* in 1776, the year in which most of the individual states were drawing up their own State Constitutions. He had considerable influence in bringing about a complete break with England, demanding independence and no compromise. He played some part in drawing up the *Declaration of the Rights of Man* in 1789 but was absent in France when the Constitution of the United States was drawn up, mainly by James Madison, in 1787. When the French Revolution began, Paine was in England, where he presently wrote the *Rights of Man* (1791) in answer to Burke's *Reflections*. Elected member for Calais in the French Convention, he was in France from

[1] *The Federalist*, No. VI.

1792 to 1801 returning then to the United States where he died in 1809 at the age of seventy-two. His life thus covers and connects the American and French Revolutions. His dissenting background connects him, moreover, with the English Revolution of the previous century. His views are summarised in the *Rights of Man* and there can be no doubt of his influence in America, in France, and even in England.

Tom Paine wrote *Rights of Man*[1] to confute Burke and takes up much of his space in doing so. He becomes more constructive when he begins to distinguish between governments, dividing them into those based on superstition, those based on power, and those based upon the common interests of society and the common rights of man. The only governments he will admit to the last category are those of the United States and France. Elsewhere,[2] however, he divides existing governments into only two classes: those empowered by election and representation and those involving hereditary succession. 'The former is generally known by the name of republic; the latter by that of monarchy and aristocracy'. His readers are left in no doubt as to which he prefers. 'Those two distinct and opposite forms erect themselves on the two distinct and opposite bases of reason and ignorance. . . .'[3] On reason, therefore, he bases 'a system of principles as universal as truth and the existence of man, and combining moral with political happiness and national prosperity'. His principles are three in number, as follows:—

I. Men are born, and always continue, free and equal in respect of their rights. Civil distinctions, therefore, can be founded only on public utility.

II. The end of all political associations is the preservation of the natural and imprescriptible rights of man, and these rights are liberty, property, security, and resistance of oppression.

III. The nation is essentially the source of all sovereignty; nor can any individual, or any body of men, be entitled to any authority which is not expressly derived from it.

He goes on to explain what the result of applying these principles will be:—

Monarchical sovereignty, the enemy of mankind and the source of misery, is abolished; and sovereignty itself is restored to its natural and original place, the nation. Were this the case throughout Europe, the cause of wars would be taken away.

He ends happily with the words:[4]

[1] *Basic Writings of Thomas Paine. Common Sense. Rights of Man. Age of Reason.* New York, 1942. See p. 88 for the Declaration of the Rights of Man.
[2] *Ibid.* p. 123.
[3] *Ibid.* p. 128.
[4] *Ibid.* p. 131.

From what we can now see, nothing of reform in the political world ought to be held improbable. It is an age of revolutions in which every thing may be looked for. The intrigue of courts, by which the system of war is kept up, may provoke a confederation of nations to abolish it: and an European congress to patronize the progress of free government . . . is an event nearer in probability than once were the revolutions and alliance of France and America.

Tom Paine's three principles are the first three included in the French *Declaration of the Rights of Man* and he may well have been the author of them. The Declaration begins with a preamble stating that all public misfortunes are due to ignorance, neglect or contempt of human rights, which are 'natural, imprescriptible, and unalienable'. The Rights listed in the French version number seventeen in all, covering the general topics of liberty, law, arrest, penalties, legal procedure, freedom of opinion and publication, the separation of powers and the sanctity of property.

In reading the considerable body of literature evoked by the American and French Revolutions, the student is necessarily struck by the contrast between theory and practice. The American doctrine of equality did not apply to women, red Indians or negroes. Frenchmen who became enthusiastic about the Rights of Man could proclaim clauses VIII and IX against a background noise provided by the guillotine. True that contrast would not invalidate the principles themselves if we could only discover the proofs of their validity. But Tom Paine and his French contemporaries generally follow the practice of Jefferson, making an axiom of the proposition they have to prove. 'We hold these truths to be self-evident. . . .' No argument can follow from such a beginning as that. In fact, however, as we have seen, these great truths became self-evident only after those who stated them had read certain older publications. The roots of the non-religious doctrine of equality are to be found in the French literature of a somewhat earlier date. To that literature we should turn for the proof of assertions later found to be self-evident.

Every student of European history is sooner or later called upon to memorise the causes of the French Revolution; one of which usually turns out to be the writings of Voltaire and Rousseau. Voltaire's direct responsibility might be difficult to prove. It is clear, on the other hand, that some ideas of the day can be traced to Rousseau. It is no doubt for that reason among others that the student is advised to read the *Social Contract*. The case for including that work as a cause of the revolution is weakened somewhat by lack of evidence that it was widely read. M. Daniel Mornet analysed the library catalogues of five hundred contemporaries of Louis XV and discovered that whereas 165 of them included *Nouvelle Heloise*, only one contained the *Contrat Social*. Easily the most popular work, incidentally, was Bayle's *Dictionnaire*, 288 copies of which figured in his list. As for J. J. Rousseau, his more popular books, like *Émile*, may have had a generally unsettling influence. The *Contrat Social*, on the other hand, supposed origin of egalitarian doctrine, had not only, as it seems, a limited circulation; it had also, in another way, only a limited effect. While Rousseau admittedly discusses politics in the abstract without expressing admiration for things as they were in France, he is far from preaching immediate revolt. He has not filled his book with sedition from cover to cover. What, after all, does it contain? It starts off bravely with the sentence 'Man is born free, and everywhere he is in chains'.[1] There follows the theory of the original contract, which is not his own, and the theory of the 'General Will', which remains rather obscure.

What, however, of Democracy? Does he in fact prove what Paine and Jefferson merely chose to assume? He does not discuss democracy until he reaches Book III, and then he writes:—

> Taking the term in its strict sense, there never has existed, and never will exist, any true democracy. It is contrary to the natural order that the majority should govern and that the minority should be governed.[2]

Democracy, he suggests, implies a small State, simplicity of manners, equality in rank and fortune and the entire absence of anything approaching luxury. Without those conditions, democracy is too liable to cause civil war and riot. 'If there were a nation of gods, it would be governed democratically. So perfect a government is unsuited to men'. Nor (see Chapter XV, Book III) will he allow that deputies or representatives can even plausibly simulate democracy. When a people sinks so low as to elect representatives—as the result, no doubt, of wealth and indolence—their freedom is lost.[3]

Jean Jacques Rousseau was a native of Geneva and had seen something of democracy in the Alpine valleys. He concluded that what was possible there might not be so practicable in other lands. The Abbé Raynal came to the same conclusion and wrote of the Swiss as follows:—

> ... From the top of their barren mountains, they behold, groaning under the oppression of tyranny, whole nations which nature hath placed in more plentiful countries, while they enjoy in peace the fruits of their labour, of their frugality, of their moderation, and of all the virtues that attend upon liberty. ... Undoubtedly, the love of riches hath somewhat altered that amiable simplicity of manners, in such of the cantons where the arts and commerce have made any considerable

[1] *The Social Contract*. J. J. Rousseau. Trans. by H. J. Tozer. London, 1924. p. 100.
[2] Rousseau. *op. cit.* p. 159.
[3] Rouseau. *op. cit.* p. 186.

progress; but the features of their primitive character are not entirely effaced, and they still retain a kind of happiness unknown to other men.[1]

They also still retained what is more important from our point of view—a clear idea of the circumstances in which democracy can flourish. This idea Rousseau also retained, expressing his preference for small States and being prepared to explain (although he never actually did so) how they might combine in a federation for mutual protection.

One of Rousseau's most significant contributions to political thought is contained in Chapter IX of Book III. It reads as follows:—

> When . . . it is asked absolutely which is the best government, an insoluble and likewise indeterminate question is propounded. . . .
>
> But if it were asked by what sign it can be known whether a given people is well or ill governed, that would be a different matter, and the question of fact might be determined.
>
> It is, however, not settled, because every one wishes to decide it in his own way. . . .
>
> . . . What is the object of political association? It is the preservation and prosperity of its members. And what is the surest sign that they are preserved and prosperous? It is their number and population. Do not, then, go and seek elsewhere for this sign so much discussed. All other things being equal, the government under which, without external aids, without naturalization and without colonies, the citizens increase and multiply most, is infallibly the best. That under which a people diminishes and decays is the worst. Statisticians, it is now your business; reckon, measure, compare.[2]

What Rousseau here suggests may not be the whole answer to the problem but it marks an enormous advance in thought. It puts him at once in a different class, and a writer like Tom Paine is not to be compared with him.

Democratic thinkers of the late eighteenth century rested their case very largely on the success of the American colonists in achieving their independence. Rousseau's background was, of course, different. He thought of Switzerland and also, at one time, of the 'Noble Savages' allegedly discovered by Captain Cook. But several other French authors were interested in interpreting the apparent success of the American experiment. And, like Rousseau, they saw that the political problem has its economic aspect. It was one of these, the Abbé Raynal, who pointed out that equality and liberty are not compatible with each other. Given equality, men stagnate. Given liberty, they are soon unequal. And liberty, he considered, was preferable.

[1] *America: Ideal and Reality.* W. Stark. London, 1947. p. 27.
[2] Rousseau. *op. cit.* p. 175.

It hath been said, that we were all born equals; but that is not true. That we had all the same rights. I do not know what rights are, where there is an inequality of talents and of strength, and no guarantee nor sanction . . . nor do I know in what sense it can be true that we enjoy the same qualities of body and of mind. There is an original inequality between men which nothing can remedy. It must last forever; and all that can be obtained from the best legislation will not be to destroy it, but to prevent its abuses. . . .

The chimerical idea of an equality of stations is the most dangerous one that can be adopted in a civilized society. To preach this system to the people, is not to put them in mind of their rights; it is leading them on to assassination and plunder. It is letting domestic animals loose, and transforming them into wild beasts. . . .[1]

Raynal nevertheless wants inequality to be kept within bounds and sees the abolition of the right of inheritance as the best means of securing this end. He also wants to ensure that trade should not predominate over agriculture. America, he considers, gains much from its primitive conditions, which give a high measure of both liberty and equality; but he notes that there is slavery there, too.

It is in the colonies that men lead such a rural life as was the original destination of mankind, best suited to the health and increase of the species: probably they enjoy all the happiness consistent with the frailty of human nature. . . .[2]

But he bids America beware of gold, of luxury, of too great inequality of wealth. He urges the Americans finally to ensure that liberty should have 'a firm and unalterable basis in the wisdom of your constitutions'.

Another French thinker, Gabriel de Mably, also faced the problem of liberty and equality but came to the opposite conclusion. 'Equality' he wrote, 'is necessary to men. Nature made it a law for our earliest ancestors and declared her intentions so clearly that it was impossible to ignore them. . . . Did she not give to all men the same organs, the same wants, the same reason?' To achieve equality he is prepared to sacrifice wealth. He thinks that poverty, as existed in Sparta, makes for happiness but he admits that the danger is one of stagnation. The remedy for stagnation lies in the institution of private property. And from that springs inequality, wealth, poverty and slavery. Essentially, he thinks 'our evils are without remedy'. But there can be palliatives and he suggests what they should be. 'I say in a word that good legislation should continually break up and divide the fortunes which avarice and ambition continually labour to amass'. As a second-best to primitive equality, he thinks it best to balance against each other the forces of Monarchy, Aristocracy and Democracy.

[1] *America: Ideal and Reality.* W. Stark. London, 1947. p. 23.
[2] Stark, W. *op. cit.* p. 33.

But what is more interesting is that Mably perceives that American political equality must be fictitious if combined with inequalities of wealth and the seeds of aristocracy imported from England.

> A spirit of commerce will, in my opinion, soon become the general and predominant spirit of the inhabitants of your cities.[1]

Wealth will result, and poverty, and then the beginnings of class war.

> With the manners we have in Europe, and which probably are already too general in America, wealth must at last usurp an absolute empire. All efforts made to oppose it will be fruitless; but it is not impossible, by many precautions, to prevent this empire from becoming tyrannical.[2]

That is the most that Mably hopes for and more perhaps than he thinks will be achieved.

Brissot was the author who admired the United States with least reservation. He was there in 1788 and published his *Travels* in 1791. He maintains that the best State is that which ensures equality by a wide distribution of property. There would always be the rich, perhaps, but we must avoid having extreme poverty. He advocates property (rather than employment) for all. The peasant farmer, he thinks, has independence, plenty and happiness in return for patience, industry and labour.

> It is in a country life in America, that true happiness is to be found by him who is wise enough to make it consist in tranquillity of soul, in the enjoyment of himself and of nature. What is the fatiguing agitation of our great cities, compared to this delicious calmness?[3]

It is, of course, the northern States he admires, and especially the people of Boston and the Quakers, for their good sense and simplicity. Of the Quakers he wrote 'Renouncing all external pleasures, music, theatres and shows, they are devoted to their duties as citizens, to their families, and to their business'. He remarks that they will have no theatre in Philadelphia. To preserve simplicity Brissot thinks it essential to restrain commerce and industry. Manufactures 'gather a multitude of individuals whose physique and morals decline together; they accustom and form man for servitude. . . .' They tend, in fact, to produce aristocracy. Brissot evidently feared (while denying) that American wealth would soon corrupt the original ideals of equality.

One other author must be mentioned and that is Chastellux, a French aristocrat, philosopher and soldier who served in America

[1] Stark, W. *op. cit.* p. 54.
[2] *Ibid.* p. 55.
[3] *Ibid.* p. 93.

during the War of Independence (1780-82) and published his impressions soon afterwards. He drew the usual contrast between North and South. He noted both the democratic constitution and the growing wealth and wondered whether they were compatible. He put the question to Mr. Samuel Adams, who maintained that the constitution balanced any growth of aristocracy by its counterpoise of monarchy and democracy. Chastellux was unconvinced and thought that, with great differences of wealth, democracy would become a meaningless form and, more than that, a dangerous fiction. Socially, he saw that approximate equality of wealth is essential to democratic rule. But he states his objection to that equality on other grounds. He cannot see that it is compatible with the arts. He loathed the Quakers as soon as he saw them. 'Great musicians', he writes 'are oftener to be met with in the courts of despots, than in republics'. He argues, further, that the man who really enjoys retirement in the country must have been educated in a city.

> . . . retirement is sterile for the man without information. Now the information is to be acquired best in towns. Let us not confound the man retired into the country, with the man educated in the country. The former is the most perfect of his species, and the latter frequently does not merit to belong to it.[1]

But Chastellux agreed with Brissot, with Mably and Raynal in one thing, that the United States would not always remain the ideal country of liberty and equality. In point of fact, the predictions made were almost immediately justified. A wealthy governing class appeared in the very first Congress and was indeed championed by John Adams, the first President after Washington. He pointed out, as against the egalitarians, that equality of property is impossible. There must always be gentlemen, he inferred, of greater wealth, intelligence and education. No pure democracy can exist. Class differences were there, as we know, from the beginning and were to become more acute. The ideal upheld was not that of equality but that of liberty. Nor is it surprising that the Americans, given their choice, should have chosen as they did. For, in coming to the New World, it was freedom they had sought.

[1] Stark, W. op. cit. p. 78.

CHAPTER XVII

Democracy justified by Utility

THE French Revolution was the result of earlier movements of which the American Revolution was the most important. It was a violent experience; so violent indeed that France has had no stable system of government since, and certainly has none now. It achieved swift and startling results—the confiscation of crown and church and noble property, the suppression of the monasteries, the abolition of tithes, the abolition of titles and the destruction of all hereditary privilege. The Revolution was accompanied or followed by the redivision of France into Departments, a new currency, the decimal system in weights and measures, a new code of laws, a new currency and a new calendar. Various political systems were tried in rapid succession. With frightful bloodshed monarchy gave way to republic, democracy to mob-rule and anarchy, and anarchy to military dictatorship. Dictatorship became monarchy, which was replaced by a republic, then by a despotism and then by a republic again. It is too early to say what the final form will be when, if ever, stability is regained.

But while the actual experience of France is not wholly encouraging, the ideas expressed at the time of the Revolution have been given almost permanent currency. These were briefly summarised at the time in the convenient slogan 'Liberty, Equality and Fraternity'. Nor was this slogan entirely meaningless. Liberty of thought, speech, religion and meeting were more or less established. Equality before the law was more or less achieved. Political equality was gained and economic equality left unattempted. Perhaps, however, the most permanent and characteristic result of the Revolution was the creation of the secular state—a thing still unknown in England or the United States. For the rest, it is not clear that the French Revolution made any notable contribution to political thought. The thinking had been done beforehand and no orator of the revolutionary era was able to progress much further than earlier thinkers except perhaps in secularism. Granted that a measure of liberty and equality was gained, no answer was found to the question already posed in America; namely, whether political equality is of much value among people economically unequal, and how liberty can be upheld in a

State where economic equality has been established by force. Generally speaking, we shall look in vain for any novelty in French political thought after the Revolution.

More interesting was the development of political ideas in England between 1776 and 1832; a development largely centred upon Jeremy Bentham. His was the intellect behind the English Radicals. Bentham was essentially a law reformer and codifier, his political thought being incidental to his initial quarrel with lawyers in general and Blackstone in particular. He wrote his *Fragment on Government* (1776) chiefly to refute Blackstone, which he did effectively and in some detail. Commenting upon one passage, he writes with gusto:

> ... on a distant glance nothing can look fairer.... Step close to it and the delusion vanishes. It is then seen to consist partly of self-evident observations, and partly of contradictions; partly of what every one knows already, and partly of what no one can understand at all....[1]

Himself a barrister, he thought poorly of lawyers as a class, describing them as:

> ... a passive and enervate race, ready to swallow anything, and to acquiesce in anything; with intellects incapable of distinguishing right from wrong, and with affections alike indifferent to either; insensible, short-sighted, obstinate; lethargic, yet liable to be driven in convulsions by false terrors; deaf to the voice of reason and public utility; obsequious only to the whisper of interest, and to the beck of power.[2]

Enough has been quoted to show that Bentham's works are well worth reading. He had, for one thing, a literary gift which was denied to many of his disciples. Using that gift, he made himself the prophet of militant atheism, the intellectual leader of middle-class revolt against aristocracy and the inspirer of most Victorian radical ideas. He was himself, of course, an eighteenth century figure, friend of the aristocrats he meant to depose and a frequenter at one time of the country houses he meant, presumably, to demolish. As a rich attorney's son he found no door closed against him; he had, therefore, none of the rebel's bitterness except perhaps where lawyers were concerned. The middle-class revolt of his day had two main aspects; the drive against all trade restraints and legalised monopolies, and the drive for political, parliamentary and municipal reform. The former movement more especially concerned the East India Company, the Corn Laws, the Church of England and all that remained of the Stuart attempts at State control and social legislation. A drive against all these evils (which have mostly now been re-introduced) might have been begun in the spirit of Rousseau or Tom Paine.

---

[1] *A Fragment on Government*. Jeremy Bentham. Ed. by F. C. Montague. Oxford, 1931. p. 152.
[2] Bentham. *op. cit*. p. 104.

But Bentham—with some help from Priestley—carefully discarded all ideas based upon religion, ethics, tradition, history or precedent. He was not interested in Social Contracts. Taking mankind as he believed it to be, he put forward, as his measure of political excellence, the principle of 'the greatest happiness of the greatest number'.[1]

This is how Bentham defines his own theory:—

> The aim of government should be the greatest happiness of all the members of the state. But what is good for one may be opposed to the happiness of many others. Unfortunately, it is impossible to enlarge indefinitely the sphere of happiness of every individual without coming in conflict with the happiness of others. Therefore, the only aim should be the greatest possible happiness of the greatest number; in a word, the common good is the right aim of government, and the proper task of a lawmaker is to discover regulations designed to bring about the greatest good to the greatest number of human beings. The just lawmaker who has equal regard for every member of the community can pursue no other aim. The determination of every point in every law, from first to last, without exception, must be directed toward the greatest good of the greatest number and must rest upon that principle. Was this ever the case?[2]

He answers 'No' and explains that government has always been for the benefit of those who did the governing.

The critic of Bentham's theory, as it is thus briefly explained, would object that 'happiness' is too vague a term. But Bentham does not leave the word undefined. Analysing it, he finds in it the elements of Subsistence, Abundance, Security and Equality. This last element he expressly denies as a fact but insists upon as a working rule of legislation—very much in the tradition of English law. Applying his main principle to the question of the inequality of worldly means, he points out that in the increase of wealth there is a law of diminishing returns. A hundred pounds or an acre of land is nothing to a millionaire, little to a man of wealth, something to a tradesman and a fortune to a labourer. It shall be given, therefore, to the man to whom it will give greatest happiness; for so only will the sum total of happiness be perceptibly increased. As a result of this reasoning, Bentham pleads for a wider distribution of property.

> The greatest sum of total happiness is to be obtained through the most equal distribution of goods. The state should thus strive towards a continual approach to equality of possession, but without impairing its three other aims which are above equality, namely, security, subsistence, well-being. Equality is, in fact, the equality of these three. For the attainment of equality, therefore, no measures should be

[1] See *Political Philosophy from Plato to Jeremy Bentham*. G. Engelmann. Trans. by K. F. Geiser. New York, 1927.
[2] Engelmann. *op. cit. Introduction to a project for a Constitutional Code.* p. 340.

applied which undermine security, disturb existence and well-being, or weaken the initiative and activity of the individual. The proper measure is the control of the right of inheritance.[1]

While thus seeking to bring about a greater degree of economic equality, Bentham was not a socialist. He considered, in fact, that 'the hostile sword in its utmost furies' would be a less dreadful prospect than the victory of socialism. But while not a socialist, he was a democrat. He wanted to sweep away monarchy and peerage and leave all power to a reformed House of Commons, itself checked by an enlightened middle class. 'An economical financial administration', he held, 'is only possible in a representative democracy'. He finds a further merit in such a regime in that 'a representative democracy—in which the supreme power is in the people who elect and reject them—will scarcely engage in war'. He strongly supported the liberty of the press as a safeguard against oppression. He thought he could have no better object in life than 'the bettering of this wicked world, by covering it over with Republics'.

Bentham believed in unlimited freedom of competition, arguing that all restrictions reduce the national wealth. Only free competition will secure the lowest prices and the best work. He was opposed to the acquisition of colonies, maintaining that one could trade with them without controlling them. Colonies were to him, in fact, yet one more instance of 'the fallacy of those artificial efforts which legislation makes to increase the country's wealth'. Curiously, his whole argument about the greatest happiness of the greatest number assumes an equality of persons, and an equality moreover in their capacity for happiness—a doubtful point—and even in their method of achieving it. Such a belief might have been justified in terms of Natural Law but Bentham believed in no such thing. Indeed, the idea of natural law or natural right had been effectively demolished by David Hume as far back as 1748, and demolished indeed to Bentham's own satisfaction. Hume had shown convincingly that the nature of human loyalty and the nature of a contract are entirely different, although both derive from a desire for a stable society. He had shown, furthermore, that ideas of morality (including the idea that a contract should be kept) are not 'eternal verities rooted in nature, but merely standard ways of behaving justified by experience . . . fixed by habit'.[2] Some of these conventions concern property, others concern government.

If the premises of Hume's argument be granted, it can hardly be denied that he made a clean sweep of the whole rationalist philosophy of natural right, of self-evident truths, and of the laws of eternal and

---

[1] *A History of Political Theory.* George H. Sabine. London, 1937. p. 508.
[2] Jeremy Bentham, *op. cit.* p. 153.

immutable morality which were supposed to guarantee the harmony of nature and the order of human society. In place of indefeasible rights or natural justice and liberty, there remains merely utility, conceived in terms either of self-interest or social stability, and issuing in certain conventional standards of conduct which on the whole serve human purposes. Such conventions may, of course, be widespread among men and relatively permanent, because human motives are fairly uniform and in their general outlines change slowly, but in no other sense can they be called universal.[1]

Hume himself ends his essay *On the Original Contract* with the words:

> New discoveries are not to be expected in these matters. If scarce any man, till very lately, ever imagined that government was founded on compact, it is certain that it cannot, in general, have any such foundation.[2]

This was an argument which Bentham accepted if others did not. He would base his government neither on a fictitious 'contract' nor on the laws of god nor on the laws of morality which men may have evolved for themselves.

> Nature has placed mankind under the governance of two sovereign masters, *pain* and *pleasure*. It is for them alone to point out what we ought to do, as well as to determine what we shall do. . . . In words a man may pretend to abjure their empire: but in reality he will remain subject to it all the while. . . .[3]

Bentham's whole argument in support of 'laissez-faire' is thus based on the assumption that human motives are selfish and that their selfishness can be turned to good account. But Bentham's own example—the example of a long life entirely spent in a selfless search for truth and the means of bettering mankind—contradicts all his own assumptions as to what human motives can be taken to be. If that life was 'happiness' to him (as it clearly was), his 'greatest happiness of the greatest number' must be given a meaning very different from the obvious meaning and very different from the sense in which he used the phrase himself.

Bentham's influence, considerable in his own day, became almost supreme in nineteenth century England after his death. His friends and followers were the Utilitarians—Ricardo the economist, Malthus the writer on population and James Mill, the historian of British India. Mill and Bentham agreed to educate the former's child to be the apostle of their teaching. Their plan was queerly successful,

---

[1] Sabine, G. H. *op. cit.* p. 509.
[2] *Social Contract.* Essays by Locke, Hume and Rousseau, with an introduction by Sir Ernest Barker. Oxford, 1948.
[3] Jeremy Bentham. *op. cit.* (Chapter I of *Introduction*).

dreadful as the results were, physically, for John Stuart Mill. Beginning to read at the age of two, he had reached the differential calculus at the age of eight, completed his formal education by the age of fourteen and had a nervous breakdown when he was twenty. He went on to become an influential writer, dominating English economic and political thought from about 1843 to about 1874. He was the prophet of the middle-class revolution, a Member of Parliament for three years and in Parliament indeed for the passing of the Reform Bill of 1867. His best-known work, perhaps, was his essay *On Liberty* of 1859. He died in 1873, leaving as his chief legacy a body of doctrine concerning 'free competition, free trade, freedom of opinion, of speech, of writing and of action'.[1]

In comparing John Stuart Mill with Bentham we must remember that they lived in different periods. Mill was not only heir to the Utilitarian philosophy; he was also a witness of its immediate results. He watched the slow process by which (with successive extensions of the franchise) the voting power in England passed from the upper to the lower middle class and so to the working class itself. There is no need to enter here into a detailed description of how this came about. The story has been told repeatedly and is exceptional only in that the English aristocracy was remarkably adroit in avoiding revolution. And yet it may be that there is occasion to remark on one or two stages of the process which are not always sufficiently emphasised. The aristocracy, firmly entrenched under the first two Hanoverian kings and justified by the success of the Seven Years War, had to meet, after 1763, George III's attempt to restore the royal power. In defeating that attempt (in America, deliberately) the great families reached the height of their power. Thenceforward their influence declined and the younger Pitt, taught by Lord Shelburne, did his best to hasten the process. He called in the middle-class to his aid. Failing in his attempt at parliamentary reform he tried to gain his purpose by other means.

> . . . He created a plebeian aristocracy and blended it with the patrician oligarchy. He made peers of second-rate squires and fat graziers. He caught them in the alleys of Lombard Street, and clutched them from the counting-houses of Cornhill. When Mr. Pitt, in an age of Bank restriction, declared that every man with an estate of ten thousand a year had a right to be a peer, he sounded the knell of 'the cause for which Hampden had died on the field, and Sydney on the scaffold'.[2]

According to Disraeli, Lord Shelburne 'was the first great minister who comprehended the rising importance of the middle class'. That is why Jeremy Bentham was invited to Bowood. His views accorded

[1] *The Social and Political Ideas of some Representative Thinkers of the Age of Reaction and Reconstruction*, 1815-65. Ed. by F. J. C. Hearnshaw. London, 1932. p. 132.
[2] *Sybil, or the Two Nations*. Benjamin Disraeli. London, 1954. p. 29.

with those of Shelburne and Pitt, and Utilitarianism essentially represents their policy, more especially on the economic side. Bentham was no tool of the politicians but he had been in close touch with one of the ablest statesmen of the day. He was going with, not against, the tide.

If comparisons suggest themselves between the history of ancient Rome and of modern Britain, the points of resemblance are not coincidental. They passed through similar phases of growth and decay. But, apart from that, the English aristocracy had been educated in the classics. People like Shelburne and Pitt—people, for that matter, like Bentham—knew all about Marius, the Gracchi, Livius Drusus and Sulla. They knew more about them than they did about King John or Queen Elizabeth. The result was that they withdrew almost instinctively from untenable positions. They gave way, moreover, gracefully. The technique, however, in which they specialised was that of retaining a ministry in office on the understanding that they would adopt the measures of the opposition. Looking back, it is difficult to recall which liberal measures were introduced by Whigs and which by Tories. More recently, it is as difficult to remember, of socialist legislation, which Act is attributable to which party. Ministers do what they realise will have to be done. The transfer of power, therefore, from the classes to the masses has been in one sense faster, in another sense slower, than is often perceived. The measures have changed more readily than the men. The transition from aristocracy to democracy was slow as represented by the composition of Parliament and Cabinet. And while the types of Prime Minister in office admittedly passed through the gradations from Lord Melbourne to Asquith, it was not until the appointment of Lloyd George in 1916 that Britain saw a Prime Minister who was not, by any contemporary standard, a gentleman.[1]

John Stuart Mill thus witnessed in his lifetime a great deal of what Bentham foresaw. Nor was Britain his only example of a growing democracy. Italy and Switzerland had modern constitutions from 1848. The United States became more democratic in character after the Civil War which ended in 1865. The constitution of Austria-Hungary, adopted in 1867, provided in Austria a House of Representatives, to which the members were directly elected from 1873. There was even a Liberal ministry in office from 1871 to 1879. The

[1] Of 35 previous Prime Ministers, 27 had been the sons of landowners. The younger Pitt and Perceval had been barristers but were well connected. Addington was the first of middle-class origin, being son of a physician. Canning was son of a barrister, Peel of a cotton manufacturer, Gladstone of a shipowner. Disraeli, the novelist, was an exception but practically all Prime Ministers down to and including Gladstone were men of wealth or family. Campbell-Bannerman (1905) broke precedent in having actually been in business as a wholesale draper, but even he was a Cambridge man. H. H. Asquith, barrister and son of a woollen manufacturer, had been educated at Balliol. Lloyd George started life without any advantage of any kind.

German Empire was brought into existence in 1871, the constitution providing for a Reichstag, elected on a system of practically universal suffrage. France became a Republic again in 1875 with a democratic constitution, a President, a Senate and a Chamber of Deputies. Switzerland had a constitutional revision in 1874 which strengthened the position of the Federal as opposed to the Canton institutions but also provided for a direct appeal to the people by referendum. Brazil became a Republic in 1889 and even Spain introduced universal suffrage in 1890. It is true that the powers of these elected assemblies varied considerably, those of the Reichstag for example, being mainly advisory, and those of the Austrian Reichsrath vested as much in the Herrenhaus as in the House of Representatives. Nevertheless there were few countries so behind the times as to refrain from going through the motions of democracy. Alexander II was about to introduce a measure of democracy in Russia when he was assassinated in 1881. It is not too great a generalisation to say that representative democracy was the fashion in the last quarter of the nineteenth century.[1]

To a conservatively-minded thinker, which John Stuart Mill was not, the course of this democratic flood was a matter for alarm. It is interesting to see how the process was viewed, for example, by Joseph Conrad, in 1885.

> . . . every disreputable ragamuffin in Europe feels that the day of universal brotherhood, dispoliation and disorder is coming apace, and nurses day-dreams of well-plenished pockets amongst the ruin of all that is respectable, venerable and holy. The great British Empire went over the edge, and yet on to the inclined plane of social progress and radical reform. The downward movement is hardly perceptible yet, and the clever men who started it may flatter themselves with the progress; but they will soon find that the fate of the nation is out of their hands now! The Alpine avalanche rolls quicker and quicker as it nears the abyss—its ultimate destination! Where's the man to stop the crashing avalanche?
>
> Where's the man to stop the rush of social-democratic ideas? The opportunity and the day have come and are gone! Believe me: gone forever! For the sun is set and the last barrier removed. England was the only barrier to the pressure of infernal doctrines born in continental back-slums. Now, there is nothing! The destiny of the nation and of all nations is to be accomplished in darkness amidst much weeping and gnashing of teeth, to pass through robbery, equality, anarchy and misery under the iron rule of a military despotism! Such is the lesson of common sense logic.
>
> Socialism must inevitably end in Caesarism.[2]

[1] See *Governments and Parties in Continental Europe*. A. Lawrence Lowell. London, 1896. (2 Vols.) See also *A Short History of Democracy*. A. F. Hattersley. Cambridge, 1930.

[2] *Joseph Conrad, Life and Letters*. G. Jean Aubry. London, 1927. 2 vols. Vol. I. p. 84.

Prophetic as this passage may seem, events were to move more slowly than Conrad anticipated. The working class did not gain control of England until the period 1910-21, nor were the results of that control immediately experienced. But there was cause for anxiety, and one man who shared that anxiety was John Stuart Mill.

Mill's anxiety was lest Bentham's democracy and Bentham's freedom might be found incompatible with each other. While government was vested in King or Peerage there might be considerable support for any proposals made to limit the power of government; especially its powers of interference in trade, in conduct, in morals and opinion. But the tendency of the nineteenth century was to secure for the people the control of the government itself.

> By degrees this new demand for elective and temporary rulers became the prominent object of the exertions of the popular party, wherever any such party existed; and superseded, to a considerable extent the previous efforts to limit the power of rulers. As the struggle proceeded for making the ruling power emanate from the periodical choice of the ruled, some persons began to think that too much importance had been attached to the limitation of the power itself. *That* (it might. seem) was a resource against rulers whose interests were habitually opposed to those of the people. What was now wanted was that the rulers should be identified with the people; that their interest and will should be the interest and will of the nation. The nation did not need to be protected against its own will. There was no fear of its tyrannizing over itself. . . .
>
> But, in political and philosophical theories, as well as in persons, success discloses faults and infirmities which failure might have concealed. . . .[1]

Mill perceives, in fact, that a democratic government may persecute a minority and abolish freedom in a way that a king neither can nor dare. So he makes his plea for liberty as against the tendency of the age.

> Apart from the peculiar tenets of individual thinkers, there is also in the world at large an increasing inclination to stretch unduly the powers of society over the individual, both by the force of opinion and even by legislation: and as the tendency of all the changes taking place in the world is to strengthen society, and diminish the power of the individual, this encroachment is not one of the evils which tend spontaneously to disappear, but, on the contrary, to grow more and more formidable. The disposition of mankind, whether as rulers or as fellow citizens, to impose their own opinions and inclinations as a rule of conduct on others, is so energetically supported by some of the best and by some of the worst feelings incident to human nature, that it is hardly ever kept under restraint by anything but want of power; and

[1] *On Liberty. Representative Government. The Subjection of Women.* Three essays by John Stuart Mill.

as the power is not declining, but growing, unless a strong barrier of moral conviction can be raised against the mischief, we must expect, in the present circumstances of the world, to see it increase.[1]

Mill then makes his plea for liberty as against the tendency of the day. He rather assumes than proves his initial position, that:

> If all mankind minus one, were of one opinion, and only one person were of the contrary opinion, mankind would be no more justified in silencing that one person, than he, if he had the power, would be justified in silencing mankind.

This view Mill goes on to illustrate with historical examples, such as those of Socrates and Christ, to show that the one may be right and mankind wrong. But, he argues, even if we suppose mankind to be right, the orthodox cannot even understand their orthodoxy until they have heard—if only to refute—the arguments against it. Beliefs accepted, he maintains, and never argued have little influence upon conduct. Apart from that, the likelihood is that the truth lies halfway between the orthodox and the heretic. Popular opinions are seldom the whole truth, and it is only by dispute that the truth can be ascertained. As for those who admit the need for free discussion but not 'pushed to an extreme', they fail to realise that unless the reasons justifying free discussion hold good in an extreme case they do not hold good at all.[2]

In Chapter 3 Mill complains again of the danger to the individual:

> . . . society has now fairly got the better of individuality; and the danger which threatens human nature is not the excess, but the deficiency of personal impulses and preferences. Things are vastly changed, since the passions of those who were strong by station or by personal endowment were in a state of habitual rebellion against laws and ordinances. . . . In our times, from the highest class of society down to the lowest, every one lives as under the eye of a hostile and dreaded censorship. . . . I do not mean that they choose what is customary, in preference to what suits their own inclination. It does not occur to them to have any inclination, except for what is customary . . . by dint of not following their own nature, they have no nature to follow. . . .[3]

He sees in this a sort of Calvinism by which everything not a duty is a sin. He pleads that originality is valuable and that people of original minds need freedom—'these few are the salt of the earth; without them, human life would become a stagnant pool'. Unfortunately, 'Originality is the one thing which unoriginal minds cannot feel the use of' and 'the general tendency of things throughout the world is to render mediocrity the ascendant power among mankind'.

[1] Mill. *op. cit.* p. 20.
[2] *Ibid.* p. 29.
[3] *Ibid.* p. 69.

No government by a democracy or a numerous aristocracy, either in its political acts or in the opinions, qualities and tone of mind which it fosters, ever did or ever could rise above mediocrity, except in so far as the sovereign. Many have let themselves be guided (which in their best times they have always done) by the counsels and influence of a more highly gifted and instructed One or Few. The initiation of all wise or noble things, comes and must come from individuals. . . .[1]

Such individuals are resisted by the lovers of what is customary. Mill then asserts that it is custom which rules the East and that it has killed progress there in killing originality.

We have a warning example in China—a nation of much talent, and, in some respects, even wisdom, owing to the rare good fortune of having been provided at an early period with a particularly good set of customs, the work, in some measure, of men to whom even the most enlightened European must accord, under certain limitations, the title of sages and philosophers. They are remarkable, too, in the excellence of their apparatus for impressing, as far as possible, the best wisdom they possess upon every mind in the community, and securing that those who have appropriated most of it shall occupy the posts of honour and power. . . . They have succeeded beyond all hope in what English philanthropists are so industriously working at—in making a people all alike, all governing their thoughts and conduct by the same maxims and rules; and these are the fruits.[2]

By the fruits Mill means stagnation. Europe, he thinks, has avoided this stagnation through the European diversity of character and culture. But this diversity, in England, is rapidly diminishing as political changes 'tend to raise the low and to lower the high'—both in station and education. Improved communications and trade have the same effect.

The demand that all other people shall resemble ourselves, grows by what it feeds on. If resistance waits till life is reduced *nearly* to one uniform type, all deviations from that type will come to be considered impious, immoral, even monstrous and contrary to nature. Mankind speedily become unable to conceive diversity, when they have been for some time unaccustomed to see it.[3]

So Mill goes on to discuss what limits there should be to the authority, not merely of the State but of society, over the individual. He has no difficulty in showing that the State and society have no right to interfere in matters which concern only the individual. He gives instances of laws based on religion rather than upon public utility; and had he lived longer could have mentioned more. He gives instances of liberty (when based on no real principle) being excessive,

[1] Mill. *op. cit.* p. 82.
[2] *Ibid.* p. 88.
[3] *Ibid.* p. 91.

as in the parent's right to educate or neglect his child. He is opposed, on the other hand, to the nationalisation of schools, for 'a general State education is a mere contrivance for moulding people to be exactly like one another'. It also 'establishes a despotism over the mind'. The most he will approve in this direction is a public examination, to ensure that parents do their duty. Not that he leaves unquestioned the right of people to become parents at all, for in an over-populated country 'to produce children, beyond a very small number . . . is a serious offence'. His argument, in short, is that questions of authority and reasonable interference should be divorced from religion and prejudice and solved on the general principle of utility.

The principle of utility certainly allows Mill to tread a narrow path between tyranny and licence. He sees dangers on either side but is more impressed by the perils of interference than the perils of neglect. Even when it does not infringe on liberty, government intervention is open, he considers, to three general objections.[1] To begin with, the individual normally knows his own business best. Even if he does not, his freedom to choose is a means of education and development. Finally the effect of state guidance is to dwarf the individual; and it is of individuals that society is composed. He describes in memorable words the situation which would result from over-centralisation.

> If the roads, the railways, the banks, the insurance offices, the great joint-stock companies, the universities, and the public charities, were all of them branches of the government; if, in addition, the municipal corporations and local boards, with all that now devolves on them, became departments of the central administration; if the employees of all these different enterprises were appointed and paid by the government, and looked to the government for every rise in life; not all the freedom of the press and popular constitution of the legislature would make this or any other country free otherwise than in name. And the evil would be greater, the more efficiently and scientifically the administrative machinery was constructed—the more skilful the arrangements for obtaining the best qualified hands and heads with which to work it. In England it has of late been proposed that all the members of the civil service of government should be selected by competitive examination, to obtain for those employments the most intelligent and instructed persons procurable. . . . [He supposes, for the sake of argument, that the State should, by this device, secure the service of all the ablest men]. . . . If every part of the business of society which required organised concert, or large and comprehensive views, were in the hands of government, and if government offices were universally filled by the ablest men, all the enlarged culture and

[1] Mill. *op. cit.* p. 133.

practised intelligence in the country, except the purely speculative, would be concentrated in a numerous bureaucracy, to whom alone the rest of the community would look for all things: the multitude for direction and dictation in all they had to do; the able and aspiring for personal advancement. To be admitted into the ranks of this bureaucracy, and when admitted, to rise therein, would be the sole object of ambition. . . . Such is the melancholy condition of the Russian empire, as shown in the accounts of those who have had sufficient opportunity of observation.[1]

Such is still the melancholy condition of the Russian Empire, as shown in the accounts of those who have had sufficient opportunity of observation. Such is also the melancholy condition, for all practical purposes, of the British Empire. Our further experience mostly goes towards proving the rule that the most successful administration produces the most complete serfdom. And Mill explains what the further disadvantages must be.

It is not, also, to be forgotten, that the absorption of all the principal ability of the country into the governing body is fatal, sooner or later, to the mental activity and progressiveness of the body itself. Banded together as they are—working a system which, like all systems, necessarily proceeds in a great measure by fixed rules—the officials are under the constant temptation of sinking into indolent routine, or, if they now and then desert that mill-horse round, of rushing into some half-examined crudity which has struck the fancy of some leading member of the corps. . . .[2]

Coming from one who never perhaps heard of groundnuts and to whom Crichel Down would have meant nothing, this last sentence reveals an almost uncanny accuracy of prediction.

Mill ends his famous essay by attempting to fix the point at which 'much of the advantages of centralised power and intelligence' can be gained 'without turning into governmental channels too great a proportion of the general activity'. The principle which he advocates is: 'the greatest dissemination of power consistent with efficiency; but the greatest possible centralisation of information, and diffusion of it from the centre'. He realises, of course, the difficulty of judging the point at which decentralisation becomes muddle. He thinks, however, that the mischief of over-administration begins when 'instead of calling forth the activity and powers of individuals and bodies, it substitutes its own activity for theirs'. He concludes finally that,

. . . a State which dwarfs its men, in order that they may be more docile instruments in its hands, even for beneficial purposes, will find that with small men no great thing can really be accomplished; and

[1] Mill. *op. cit.* p. 135.
[2] *Ibid.* p. 138.

that the perfection of machinery to which it has sacrificed everything, will in the end avail it nothing, for want of the vital power which, in order that the machine might work more smoothly, it has preferred to banish.[1]

Far longer than his essay on *Liberty* is Mill's essay on *Representative Government*.[2] He asks in Chapter II what is the criterion of a good form of government. He answers that government should be judged, in the first place, by the degree in which it tends to increase the sum of good qualities in the governed, taking these both collectively and individually. It should be judged, in the second place, by the efficiency with which it harnesses these qualities for public ends. Only a 'completely popular government' has this character. But direct democracy, as he admits, is possible only in a small town. Democracy on a larger scale must be representative, and representative government is therefore 'the ideal type of the most perfect polity', although not all peoples are fit to have it or able to do their duties under it. He then goes on to a detailed description of an extended suffrage, methods of election, ballot, duration of elected office, second chambers, executive, federations and colonies. Basically, his argument is more convincing than all earlier reasonings about natural law, implied contracts and the rights of man. Mill very properly holds that government is to be judged by results, not by theories as to how it may have originated. Whether his two criteria are the best is another matter and raises some doubt as to what 'good qualities' are. But, without criticising the validity of his reasoning, let us note what his conclusions are. He believes in representative democracy, with votes for all. While he does not assert (and indeed practically denies) that all men are born equal, he does urge that they should have equal rights as citizens and voters. He advocates political equality.

The inherent contradiction in Mill's position is obvious. His argument about political equality can lead only to socialism. There can be no equality between millionaires and paupers. Votes for all are a mockery where there are vast differences in wealth. If citizens are to be politically equal it is absurd to allow one man to control six newspapers while another controls nothing—not even himself. But how can these inequalities be prevented? By just such governmental interference and confiscation as Mill has already rejected in the name of liberty. His two doctrines are incompatible. He wants to equalise citizens as voters while simultaneously freeing them as traders. The result can only be the nationalisation of industries, the probably fatal results of which Mill was himself the first to point out. The measures taken to ensure equality—the measures taken indeed as a result of

[1] Mill. *op. cit.* p. 141.
[2] *Ibid.* p. 157.

that equality—are those certain to destroy the freedom in which Mill so passionately believed. He was manifestly uneasy about his whole position. He played with and even recommended devices like proportional representation and even plural voting for the highly educated or intelligent. He opposed secret voting and the payment of deputies while demanding votes for women. In some of his arguments it is difficult to see even the principles of Utilitarianism; he seems rather to be guided by mere preference. But no devices of voting or electing could help him to escape from the dilemma in which, like so many later theorists, he had become involved. To his main problem he could find no answer; probably because there is none.

CHAPTER XVIII

Democracy carried to its Logical Conclusion

JEREMY BENTHAM'S doctrine that the individual knows his own business best remained the gospel in England until about 1874. The industrialisation of Britain between about 1840 and 1874 was unhampered by State interference except in very minor details. To say that this was due to Bentham's influence would, of course, be wrong. But those who had already decided against intervention could and did quote the utilitarians when justifying their inaction. The unimpeded growth of the manufacturing towns brought wealth to many, and with wealth came political power. The English aristocracy, reinforced successively by West India Merchants, East India Nabobs, Shipping Magnates and Cotton Manufacturers, was expanded again to include Hardware Manufacturers, Stockbrokers, Railway Directors and Engineers. We read much in the literature of the period of the social difficulties experienced by the newly prosperous; nor were these wholly imaginary. But the two basic facts were these: the successful manufacturers mostly wanted to join the aristocracy and the aristocracy would usually admit them. It would perhaps be truer to say that it was the manufacturer's wife who wanted to be a lady and her daughter who became one. The effect, however, was the same. Had the newly rich wanted to destroy aristocracy as such, and had the aristocracy been exclusive, the history of England would have been different. There would have been revolution.

As it was, the privileges of aristocracy were extended to an ever-widening circle. This probably happens in any aristocracy. In England it was accelerated, however, by the development of the public schools (a by-product of the railways) as a device for assimilating the middle class into the aristocracy. These schools catered not only for the wealthy but for the merely professional and aspiring. Partly as a result of this educational device there was soon very little social gulf between those with five thousand and those with fifty thousand a year; and less, if anything, between those with two and those with six generations of established wealth behind them. Clergy, Lawyers and Physicians claimed to rank as gentlemen. Bankers tried to look like Lawyers and Schoolmasters dressed as Clergy, the Merchant had his commission in the Volunteers and the Moneylender his place in the country. A sort of shabby gentility extended down to commercial travellers and clerks. There was no threat to aristocracy from those who believed themselves to be on the fringes of it.

There were always, however, a number of the more or less prosperous who were opposed to aristocracy on principle. These were the nonconformists, sundered from their social betters by an abyss of their own digging. Some of the seventeenth century sects still survived but these were somewhat overshadowed by the Methodist groups of eighteenth century origin. The Victorian nonconformists were well fitted to take advantage of the economic opportunities of their day and many of them became prominent in the life of the industrial towns. It was always manifest that the nonconformist (unless a Quaker) could not be a gentleman as well. He disapproved of the gentry as frivolous and immoral, addicted to wine, gambling, horse-racing, theatre-going and profanity. He did not aspire to join them in the hunting field or the officers' mess. He did not wish to be seen in the ballroom, on the grouse-moor or even in the bar parlour. He disapproved of the public schools and his sons were as effectively excluded from college by their upbringing as by the law. His surplus energies went in organising temperance societies and sabbath-day schools. He came nearest to conviviality at a Chapel tea-party and nearest to pleasure in deploring the moral shortcomings of others. The nonconformist was the natural leader of democracy. It was under his guidance that the more extreme liberals became socialists. The result is that English, as opposed to continental, socialism has always retained an aura of dissent, a faint taste of cocoa and a just perceptible odour of pitch-pine pews. It is connected, not of necessity but by historical association, with total abstinence, adult education and that slight untidiness which goes with home-woven tweed. Many of those concerned in the early Labour movement had, in addition, some family connection with earlier Radicals or with the Chartist Movement of 1838-48. They knew about Robert Owen and had read the works of John Stuart Mill.

Although, however, there were drawing-room Marxists before 1874, it was not they who began the move towards socialism. It was the Tory leader, Disraeli, who took the decisive step; not perhaps through any belief in democracy but from a recognition of the inevitable. He had a great sympathy for the working man but few illusions about democracy as such.

> . . . If you establish a democracy, you must in due season reap the fruits of a democracy. You will in due season have great impatience of the public burdens combined in due season with great increase of the public expenditure. You will in due season reap the fruits of such united influence. You will in due season have wars entered into from

passion, and not from reason; and you will in due season submit to peace ignominiously sought and ignominiously obtained, which will diminish your authority and perhaps endanger your independence. You will, in due season, with a democracy find that your property is less valuable and that your freedom is less complete.[1]

It was Disraeli, nevertheless, who introduced the Reform Bill of 1867, doubling the number of voters. The Liberals gained the first election on the new register but the newly enfranchised artisans soon turned against liberalism. They wanted, not the protection of private enterprise against interference but the protection of the working man against private enterprise. They wanted exactly what the Benthamites had always denied them. They voted, therefore, for the Conservatives, bringing Disraeli back to office in 1874. And it was Disraeli who gave the British their first experience of virtually socialist legislation. An Act of 1874 limited the working week to 56 hours. By an Act of 1875, the Trades Unions were legalised. A Public Health Act of 1876 and an Artisans' Dwelling Act were fresh evidence of a new trend in legislation. Disraeli might be accepted by the aristocrats but he had been brought into power by working-class votes.

From about 1875 the English socialists began to diverge from the Liberal Party of which they had once formed the left wing. The two working-class members of parliament elected in 1874 found themselves more often voting with the Conservatives. But the views of other socialists began to become more extreme. This was partly due to the great Trade Depression of 1877-78, which seemed to prove what the Marxists said about the impending doom of capitalism. Then came the bad harvest of 1879.

> . . . It rained continuously. Everywhere the harvest blackened in the fields, and farmers were faced with ruin, landlords with depleted rentals. In England and Wales alone three million sheep died of rot. Meanwhile industry struggled against one of those periodic slumps which seemed inseparable from the capitalist system . . . for industry the trade depression of the early eighties was only a passing phase. . . . But for English agriculture the blackened crops of 1879 and the years of continued rain and cold that followed marked the end of an era. It never recovered.[2]

This turning point in the national way of life was another factor in the rise of socialism. It could hardly have achieved the same measure of success in a largely agricultural society.

While parting company with the liberals the early socialists also tended to differ among themselves. Most of the socialist societies were more or less united in the Social Democratic Federation, which

[1] *Life of Disraeli*. Monypenny and Buckle. Vol. I. p. 1608.
[2] *English Saga, 1840-1940*. Arthur Bryant. London, 1953. p. 267.

was inspired by Marxism and led by H. M. Hyndman. There was also, however, the Independent Labour Party, led by James Keir Hardie and drawing its support from the Trades Unions. Then there was founded, in 1885, the Fabian Society, with a more intellectual membership gathered round Sidney Webb, H. G. Wells, and George Bernard Shaw. Before that, in 1884, the Social Democratic Federation —which had failed to obtain much working-class support—split in two. The Federation lived on, with Hyndman and John Burns as leaders, but William Morris, Crane, Bax, Eleanor Marx and their friends left it to form the Socialist League, which ultimately died out. It is doubtful whether William Morris can be counted as a socialist at all. He should rather perhaps be classed, with Gandhi, as a democrat who saw the evil in industrialism itself irrespective of its private or state ownership. He wanted to reverse the whole trend of the period in which he lived. The genuine socialists, including Webb and Shaw, accepted industrialism and were mainly concerned with its immediate and less immediate implications.

Events which mark the progress of the Labour Movement are the Trafalgar Square riots of 1887, led by John Burns and Cunninghame Graham; the London Dock strike of 1889; the publication of William Morris's *News from Nowhere* in 1890; the Trades Union Congress reaching a membership of about 1,200,000 in 1892; and finally, in 1899, the decision of the Trades Union Congress to seek to gain increased representation for the Labour Movement. This led to fifteen Labour candidates standing for Parliament in 1900, of whom two were elected. In 1906 there was an electoral triumph for Liberal-Labour candidates, twenty-nine being elected, the Miners' Federation gaining fourteen seats for itself. It was not very clear, at this stage, what the Labour Party's principles were. Their programme and party organisation began to appear in 1908. This narrative omits, however, the most important aspect of the Movement. For Liberals and Conservatives each adopted virtually socialist measures in response to, or anticipating, Labour demands. These included the Local Government Act of 1888, the Housing Act of 1890, the Act by which education was provided free of charge in 1891, the imposition of Death Duties in 1893 and the Workmen's Compensation Act of 1897. Both through central and local governments, the members of the Fabian Society were able to secure many of their objects even before 1906.

Between 1906 and 1914 there were many further reforms, many of them initiated by Lloyd George, then Chancellor of the Exchequer. Acts provided for the feeding and medical inspection of school-children, for limiting the coal miner to an eight-hour working day, for fixing a minimum wage in certain industries, for setting up Labour

Exchanges, for Housing and Town Planning and for Old Age Pensions. The House of Lords, attempting to resist Lloyd George's Budget of 1909, lost its effective power under the Parliament Act of 1911. When Lloyd George became Prime Minister in 1916 the English Revolution had been virtually accomplished. The War finished what pre-war legislation had begun. The way was prepared for the first Labour Government of 1923, the General Strike of 1926 and the second Labour Government of 1929. Roughly speaking, Britain had become a pure democracy by 1910, with an evident tendency towards socialism. Successive Ministers, of whatever party, had to compete for votes by offering higher benefits to the poor and laying heavier taxes on the rich. The levelling-out process may not be complete but the trend is towards its completion and the achievement of a virtually socialist society.

The British experience in progressing from democracy to socialism was closely paralleled in other countries as from about the same period. Socialism was strongly established in Germany from the 1860's and led to legislation of a more or less socialist character. Ferdinand Lassalle had led the German Workers Union until his death in 1864, the Union thereafter merging with the Marxists to form the Social-Democratic Party in 1875. This was suppressed by Bismarck in 1878 after an attempt had been made to assassinate the Emperor. Socialism revived, nevertheless, and Bismarck tried to forestall the movement by legislation of his own, which was continued after his fall in 1890. Trade Laws were introduced in 1881 and subsequently; compulsory insurance against sickness in 1883; insurance against industrial accidents in 1884; old age pensions in 1889; and a Workers' Protection Law, which restricted the hours of work in 1891. The Socialists were not discouraged and by 1903 they numbered three million voters and held eighty-one seats in the Reichstag. Their success was limited, however, by their Marxist violence and talk of revolution. They lost their influence in 1914.

The French Socialists, well established by 1880, were also under Marxist influence but suffered from disagreement among themselves. They had split by 1890 into four groups, the French Labour Party, the Federation of Socialist Workers, the Socialist Revolutionaries and the Anarchists. Members of the last-named group managed to assassinate the President of the Republic in 1894. Despite such episodes as that the various groups (by now well represented in the Chamber) managed to agree on a programme in 1896. This was the work of Jaurès and Millerand and led to socialist success in the elections of 1902. But Marxist dogmatism soon produced fresh disagreements as a result of which the moderate socialists took office as liberals. One of these, Briand, was Prime Minister in 1906. Jaurès devoted himself to pacifist propaganda and was assassinated in 1912.

Socialism in Italy dates from about 1890 but was made illegal in 1894. More socialists having been elected at the elections of 1895, the party was again legalised. The liberals, moreover, introduced (in 1896-1905) compulsory insurance against industrial accidents and sickness, old age pensions and further legislation concerning public health, hours of work, subsidised housing and labour exchanges. The Italian Socialists thus gained an indirect success and were still numerous when Mussolini was editing the *Avanti* in 1912. They organised a General Strike in Emilia in 1914 but their activities were then cut short by the beginning of the First World War.

Socialism in the United States appeared in 1910 when Woodrow Wilson was first heard of as Democratic candidate for the Governorship of New Jersey. Wilson was then regarded as a conservative. When elected as President, however, in 1913, he proclaimed the *New Freedom*. This involved a graduated income tax in favour of the poor, a basic eight-hour day for railwaymen and other workers and the establishment of Boards of Mediation to arbitrate in industrial disputes. It was a small beginning, although a foretaste of F. D. Roosevelt's *New Deal* of 1933, but it was an illustration of the fact that even the United States was experiencing, belatedly and to a limited extent, the influence of socialist ideas.

The general conclusion to be drawn is that democracy in Europe, fairly widely established by 1875, began its movement towards socialism in about that year. The movement developed strongly in the period 1880-1900, most Socialist ideas having reached their virtually final form by about 1895. There was a peak of political success in 1902-1906 but soon afterwards a loss of direction and impetus. The Marxist groups still demanded revolution as an end in itself, as an essential step in progress. The more moderate groups found that their original demands had been largely met and that what remained of their programme seemed within reach by constitutional means. One formerly regarded as a rebel could end, like Sidney Webb, with a peerage. There was a pause during which the extremists, who now held the initiative, prepared the way for the next move. Socialism in its democratic form was intellectually finished before 1912; finished, in fact, before it reached America at all. It was stagnant after the First World War when the counter-offensive began. It needed no killing. It was already dead.

In the field of strictly political ideas, the Socialists had little to contribute. Accepting the liberal notion of political equality, they simply pointed out that it was meaningless unless coupled with economic equality. They merely carried the doctrine to its logical conclusion. Some of them, it is true, wrestled with the basic idea of

Equality, trying to justify it in other than religious terms. Such is the book called *Equality* by R. H. Tawney, published in 1931 and dedicated to Sidney and Beatrice Webb. Tawney does not so much defend Equality as ask what justification there can be for inequality. He concludes that,

> . . . it is the mark of a civilised society to aim at eliminating such inequalities as have their source not in individual differences, but in its own organisation, and that individual differences, which are a source of social energy, are more likely to ripen and find expression if social inequalities are, as far as practicable, diminished.[1]

Other authors have struggled with the same problem, notably David Thomson,[2] but usually with the air of finding reasons for something already generally agreed, a policy which no sane man could really propose to reverse. Apart from discussions such as these, the British Socialists have mostly been glad to accept Parliamentary Government as they found it. The Webbs once proposed having two Parliaments instead of one but the rest have shown little interest in political theory or in any but economic reforms. Political wisdom ends for them with the establishment of Universal Suffrage.

While there is little to say about the political thought of the Socialists, it would be wrong to conclude this chapter without mention of the two thinkers of the Socialist period in Britain, whose views, in retrospect, seem most significant. One of these was George Bernard Shaw, an important member of the Fabian Society in its early days but never an accepted leader of the Labour Party. He was the most original thinker the English Socialists ever had among them and he proved too original at times for their liking. What is especially interesting, however, about his line of thought is that he came to think socialism more important than democracy. For him, as for many less gifted, socialism itself had become the aim and democracy at best the means. Democracy for him came to have a special meaning; one which the actual politicians may have shared but could never have publicly avowed.

> Democracy means the organization of society for the benefit and at the expense of everybody indiscriminately and not for the benefit of a privileged class.
>
> A nearly desperate difficulty in the way of its realization is the delusion that the method of securing it is to give votes to everybody, which is the one certain method of defeating it. Adult suffrage kills it dead. Highminded and well-informed people desire it; but they are in a negligible minority at the polling stations. Mr. Everybody, as Voltaire called him—and we must now include Mrs. Everybody and

[1] *Equality*. R. H. Tawney. London, 1951.
[2] *Equality*. David Thomson. Cambridge, 1949.

Miss Everybody—far from desiring the great development of public organization and governmental activity which democracy involves, has a dread of being governed at all. . . .[1]

He goes on to explain the ignorance and indifference of the voter and the reluctance of the intelligent person to take any part in politics. Only a few are fit to take part in public affairs.

I do not see any way out of this difficulty as long as our democrats persist in assuming that Mr. Everyman is omniscient as well as ubiquitous, and refuse to reconsider the suffrage in the light of facts and commonsense. How much control of the Government does Mr. Everyman need to protect himself against tyranny? How much is he capable of exercising without ruining himself and wrecking civilization? Are these questions really unanswerable? I think not. . . .

It is a matter of simple natural history that humans vary widely in political competence. They vary not only from individual to individual but from age to age in the same individual. In the face of this flat fact it is silly to go on pretending that the voice of the people is the voice of God. When Voltaire said that Mr. Everybody was wiser than Mr. Anybody he had never seen adult suffrage at work. It takes all sorts to make a world; and to maintain civilization some of these sorts have to be killed like mad dogs whilst others have to be put in command of the State. Until the differences are classified we cannot have a scientific suffrage; and without a scientific suffrage every attempt at democracy will defeat itself as it has always done.[2]

Although he concedes that average or representative people should have the means of voicing their grievances,[3] he maintains that 'The legislators and rulers should, on the contrary, be as unrepresentative of Everyman as possible, short of being inhuman'. He wants to have people classified and graded according to their political competence, not to abolish elections altogether but to eliminate all candidates without the necessary mental and moral qualifications for office. He writes an interesting chapter (Chap. XXXVI *op. cit.*) on the kinds of test which might be used to grade citizens according to their political competence. And he complains, in his summary[4] that 'we never dream of asking whether a Secretary of State has ever heard of Macaulay or Marx, nor even whether he can read the alphabet'.

There is much in this of lasting value and interest but he does not explain how to take the franchise from people who have quite recently been granted it. He discards democracy—using the word to describe something else—and demands a new and better constitution. But who can approve it in a democratic state? Who can persuade the people

---

[1] *Everybody's Political What's What.* Bernard Shaw. London, 1944. pp. 40-41.
[2] Bernard Shaw. *op. cit.* pp. 45-46.
[3] That is, in a second or Social Parliament as proposed by the Webbs.
[4] Bernard Shaw. *op. cit.* p. 366.

to surrender the most part of their theoretical or actual powers? Who but a dictator could create and empower the aristocracy which Shaw wishes to see established? And how, except by revolution, could the dictator gain office himself? In defining the word democracy afresh, Shaw emphasises his view that society should be organised for the benefit of all, not merely for the benefit of a privileged class. He was not content, for example, to see it organised for the benefit of a privileged working class with a fifty-one per cent majority. He believed in equalising income sufficiently to abolish classes but he had ceased to believe in the wisdom of the people. He had seen it at work for too long.

Contemporary with Bernard Shaw and with a brain as original was Hilaire Belloc (1870-1953), whose preferences were diametrically opposite but whose conclusions were, in one respect, almost the same. Belloc was a liberal democrat and utterly opposed to socialism. And whereas Shaw was ready to jettison democracy when he found it inconsistent with socialism, Belloc rejected socialism as inconsistent with democracy. They agreed, that is to say, on the central fact of their being incompatible. One of Belloc's most remarkable works is *The Servile State*, written in 1912. That book and the *Party System* (1911) resulted from his experience as a Liberal Member of Parliament, for Salford, from 1906 to 1910. In other words, Belloc entered Parliament as one of the triumphant Liberals of 1906 and witnessed, from a back bench, the passing of the more or less socialist legislation which led up to the Parliament Act of 1911. His conclusion was that Britain had taken a road which could lead only to slavery. As an historian he knew how difficult it is to prevent slavery, and he made this clear in a sentence which is the starting point of his argument:

> In no matter what field of the European past we make our research, we find, from two thousand years ago upwards, one fundamental institution whereupon the whole of society reposes; that fundamental institution is Slavery.[1]

He reminds us that the freedom of the proletariat is a recent and precarious state of affairs to be maintained only by ceaseless democratic vigilance. A Capitalist State, democratic in theory but with vast differences in economic status, is, he points out, essentially unstable. It is a pyramid balanced upon its apex. It can be upset at any moment by a democratic attack on the wealthy or a capitalist attack on democracy. The theory of equality and the concrete facts are too much at variance for stability to be achieved.

> If the Capitalist State is in unstable equilibrium, this only means that it is seeking a stable equilibrium, and that Capitalism cannot but be transformed into some other arrangement wherein Society may repose.

[1] *The Servile State*. Hilaire Belloc. London, 1912. p. 31.

There are but three social arrangements which can replace Capitalism: Slavery, Socialism, and Property. . . .

The problem turns, remember, upon the control of the means of production. Capitalism means that this control is vested in the hands of few, while political freedom is the appanage of all. If this anomaly cannot endure, from its insecurity and from its own contradiction with its presumed moral basis, you must either have a transformation of the one or of the other of the two elements which combined have been found unworkable. These two factors are (1) The ownership of the means of Production by a few; (2) The Freedom of all. To solve Capitalism you must get rid of restricted ownership, or of freedom, or of both.[1]

The abolition of restricted ownership can be brought about in two ways, either by redistributing property among the many or by vesting it in the State. 'The essential point to grasp is that the only alternative to private property is public property'. The choice is between Distributism and Socialism. But the redistribution of property, in an industrial state, is politically and even technically difficult. It might follow some external catastrophe but could hardly be done from within, without so disturbing 'the whole network of economic relations as to bring ruin at once to the whole body politic'.[2] The difficulty, in fact, of 'redistributing' a railway system would be less formidable than that of persuading the employees to accept property in the railway (with its attendant risks) instead of a secure living wage. Belloc concludes, reluctantly, that Capitalist modes of thought and the division of society into employers and employed, must present an almost impossible situation to the distributist reformer. He wants to take from those who are unwilling to relinquish in order to give to those who are unwilling to receive. In practice, therefore, it is only the socialist who makes any progress.

The Socialist movement . . . is itself made up of two kinds of men: there is (a) the man who regards the public ownership of the means of production (and the consequent compulsion of all citizens to work under the direction of the State) as the only feasible solution of our modern ills. There is also (b) the man who loves the Collectivist ideal in itself, who does not pursue it so much because it is a solution of modern Capitalism, as because it is an ordered and regular form of society which appeals to him in itself. He loves to consider the ideal of a State in which land and capital shall be held by public officials who shall order other men about and so preserve them from the consequences of *their* vice, ignorance, and folly.

These types are perfectly distinct, in many respects antagonistic, and between them they cover the whole Socialist movement.[3]

[1] Belloc. *op. cit.* pp. 97-98.
[2] *Ibid.* p. 110.
[3] *Ibid.* pp. 121-122.

The Socialist party, comprising these divergent elements, finds itself confronted with the formidable entrenchments of Capitalism, strengthened with the barbed wire of legal, moral and technical entanglement. The assault is not going to be easy. There is a parley. The Socialist leader says to the Capitalist 'I desire to dispossess you, and meanwhile I am determined that your employees shall live tolerable lives'.[1] The Capitalist shows that the attempt to evict him can lead only to disaster. But he is willing to compromise. While retaining his position, he will make the workers' lives more tolerable —provided they will accept certain conditions, to be agreed.

> This idealist social reformer, therefore, finds the current of his demand canalised. As to one part of it, confiscation, it is checked and barred; as to the other, securing human conditions for the proletariat, the gates are open. Half the river is dammed by a strong weir, but there is a sluice, and that sluice can be lifted. Once lifted, the whole force of the current will run through the opportunity so afforded it; there will it scour and deepen its channel; there will the main stream learn to run.[2]

In other words, nearly everything that the humanitarian socialist wants can be achieved. He can end the suffering and insecurity of the poor, provided they will accept a diminution of their freedom; for that is what the attached conditions will amount to. The Capitalist cannot give them security unless they will do as they are told. The idealist Reformer will find that he has brought about the Servile State. What of his colleague, the lover of statistics? He is still less likely to risk a frontal assault, without even moral indignation to drive him on. He finds, in fact, that all he really cares about—a tidy system and a high salary for himself—can be gained with relative ease.

> To such a man the Servile State is hardly a thing towards which he drifts, it is rather a tolerable alternative to his ideal Collectivist State, which alternative he is quite prepared to accept and regards favourably. . . .
> The so-called 'Socialist' of this type has not fallen into the Servile State by a miscalculation. He has fathered it; he welcomes its birth, he foresees his power over its future.[3]

Belloc saw the beginnings of the Servile State in the National Insurance Act of 1911, partly because the definition of the persons to be compulsorily insured drew the line between the proletariat and the free, and partly because, to the threat of unemployment could now be added the threat of a deprivation of savings.

[1] Belloc. *op. cit.* pp. 124-125.
[2] *Ibid.* p. 125.
[3] *Ibid.* pp. 129-130.

A man has been compelled by law to put aside sums from his wages as insurance against unemployment. But he is no longer the judge of how such sums shall be used. They are not in his possession; they are not even in the hands of some society, which he can really control. They are in the hands of a Government official. 'Here is work offered you at twenty-five shillings a week. If you do not take it you certainly shall not have a right to the money you have been compelled to put aside. If you will take it the sum shall still stand to your credit, and when next in my judgment your unemployment is not due to your recalcitrance and refusal to labour, I will permit you to have some of your money: not otherwise'. Dovetailing in with this machinery of compulsion is all that mass of registration and docketing which is accumulating through the use of Labour Exchanges. Not only will the Official have the power to enforce special contracts, or the power to coerce individual men to labour under the threat of a fine, but he will also have a series of *dossiers* by which the record of each workman can be established. No man, once so registered and known, can escape; and, of the nature of the system the numbers caught in the net must steadily increase until the whole mass of labour is mapped out and controlled.

These are very powerful instruments of compulsion indeed. They already exist. They are already a part of our laws.[1]

Belloc lived long enough to see the logical conclusion of the process; the legalised 'direction' of labour. The Servile State had arrived, as he had predicted in that final paragraph with which his book is brought almost to its close:

The internal strains which have threatened society during its Capitalist phase will be relaxed and eliminated, and the community will settle down upon that Servile basis which was its foundation before the advent of the Christian faith, from which that faith slowly weaned it, and to which in the decay of that faith it naturally returns.[2]

[1] Belloc. *op. cit*. pp. 175-176.
[2] *Ibid*. p. 183.

PART IV

Dictatorship

CHAPTER XIX

Democracy in Decline

HILAIRE BELLOC tried to show that, in an industrial community at least, democracy will tend to turn into Socialism or else into that compromise which exists in what he termed the Servile State. Subsequent events have gone some way to justify his theory. They have also, however, led many to suspect that the alternative offered is an unreal one; that there is a distinction here without a difference. In Britain, at any rate, we have seen private enterprise swept away by combines, price-rings and trade associations to the point at which nationalisation, when it comes, makes little apparent difference. When the possible employers in a particular trade have been reduced, by successive mergers, to perhaps half-a-dozen; when these few Boards of Directors, perhaps with an overlapping membership, have reached agreement with each other about prices, wages and quality of product, they cannot resist nationalisation in the name of free competition for (as everyone knows) there is none. In a period, moreover, of impending slump they may actually welcome nationalisation as tending to fix salaries at a level which future profits might not otherwise justify. To the employees the change may be welcome for the same reason. To the consumers the change will probably make no difference at all. Socialism and the Servile State would appear to be much the same thing. In either form of democracy the voters have traded their liberty in exchange for secure wages. In each, democracy remains effective enough to ensure that the level of wages is at least maintained. In neither form is democracy very consistent with freedom.

Modern European democracy, in a more or less socialist form, reached its highest level of popularity in 1918. The First World War could be represented as a conflict between obsolete and progressive countries; between despotism and democracy. Its immediate and most spectacular result was the collapse of monarchy in Germany, Austria-Hungary and Russia. The world could be re-shaped according to the views of the democratic countries, Britain, France and the United States. More than that, the result of the war had seemed to show that the democratic way of life could produce armies which were actually more effective than those ordered into battle by despots. The soldiers of democracy had something, it was thought, for which they could fight. Athens must eternally prove superior to Sparta, Grant must always triumph over Lee. The making of peace was to be the work of genuine democrats—Briand, son of an innkeeper of Nantes, Lloyd George, son of an itinerant teacher and brought up by a cobbler, and Woodrow Wilson, the college president and idealist. The future of the world seemed brighter than ever before.

What is extraordinary, in retrospect, is the speed with which the vision disappeared. Readers of Plato and of Karl Marx might have expected to see democracy collapse in anarchy and revolution. Readers of John Stuart Mill might have questioned whether socialism was compatible with liberty. But none surely would have expected it to collapse as quickly as it did. Representative Democracy had become the vogue by about 1875. It had led to Socialism, which was widespread in 1895 and triumphant by about 1910. By 1930 the period of socialistic democracy was practically over. 'Socialism' wrote Joseph Conrad 'must inevitably end in Caesarism', but even those who shared his fears would hardly have dared to predict that the socialist era would be as brief as it proved to be.

In considering the question of how long a democratic phase of government may be expected to last, we can appeal to reason, to history and to recent experience. Merely theoretical discussion would lead us to expect one of two things. Either the proletariat would establish a socialist state or it would fail as against middle-class opposition. If it succeeded, the State would acquire such an accumulation of centralised power—political, economic, religious and cultural —that some of the former upper class would be goaded into revolt. Supposing the conspiracy or rising should attract any measure of support, in the name of freedom, the strongest personality in the government would make himself dictator during the emergency: thereafter, the rising crushed, he would remain dictator as a precaution against any future threat of the same kind. In the opposite case, supposing that the socialist police state has not been firmly established, the middle classes might rally to protect their lives and property. In the struggle they will appoint a leader or more probably allow the leader to appoint himself. By the time the conflict ends in a middle-class victory, the leader will have become dictator; and he must remain dictator, this time in a capitalist police state, to prevent the proletariat rising again. Civil War of this kind seems likely to produce dictatorship in any case; nor do dictatorships of different origin differ from each other as much as might be supposed. For the dictator, in the last resort, is not so much a master of intrigue and cruelty as a man with sufficient moral courage to open fire. It is sometimes thought that the invention of automatic weapons has ended for ever the effectiveness of the mob, putting all the trump cards in the hands of whatever government there is. But revolutions are not brought about, have never been brought about, by weapons; nor is it by weapons that a rising is suppressed. Governments which collapse when mobbed are usually lacking not weapons but courage. At some point in a situation of growing disorder someone must give the order to fire or charge. In a capital city—with the certainty that half the casualties will be innocent bystanders—this requires a fair amount of courage. It is easiest for a foreigner, a Prince Rupert, a Napoleon, a General Dyer; and easier still if the troops are also foreign—Scottish mercenaries in Paris, Swiss mercenaries in Rome or German mercenaries in Algiers. But the risk is considerable, for the man who takes the responsibility may never be forgiven by the people and may easily be disowned by his own side. That is why a feeble government will allow riot and bloodshed to go on for days while its leaders twitter among themselves about humanity. Some twenty cartridges will disperse the average crowd but a man like Napoleon does not stop at that; he cheerfully uses artillery. The smoke has hardly cleared before he finds himself dictator.

Once a man has become dictator he cannot, usually, abdicate. If he does, the enemies he has made will kill him. Sulla resigned, it is true, and lived for a year. But Julius Caesar could not have resigned —he was murdered even while still in office. Pompey could not have resigned, nor Cromwell, nor Napoleon. It is the knowledge of his own danger that drives the dictator on to eliminate his opponents. Nor does it very much matter whether he began, like Julius Caesar, as a democratic leader, or like Sulla as the saviour of the oligarchs. Once in office he must rule as he can. That is why Gandhi was supremely right in maintaining, as he did, that an egalitarian democracy cannot be achieved by force but only by persuasion. Once violence has been used, the feelings aroused will make further violence unavoidable. And in a state of tension and fear the party led by one will always (given anything like equal chances) defeat the party led by a committee. There are therefore abstract reasons for doubting whether socialism, as a phase in the decline of democracy, can be expected to last for long. There are abstract reasons again for supposing that it will lead to dictatorship.

Does history, generally, bear out this conclusion? For early civilisations the evidence is scanty. We know that ancient Egypt had a form of revolution against a ruling class. The sage Ipuwer bewailed the results in phrases which suggest what had happened. 'The wealthy are in mourning. The poor man is full of joy. Every town says "Let us suppress the powerful among us"'. 'The son of a man of rank is no (longer) distinguished from him who has no such father'. 'Those who were clad in fine linen are beaten. Noble ladies suffer like slave girls'. 'All female slaves are free with their tongues. When their mistress speaks, it is irksome to the servants'. 'Princes are hungry and in distress'. 'Serfs become lords of serfs'. 'The corn of Egypt is common property'. 'The chiefs of the land flee. Noble ladies go hungry'. 'No craftsman works. . . .' This is certainly a fair description of a revolution and the sage goes on to describe the results. 'Plague is throughout the land. Blood is everywhere. Death is not lacking'. The next known event is the proclamation of Intef or Antef of Thebes as the first king of the Eleventh Dynasty, about 2160 B.C.[1]

In ancient Greece the examples of democracy turning into dictatorship after a phase of socialism were so numerous that the Greek thinkers felt justified in regarding that sequence as almost a law of nature. In ancient Rome the episode of democracy and socialism was relatively brief but quite recognisable. It is only, however, of modern times that we have such full information as to be quite certain what happened. And that historical experience is incomplete in the sense that it is still going on. No one could attempt to deduce a law from what is, after all, only a single example.

But one aspect of quite recent experience is the way in which a democratic government may lose support even before its 'levelling' policy has gone very far. On this subject Gopinath Dhawan is admirably precise:

> In recent years Parliamentary Government has been subjected to severe criticism. Thus the system of elections; the slow-moving procedure; the incapacity of the system, due to centralization and congestion of business, for the really creative work of social and economic planning; the dictatorship of the cabinet; the increasing power of permanent officials; the failure of the system to induce the citizen to participate actively in political life; the absence of approximate economic equality—all these weak points have been assailed by many critics. To Gandhiji [i.e. Gandhi, as usually spelt] democracy remains unachieved more on account of the prevailing belief in the efficacy of violence and untruth than on account of mere institutional inadequacy. Democracy is really vitiated by the wrong ideas and ideals that move men.[2]

Impatience with democracy had become fairly general before a quarter of the twentieth century had passed. Bernard Shaw describes how real socialism had been frustrated in England by the party system and by universal suffrage. While attributing this to the cunning of Disraeli, he admits that things were no better in Germany or France.

> . . . As nothing parliamentary happened either in Germany or anywhere else, the proletariat became more and more disappointed and disgusted with parliamentary government without understanding

[1] *The Steppe and the Sown.* H. Peake and H. J. Fleure. Oxford, 1928. pp. 142-143.
[2] *The Political Philosophy of Mahatma Gandhi.* Gopinath Dhawan. Ahmedabad, 1951. p. 334.

what was the matter with it. Anarchists, Syndicalists, and Guild Socialists, crushed by Fabianism, raised their heads again and were able to shew that militant city mobs were more feared by despots than parliamentary Labour Parties by the Capitalist oligarchy. Despotic dictators came into fashion as fast as Lib-Lab prime ministers lost face. Peter the Great building a new capital city on the Neva; Napoleon sweeping out Augean stables, breaking rusty chains, draining marshes, making roads for world traffic, and opening a career to the talents in a blaze of revolutionary glory; his nephew Haussmanising Paris and Mussolini rebuilding Rome; Primo de Rivera and Hitler covering their countries with up-to-date roads, were contrasted with the British parliament's helpless inability to build a bridge over the Severn, and the impotence of Liebknecht and Bebel under the heel first of Bismarck and then of the Kaiser. No parliament could either abolish unemployment, the most dreaded affliction of the proletariat, or treat the unemployed decently. . . . Adolf Hitler and Benito Mussolini found, as Cromwell had found before them, that . . . they could get anything they wanted done, and sweep all parliamentary recalcitrants into the dustbin, alive or dead. To the people it seemed that the dictators could fulfil their promises if they would, and that the parliamentary parties could not even if they would. No wonder the plebiscites always gave the dictators majorities of ninety-five per cent and upwards.[1]

Gandhi, the more profound thinker, says plainly that democracy cannot work if the voter's chief aim is to benefit himself. In his view (and he is obviously right) no good can come of the violence which a state confiscation of private wealth must involve. Bernard Shaw sees that the kind of socialism he wants will never be voted by any electorate he knows. A moderate socialism, in fact, with the voters seeking a secure wage and no responsibility can produce only Belloc's Servile State. Real socialism, on the other hand, brought about by an extremist group, will mean violence, and violence will mean dictatorship. But what is significant about Bernard Shaw's viewpoint is his admission that dictatorship, when it comes, is actually what many people want. The democracy that does not fail through socialist violence fails through mere incompetence; and through an incompetence which has become notorious, public and measurable.

It has been suggested on an earlier page (see p. 173) that the defects of Athenian democracy appeared in the disunion produced by socialist measures; in public finance; and in external affairs. How far does recent experience confirm the view that democracy is liable to fail in those particular directions? It would be a study in itself to analyse the history of European democracy since 1900, and further volumes would be needed to cover the history of democracy elsewhere. All that can be done here is to show that the Athenian defects

[1] *Everybody's Political What's What.* Bernard Shaw. London, 1944. p. 263.

are not unknown to-day; which is not the same thing as to show that they are universal.

The best example of democratic disunity producing disaster is afforded by the fall of France in 1940. Not all the circumstances of the collapse are relevant to the present purpose nor were all its causes even political. What is clear, nevertheless, is that the French were so divided among themselves that their military effort came to nothing. More to the point, they quickly produced a government which was virtually collaborationist, led by an aged general whose love for France was less perhaps than his detestation of socialism in its French form. The earlier manifestations of disunity—Boulangism, the anti-Dreyfus agitation, the politics of the *Action Française*—all foreshadowed what would sooner or later take place. Elsewhere in the world believers in democracy took heart from the triumph of the First World War. But the French had been defeated in that war and saved only by their allies. Their feeling when war ended was not one of elation but of dread. Their fear of German revenge was justified by events but it produced no sort of unity. French society had been destroyed in successive revolutions, leaving nothing but left-wing malcontents whose spiritual home was in Soviet Russia and right-wing malcontents whose spiritual home was in Italy or Spain.

> From Germany's exit from the League of Nations in October, 1933, a sub-revolutionary period set in for France. Both the Italo-Abyssinian War and the Spanish Civil War tore the tissue of France's national opinion to shreds, set all antagonisms ablaze and produced the well-known historical phenomenon of some Conservatives' preference for a foreign invader to the victory of the progressive social forces in his own country. . . .[1]

The French armies did not fight; they disintegrated. Nor is their any sign of recovered unity since 1945. As a world power France no longer exists.

For an example of the dangers of democratic finance we need go no further than England. And yet the tendency to build up an enormous civil service, such as existed at Athens, is universal and not even directly connected with democracy. What is distinctively democratic is the force which prevents any reduction in the establishment which has been built up. The increase in itself is due to a law of growth which affects every administrative office; a law which has yet to be fully investigated, the workings of which are manifest although not yet reduced to a satisfactory formula. The obvious fact is that anyone appointing an administrator to do a certain continuing task, assisted by two clerks, will find (after two or three years) that the original official is now assisted by two others, dividing the work between them, and each of these aided in turn by two clerks. A year

[1] *The Future of Government.* H. Finer. London, 1946. p. 80.

or two later the official first appointed will need a higher salary in order to control two sub-departments, each of which will comprise a head and two or more assistants, each again with clerks to assist him. By then there will have to be an establishment officer in addition, to deal with problems of emoluments and leave. So much is common knowledge. What is less widely realised is that the increase in staff is governed by a law of growth which is not related in any way to the amount of work to be done.[1] The volume of outside correspondence may be constant, it may have diminished; it may even have increased. But the staff will multiply in any case and at approximately the same speed, all working as hard as (and some working harder than) before. In a commercial concern this process will not continue unchecked for ever and may be reversed promptly in a period of slump. Under a monarchy the process may be undone when the king wants the money for something else, if only for a new mistress. But no one can reduce the civil service in a democracy. No one can economise on staff in a nationalised industry. To do so would be to lose votes on a big scale. There is hardly a modern state not grossly overburdened with unproductive clerks and officials, and Britain perhaps as over-burdened as any. But there is no remedy for it under a democratic form of rule.

Lastly, there is the question of foreign and colonial policy. So far as Great Britain is concerned, it must be remembered that democratic measures were for long introduced by aristocratic men. No revolution came to break the older traditions and the process of democratic dilution has not been completed even yet. Even after Lloyd George began to found the Welfare State, diplomacy and the armed services remained in aristocratic hands—so much so that there were fears of armed revolt over Ulster in 1914. The result was that the diplomatic preparation for the First World War was admirable. It was conducted, that is to say, solely with regard to national interests. There was little confusion about ideological aims. It took even longer for democracy to affect the Army and Navy, both remaining under more or less aristocratic leadership throughout and after the Second World War. To judge the effectiveness of democratic foreign policy we must turn to the British record between 1916 and 1940. Of democratic war leadership there is as yet no British example at all. All that can be noted on that score is that the British turned with relief to an aristo-cratic leader in 1940, leaving the direction of the war thereafter to him and to senior officers who equally dated from the old regime. The results of throwing the services open to talent cannot be known until another decade has passed. We know, in the meanwhile, that the age of Pericles is over.

[1] See *The Economist*, Nov. 19th, 1955.

Would it be fair to say that British foreign policy in 1916-1940 reproduced all the Athenian mistakes? That the foreign policy itself was all but suicidal is obvious from the facts. In 1914 Britain faced up to the German aggressor in firm alliance with Russia, France and Japan, thereafter obtaining the alliance of Italy, Roumania, China and the United States. Diplomatically outmanoeuvred, the Kaiser had Austria, Turkey and Bulgaria as his only allies. In 1939, by contrast, Britain went to war against the same aggressor with France and Poland as her only allies. Germany was then in alliance with Austria and other satellite countries and enjoyed, in addition, a diplomatic understanding with Italy, Spain, Japan and Russia. As against that, Great Britain had no understanding with the United States, which in fact remained neutral until attacked. Nor was this all. For there was actually a moment in 1939-40 when Great Britain, already at war with Germany and still unaided by the United States, was actually aiding Finland against Russia with every likelihood of having in consequence to fight the Russians as well. As it proved no easy task, in the end, for Great Britain, Russia and the United States to defeat Germany by their combined efforts, an attempt by Great Britain to fight both Germany and Russia, and without American help, would have been magnificent. But is that war? More to the point, is that foreign policy? Disraeli had uttered a specific warning that, under a democracy 'You will in due season have wars entered into from passion, and not from reason'.[1] On the face of it, the failure of British foreign policy would seem to have been complete.

It is not enough, however, for our present purpose, to show that British foreign policy had failed, even though the fact is beyond dispute. We have to show that it failed through being democratic. Mistakes in foreign policy are not confined to democracies, as the Kaiser proved in 1914. What we have to ascertain is whether the mistakes made were of a kind to which democracies are peculiarly liable. Were they brought about, in fact, by the pressure of public opinion? Or were the disasters due to circumstances unrelated to any form of rule? In considering this question the basic fact to realise is that the British Empire began to disintegrate in 1921. A result of the Washington Conference was to weaken, not only the Royal Navy but the entire British position in the Far East. This was the first step in a process which was to involve the loss of India. Behind this process was the realisation in Britain that a democracy has no right to govern an empire. British voters could not logically deny to the Hindoos the political privileges they claimed for themselves. When, moreover, the British forgot the weakness of their moral position the Americans were always quick to remind them of it; being in fact (as it happened) less sensitive about American imperialism than British. As a background, therefore, to British foreign policy was the weakening of the Empire generally and the steady deterioration of the position in the Far East; due in part to American pressure but also in part to the moral sentiments of the British voters whose sentiments joined happily with their preference, for the money saved on warships could be (and was) spent on social benefits for themselves.

While it may be admitted, however, that the disintegration of the Empire (or the beginnings of it) made the statesman's task more difficult, it could be urged that the moral position of Britain was an asset and that the purity of British motives would make friends to take the place of subjects. No true democrat could accept it as a valid criticism of British policy that the principles of freedom were allowed to prevail in the Empire over mere principles of strategy. So that it is to foreign policy in the narrower sense that we must look for proof of democratic weakness. There are three aspects of this which seem worthy of study; the methods used, the aims in view and the specific results. As regards the methods there can be few better witnesses than Sir Harold Nicolson, who writes:

> The essential defect of democratic policy can be defined in one word, namely 'irresponsibility'. Under a monarchic or oligarchic system the 'sovereign' who enters into a contract with some foreign State feels himself personally 'responsible' for the execution of that contract. For a monarch or a governing class to repudiate a formal treaty was regarded as a dishonourable thing to do, and would have aroused much criticism both at home and abroad. Now, however, that the people are 'sovereign', this sense of individual or corporate responsibility no longer exists. The people are in no sense aware of their own sovereignty in foreign affairs and have therefore no sense of responsibility in regard to treaties or conventions entered into with other Powers, even when they have themselves, through their elected representatives, approved of those treaties. They are honestly under the impression that their own word has not been pledged and that they are therefore fully entitled to repudiate engagements which they may subsequently feel to be onerous or inconvenient. . . .[1]

This might seem exaggerated but it is more than borne out by the facts.

> The chief asset with which the Labour party approached the conduct of British foreign policy was that it had no past to be ashamed of and no heritage to live down. It had played no part in the secret diplomacy preceding the war or in the peace settlement. . . . It had no responsibility for the blockade or the armed intervention against Soviet Russia. It had, in opposition, denounced these policies and proclaimed that it would never be bound, as a government, by secret treaties or arrange-

[1] *Curzon, the last phase*. 1919-1925. H. Nicolson. London, 1934. p. 391.

ments with foreign nations which it might find in existence when it assumed power. Its advocacy of a just peace and its insistence upon the reconciliation of the victors and the vanquished had an immense appeal to a world divided by hostility and suspicion. It was on such a basis that Labour was prepared to inaugurate a new era of international good will and co-operation.[1]

It is not obvious, at first sight, why a refusal to abide by earlier agreements (if only secret ones) should in itself banish suspicion or attract goodwill. Even, however, if it did, the principle here upheld seems to combine idealism and duplicity in a way which foreign governments might eventually find confusing. In comparing this new type of diplomacy with that prevalent before 1914, Sir Harold Nicolson points out where the danger lies:—

> The main distinction, therefore, between the methods of the new and those of the old diplomacy is that the former aims at satisfying the *immediate* wishes of the electorate, whereas the latter was concerned only with the *ultimate* interests of the nation. It is, very largely, a difference in the time available. The old diplomatist, negotiating as an expert with fellow experts, was able to approach his problems in a scientific spirit, with due deliberation, and without regard to immediate popular support. Such a system was obviously open to abuse and danger. Yet democratic diplomacy is exposed to its own peculiar maladies which, in that they are less apparent, are even more insidious. In its desire to conciliate popular feeling it is apt to subordinate principle to expediency, to substitute the indefinite for the precise, to prefer in place of the central problem (which is often momentarily insoluble) subsidiary issues upon which immediate agreement, and therefore immediate popular approval, can be attained.[2]

This is the other aspect of open diplomacy as conceived by the Labour Party. But Sir Winston Churchill makes it plain that no one political party was responsible.

> . . . Delight in smooth-sounding platitudes, refusal to face unpleasant facts, desire for popularity and electoral success irrespective of the vital interests of the State, genuine love of peace and pathetic belief that love can be its sole foundation, obvious lack of intellectual vigour in both leaders of the British Coalition Government . . . the strong and violent pacifism which at this time dominated the Labour-Socialist Party, the utter devotion of the Liberals to sentiment apart from reality . . . the whole supported by overwhelming majorities in both Houses of Parliament: all these constituted a picture of British fatuity and fecklessness which, though devoid of guile, was not devoid of guilt, and, though free from wickedness or evil design, played a definite part in the unleashing upon the world of horrors and miseries which, even

[1] *British Labour's Foreign Policy*. Elaine Windrich. Stanford, California, 1952. p. 32.
[2] Nicolson. *op. cit.* pp. 185-186.

so far as they have unfolded, are already beyond comparison in human experience.[1]

These are grave words and written by one who, perhaps beyond any other, is in a position to know the facts.

So much for the methods. What of the aims? In dealing with these it becomes necessary to ignore the period before 1933. It was an epoch, for the democratic states, of a rather unpractical idealism, exemplified (to take one instance) by the Kellogg Pact of 1928, which either meant the millenium had come or else meant nothing at all. By 1933, however (or at latest by 1934) the 'disarmament' period was over and Adolf Hitler was already in power. Thenceforward it becomes more possible to discover what the British aims were supposed to be. One principle of British foreign policy has always been to oppose whatever Power threatens to become dominant in Europe. By 1934 that Power was, for the second time, Germany. To keep Germany in its place an alliance was needed of Great Britain and France with Russia or Italy or both. Nor was this theoretically impossible. Hitler's hatred of Russia was known. Mussolini's anxiety to maintain Austrian independence was known. But such an alliance required, to begin with, the strong and consistent support of Great Britain and France. And French policy was not even consistent with itself. On the one hand, France had made alliance with Czechoslovakia, Yugoslavia and Roumania. On the other hand, the money which should have been spent on mobile forces (if the French alliance was to help the Czechs) was spent from 1930 on the static defences of the Maginot Line. These defences, if completed, might or might not have saved France: they could not have saved the Little Entente. Great Britain was filled, by contrast, with high-minded people who at the same time denounced Germany, denounced Italy and opposed rearmament.

When a feeble government proposed to strengthen the Royal Air Force in July, 1934, the Labour and Liberal Parties moved a vote of censure. Mr. Attlee denied the need for more aircraft and denied that greater strength would make for peace. Mr. Winston Churchill reminded the house that 'our weakness does not only involve ourselves; our weakness involves also the stability of Europe'. He also pointed out that the Labour and Liberal parties and press were foremost in abuse of Germany.

> . . . But these criticisms are fiercely resented by the powerful men who have Germany in their hands. So that we are to disarm our friends, we are to have no allies, we are to affront powerful nations, and we are to neglect our own defences entirely. That is a miserable and perilous situation.[2]

[1] *The Second World War.* Winston S. Churchill. Vol. I. pp. 69-70.
[2] Churchill. *op. cit.* Vol. I. pp. 92-93.

It was to become more perilous still. For Italy, seeing that there was nothing to fear from France or Britain, invaded Abyssinia in 1935 and drove high-minded Englishmen into still more startling inconsistency. Mr. Attlee demanded 'effective sanctions, effectively applied' against Italy, while maintaining that 'We think that you have to go forward to disarmament. . . .' Earlier in the same year the League of Nations Union had organised a Peace Ballot in which over ten million people by demanding reduction of armaments, gave a misleading impression of their views to the rest of the world.[1] Mussolini, thinking the British negligible, decided to look for friends elsewhere. At this stage there was something to be said for conciliating him as Hoare and Laval wanted to do; and more for sinking the Italian fleet as others would have preferred; but the policy chosen combined all that was dangerous in either alternative. Next year, in 1936, the Spanish Civil War, in which a now hostile Italy was involved, offered a splendid opportunity for an agreement with Russia. The chance was missed and the end of the war found Britain on bad terms with Germany, Italy, Russia and, for that matter, Spain.

Throughout this period, however, of recurring crises, Britain and France had one loyal ally, not a great power but a firm friend, and that was Czechoslovakia. At Munich in 1938 that one ally was abandoned, betrayed by France with British connivance and despite the protest of Russia. Churchill denied at the time 'that security can be obtained by throwing a small State to the wolves'[2] but that was exactly what Chamberlain had agreed to do. By snubbing Russia he played into Hitler's hands, preparing the way for the later agreement between Russia and Germany. By sacrificing Czechoslovakia he demonstrated just what the Franco-British alliance was worth to any other potential ally. By the same act he threw away the Czech Army and the Skoda armaments factory. He threw away, finally, a year; delaying the inevitable war by a period during which German strength increased far more rapidly than British.[3] Having done this, Chamberlain returned to have his policy endorsed by an overwhelming majority in the House[4] and by a still larger majority of the British public.

It is not to our present purpose to draw up an indictment of individuals or political parties. The object is merely to show that one leading principle of British foreign policy—a principle firmly adhered to throughout most of three centuries—a principle vindicated afresh in 1914—was reversed during the period from 1933 to 1939. It was reversed by a democratically elected government, reversed with popular approval, reversed with the full consent of Parliament. This

---

[1] 'Its name overshadowed its purpose'. Churchill. *op. cit.* Vol. I. p. 232.
[2] Churchill. *op. cit.* p. 238.
[3] See Churchill. *op. cit.* pp. 262-265.
[4] By 366 votes to 144.

principle is only one of several. It is chosen for illustration here because it exemplifies the specific dangers of democratic rule; the refusal to abide by agreements, the refusal to pay for defence, the ready betrayal of allies and the failure to combine with others against a common danger. Said Disraeli 'you will in due season submit to peace ignominiously sought and ignominiously obtained' and events were to justify his prophecy. Democrats have claimed that the will of the people is always right. But can it be the will of a people to prepare their own destruction?

CHAPTER XX

The Caudillos

DICTATORSHIP is the natural sequel to the anarchy which results, very often, from the collapse of democratic rule. Dictatorship is usually, however, by its nature a short-lived experiment, limited to a single lifetime and giving way to another form of rule. Were we to judge from the history of dictatorships in the ancient world, we should conclude that the dictator is raised to his pedestal by fairly general consent. Once there, he cannot descend for fear of his enemies; nor do others want him to descend, for fear of renewed confusion. So he remains in power until his death, not necessarily attributable to old age. There is a marked tendency for dictatorship to turn into monarchy, and this trend appears again in modern history. The career of Oliver Cromwell is thus very true to pattern. Towards the end of his life it was obvious that monarchy had to be revived, whether with Cromwell as king or under Charles II restored. There was a phase of doubt as to who the king should be but none about the need for monarchy as such. And just as Cromwell prepared the way for Charles II, so did Napoleon prepare the way for Louis XVIII. His intention was to found a new dynasty but, failing in that, he merely ensured the restoration of the old. There is much evidence, in fact, to suggest that dictatorship is likely to be only a temporary expedient in a State with any tradition of unity. Dictatorship as a recurrent pattern of rule would seem more characteristic of States in which no such unity exists and in which monarchy is, for some reason, difficult to establish.

All modern dictatorship owes its inspiration to Simon Bolivar and, through him, to Napoleon. It is to South America that we must look, in the first instance, for dictatorship introduced and perpetuated as an admitted necessity; defended by thinkers of integrity and seen by historians as a positive good. This attitude towards dictatorship must be understood, however, in relation to its geographical and economic setting. South America has offered to its rulers a political problem which was initially almost insoluble. The continent is vast, largely tropical and jungle-covered, climatically exhausting to the immigrant, broken by mountains and periodically afflicted by hurricanes, earthquakes and floods. Its original Inca and Aztec rulers had been able, nevertheless, to organise the stable monarchies which the Spaniards found there in about 1500. Some three centuries of Spanish colonial rule reduced the Indian population from perhaps twenty-five million to about nine million in the early nineteenth century. By the same period the Creole white or semi-white population amounted to five million, thinly spread over an enormous territory. The Spanish social and political structure was aristocratic, all power being vested in the officials and higher clergy from Spain and the resident horse-riding landowners of Spanish descent. These ruled over a listless and improvident population of serfs and slaves. There was little or no middle class because of the rigid commercial restrictions which monopolised some trades and forbade others. Of intellectual activity there was very little sign.

If some South American handicaps were attributable to nature, others were certainly attributable to Spain.

> Spanish America received a poor heritage from the mother country: a class system, little experience in self-government, a wealthy, powerful and intolerant established church, intellectual repression, and a poor, illiterate and superstitious population. . . .[1]

Upon this practically medieval world there burst suddenly the potent ideas of nationality, independence, secularism, democracy and freedom. The Creoles were to experience the Reformation, the American War of Independence and the French Revolution. They were to experience them, moreover, at the same time, adding (for the sake of variety) some scenes borrowed from the Wars of the Roses and others from the America of Buffalo Bill. Theirs was a history in which St. Dominic, Don Quixote, Garibaldi, John of Gaunt and Al Capone were all contemporaries and at variance with each other. Their swiftly-moving drama passed abruptly from the cloister to the wild-west saloon, from the world of Francis Drake to the world of Jeremy Bentham. Nor was their confusion merely of the mind. Their wars of liberation lasted fourteen years, leaving three million exhausted and impoverished Creoles, free now from Spanish rule, to govern themselves as well as they might. They were full of new ideas but without experience of administration. They were full of noble aspirations but had no money at all.

From the confused story of the Wars of Liberation there emerges the one great reputation; that of Simon Bolivar. He was of aristocratic birth, brought up at Caracas in the Vice-Royalty of New Granada.

> If he had not been a great horseman, he would never have reached his goal, would never have held his own in battle, on mountain paths and mountain passes, and, in spite of all the noble feelings which later moved him to ever-greater deeds of daring, would never have become

---

[1] *Historic Evolution of Hispanic America.* J. Fred Rippy. New York, 1932. p. 336.

a man of action. A horseman, and only a horseman, could become the liberator of the plains and mountains of South America.[1]

His education, begun in South America, was continued in Spain (1800-1801) and later in the France of the Consulate. He admired Napoleon as a soldier, as the hero of the Republic, as the genius of freedom. He had no use for him as Emperor and would not even attend the coronation, considering him from that moment a tyrant and a bar to progress. His education was completed in Milan and Rome, where he probably met Lamartine, Madame de Staël, Chateaubriand and (possibly) Lord Byron. He returned to South America at the age of twenty-three, having read widely and met many of the distinguished men and women of the day. He was familiar with the works of Spinoza, Rousseau, Montesquieu, Machiavelli, Voltaire and Hobbes. Returning to his ancestral home, he was there when the news arrived of Napoleon's conquest of Spain. Venezuela was declared an independent state in 1810. Bolivar's military career began soon afterwards and in 1812 he set out, with five hundred men, to liberate South America from all that remained of Spanish rule.

Most of what followed is not to the present purpose. What is significant is his answer to the problem created by his military success. How was South America to be governed? He dreamt at one time of a united continent, even of the two Americas forming a single state with a capital at the Isthmus of Panama. This was fantasy. When he liberated Venezuela, however, he proclaimed it a republic and summoned a Congress at Angostura. His opening speech to the delegates has survived and is proof of the close attention he had paid to political theory.

> ... Nature endows us with the desire for freedom at our birth, yet men, whether from apathy or inborn inclination, suffer the chains laid upon them. It is a terrible truth that it costs more strength to maintain freedom than to endure the weight of tyranny. Many nations, past and present, have borne that yoke; few have made use of the happy moments of freedom and have preferred to relapse with all speed into their errors. For it is people rather than systems which lead to tyranny. The habit of subjection makes them less susceptible to the beauty of honour and progress, and they look unmoved on the glory of living in liberty under self-made laws. But are there any democratic governments which have combined power, prosperity and long life? Was it not rather aristocracy and monarchy which created the great and durable empires? Is there any empire older than China? What republic ever lasted longer than Sparta or Venice? Did the Roman Empire not conquer the world and the French monarchy last for fourteen hundred years?[2]

[1] *Bolivar, the life of an Idealist*. Emil Ludwig. Trans. by M. H. Lindsay. London, 1947.
[2] Ludwig. *op. cit.* pp. 149-50.

Bolivar became President under the new constitution of a State in which his military power was already supreme. He saw himself as 'a predestined man' and added 'The man is a fool who mistakes the blessings which Providence pours on his head. At this very moment we are beloved of God and must not leave His gifts unused!'[1]

After an absence of five years, Bolivar returned to Colombia to find it torn by intrigues, some wanting to make him king, some wanting to depose him altogether. He replied in public:

> 'The voice of the nation has forced supreme power upon me. I shall abhor that office to my dying day, for it is the cause of suspicion that I am aiming at the crown. Who can imagine me so blinded that I could desire to descend! Do these men not know that the name of *Libertador* is more glorious than any throne? Colombians! I have once more taken the yoke upon me, for in time of danger it would be hypocrisy, not modesty, to shirk it. But if my action means anything else than that I wish to safeguard the rights of the people, let no man count on me!'[2]

He wrote, however, to Paez:

> I am weary of this way of life and desire nothing but my release. I tremble lest I may descend from the heights to which fortune has raised my name. I never wished for power. It used to oppress me; now it is killing me. But Columbia moves my heart. I see our work being destroyed and future centuries passing verdict upon us as the culprits. That is why I remain in the place to which the voice of the people has called me. . . .[3]

Not only did he remain in that position. He came to see that a dictatorship was needed and that the constitution must, if necessary, be ignored. He wrote in that sense to Santander.

> The dictatorship must bring a total reform with it. Our organization is an excess of ill-applied power, and hence harmful. You know that I find administration, sedentary work, tedious. Dictatorship is in vogue; it will be popular. The soldiers want coercion and the people provincial independence. In such confusion, a dictatorship unites the whole. If the nation would authorize me, I could do everything. You speak of a monarchy . . . am I now to descend to a throne? Your letter hurts me. If you want to see me again, never speak again of a crown.[4]

Bolivar was dictator of Colombia for eighteen months, 'the supreme leader chosen by the people, but neither a tyrant nor a despot'. He saw clearly what had to be done but also saw that 'there is one great difficulty in our way'. 'Colombia' he wrote, 'is perishing because its leader is not ambitious enough'. He had too little love of power, too great a dislike of tyranny. When the last Spaniards had

[1] Ludwig. *op. cit.* p. 176.
[2] *Ibid.* p. 256.
[3] *Ibid.* pp. 257-258.
[4] *Ibid.* p. 262.

been driven from South America, the liberated republics fell into confusion, fighting each other and fighting within themselves. Bolivar narrowly escaped assassination and listened afresh to those who urged importing royalty from Europe. He decided that it was impossible.

> Who is there to become King of Colombia? No prince will come from abroad to take over a country in this state of anarchy as a hereditary monarchy without guarantees. Debts and poverty cannot support princes and courts. Further, the lowest class would fall into destitution and would dread inequality, while the generals and ambitious men in all classes would not be prepared to lose their power. A country dependent on an individual runs a gambler's risk every day. . . . No European prince will mount these royal gallows.[1]

Nor would he mount it himself. He resigned office in 1830 and died shortly afterwards, summing up his career with the words 'There have been three great fools in history: Jesus, Don Quixote and I'.

The basic trouble in South America was, of course, religious. The rising against Spain had been spontaneous, uniting most of the Creoles against an outside domination. It was headed by men of liberal views, fired by the example of America and inspired by doctrines from France. But these were fundamentally opposed by others who, while wanting liberation, were in all other respects conservative. Against visionary anti-clericals were arrayed catholic and slave-owning aristocrats with a Spanish dislike for government in any form. With a poor and illiterate population and with this lack of unity among the politically active, a monarchy was the only possible solution. But monarchy was detested by the liberals who had headed the revolt. Bolivar saw the practical need for kingship but would not renounce all his republican views in order to be crowned. How could he who had been too shocked to attend Napoleon's coronation now accept a crown for himself? He could see that the constitutions being drawn up by the liberals, 'the inventions of well-meaning visionaries',[2] were utterly futile but he could see no alternative but dictatorship. He died leaving the problem unresolved.

What followed was a prolonged period of political instability throughout South America; phases of disorder alternating with phases of dictatorship. Few of the dictators have had anything like Bolivar's political scruples.

The South American dictator is the caudillo or military leader, leader of a party; sometimes leader of an intellectual group, more often leader of a military class. Politics were confused in the nine-

---

[1] Ludwig. *op. cit.* p. 295. The fate of Maximilian was to show that Bolivar was right in this as in so much else.
[2] *The Evolution of Modern Latin America.* R. A. Humphreys. Oxford, 1946. See p. 79 *et seq.*

teenth century by the mutual hostility of landowner and peasant, oligarch and half-breed, catholic and secularist, country and town, Sierra and seacoast, military and civil.

> Each party supports a leader, an interest, a dogma; on the one side a man beholds his own party, the missionaries of truth and culture; the others are his enemies, mercenary and corrupt. Each group believes that it seeks to retain the supremacy in the name of disinterested virtue and patriotism. Rosas used to call his opponents 'infamous savages'. For the gang in possession of power, the revolutionaries are malefactors; for the latter the ruling party are merely a government of thieves and tyrants. There are gods of good and evil, as in the Oriental theogonies. Educated in the Roman Church, Americans bring into politics the absolutism of religious dogmas; they have no conception of toleration. The dominant party prefers to annihilate its adversaries. . . .[1]

Revolutions have followed one after another. The Republic of Bolivia had sixty revolts, ten constitutions and six presidents assassinated between 1826 and 1898. Peru had forty revolts and fifteen constitutions in about the same length of time. Ecuador had twenty-three dictators in about eighty years, Venezuela had fifty-two risings in seventy years.[2] The Dominican Republic had forty-three presidents in seventy-two years. Mexico had eight revolutions and thirty-seven governments between 1828 and 1867. Chile had three constitutions and ten governments in seven years, five revolutions between 1827 and 1829. Throughout South America the pattern was much the same. The aristocracy of the *hacienda* was allied with the church against the liberals—the Whites versus the Reds, the 'Bigwigs' versus the Radicals. There was no stability except under the more successful dictators. Thus, Rosas ruled Argentina for twenty-three years, Francia ruled Paraguay for twenty-six years, Gomez ruled Venezuela for twenty-seven years and Diaz ruled Mexico for thirty-four. Some of these dictators ruled extremely well—Cardenas, Pardo,[3] Blanco and Juarez for example—while others ruled badly. But everyone could see that even a bad dictator was preferable to the periods of anarchy which followed each dictator's death. The one exception to the rule was Brazil. There a monarchy had been established in 1824, providing peace until 1889. Then a bloodless revolution led to the establishment of a Republic in 1891. The sequel is as significant as the earlier part of the story, for Brazil came under a dictatorship in 1930 and was ruled very competently by Vargas until 1945.

It is difficult to make a coherent story out of events in their nature so confused. But it would be roughly true to say that most of the

[1] *Latin America: its rise and progress.* F. G. Calderon. London, 1919. p. 369.
[2] *Ibid.* p. 103 *et seq.*
[3] *Peru.* C. R. Enock. London, 1925.

South American Republics were still experiencing alternate dictator-ship and chaos in 1850. By 1870 there was a slight tendency towards more settled administration, a reflection of democratic trends in Europe. This tendency became more marked after 1900 as the influence of the United States was established over Cuba and Panama. At much the same time South America was becoming a principal source of grain and meat for the European market. Ameri-can capital began to be invested in Brazil and Peru and British capital in the Argentine.

> Between 1913 and 1929 the history of Latin America was charac-terized by important political and social changes and notable material progress. In several countries the middle and lower classes became more assertive and exercised no little influence over governmental policy. In others strong executives revealed greater interest in the masses and inaugurated systems of social welfare under state control. Of the seven new constitutions framed in as many countries, at least five were significant because of their provisions with reference to labor; and everywhere the period was marked by unprecedented social legislation.[1]

Growing prosperity in 1914-18, in creating a new middle class, hurried South America on from dictatorship to democracy and from democracy to socialism. By 1920 Chile, for example, had a vastly expanded and burdensome civil service. More or less socialistic legis-lation characterised the period from 1920 to 1925 and the various left wing parties then gained considerable influence during that period.[2] Socialism was also attempted in other States, notably in Uruguay from 1903 and (after 1911) in Mexico. But socialism, and even democracy, rested upon insecure foundations. The population was racially mixed and the Indians were still living in the Middle Ages.[3] Progress had been far too rapid and superficial. The result was that the trade depression of 1930-31 brought about revolutions in twelve out of twenty Latin American republics. Following a period of chaos there was a general return to dictatorship. Chile was ahead of the fashion in having Carlos Ibáñez as dictator in 1927. Brazil had Vargas as dictator from 1930, Mexico had Cardenas from 1934. Uruguay had a dictatorship from 1933 and Guatemala from 1931. In the Argentine, one of the most prosperous states, there was dictator-ship from 1931 almost to the present day.[4] By 1930, incidentally,

[1] *Historical Evolution of Hispanic America.* J. Fred Rippy. New York, 1932. p. 272.
[2] *Chile: an outline of its geography, economics and politics.* G. J. Butland. London, 1951. p. 42 *et seq.*
[3] See Rippy. *op. cit.* p. 433 *et seq.* In 1929 there were in South America 34 million white people, 30 million mixed, 26 million negroes and mulattoes and 20 million Indians.
[4] Juan Peron, the recent dictator, became President in 1946 and followed the example of the European dictators rather than that of previous Caudillos. It is interest-ing that the Argentine should have had a dictatorship before, during and after the Hitler period of 20th Century Europe.

Europe was beginning to follow South American precedent, producing new theories to justify what had for long been the established practice in Colombia, Paraguay, Bolivia and Ecuador. Nor was the South American example unnoticed by European critics of democracy. Francia, for example, dictator of Paraguay from 1813 to 1840, was particularly admired, as was Diaz later on.

> When he died Francia was mourned by his people, a people about to reveal in warfare a Spartan tenacity, a tranquil heroism. . . . Francia had formed a proud and warlike race. He was the most extraordinary man the world had seen for a hundred years, said Carlyle in one of his Essays—a Dominican ripe for canonisation, an excellent superior of Jesuits, a rude and atrabilious Grand Inquisitor. The Scottish historian praises the grim silences of Francia—'The grim unspeakabilities'— that mute solitude in which remarkable men commune with the mystery of things.[1]

The fact that South America raced through so much political experience in so short a time must not blind us to the nature of the process. Monarchy was what most of the States needed and it was to dictatorship (as a substitute for monarchy) that most of the States continually returned. There are grounds for believing that, without an initial period of monarchy, the later development of democracy is not even possible; not, at least, in a State of any size or any diversity of population.

Resembling each other in language and race, and in the general nature of their problems, the South American Republics are a sort of modern equivalent of the Greek City States. They have presented, at different times, examples of nearly every form of rule. It is to be expected, therefore, that they should have produced their own political theorists, profiting by so many object lessons, so many tales of success and failure. Nor is such an expectation disappointed in the event. Most of the theorists were liberals, teaching the doctrines of Bentham, Toqueville and John Stuart Mill. Many were more or less influenced by Alphonse Lamartine (1790-1869), especially after the revolution in France of 1848. Chief of the liberal theorists was Lastarria of Chile but after him came Bilbao, founder of the Society of Equality, exiled for blasphemy and sedition. Montalvo in Ecuador was of the same school of thought, an opponent of the Church, but an admirer of Christianity. He was also, however, and significantly, an admirer of Bolivar, whom he compares with Napoleon rather to the latter's disadvantage. From Montalvo we learn something of the way in which the best of the Caudillos were regarded in his day. Writing of Napoleon but thinking more of Bolivar, he says:

---

[1] *Latin America, its rise and progress.* F. G. Calderon. Trans. by B. Miall. London, 1919. p. 195. See also *Paraguay.* W. H. Koebel. London, 1919. Chap. X. (pp. 164-179).

In Napoleon there is something more than in other men; a sense, a wheel in the mechanism of understanding, a fibre in the heart. He looks across the world from the Apennines to the Pillars of Hercules, from the pyramids of Egypt to the snows of Russia. Kings tremble, pallid, and half-lifeless; thrones crack and crumble; the nations look up and regard him and are afraid, and bend the knee before the giant.[1]

He thus comes near to being an apologist of dictatorship. That could not be said of Vigil or Sarmiento, liberal thinkers respectively of Peru and the Argentine. All these looked chiefly to France for their ideas and others, between 1848 and 1858, regarded Lamartine as a 'demi-god, a second Moses'. They quoted with approval his saying that democracy is, in principle, the direct reign of God; the application of Christian ideas to the world of politics.[2] Almost alone among these theorists was Alberdi, who pleaded for monarchy.

'The Republic has been and is still the bread of Presidents, the trade of soldiers, the industry of lawyers without causes, and journalists without talent; the refuge of the second-rate of every species, and the machine for the amalgamation of all the dross of society.[3]

It is a fair description and Calderon adds his comment that 'amid the sterile enthusiasm of romantic politicians his book stands out, in its gravity, sobriety, common sense, and realism, like a lesson for all time'.[4] It was not however a lesson that his countrymen were willing to learn. Neither, on the other hand, have European political theorists shown much interest as yet in the experience or the political thought of South America.[5] In the histories of the future the ideas of Lastarria, Montalvo and Alberdi would seem to deserve at least as much space as we now devote to those of Tom Paine or Graham Wallas.

[1] Calderon. *op. cit.* See Chap. I. Book V. (pp. 235-248).
[2] *Ibid.* p. 244.
[3] *Ibid.* p. 246.
[4] *Ibid.* p. 247.
[5] See, however, *Dictatorship. Its History and Theory.* A Cobban. London, 1939. pp. 144-159.

CHAPTER XXI

Twentieth Century Dictatorship

THROUGHOUT the first half of the present century dictatorship
has been, beyond dispute, the characteristic form of rule.
Thinkers of the English-speaking world have tended, it is true, to
consider dictatorship as no more than a momentary deviation from
the path towards democracy. They attribute just the same permanence
to democratic government that their forefathers attributed in turn to
monarchy and aristocracy. But there is no particular reason for supposing that democracy will last any longer than the earlier forms of
rule; and historical analogy would incline us rather to doubt whether
it will even last as long. Predictions, however, are not to the present
purpose. The plain fact is that democracy passed its peak of popularity in about 1918.[1] There was a moment at the end of the First
World War when monarchies had collapsed in Germany, Austria
and Russia and when the fate of the world was to be decided by the
United States, the British Empire and France. The future was to be
made safe for democracy. At that very moment the first of the new
totalitarian states was founded in Russia by Lenin and the second
in Poland by Jozef Pilsudski, who remained in office until his death
in 1935. It was the beginning of a landslide.

It was Italy that now led the way, Mussolini becoming dictator
there in 1922. Dictatorships were founded thereafter in this order:
Spain (1923), Turkey (1923), Chile (1927), Greece (1928), Brazil
(1930), Dominican Republic (1930), Argentine (1931), Guatemala
(1931), Portugal (1932), Uruguay (1933), Austria (1933), Germany
(1933), Mexico (1934), Greece (again, in 1936), and France (1940).
The student confronted by this list must find it difficult to talk of the
inevitable progress of nations towards parliamentary rule with
universal suffrage. Nor must he forget that there were significant
tendencies towards dictatorship in countries which finally opposed
the trend. As against that it may be argued that the triumph of the
English-speaking peoples in 1945, with the collapse of the dictatorships involved in the Second World War, showed that democracy

[1] It is perhaps significant that Oswald Spengler's book *The Decline of the West*
appeared in 1918 and had an instant and widespread circulation; as much perhaps on
the strength of its title as on its contents. Some ninety thousand copies were sold in a
few years and it was translated into many languages. See *Social Philosophies of an age
of Crisis*. P. A. Sorokin. London, 1952. Chap. IV. p. 72 *et. seq.*

was very much alive. The trend should accordingly have been reversed. In point of fact, however, the trend has continued, with new dictatorships set up in Rumania (1940), Yugoslavia (1944), the Argentine (1946), Nationalist China (1946), Paraguay (1947), Thailand (1947), Peru (1948), Communist China (1949), Vietnam (1949), Venezuela (1952), Egypt (1952), Cuba (1952) and Colombia (1953). No exact statistics are possible, for a dictatorship is not easy to define, but there are grounds for supposing that dictatorship is still on the increase and might extend at any time to such countries as Indonesia and South Africa.

There is room for disagreement about the details of this general tendency. Was Lenin a dictator? Was Venizelos? But there can be no question, surely, that the tendency exists. There may be more democracies than ever, and more still to be created as a result of colonial territories becoming autonomous. The nineteenth century liberal impetus has not been lost in the more remote parts of the world. But the surge of these distant waves is clearly the result of a central movement that has itself ceased. Democracy died long ago as a creed and an inspiration. It died in the middle of the First World War, just before the moment of its apparent triumph.

> The question, whether men will rise towards the higher standard which the prophets of democracy deemed possible has been exercising every thoughtful mind since August 1914, and it will be answered less hopefully now than it would have been at any time in the hundred years preceding. That many millions of men should perish in a strife which brought disasters to the victors only less than those it brought to the vanquished is an event without parallel in the annals of the race. There has probably been since the fifth century no moment in history which has struck mankind with such terror and dismay as have the world-wide disasters which began in 1914, and have not yet passed away. The explanations of the facts are no more cheering than the facts themselves. . . . Knowledge has been accumulated, the methods and instruments of research have been improved . . . but the mental powers of the individual man have remained stationary, no stronger, no wider in their range, than they were thousands of years ago, and the supremely great who are fit to grapple with the vast problems which the growth of population and the advances of science have created come no more frequently, and may fail to appear just when they are most needed.[1]

So wrote James Bryce in a book published in 1929, compiled before the trade depression had even begun. And there can be no doubt that he was right. The liberals lost their faith when they discovered that democracies can kill. Democracy, which had been thought to provide the answer to all problems, had already been found

[1] *Modern Democracies.* James Bryce (Viscount Bryce). 2 Vols. London, 1929. Vol. II. p. 667.

lacking the answer to one; the problem of war. It was soon to be found equally devoid of an answer to a second problem; the problem of peace. But even before that second discovery the institution had begun to collapse. To quote Bryce again:—

> In the form which it has almost everywhere taken, that of government by a representative assembly, democracy shows signs of decay; for the reputation and moral authority of elected legislatures, although these, being indispensable, must remain, have been declining in almost every country. In some they are deemed to have shown themselves unequal to their tasks, in others to have yielded to temptations, in others to be too subservient to party, while in all they have lost some part of the respect and social deference formerly accorded to them. Whither, then, has gone so much of the power as may have departed from them? In some countries it would seem to be passing to the Cabinet—England is often cited as an example—in others to the directly elected Head of the State, as for instance to the Governors in the several States of the American Union. In France, though there has been no definite change, calls are heard for a strong President, and in Argentina the President already overtops the Chambers. What is common to all these cases is the disposition to trust one man or a few led by one, rather than an elected assembly.[1]

Writing a decade later and writing in fervent defence of democracy, Eduard Beneš had to admit that the democratic governments had been widely criticised.

> The deficiencies, weaknesses, and of course great mistakes of the individual democracies, which it was apparently impossible to avoid, are the third category of facts which played a specially important role in the downfall of European democracies. There were the excesses of the party system, its mistakes and exaggerations; the slowness and inefficiency of democratic methods of work and leadership during times of crises and at moments when quick actions and quick decisions were necessary; the partiality, corruption and incapacity of bureaucracy, subjugated very often to the exaggerated party spirit; the deficiencies, mediocrity and mistakes of the democratic leaders.[2]

If Beneš was aware of such criticism, others without his democratic idealism were still more ready to see where democracy had failed. These others had as their basic motive a dislike of the socialism (or communism) to which democracy—except in a small and simple community—was obviously bound to lead. We read in *Mein Kampf* that Adolf Hitler (then aged nineteen) attended the Chamber of Deputies at Vienna for a year. Critical from the first, he listened to confused debates at which everyone shouted. He also listened to bored debates when scarcely anyone was there. He finally concluded

[1] Bryce. *op. cit.* Vol. II. p. 632.
[2] *Democracy Today and Tomorrow*. E. Benes. London, 1939. p. 61.

that 'the institution itself was wrong in its very essence and form'. Merely to abolish it, on the one hand, would be to reinstate the Habsburgs in absolute power. To leave it in existence, on the other hand, would be to open the gates to socialism.

> Democracy, as practised in Western Europe to-day, is the fore-runner of Marxism. In fact the latter would not be conceivable without the former. Democracy is the breeding-ground in which the bacilli of the Marxist world pest can grow and spread. By the introduction of parliamentarianism democracy produced an abortion of filth and fire, the creative fire of which, however, seems to have died out.[1]

To abolish parliament without restoring monarchy could only mean finding a form of rule different from either. Hitler was typical of many in wondering whether some form of dictatorship might not be preferable. In their opposition to social democracy these middle-class spokesmen were neither more nor less selfish than the trades-unionists they sought to oppose. They could point, moreover, to very real defects in democratic governments of the day. They could find valid reasons for advocating a form of government which might seem, at the outset, more efficient. It is essential to realise that dictatorship was not merely imposed by military force. That there was normally an element of violence in the process by which the dictators gained power is true. There was also, however, considerable support from the public at large; and without that support the rise of most dictators would scarcely have been possible.

Not all dictators came into power on the heels of a collapsing socialist democracy. Some were installed, as we shall see, in countries where democracy was hardly known. But the tendency for dictatorship to succeed democracy, after a period of confusion, was exemplified in several countries of which Italy was perhaps the first. Italy had shown liberal-labour tendencies in 1912-14 which were checked momentarily when Italy entered the war against Germany and Austria. Overwhelming defeat followed at Caporetto in October, 1917. Rallying quickly the Italians managed, with Allied help, to defeat the Austrians in 1918 at Vittorio Veneto. They afterwards convinced themselves that they had won the war, being cheated by the French and British of their proper reward. They had been deceived by President Wilson. Their own assessment of their contribution to victory differed sharply from the assessment of others and Baron Sonnino had little success, therefore, in his efforts to sustain the Italian claims. The government was discredited by that failure and the Socialists began to recruit masses of adherents from among the disillusioned and resentful. The Socialist Party had opposed the war

[1] *Mein Kampf.* Adolf Hitler. Trans. by James Murphy. 2 Vols. London, 1939. Vol. I. p. 78.

and its members could now regard it as a virtual defeat; just such a defeat, in fact, as had preceded the revolution in Russia. Impressed by this analogy, the Socialist Party affiliated to the Communist International in March, 1919, before achieving a striking success in the General Election of November. The Socialists won, it is true, only 156 seats out of 508. They were, nevertheless, the strongest single party, supported by a third of thê voters and gaining a proportionate control in local government. Rather surprised by their own success, the Socialist leaders failed to grasp their opportunity. Uttering the slogan 'The Revolution is not made. The Revolution comes',[1] they allowed their movement to spend itself in pointless demonstrations. Climax to a period of confusion was the occupation of the North Italian factories in September, 1920. In the course of this episode half a million workers were in possession of six hundred factories, with armed guards posted and elected committees in control. Nor did they withdraw until promised a twenty per cent wage increase and a share in the future management.

Now was the moment for revolution.

> Had the leaders of the General Confederation of Labour and of the Socialist Party wished to strike a decisive blow, here was the opportunity. . . . The bankers, the big industrialists and big landlords waited for the social revolution as sheep wait to be led to the slaughter. If a Communist revolution could be brought about by the bewilderment and cowardice on the part of the ruling classes, the Italian people in September, 1920, could have made as many Communist revolutions as they wished.[2]

This was proved by the earlier events in 1920—railway strikes, agricultural strikes in Ferrara and Lombardy, rioting in the streets and even fisticuffs in Parliament. The government headed by Nitti and later by Giolitti was composed of liberal pacifists who had in 1919 agreed to improve the universal suffrage (introduced in 1912) by proportional representation. They were faced in consequence with a variety of political parties. These did not include the Fascisti, however, who failed at this time to win a single seat. Giolitti met the situation in the factories by a policy of inaction and the workers realised that they must either stage a revolution or retreat from their position. They shrank from a Communist Revolution (many being Catholics) and so lost the initiative.

It was during the lull which followed the workers' withdrawal in 1920 that the reaction began. Failing actual revolution, it was inevitable that the professional classes, ex-officers and students should rally to defend themselves. The Fascist party, opposed to

---

[1] *Fascism and Social Revolution*. R. Palme Dutt. London, 1934. p. 97.
[2] G. Salvemini, quoted in R. Palme Dutt. *op. cit.* p. 98.

Communism, attacked and burnt the Labour Party headquarters at Bologna in January, 1921. Encouraged by this success (and more by the failure of the police to interfere), people of wealth began to contribute to Fascist funds. Membership of the party, insignificant in 1920, rose to 248,000 in the following year. Between January and April, 1921, the Fascists attacked and destroyed Labour Party Offices and Clubs, inflicting and sustaining casualties and gaining further support. In the elections of May, 1921, only 35 Fascists were elected as against 122 Socialists and 16 Communists. It was not, however, by votes that the Fascists could hope to win. Following Giolitti's resignation in July, 1921, the liberals lost any cohesion they had ever had. By November the Fascists had drawn up a programme and a creed, primarily designed to attract further middle-class support.

> The Confederation declares that the increase of production and means of production implies, not only the increase of the productive types, but at the same time the increase of the middle classes and an ever-growing diffusion of wealth and property; which also means that it will afford to the proletarian élites the possibility of acquiring and directly managing the instruments and materials of production and of rendering themselves indispensable both socially and technically.[1]

Organised now on military lines, the Fascists went into action afresh, captured Milan in August, 1922 and prepared for the march on Rome. One significant Fascist proposal made at this time was to minimise the functions of the State.

> . . . We have had enough of the State railwayman, the State postman, and the State insurance official. We have had enough of the State administration at the expense of the Italian tax-payer, which has done nothing but aggravate the exhausted financial condition of the country. . . .[2]

Under battle-cries such as this, inspiring if slightly obscure, the Fascists went forward to their bloodless revolution of October 28th, which resulted in Mussolini becoming Prime Minister, at the King's invitation, on the 30th. He secured full powers from the House of Representatives by a vote of 275 to 90, announced a programme of 'Order and Economy', and gained a firm majority in the general election of 1924. Among his first achievements in office was the reduction of the public pay-roll.

> . . . Mussolini realised that Italy was suffering, in common with most Southern countries, from a plethora of officials and State employees. He began by amalgamating overlapping ministries and suppressing superfluous offices. A ruthless cutting of staffs in the various ministries

[1] *Three Master Builders and Another*. P. H. Box. London, 1925. Manifesto quoted on p. 158.
[2] *Ibid.* quotation on p. 169.

was inaugurated, designed to discover the exact point at which the services could be maintained in a state of efficiency. In the six months ending 30th April, 1923, 17,232 men were dismissed from the railways, which since the war had become under the State management hopelessly over-staffed and inevitably insolvent. Notice was given that by the end of 1923 the staff must be reduced by another 300,000. The stupendous disorder of the State railways can be gauged by the fact that after these amputations, they increased in efficiency.[1]

This policy of 'Order and Economy' also allowed Mussolini to abolish death duties, reduce direct taxation and repeal much of the socialist legislation passed by the liberals. The middle classes thus won over, Mussolini next turned to console the workers and eventually (under the pressure of war) went far towards re-introducing the economic controls he had just abolished.[2] However inconsistent its policy, Fascist government could count at one time upon a great measure of popular support. Nor was there any display of Italian grief when 'the whole Parliamentary structure of government in Italy crumbled like a stucco facade'.[3] Mussolini had something better than parliamentary support in a Catholic country where the Pope (Pius XI) regarded him—after the concordat of 1929—as 'the incomparable Minister'.[4] Nor was Mussolini at fault when he said that 'Never have peoples been yearning for authority, leadership, and order as they are now'.[5]

> The Dictatorships of to-day were thrown up by the swirl of events, but they have developed an authoritarian philosophy to buttress their thrones. Bolshevist, Fascist and Nazi agree in repudiating nineteenth-century Liberalism as a creed outworn. . . .
>
> 'Liberalism only flourished for half a century' echoes Mussolini. 'It was born in 1830 in reaction against the Holy Alliance. It is the logical, and indeed historical, forerunner of anarchy. . . .'[6]

The story of democracy and dictatorship in modern Germany is not strikingly different. A strong liberal movement in the late nineteenth century had turned towards socialism and gained a measure of socialist legislation in Bismarck's time. Defeat in the First World War had combined with the example of Russia to bring about the revolution of 1918. In this revolution the proletariat gained power.

> A Council of People's Commissars, responsible to the Workers' and Soldiers' Councils, was appointed, consisting of three majority Social

[1] *Ibid.* p. 174.

[2] *Dictatorship.* A. Cobban. London, 1939. p. 129.

[3] Cobban. *op. cit.* p. 127.

[4] *The Official Life of Benito Mussolini.* Georgio Pini. Trans. by Luigi Villari. London 1939.

[5] *Ibid.* p. 244.

[6] *Dictatorship in Theory and Practice.* G. P. Gooch. London, 1935. (Conway Memorial Lecture).

Democrats, and three Independents. The forms which had thus to be adopted revealed how completely the pressure and demand of the masses in the moment of revolution was towards the Soviet Republic. . . .[1]

The same events appeared differently to another, closer, observer.

. . . The great middle stratum of the nation had fulfilled its duty and paid its toll of blood. One extreme of the population, which was constituted of the best elements, had given a typical example of its heroism and had sacrificed itself almost to a man. The other extreme, which was constituted of the worst elements of the population, had preserved itself almost intact, through taking advantage of absurd laws and also because the authorities failed to enforce certain articles of the military code.

This carefully preserved scum of our nation then made the Revolution. And the reason why it could do so was that the extreme section composed of the best elements was no longer there to oppose it. It no longer existed. . . .[2]

It is the fashion among communists to bewail the fact that the German workers missed their chance in 1918-23, failing to secure their position as they might have done by dispossessing the wealthy, taking over the key industries and arming themselves against middle-class revolt. That they failed to make the most of their opportunity is clear. It is at least equally clear that they furthered their own ends to a very considerable extent. The Weimar Republic was a Social Welfare State. Rents had been frozen during the war and comprehensive schemes of social insurance had been introduced even earlier. In November, 1918, fresh legislation secured the right to form trades unions and the right to strike. Similar reforms introduced the eight-hour day, provided for collective labour agreements and allowed workers a share in the control of industry. Fixed wage scales were agreed by arbitration and Conciliation Boards formed to settle labour disputes—Boards empowered to give legally binding decisions as from 1923. Factory Councils existed from 1920 and in 1923 a 'Degree against the abuse of economic power' placed the Cartels under what was virtually state control. There was even a National Economic Council with 326 members and labour interests amply represented. Means Tests were abolished in 1927, by which date most trade union objectives had been more or less achieved.[3]

The working class gained something, therefore, under the Weimar Republic. The middle class, by contrast, lost everything. The inflation of 1923 destroyed their savings and left them resentful, insecure and

[1] *Fascism and Social Revolution*. R. Palme Dutt. London, 1934. pp. 110-111.
[2] *Mein Kampf*. Adolf Hitler. Trans. by James Murphy. London, 1939. p. 428.
[3] See *The Weimar Republic*. G. Scheele. London, 1946.

almost ready to revolt. Hayek has very properly pointed out that the type of socialism which gives security to skilled workmen, fixing wages and preventing unemployment, actually diminishes the security of everyone else.[1] The impoverished middle class had been left out in the cold. The National Socialists or Nazis in Germany were largely drawn from this middle class, a 'white collared proletariat' of lawyers, teachers and engineers who retained pretentions to power but whose actual income was far less than that of an engine driver or other skilled artisan. They were not opposed to Socialism as such but they 'expected a place in that society very different from that which society ruled by labour seemed to offer'. To an opposition comprising an aristocracy and army were added middle class elements and even such of the lower classes as were outside the privileged bodies, the trades unions of skilled workers. Adolf Hitler arose as leader of this opposition and made much of the fact that the Socialist leaders were, some of them, pacifists, Jews or both. In a speech delivered in September, 1923, he asked:

> How are States founded? Through the personality of brilliant leaders and through a people which deserves to have the crown of laurel bound about its brows. Compare with them the 'heroes' of this Republic! Shirkers, Deserters, and Pacifists: these are its founders and their heroic acts consisted in leaving in the lurch the soldiers at the front . . . while at home against old men and half-starved children they carried through a revolutionary coup d'etat. They have quite simply got together their November-State by theft! In the face of the armies returning wearied from the front these thieves have still posed as the saviours of the Fatherland! They declared the Pacifist-Democratic Republic. . . .[2]

Hitler attacked democracy as such, considering that it led directly to Bolshevism.

> . . . At all times it has been the principles of Democracy which have brought peoples to ruin. And if Germany has fallen in the last fourteen years that was only because the representation of the principles of Democracy was carried to such lengths that its fathers and representatives in Germany did as a matter of fact stand even below the average of those numbers whose supremacy they preach. They themselves have been so mediocre, so small, such dwarfs that they possess no right whatever to raise themselves above the masses. Never has any system or any Government left its place in a more melancholy, more miserable, more mediocre fashion than did the representatives of the present system.[3]

[1] The Road to Serfdom. F. A. Hayek. London, 1944. Chap. VIII.
[2] The Speeches of Adolf Hitler. Ed. by N. H. Baynes. 2 Vols. Oxford, 1942. Vol. I. p. 81.
[3] Hitler. op. cit. p. 256.

Hitler voiced a less personal criticism of democracy in deploring the fate of a country in which the government represents a particular class.

> ... for then the regime will be dependent upon the wishes of individual economic groups and will thus become the servant of one-sided economic interests, and therefore be incapable of rising above the natural economic hopes of individuals in order to protect the justifiable interests of the community. But a Government cannot serve the interests of employers on the one hand or of workmen on the other, it cannot serve city or country, trade or industry, but exclusively the whole people. . . .[1]

There was sufficient substance in arguments such as these to gain for Hitler a measure of genuine support from those honestly convinced that he was right. This support was not considerable, it is true, until after the economic crisis of 1929. By April, 1932, nevertheless, the National Socialists polled nearly thirteen and a half million votes; votes for a party leader whose avowed aim was to make himself dictator. It is incidentally manifest that, had Hitler died at that point, the dictatorship would have gone to someone else. Bruning had been ruling dictatorially, for that matter, from 1929 and many assumed that this conservative reaction would continue. 'I think it is a safe prophecy' wrote H. J. Laski, 'that the Hitlerite movement has passed its apogee'. This prophecy was uttered on November 19th, 1932.[2] Hitler came to power on January 30th, 1933.

The notoriety of these two examples, that of Italy and that of Germany should not persuade us to base any conclusion upon those examples alone. It would not be true to say that all social-democratic governments end in dictatorship. Nor would it be true to say that dictatorships arise in no other way. As against that, it must be conceded that the tendency exists and that many modern dictatorships did in fact arise on the ruins of some experiment in democracy. Dr. Alfred Cobban recognises this in his study of dictatorship and goes so far as to say that 'The historic task of many parliamentary systems appears to have been to prepare the way for the sovereignty of a dictator'. He continues:

> Dictatorship in modern times has arisen so often out of so-called democratic institutions that it seems almost as though it could not appear where there had been no previous attempt at self-government; but whereas the decline of traditional authorities is an invariable prerequisite of dictatorship, the establishment of what might be called a democratic government is not always to be found among the events preceding its rise. In the Greek cities, for example, we often seem to

---

[1] Hitler. *op. cit.* p. 453.
[2] *Daily Herald*, quoted in R. Palme Dutt. *op. cit.* p. 124.

pass directly from the overthrow of an aristocracy to the rule of a tyrant. In the modern world, however, a positive attempt at government by the people, however false or fleeting, has nearly always intervened between the fall of an hereditary monarchy, and the establishment of dictatorial rule.[1]

But if the examples briefly cited afford no foundation upon which to base an invariable rule governing the origin of dictatorship, they are equally insufficient to prove that dictatorship is manifestly harmful. Any detailed study of dictatorship in modern history must certainly reveal examples to the contrary.[2] Count Carlo Sforza had to admit that Porfirio Diaz governed Mexico well.[3] Most historians will admit that there was much to say for Eleutherios Venizelos and more to say for Mustafa Kemal. Pilsudski, Primo de Rivera, Dollfuss and Salazar have their admirers still. And even in the instances cited of frankly tyrannical rule it is not always clear that the possible alternatives would not have been worse. In a comparison of tangible achievement many dictatorships might be found to have a better record than many democracies. The main objection to dictatorship is not that it is inefficient or harsh but simply that it cannot last more than a lifetime and that its termination may involve civil war. The final criticism of dictatorship comes not from its enemies but from its defenders. For the more fervent they are in a dictator's praise, the more hopeless (they imply) will the situation be when he dies.

> We must not forget that Mussolini is the man who gave himself entirely to the great cause, animating it by his intelligence and his robust military temperament. Fascism does not make an idol of him, but it admires him for his political correctness, for the clearness of his outlook, and for his wisdom in action. Above all, it knows that, without Mussolini, it would be like an orphan or a crippled child, and that, without his vivifying inspiration, it would eventually fall under the blows of a victorious enemy.[4]

The sternest critic of fascism can add little to that.

[1] *Dictatorship, Its History and Theory.* Alfred Cobban. London, 1939. p. 260.
[2] See *Dictatorship in the Modern World.* Ed. by G. S. Ford. Minnesota, 1935-37. See also *The Story of dictatorship from the earliest times till to-day.* E. E. Kellett. London, 1937.
[3] *European Dictatorships.* Count Carlo Sforza. London, 1932.
[4] *The Fascist Movement in Italian Life.* P. Gorgolini. Trans. by M. D. Petre. London, 1923. p. 213.

CHAPTER XXII

The Theory of Dictatorship

T HE part played by authors in shaping the political destinies of
mankind has often been exaggerated. Few dictators have seized
power with a weapon in one hand and a textbook in the other. What
they have done, however, more especially in recent times, has been to
choose from the available literature such books as seemed useful in
exhorting the faithful or persuading the public. By the books thus
chosen they have been influenced in details, at least, of policy. We
shall not overestimate that influence if we remember that the dictator
chose the book from among a dozen others, all containing less
palatable advice; it was not the author who chose the dictator from
among a group of other candidates. Within these limits it is clear
that authors have had their influence, both upon dictators and upon
the peoples they ruled. Not all dictators have been illiterate.
Mussolini, while remarking that 'The reality of experience is far
more eloquent than all the theories and doctrines of all languages
and all bookshelves',[1] was careful to emphasise that he had his
cultural side. His official biographer tells us of him that,

> As a young man he devoted long hours to the study and the trans-
> lation of German authors, such as Nietzche, Schopenhauer, Stirner,
> Weininger, Marx, Schiller, Klopstock, von Platen, Heine, Goethe and
> Hegel. His favourite Italian authors are Dante, Carducci, Oriani,
> Foscolo, Pareto; his French favourites are Sorel, Blanqui, Balzac,
> Le Bon. He reads and re-reads Plato, and likes to discuss Phaedon's
> arguments on the immortality of the soul. Occasionally he reviews
> some new publication. He listens to the operas of Wagner, Verdi, and
> Puccini, but 'I adore Beethoven', he says. . . .[2]

Had he in fact read as widely as this? He probably had in so far as a
journalist ever reads anything. He had certainly read Sorel. What of
the other dictators? Bolivar had read a great deal and so no doubt
had Venizelos. Adolf Hitler had read within the narrow range of his
own ideas, being willing and even eager to compare the theories of
Chamberlain with those of Rosenberg. He had read Möller van den
Brück's book, *The Third Realm* (1922) in which liberalism is denounced

---

[1] *The official life of Benito Mussolini.* Georgio Pini. Trans. by Luigi Villari. London,
1939. p. 229.
[2] *Ibid.* p. 241.

as the gospel of anarchy and liberals as persons who consider their own interests, never those of society or the State. He had read with interest the works of Schopenhauer and Carlyle's biography of Frederick the Great.[1] He had read Machiavelli's *Prince*.[2] He is more remarkable, however, in having written and published his bible and manifesto long before he came to power. As it contained the detailed programme of all that he intended to do, it might have been of considerable value to the Ministers of the democratic states. He evidently relied, however, upon their never having read that (or, in some cases, anything else)—or upon their not believing it. Events were to justify his confidence but it is an aspect of his career which is surely unique. Apart from that, *Mein Kampf* gives us an unusually clear and frank picture of his mental development as also of his mental limitations. He had gained inspiration from a number of sources. Studying what he had read we know also by what authors he was indirectly influenced. We can trace his ideas to their origin. The same is true of Mussolini. And, having so traced the ancestry of modern dictatorship we must agree that it is worthy of study.

'Sorel is the key to all contemporary thought' wrote Wyndham Lewis,[3] and Benedetto Croce regarded Sorel as the only original socialist thinker other than Karl Marx. In a sense, this is true, but to begin with Sorel would be to ignore Nietzche, which hardly seems possible. For whereas socialism will normally lead to dictatorship, whether as a result of its success or failure, the gospel of the Superman reaches the same goal by a different route; and would reach it just the same even if no such doctrine as socialism had ever been evolved. The Superman idea was to some extent endemic in Germany and can be traced to Fichte (1762-1814) and even to Kant (1724-1804). Kant taught, among other things, that the united will of the people could be embodied in and represented by a single individual. The same idea appears in the later works of Fichte (1762-1814). This philosopher held that the progress of mankind is not attributable to peoples as a whole but to the creative genius of heroes and scholars— 'Heroes who left their age far behind them, giants among surrounding men in material and spiritual power'.[4] Intellectual giants such as these should be the rulers as well as teachers of mankind. They should appoint the wisest and greatest among them to be the supreme dictator. Fichte was rather vague about the process of election and succession but concluded hopefully that it could be left to the hand of God. 'Sooner or later a man will arise who is both the ruler of his

[1] See *Hitler's Table Talk*. Trans. by H. R. Trevor-Roper. London, 1953. pp. XXIX, 89, 358. See also *Mein Kampf*. Adolf Hitler. 2 vols. London, 1939. p. 256, 227.
[2] *Hitler Speaks*. Herman Rauschning. London, 1939. p. 267.
[3] *The Art of being Ruled*. Wyndham Lewis. London, 1926. p. 128.
[4] *From Luther to Hitler, the History of Fascist-Nazi political philosophy*. W. M. McGovern. London, 1946. p. 255.

country and the most just of his countrymen. Such a man will certainly find a way to establish the succession of the best'.[1] It is an optimistic conclusion, and worldly experience would suggest that a meeting of intellectuals, summoned to elect the wisest of them all, might prove more acrimonious than Fichte seems to anticipate.

Another exponent of the German love of authority was Hegel (1770-1831) for whom the State was the Divine Idea as it exists on earth. He regarded Alexander, Caesar and Napoleon as so many unconscious agents of the World Spirit, meeting their death only when their earthly mission had been fulfilled. To the national State of the nineteenth century Hegel assigned a permanence as representing the final and perfect development of political institutions, created by the World Spirit working through man. He assigned to the State, moreover, an importance which he denied to the individual. The State to him was an end in itself and had 'the highest right over the individual, whose highest duty in turn is to be a member of the state'.[2] States have unequal value, however, and at a given period the dominant idea of that period 'is embodied in a dominant people'.[3] The mere success of that people is proof of their being more in accord with the World Spirit than the others. Hegel considered that monarchy is essential to good government and achieves its perfection in its constitutional form. All this was acceptable doctrine in the Prussia of his day and well calculated to transform the professor of 1818 into the University Rector of 1830. To one not fascinated (as the Germans were) by the obscurity of his diction, Hegelian dialectic might seem no more important than that. Hegel, however, whether profound or not, was certainly important, if only through the historical role of his disciples, Karl Marx, Friedrich Engels and Ferdinand Lasalle. It is perhaps significant that in Hegel the arguments for dictatorship and the arguments for socialism can be traced to a common source.

In the development, however, of the doctrine of Superman, it is easy to exaggerate the part played by German professors of philosophy. It is true that potential dictators, like Mussolini, could turn for inspiration to Hegel. But they would gain more encouragement by going direct to the source of Hegel's inspiration: the Prussia of Bismarck, as heir to the Prussia of Frederick the Great. In so far as authors were to provide inspiration, the two that mattered most were probably Thomas Carlyle and Friedrich Nietzsche, not so much because of their profundity as because of their literary gifts. The arguments for dictatorship are largely emotional and aesthetic and need poetic rather than purely intellectual expression. Carlyle was too much of a literary man to spend much time on Kant or Fichte,

[1] *Ibid.* p. 255.
[2] *Ibid.* p. 300.
[3] *Ibid.* p. 318.

fervently as he professed to admire them both. Nor was he himself a systematic thinker on political problems. His views are implicit, rather, in what he had to write about the *French Revolution, Heroes and Hero-Worship* and *Frederick the Great*. History was to him 'the biography of great men'—of men like Luther, Oliver Cromwell and Goethe. He had nothing to say in praise of hereditary monarchy, aristocracy or plutocracy, but neither can we find that he liked democracy any better. He could see in it nothing but 'a swift transition towards something other and farther' for the people were, after all, 'mostly fools'. Rule must be vested in the wise few, not in the innumerable and foolish. Over the few he would set a single ruler—a king. He wanted to see '. . . Hero-kings, and a whole world not unheroic. . . .'[1] How is the king to be appointed? Carlyle does not say, but his expressed admiration for Cromwell and Napoleon is at least suggestive. He infers that the hero will arise to meet the need of the day.

From a bare recital of this lame conclusion it might well be thought that Carlyle's disciples would be few. But his strength, his appeal as an author, does not lie in argument but in a picturesque violence. He does not so much preach violence as exemplify it attractively. He does not so much defend dictatorship as describe it in terms of hero-worship. How does he define heroism?

> The Hero is he who lives in the inward sphere of things, in the True, Divine, and Eternal, which exists always, unseen to most, under the Temporary, Trivial: his being is in that; he declares that abroad, by act or speech as it may be, in declaring himself abroad. His life, as we said before, is a piece of the everlasting heart of Nature herself: all men's life is,—but the weak many know not the fact, and are untrue to it, in most times; the strong few are strong, heroic, perennial, because it cannot be hidden from them.[2]

Heroes, as thus defined, are born from time to time, and it is upon these that all depends.

> To me. . . . 'Hero-worship' becomes a fact inexpressibly precious; the most solacing fact one sees in the world at present. There is an everlasting hope in it for the management of the world. Had all traditions, arrangements, creeds, societies that men ever instituted, sunk away, this would remain. The certainty of Heroes being sent us; our faculty, our necessity, to reverence Heroes when sent; it shines like a pole-star through smoke-clouds, dust-clouds, and all manner of down-rushing and conflagration.[3]

Apart from prophets, Carlyle finds that Cromwell fits best into his

[1] McGovern. *op. cit.* p. 200.
[2] *Carlyle's Theory of the Hero.* B. H. Lehman. North Carolina, 1928. p. 41. See also *Carlyle and Hitler.* H. J. C. Grierson. Cambridge, 1933.
[3] *Sartor Resartus: Lectures on Heroes, etc.* T. Carlyle. London, 1892. pp. 336-337.

idea of the heroic role. He cannot summon up quite the same feeling about Napoleon.

> . . . I find in him no such *sincerity* as in Cromwell; only a far inferior sort. No silent walking, through long years, with the Awful Un-namable of this Universe; 'walking with God', as he called it; and faith and strength in that alone: *latent* thought and valour, content to lie latent, then burst-out as in blaze of Heaven's lightning! Napoleon lived in an age when God was no longer believed . . . he had to begin not out of the Puritan Bible, but out of poor Sceptical Encyclo-pédies. . . .[1]

This last disadvantage, almost excluding Napoleon from the ranks of the heroes, was shared by most of those who came later still in history. Carlyle, contemporary as he was of (say) Abraham Lincoln, could find no heroes in his own day, save Goethe. He makes it clear, nevertheless, in *Past and Present* that further heroes are to be expected. More than that, they are to be recognised. Of the Hero, he writes

> . . . His place is with the stars of heaven. . . . To this man death is not a bugbear; to this man life is already as earnest and awful, and beautiful and terrible, as death.
>
> Not a May-game is this man's life; but a battle and a march, a warfare with principalities and powers . . . a stern pilgrimage through burning sandy solitudes, through regions of thick-ribbed ice. He walks among men; loves men, with inexpressible soft pity—as they *cannot* love him: but his soul dwells in solitude, in the uttermost parts of Creation. In green oases by the palm-tree wells, he rests a space; but anon he has to journey forward, escorted by the Terrors and the Splendours, the Archdemons and Archangels. All Heaven, all Pande-monium are his escort. The stars keen-glancing, from the Immensities, send tidings to him; the graves, silent with their dead, from the Eternities. Deep calls for him unto Deep.
>
> Thou, O World, how wilt thou secure thyself against this man? . . . He is thy born king, thy conqueror and supreme lawgiver: not all the guineas and cannons . . . under the sky can save thee from him. . . . Oh, if in this man, whose eyes can flash Heaven's lightning . . . there dwelt not, as the essence of his very being, a God's justice, human Nobleness, Veracity and Mercy—I should tremble for the world. But his strength, let us rejoice to understand, is even this: The quantity of Justice, of Valour and Pity that is in him. To hypocrites and tailored quacks in high places, his eyes are lightning; but they melt in dewy pity softer than a mother's to the downpressed, maltreated; in his heart, in his great thought, is a sanctuary for all the wretched. This world's improvement is forever sure.[2]

Improvement there will be but Carlyle makes it clear that nothing of this sort is to be expected of a Parliament.

[1] Carlyle. *op. cit.* p. 363.
[2] *Ibid.* p. 297.

A Government such as ours, consisting of from seven to eight hundred Parliamentary Talkers, with their escort of Able Editors and Public Opinion; and for head, certain Lords and Servants of the Treasury, and Chief Secretaries and others who find themselves at once Chiefs and No-Chiefs, and often commanded rather than commanding,—is doubtless a most complicate entity, and none of the alertest for getting on with business![1]

Indeed, he turns with relief from Parliament and gazes with some respect at the Horse Guards. By comparison, he feels that the War Office has achieved something, created an army out of 'runaway apprentices, starved weavers, thievish valets'. The soldier offers a kind of reality—'He is a fact and not a shadow'. Then he continues:

> . . . Most potent, effectual for all work whatsoever, is wise planning, firm combining and commanding among men. Let no man despair of Government who looks on these two sentries at the Horse-Guards, and our United-Service Clubs! I could conceive an Emigration Service, a Teaching Service, considerable varieties of United and Separate Services, of the due thousands strong, all effective as this Fighting Service is; all doing their work, like it;—which work, much more than fighting, is henceforth the necessity of these New Ages we are got into! Much lies among us, convulsively, nigh desperately *struggling to be born*.[2]

Carlyle calls for a military efficiency in combating Falsehood, Nescience, Delusion, Disorder and the Devil. He asks that something of the British competence displayed in war should be mobilised against bad drainage and dirt and soot. Forty soldiers, he points out, will disperse the largest Spitalfields mob. Why should governmental energy be confined to that? He wants government to 'order all dingy Manufacturing Towns to cease from their soot and darkness'—a plea still being made by others a century later and with as little result. He demands an education service and a Captain-General of Teachers. He wants to see vigorous action and doubts whether he will ever see it in Parliament.

It is at that point that he tends to lose the sympathy of those who are otherwise to be counted among his British admirers. Dr. G. M. Trevelyan, profoundly shocked, finds that Carlyle's genius declined after 1851.

> Fortunately Carlyle's later and worse doctrines in dispraise of Parliamentary government had singularly little influence on the English, even during those last years when his countrymen so much revered him. There was indeed no period in our history when Parliamentary government was so universally acceptable, and despotism more abhorred.[3]

[1] Carlyle. *op. cit.* p. 297.
[2] *Ibid.* p. 275. *Past and Present.*
[3] *Carlyle, an Anthology.* G. M. Trevelyan. London, 1953. Introduction, p. 5.

This may well be true, even of the year 1843 when he was writing *Past and Present* and long before his genius had, in Trevelyan's view, deteriorated. But it is that very fact, supposing it admitted, that makes his criticism more striking. It is not the unreformed Parliament he is attacking, nor the corruption of the early twentieth century. The Parliament he dismisses as hopelessly inactive and useless can clearly be taken as Parliament at its best. It has never, surely, had a comparable prestige before or since. His objection to Parliament is not that it is particularly corrupt or unrepresentative. Nor would he think the better of it were Parliament to be made more democratic. His complaint is merely that it does not work.

Akin to Carlyle in some ways but born at a later date was Friedrich Nietzsche (1844-1900). If the other apostles of violence and heroism were, without exception, academic and sedentary, Nietzsche was practically an invalid. He was a believer, nevertheless, in the German equivalent of Carlyle's hero; the Superman. In his own words, 'humanity must always act so as to bring men of genius into the world—this is its task; it has no other'.[1] He is less precise about the method to be chosen but emphatic that it can be done. One essential condition for the cultivation of genius is, he maintains, the institution of slavery. 'The misery of the men who struggle painfully through life must be increased to allow a small number of Olympic geniuses to produce great works of art'.[2] Another essential condition is the creation of an élite, a superior class from which the Superman can spring to a yet greater height. There is therefore, he concluded, a morality of masters and a morality of slaves. The masters despise weakness, cowardice, flattery and humility but respect strength, audacity, deceit and even cruelty. The principles of conduct maintained among themselves are not applied to inferiors. The slaves have a different morality. They detest all that is violent, hard, terrible and destructive. They applaud the slave virtues of pity, benevolence, industry, humility and patience. Typical products of the slave mentality are the Jews who have equated misery with virtue, happiness with vice. Christianity, adopting the Jewish scale of values, has exalted the weak, consoling them with tales of a future happiness. These Christian ideas, spreading widely, have represented the triumph of the slave morality. This triumph of a religion of suffering has brought Europe to a state of decadence. Mediocrities rule who dare not even keep order. The chief symptom of decadence is democracy. The fashion is to demand a Society of equals, without masters or slaves, rich or poor, rulers or subjects. Nothing is to be left but the herd. Only the Superman can finally save mankind from this levelling

[1] *Schopenhauer as Educator*, sec. 6. Quoted in *The Gospel of Superman*. H. Lichtenberger. Trans. by J. M. Kennedy. London, 1926.
[2] Lichtenberger. *op. cit.* p. 61.

tendency but it is the task of men as they are to recreate the conditions which will favour the Superman's rise.

The gospel of Superman did not appeal to all but it did appeal to George Bernard Shaw, the non-democratic socialist. He gave expression to his belief in the play *Man and Superman*, first published in 1903.[1] In a sort of postscript to that he writes:—

> The need for the Superman is, in its most imperative aspect, a political one. We have been driven to Proletarian Democracy by the failure of all the alternative systems; for these depended on the existence of Supermen acting as despots or oligarchs . . . [who were not forthcoming]. . . .
>
> Now we have yet to see the man who, having any practical experience of Proletarian Democracy, has any belief in its capacity for solving great political problems, or even for doing ordinary parochial work intelligently and economically. Only under despotisms and oligarchies has the Radical faith in 'universal suffrage' as a political panacea arisen. It withers the moment it is exposed to practical trial. . . .[2]

His preference may have been for a democracy of Supermen but the fact remains that he was attracted by the idea of dictatorship, going so far as to express a guarded approval of Mussolini.[3] Views of this kind were virtually echoed by two of his outstanding contemporaries, Hilaire Belloc and H. G. Wells. Nor, as late as 1928, had Shaw greatly changed his views. He knew that dictatorship has its major weakness in the succession difficulty but he also knew that democratic politicians had failed and failed repeatedly to solve even the simplest problems of the age. Universal suffrage he regarded as a delusion and a disappointment.

> At all events the bunch of carrots which for a whole century kept the electoral donkey pursuing it has now been overtaken and eaten without giving the poor beast the least refreshment. This is why Parliament has been pushed aside by Fascist Leaders in Germany and Italy, and reduced in Russia to a congress which meets at long intervals to ratify reforms, but has no effective hand in initiating them.[4]

He also saw that dictators could and did succeed where parliaments had failed.

> . . . All your wouldbe dictator has to do is to deal with fools according to their folly by giving them plenty of the stuff they like to swallow whilst he sets to work energetically on reforms that appeal to everyone's commonsense and comfort, and stops the more obvious abuses

---

[1] *Man and Superman. A Comedy and a Philosophy.* By Bernard Shaw. London, 1931. See pp. 184-5.
[2] Shaw. *op. cit.* p. 184.
[3] See Dutt, R. P. *George Bernard Shaw.* London, 1951.
[4] *The Intelligent Woman's Guide to Socialism, Capitalism, Sovietism and Fascism.* Bernard Shaw. London, 1949. p. 476.

of the existing order. His first step will be to abolish all the little councils of elderly local tradesmen. . . . He will substitute energetic and capable young prefects with absolute powers from himself to clean up the provinces; and by this he will not only effect a speedy improvement in local government, but will do it in a way which exactly fits in with the popular desire to get rid of a lot of vulgar old tradesmen and employ some superior person to set things right.[1]

He emphasises that these and more ruthless measures will be popular.

. . . When the Leader speaks of the Liberals and their bag of rights and liberty with masterful contempt, and calls for discipline, order, silence, patriotism and devotion to the State of which he is the embodiment, the people respond enthusiastically and leave the Liberals to rot in the penal islands, concentration camps, and prisons into which they have been flung. . . .[2]

Fascism also gets rid of the absurdity of a senselessly obstructive Party Opposition, resulting in parliaments where half the members are trying to govern and the other half trying to prevent them. . . .[3]

In the final analysis, Bernard Shaw's main objection to Fascism is that it is not Socialism—although (as he admits) closely resembling it. He considers that Fascism is doomed simply because it is capitalistic. He considers that liberal democracy is also doomed and for the same reason. In the meanwhile, of the two evils, he prefers Fascism 'in so far as it produces a United Front with a public outlook'.

If Fascist or Nazi ideas could be as attractive as this to a great Irishman, who finally condemned them as childish, they naturally appealed more forcibly to people with wilder emotions and fewer brains. Outstanding among these, and wielding considerable influence in Germany, was Houston Stewart Chamberlain (1855-1926), an Englishman who went abroad for his health, first to Austria and then in 1900, to Germany. His principal work was entitled 'The Foundations of the Nineteenth Century', and was published in 1899. Chamberlain took some of his nonsensical doctrines about racial purity and inequality from Gobineau (1816-1882) but is more interesting, or more to our present purpose, when he discusses democracy.

To tell the truth, all nations of the earth are sick and tired of parliaments; tired of the sacred general franchise; tired of the ever-running flow of oratory, which threatens to drown the whole of the civilised world, as in a new Deluge.

He asks what part the people should play in government and answers his question thus:—

[1] Shaw. *op. cit.* p. 479.
[2] *Ibid.* p. 480.
[3] *Ibid.* p. 481.

The people will be the unconscious root, supplying nutriment, the reserve of forces, and will then prove themselves as efficient as now in the German army. As soon as the people are brought to silence, their voice is most distinctly heard. Their speech is not dialectic, but something which far surpasses it. A monarch may be represented, a class, a profession—a people cannot be represented. The people are nature, and a Mr. Müller or Mr. Meyer is as little able to represent them as he is to represent a mountain or a wood. This pretended representation of the people does nothing but destroy the real vigour of the people and cause a chaos. It causes restlessness and, therefore, anxiety. It consumes every root fibre which would have served to sustain life. It stultifies by its debate and nullifies all great plans by its disputes. In addition to this, like a monstrous dragon, it swallows mountains of strength and oceans of time, all of which are lost for ever for the life of the nation. The people naturally recognise and foster great characters; parliament invariably refuses to tolerate any talent that arises above mediocrity. . . .[1]

Central to the groups of thinkers who had come to regard liberal democracy with contempt was Richard Wagner (1813-1883). If Strauss may be said to have composed the background music for the Holy Alliance, Wagner certainly provided the musical accompaniment for the drama of dictatorship. It was he too who was responsible for those cavorting Nibelungs and Valkyries which played what seems to be (at first sight) an unnecessarily prominent role in the politics of the Third Reich. He was central to this school of thought in that he was for years a close friend of Nietzche, who wrote in his defence; a composer greatly admired by Bernard Shaw;[2] and the father-in-law of Houston Stewart Chamberlain. Wagner was sufficiently active in the Dresden insurrection of 1848-49 to suffer years of exile in Switzerland. He was sufficiently prolific to leave behind him ten volumes of published prose. It was, nevertheless, his music which had the greater effect in furthering the emotional cause, in stilling the voice of reason, in heightening the operatic effect of violence as its own excuse. Adolf Hitler could find in *Tannhäuser* or *Lohengrin* any inspiration he might fail to draw from mountain scenery or tea-time buns. The mad King Ludwig of Bavaria had pensioned Wagner in the first place and a later Bavarian hero was to be carried away more fatally by the dramatic force of drums and wind. Adolf Hitler first became obsessed with Wagner in his Vienna days when he saw *Tristan* thirty or forty times; ever afterwards maintaining that this is Wagner's masterpiece. His first contact with the Wagner family was

[1] *The Ravings of a Renegade; being the War Essays of Houston Stewart Chamberlain.* Trans. by G. H. Clarke. London, 1915.
[2] See *Major Critical Essays. The Perfect Wagnerite.* G. B. Shaw. London, 1948. pp. 187, 244, 245. Wagner, originally a friend of Bakunin, was much influenced by Schopenhauer's treatise on 'The world as Will and Representation' in which instinct and reason are contrasted. Wagner also hated the Jews.

indirectly through the son-in-law—('Houston Stewart Chamberlain wrote to me so nicely when I was in prison')—but he evidently met Wagner's widow, Cosima, for the first time in 1925. He had just emerged from jail and went to stay with Frau Bechstein at Bayreuth for the Festival. The Wagners, Cosima and Siegfried, lived a few yards away, and a friendship began, with drives into the Franconian mountains and evenings at the opera with Cleving at his best in *Parsifal*. 'I was also present' said Hitler in 1942, 'at the *Ring* and the *Meistersinger*. The fact that the Jew Schorr was allowed to sing the role of Wotan had the effect of a profanation on me. Why couldn't they have got Rode from Munich?' Despite this shock, the visit was a success. Hitler remained on Christian-name terms with the Wagners, remarking afterwards that it was Cosima's merit 'to have created the link between Bayreuth and National Socialism'. The link was certainly there. Hitler owned several of Wagner's original scores and would sigh, on occasion, 'What joy each of Wagner's works has given me!'[1]

It is easy to see what is absurd in Wagnerian politics, even when related to the portentous conclusions of German philosophers, stated with all the violence of the sedentary, the bookish and the sick. It is easier still, however, to forget that theories generally false may be based on some beliefs that are perfectly true. And the truth which lurks amid the Fascist falsities is that liberal democracy is dreary, deadening and dull. That is not a theory but a fact; and when Chamberlain said that people are sick and tired of parliaments, he was telling the literal truth. The spectacle of drab little men moving amendments to drab little proposals is seldom inspiring. It lacks the pageantry which the normal human being needs. The enthusiast can explain its significance to schoolboys and may even gain their reluctant assent. But the pageant of a coronation needs no explanation. The critic who grumbles about the cost is answered not by arguments but by the clatter of the cavalry, the thunder of the psalm, the glitter of the sword blades and the spine-shivering shrillness of the trumpets' chord. Words are worse than useless. The thing explains itself. And that is exactly what the average modern legislature fails to do. Its proceedings are usually as colourless as its ideas. Round its prim procedure there hangs the slight but unmistakable smell of political corruption. Its atmosphere is heavy with failure; failure to achieve anything, failure to agree and failure even to arouse any public interest in what has been attempted.

[1] See *Hitler's Table Talk*. Trans. and edited by H. R. Trevor-Roper. London, 1953. pp. 147, 240-242 and 283. Oswald Spengler, whom Hitler consulted before the former died in 1936 saw in *Tristan* the finale of western music. He also points out the affinity between Wagner and the painter, Manet 'which Baudelaire with his unerring flair for the decadent detected at once'. See *The Decline of the West*. Oswald Spengler. 2 vols. Trans. by C. F. Atkinson. New York, 1947. Vol. I. p. 292.

Among the nineteenth-twentieth century thinkers who most clearly perceived this failure was Georges Sorel (1847-1922). Unlike many political theorists, he had some practical experience; not of politics but of roads and bridges.[1] As a Frenchman and, after his retirement, a Parisian by choice, he was privileged to contemplate perhaps the least inspiring of the uninspired republics. His views veered from socialism to syndicalism, from royalism to anarchy. He can be quoted in defence of many political creeds. The syndicalists, whose prophet he once was, bequeathed to Mussolini a single (and useful) constructive idea; that of providing for the political representations of trades and professions rather than of areas or places. But that is not Sorel's importance in the present context. His *Reflections on Violence*, which first appeared in 1906, emphasise the need for an irrational and romantic heroism. Among the first to apply psychology to politics, he held that a political movement needs not a rational creed but a *myth*. Without a mythology it cannot succeed. He dismissed the socialism of Sidney Webb as the typical product of a second-class mind.[2] He rejected statistical arguments and called for a myth, defined as 'a body of images capable of evoking sentiment instinctively'.[3] His chosen myth was that of the General Strike, considered as a political panacea. He rejected the myth of the Barricades, observing sorrowfully that 'Civil war has become very difficult since the discovery of the new firearms, and since the cutting of rectilinear streets in the capital towns'. This was a natural reflection for a revolutionary Parisian living in the Paris replanned by Haussmann for Napoleon III, and his general strike was a poor substitute for something better. His own chosen myth came to little in France and to less in the England of 1926. But the idea of the Myth has taken root.

> Experience shows that the *framing of a future, in some indeterminate time*, may, when it is done in a certain way, be very effective, and have very few inconveniences; this happens when the anticipations of the future take the form of those myths, which enclose with them all the strongest inclinations of a people, of a party or of a class, inclinations which recur to the mind with the insistence of instincts in all the circumstances of life; and which give an aspect of complete reality to the hopes of immediate action by which, more easily than by any other method, men can reform their desires, passions, and mental activity.[4]

[1] Bernard Shaw very rightly observes that Wagner also had practical experience. 'It is possible' he observes 'to learn more of the world by producing a single opera, or even conducting a single orchestral rehearsal, than by ten years reading in the library of the British Museum'. Wagner is thus contrasted favourably with Karl Marx. See Shaw. *op. cit.* p. 244.

[2] *Reflections on Violence.* Georges Sorel. Trans. by T. E. Hulme. London, 1915. See also *The Myth of the State.* Ernst Cassirer. Yale, 1946.

[3] *Ibid.* p. 75.

[4] *Ibid.* p. 133.

Later in the same book Sorel asks what motive can inspire the worker in a socialist state, what motive comparable with that which inspires a soldier in battle.

> Economic progress goes far beyond the individual life, and profits future generations more than those who create it; but does it give glory? Is there an economic epic capable of stimulating the enthusiasm of the workers?[1]

If no such epic has been found in modern times, it is certainly not from any lack of energy in the search. From Mussolini's Pontine Marshes to Stalin's films about increased production we have seen the myth triumphant over fact or even probability. Sorel believed not in laboured reasoning but in mythology and resulting action. For representative assemblies he had no use at all.[2]

> Government by all the citizens has never been anything but a fiction; but this fiction was the last word of democratic science. No one has ever been able to justify this singular paradox according to which the vote of a *chaotic majority* is made to appear to be what Rousseau calls the general will which cannot err. In spite of their distrust of the utopians of the eighteenth century, socialist writers often reproduce Rousseau's idea: they say that the state will no longer exist because, classes having disappeared, there will no longer be oppression in society and that then the public administration will truly represent the whole of the citizens. These affirmations are without a vestige of proof. . . .[3]

His dislike of parliamentary government was intensified by the First World War and he wrote bitterly of the Allies' treatment of Germany and Italy.

> I am only an old man, whose life is at the mercy of the smallest accident; but may I before descending into the grave, witness the humiliation of the arrogant bourgeois democracies today so cynically triumphant![4]

It is a matter for doubt whether his wish was granted him. Dying in 1922, he had not lived long enough to see the humiliation of Munich. He had, however, witnessed the Washington Naval Treaty of 1921, the beginning of a process which would lead in the end, if not to Munich, at least to the fall of Singapore.

Sorel left behind him not only his works but his disciples. Vilfredo Pareto survived him, it is true, for only a year, but Sorel's thought is reflected in the works of Marinetti, Palmieri and the other Fascist

[1] Sorel, *op. cit.* p. 293.
[2] See *From Luther to Hitler.* W. M. McGovern. London, 1946. p. 432.
[3] *Georges Sorel, Prophet without Honor.* A study in anti-intellectualism. Richard Humphrey. Harvard, 1951. p. 70.
[4] Humphrey. *op. cit.* p. 21.

apologists. Nor is it absent in the works of Benedetto Croce, who points out that the scope of the Myth in politics has been widened by elementary education:

> Popular education, which the liberal nineteenth century enthusiastically inaugurated, has not fulfilled the hope of making the masses politically intelligent. They have become more the prey of emotional propaganda, drawing its strength from passion and imagination. . . . What the people want is not truth but some myth which flatters their feelings, and the first and unwelcome truth they need to be taught is to distrust the demagogues who excite and intoxicate them. . . .[1]

Above all, we know of Sorel's influence upon Mussolini, who said in 1932:

> Every revolution creates new forms, new myths and new rites and the would-be revolutionist, while using old traditions, must refashion them. He must create new festivals, new gestures, new forms which will themselves become traditional.[2]

By 1932 the myth had indeed been established in the world. It was not, however, the myth which Sorel had wished to see installed. It was the myth of the all-seeing, all-knowing and all-powerful Leader; the dominant political theme of the twentieth century. We have seen democracy turn into dictatorship and we have seen some dictatorships collapse under the impact of military defeat. There are many to-day who expect to see these dictatorships replaced by democracy. Neither, however, in historical example nor in political theory can we find much reason to think this probable. After a dictator we should rather expect to see a King.

---

[1] *My Philosophy.* Benedetto Croce. Trans. by E. F. Carritt. London, 1949. p. 90.
[2] Quoted in McGovern. *op. cit.* p. 549.

CHAPTER XXIII

Dictatorship in Decay

NOT all the arguments for dictatorship are either dishonest, romantic or false. We have seen what arguments have been used and those of substance can evidently be reduced to three. They are worth re-stating now. First of these is the argument which springs from the fact of genius. Persons with what appears to be divine inspiration—Gautama, Joan of Arc or Gandhi—are relatively few in the story of mankind. In retrospect it is often found that they were uncannily right when everyone else was wrong. We feel, looking back, that the people among whom they lived would have fared better had they done exactly what they were told to do. Is it not the sensible course to do what genius says should be done? Would not the Greeks have done well to make Socrates their leader? Would not the French have done better to instal St. Joan in supreme power? Were not the people of India wise to obey Gandhi as much as they did, and would they not have been wiser still had they obeyed him even more implicitly? To believers in God there can be nothing very unreasonable in obeying those whom God has inspired. Non-believers, on the other hand, are usually ready to admit the fact that genius exists. If genius is known and admitted in music and painting—if John Sebastian Bach and Michaelangelo had genius—why should we question that there may be genius too in politics? Christopher Wren was apt to differ from his contemporaries in matters of architecture and engineering, and events have almost invariably proved that he was right and they were wrong. Are there no statesmen as prescient, and if there are, should we not entrust the supreme authority to them?

To this argument many would reply that the genius may, by persuasion, gain acceptance of his ideas, achieving by example and argument what we do not allow him to achieve by force. To this Adolf Hitler has the answer:

> Is it an indispensable quality in a statesman that he should possess a gift of persuasion commensurate with the statesman's ability to conceive great political measures and carry them through into practice? . . .
>
> What shall the statesman do if he does not succeed in coaxing the parliamentary multitude to give its consent to his policy?[1]

[1] Hitler. *op. cit.* p. 79.

As an answer this is sufficient. Vision and strength are not necessarily accompanied by the arts of the demagogue. A genius apt for
command cannot always stoop to persuade. More than that, the
serene certainty of the man of vision is not always easy to convey.
The more clearly he can see what has to be done, the fewer reasons
he has to convince anyone else. The conclusion most easily explained
to others is the conclusion reached by long and exhaustive elimination. The conclusion most difficult to explain is the one reached in a
flash—by a stroke, in fact, of genius. Not every man of genius has
both the flash of inspiration *and* the wit to invent, afterwards, the
argument which even the densest colleague will accept.

The second argument for dictatorship is that any great political
achievement is a work of art and that a work of art implies an artist.
This is most obvious in architecture and planning. To re-plan the
centre of London as Wren wished to re-plan it after the Fire of
London implied, for success, a genius invested with dictatorial powers.
The genius was available but the dictator was not. Historians were
apt to wonder why nothing was done but need wonder no longer
since they have seen exactly the same opportunity missed again in
exactly the same way. Napoleon III had the power denied to Charles
II and George VI, and modern Paris is the result. Wherever there is a
city, a cathedral or a palace of monumental character and seemingly
inevitable design, its plan is normally the concept of a single human
brain. It is, in short, a work of art and subject to the same conditions
in the making as apply to a painting, a statue, a concerto or an ode.
Things of this kind are seldom the result of collaboration, rarely
affected by a majority vote, and never safely attributable to a
committee. The artist normally signs his work, accepting full responsibility for it. And when he leaves out the signature it is often
because none is needed. No seventeenth century general had to be
told that a fortress had been planned by Vauban; he could see that for
himself. A modern art critic will as readily—if not quite as certainly—
—attribute a canvas to Rembrandt or Vermeer.

Between the planning of a palace and the founding of a city the
difference is only one of degree. The founder of a city may well be the
founder of the state or colony of which it is to be the capital. It is
natural for him to plan the streets and bridges, the boundaries and
the roads. He will reserve the parks and name the hills. Then he will
deal with the drainage and water supply, laying down what is to
constitute an offence against public health. He will define the limits of
the harbour and decide what dues shall be paid for anchorage or
ballast. This will compel him to decide whether the local and harbour
authorities are to be distinct; if they are, he must draft a constitution
for each; and indeed a code of laws. But laws will require amendment

or repeal from time to time, which implies a legislature. They must be enforced, which implies an executive. . . . At what point in this scheme of work should the single artist, with his vision of the completed whole, give place to a committee representative of the different interests? The answer is not obvious, and the founder of a colony might be forgiven for regarding the whole thing as a single work of art, and himself the artist whose signature it will bear to all eternity. Should he later, however, rise to high rank in a country already long established but in a state of disorder and chaos, he will not think that the problems to be solved are markedly different from those of the new colony he formerly ruled with such success. The canvas may be old but his skill has, if anything, matured. Given a free hand, he could make something of it yet. If the state is to be a work of art, there must be an artist: and an artist is essentially a dictator.

The third argument for dictatorship is that a swift decision, one way or the other, is often preferable to an endless argument. This was recognised from an early period at sea, where the oldest law still in force runs thus:— '*In a ship one man is master*'. It is nowhere stated that the one man is the wisest, the oldest or the most experienced. All that we know about him is that he is one, the master; and not a committee. Committees at sea have been tried but results have shown that it is better to decide on something, on anything, rather than hold a debate as to which policy is best. When a vessel is on a dangerous lee shore, safety may lie in beating out to sea or, alternatively, in dropping anchor where she is. There may be cogent arguments to put forward in support of either policy. There may well be two schools of thought, and possibly a third group eager to find a compromise acceptable to both. But long and sad experience has shown that a prolonged discussion would be unwise. It is better to let the master decide and compel the rest to obey. For the master's decision (irrespective of his ability) has a fifty per cent chance of being right, while the delay caused by an argument has a hundred per cent chance of being wrong.

What is obviously true at sea is almost as manifestly true in a time of crisis on land. In a battle, a revolution or riot, the promptness of a decision is often more important than the decision itself. Victory may result from going to the left or to the right. It may in fact be attained equally by either route. But it seldom results from a mere inability to decide upon one or the other. Nor is this consideration paramount only on the battlefield. The reasoning which induces us to place one general in command of an army will equally lead us to place one headmaster in charge of a school, one leader in charge of an alpine expedition, one producer in charge of a play, one surgeon in charge of an operation, one physicist in control of a nuclear physics laboratory or one Commissioner in charge of the Metropolitan Police. We entrust a certain kind of responsibility to an individual, not primarily because he is outstanding but simply because he is singular. Granted the wisdom of this practice, the question rises as to where it should begin and end. The office of dictator was a Roman expedient to deal with a crisis in public affairs. But such a crisis, with prompt decisions needed the whole time, may last for years. A state may be so situated, in fact, as to be in a perpetual state of crisis. Are there not states then so situated, at least at a certain period, in which a dictatorship is advisable—or even essential?

Here then are the three chief arguments for dictatorship in general, based respectively upon the use to be made of genius, the unity of conception required to produce a work of art and the need for a single chief if quick decisions are to be made. Such arguments have been used to justify any dictatorship at any period of history. But the present century has certain technical features which, while lending additional point to the arguments previously used, amount to a new argument in themselves and one applicable to the present time. The first feature to observe concerns the art of war. We have all read history books which emphasise the changes in the art of war which accompanied the Renaissance. Firearms, we were told, made the armoured knight obsolete. He became vulnerable to a hand-gun which the mere serf could fire. His castle became vulnerable to cannon. And so political power tended to pass from the nobility to the king; and also, in some degree, to the peasantry. Feudalism, we were taught to infer, was finished. Not all the facts cited in support of this theory are strictly accurate but there is probably something in the theory. What is less frequently remarked is the way in which the whole tendency has now been reversed. The great period of democracy in Europe was in fact the period of massed infantry, with God tending to favour the big battalions. The War of 1870 was mainly fought with rifle and bayonet and the First World War was not dissimilar in that respect until its close. Since 1917 the infantry mass, the conscript army, has given place to the armoured column and the defended locality. So far as the social implications of war are concerned, the conditions to-day are more nearly medieval. The armoured knight is in the field again with his team of assistants. It is true that it takes the efforts of an entire community to maintain him there, but this was equally true in the Middle Ages, when the Feudal system was in fact the organization through which this was done. It may be thought premature to forecast what the political results of this change may be. We can at least note, however, that conscript armies and massed voting went out of fashion at about the same time.

Just as the new techniques of industry weaken the general position of the workers in the productive process as a whole, so do the new techniques of warfare weaken the potential position of the workers in a revolutionary crisis. Street barricades and pikestaffs, even plus muskets, are not enough against tanks and bombers.[1]

Parallel with changes in the art of war have been the technical changes in the art of peace. Some of these have been summarised in a study made of the Managerial Revolution by James Burnham, from which the above passage is quoted. He points out that the social position of the working class has deteriorated sharply of recent years. The skilled worker has been largely superseded by the classes above and below him; that is, by the experts in engineering and production planning (who are highly specialised and elaborately trained) and by the packers and sorters and fasteners (who are hardly trained at all). Skilled workers of the old trade-union type are at once less important and less numerous. They could not, by themselves, run the motor-car factory. It is doubtful whether they could produce a single car. They no more ask a share in the management than do the share-holders. In so far as democratic Parliaments have represented capital and labour, Burnham accounts for their decline in usefulness by ex-plaining that neither capital nor labour is now as important as management and that managers and experts do not work through parliament at all. The decisions that matter are taken in the United States by bodies like the T.V.A. and in Russia by the Four Year Plan Commission. Parliaments have not been abolished so much as quietly by-passed by people whose time is too valuable to waste in that sort of debate.[2] These technological changes are fairly consistent with dictatorship of the right kind. They are not at all consistent with rhetoric about self-evident truths or the sacred mission of the proletariat. The time for politics, in that sense, has passed.

Comparable in importance to the production expert is the psy-chologist. Critics of the positive achievements of psychology have often failed to notice its negative effects. It was relatively easy for a politician of the mid-nineteenth-century—the Marxist period, as we may call it—to count the votes and announce the Will of the People. It seemed relatively easy in Victorian England to discover whether the voters wanted Disraeli or Gladstone. But the whole democratic theory has been undermined by the psychologist with a process which began to attract public attention in about 1920.[3] It may have begun with intelligent people looking back upon the part they and others had played in the war mania of 1914-18. It took the form of a serious

[1] *The Managerial Revolution.* James Burnham. London, 1942. p. 50.
[2] See Burnham. *op. cit.* p. 138.
[3] See *The group mind.* W. McDougall. Cambridge, 1920. *Instinct and the unconscious.* W. H. R. Rivers. Cambridge, 1920. *Instincts of the herd in peace and war.* W. Trotter. London, 1920 and *Decline of the West.* O. Spengler. New York, 1926.

attempt to determine why people think, vote and react as they do. The results could not be otherwise than profoundly disturbing to a believer in democracy. For one thing, it appeared that the views of a person as an individual are often quite different from his or her views as one of a crowd. Freud and McDougall pointed this out and even tried to decide between the merits of the two opinions the same individual might express. Such an inquiry has its interest but is not our present concern. The important fact, politically, is that the difference exists.[1] Research also reveals that

> . . . in a group of three, one person who knows his mind will obtain a majority vote in three times out of four provided that the other two members vote at random. About the same degree of control can be exercised by a bloc vote of 3 over an indifferent population of 20.[2]

It is true that the word 'indifferent' limits the influence of the few to matters on which the majority have no decided views. But other investigations show that the views fervently held by the majority are susceptible to mental disturbances, mass hypnotism and panic. Research by mass observation showed that the British public completely reversed its opinion about conscription during ten days in 1939. Between the 21st and 26th April, fifty-three per cent of those questioned thought that voluntary recruitment was preferable, thirty-nine per cent wanted compulsion, eight per cent expressed no opinion. Conscription was approved in the House of Commons on 27th April. Between the 2nd and 5th May it was found that, of those questioned, fifty-eight per cent were in favour of conscription, thirty-eight per cent opposed to it and four per cent were still at a loss. Nothing had happened in the meanwhile to justify this sudden change of attitude. Some fifteen per cent of the people had changed their minds and four per cent previously without an opinion found that they had acquired one.[3] Doris Langley Moore concludes that 'As a matter of deplorable truth, multitudes of people do not know what they want. . . .' In the light of this sort of evidence, talk about the Will of the People loses much of its force. The trained investigator is apt to ask what *sort* of will is to be considered sacred—the views of individuals, the views of the same individuals when herded together, the views of the herd on Tuesday or the views of the herd on Sunday afternoon? The suspicion is bound to dawn that the minority of people who reply 'Don't know' are merely more honest than the rest.

Contemporary with the advance of psychology (and closely connected with it) was the development of commercial advertising.

[1] *On the objective study of crowd behaviour.* L. S. Penrose. London, 1952. pp. 2–5.
[2] *Ibid.* p. 6.
[3] *The Vulgar Heart: An Enquiry into the Sentimental Tendencies of Public Opinion.* D. L. Moore. London, 1945. See pp. 54–55.

It became daily more apparent, between the two World Wars, that goods do not, of necessity, sell on their merits but through a process of almost hypnotic suggestion. This has always been partly true but it remained for the modern expert to make the process of suggestion a science. Sales were found to depend upon an adroit combination of colour, form, visual suggestion and the written word. Cunning appeals were directed to the basic instincts of hunger, thirst, fear and sex. Results were plotted and graphs were drawn, the more cynical finally concluding that the usefulness (if any) of the thing to be sold was irrelevant to the success of the campaign. Experience in advertising went further to undermine the liberal idea of democracy. For if the people could be coaxed into buying the worse—and even the more expensive—of two rival products, it was manifest that they could be coaxed by the same means into voting for the worse of two rival candidates for office. It was also increasingly evident that the man already in office—and more especially the dictator—could use the considerable resources of government (schools, newspapers, posters, leaflets, films and radio) to retain the confidence which he possibly deserved to forfeit. Examples multiplied of this being done.

Faced with this evidence, the democrat will maintain that the real will of the people can be ascertained and that the common sense of the electorate will assert itself in the end. But the deathblow to this theory comes from the accounts received of witch-hunts and treason trials. We are by now familiar with the spectacle of accused persons entering the witness box in totalitarian courts and calmly confessing to the treason which will ensure their condemnation. We are told that such confessions are extorted by fear, as would indeed seem most probable. What is significant, however, is that the psychological treatment used has actually, in many instances, convinced the victim of his own guilt. He will tell a detailed and circumstantial story, describing events which never happened and naming accomplices of whom he had never previously heard. Persons accused of witchcraft in the seventeenth century seem to have done the same. Victims of this sort of treatment are not giving evidence under duress. They believe what they are saying. They are instances (in an extreme form) of the success attributable to methods of suggestion. But milder methods produce results almost as striking. The child enrolled in the Hitler Youth ends with a mind so filled with legend as to be unreceptive of fact. The American voter is so conditioned by propaganda about communism that he will refuse to recognise the existence of China. The British voter is so conditioned by propaganda about Parliament that he thinks the party system is inevitable. The British housewife has been so conditioned by advertisement that she will buy the worse instead of the better product. At what point in this series does suggestion end? At what point does free will begin? There is no possible answer. The study of the art of suggestion has made nonsense of democratic theory. It has also provided the dictator with a technique, not of oppression but of gaining a continued and willing assent to his rule.

So far we have been considering the theory of dictatorship and the means by which twentieth century dictatorship has been sustained. It might well be asked what this has to do with dictatorship in decay. The answer is that its merits and defects are the same, its success and decay simultaneous. The dictator rules, as we have seen, by virtue of his inspiration, by virtue of his artistry and by virtue of his ability to make firm and rapid decisions. He rules in this century, moreover, in a world unsuitable for democracy and at least technically favourable for dictatorship. But dictatorship soon becomes decadent. That feeling of inspired genius by which the dictator is at first sustained, and for which he is admired, makes him impatient of contradiction. He will have no one near him of comparable ability. He demands obedience and resents opposition. How must he regard those who criticise the plans of the destined leader? They are stupid. Worse, they are disloyal. As Hitler himself observed:

> . . . the majority can never replace the man. The majority represents not only ignorance but also cowardice. And just as a hundred block-heads do not equal one man of wisdom, so a hundred poltroons are incapable of any political line of action that requires moral strength and fortitude.[1]

So a dictator will tend to surround himself with men less able than himself—with men beside whom he cannot be made to look small—with men unlikely to have views of their own. He wants obedience, help, sympathy and admiration. He does not want to be told that his facts are wrong or his policy mistaken.

As an artist he is even less patient of criticism. The whole point in appointing one supreme planner is to ensure the unified conception of the plan. But what will become of the central theme if there are to be niggling amendments by ignorant busybodies—by people too small to appreciate the grand outline of the master plan? The sense of purpose will be lost. Sweeping lines and generalisations will become blurred and indistinct. Rules will be loaded with exceptions. Better to ignore all paltry objections and keep the main object in view! The same reasoning applies to the leader's swift and final ruling. This becomes far more difficult if advisers are going to talk over every issue. It becomes a question indeed whether the adviser who emphasises imaginary obstacles can be whole-heartedly behind the national effort. Is it not more probable that he wishes that effort

[1] Hitler. *op. cit.* p. 81.

to fail? Has he not, for that matter, been bribed by the other side? What is needed is, first and foremost, loyalty. So the leader must be surrounded by the loyal, the steadfast, the reliable; not men who make difficulties but those who suggest expedients. To put the case more briefly, only the second-rate are wanted, and those only while they remain consistently acquiescent. If brilliance is wanted at all, it will be on the advertising side, in explaining the orthodox view to the people, or perhaps to other countries.

The dictator who assumes responsibility for all major decisions, surrounding himself with mediocrities so as to be unrivalled and un-opposed, must live under an appalling strain. He is as subject as other people to illness and overwork. To normal ailments he must add the strain of public life and the fear of assassination. To relax for more than a short time would be to admit that others can govern as well as he—an impossible admission for one who claims to be unique. Even if he does not fall sick, he will grow old. As time goes on, inspiration will fail. Large scale and long-term plans will have less attraction for a man who no longer expects to see them fulfilled. The dictator will begin to suspect that his decisions will be reversed as soon as he dies. Fatigue sets in and he is no longer able to decide instantly upon a policy. He is no longer the man he was. He sees this fact reflected in the faces of his staff. Are they (or is this imagination?) exchanging significant looks behind his back? Do they dare to think that he, the Leader, is losing grip? This is the point at which dictatorship begins to suffer from the disease which earlier proved helpful. The legend, the myth begins to react on its inventor. No one dares to tell the Leader what is actually happening. Sober facts he will regard as pessimism; and pessimism as disloyalty. So bad news comes to be increasingly hidden from him. Worse still, he comes to believe his own propaganda. The deceiver of others ends even by deceiving him-self. He lives finally in a world of unreality, in a world of his own imagining. From then he can be regarded as practically insane.

The life of Adolf Hitler offers, not the only example of this tendency but the example of which we have the fullest data. *Mein Kampf* is the work of a sane man, unbalanced in some of his hatreds but realistic in judging what could and could not be done. Sane he re-mained for many years, revealing a remarkable flair for politics and even for strategy. 'He was a systematic thinker'[1] says one historian. 'Never' says another 'was Hitler's ability more clearly shown than in the way he recovered from this set-back' [i.e. of 9th November, 1923]. It was in these words that Hitler addressed the court which tried him:—

The man who is born to be a dictator is not compelled; he wills it.

[1] *Hitler's Table Talk*. 1941-44. Ed. by H. R. Trevor-Roper. London, 1953. p. viii.

He is not driven forward, but drives himself. There is nothing immodest about this. Is it immodest for a worker to drive himself towards heavy labour? Is it presumptuous of a man with the high forehead of a thinker to ponder through the nights till he gives the world an invention? The man who feels called upon to govern a people has no right to say: If you want me or summon me, I will co-operate. No, it is his duty to step forward.[1]

These are the words of a remarkable man, a man of intellect and vision. Nor is the man described by Rauschning in 1932-33 other than sane. As the war approached, however, and after it had begun, Hitler began to assume heavier and heavier responsibilities, trusting nobody. He made himself Minister for War in 1938. In 1941 he assumed the command of the army (O.K.H.) in addition to the command of the armed forces as a whole (O.K.W.). In January, 1942, he could speak of his 'unbounded confidence, confidence in myself, so that nothing, whatever it may be, can throw me out of the saddle, so that nothing can shake me'.[2] That represented the high-water mark of his belief in himself and his destiny. Three months later, in March, his hair was grey and he had fits of giddiness. He had by then convinced himself that he had saved the situation by superseding his Army High Command. He drew up his plans for victory over Russia in 1942. Halder, who warned him of the Russian strength, was shouted down.[3] Hitler quoted Nietzsche and Clausewitz and removed the generals who disagreed with him. Goebbels wrote that 'As long as he lives and is among us in good health, as long as he can give us the strength of his spirit, no evil can touch us'.[4] Hitler now demanded and was given by law still further and more absolute powers. He personally directed the drive of 1942 against Stalingrad and towards the Caucasus and it is generally recognised that he could have gained either objective if he would only have restricted himself to the one. It was a major strategic error, made worse by Hitler's refusal to believe his own intelligence reports.

> When a statement was read to him which showed that Stalin would still be able to muster another one to one and a quarter million men in the region north of Stalingrad (besides half a million more in the Caucasus), and which proved that the Russian output of first-line tanks amounted to twelve hundred a month, Hitler flew at the man who was reading with clenched fists and foam in the corners of his mouth, and forbade him to read such idiotic twaddle.[5]

By November, 1942, Hitler had sustained a definite and large-scale defeat.

[1] *Hitler, a Study in Tyranny*. Alan Bullock. London, 1952. p. 106.
[2] *Ibid*. p. 614.
[3] *Ibid*. pp. 616-617.
[4] *Ibid*. p. 617.
[5] *Ibid*. p. 628.

In the course of 1943 Hitler, who looked fifteen years older (according to Goering) since the war began, experienced a trembling of his left arm and left leg. He was taking drugs constantly and receiving daily injections. By the winter of 1944-45 he was meeting all opposition or warning with hysterical outbursts of rage. 'He had', says Guderian, 'a special picture of the world, and every fact had to be fitted into that fancied picture. As he believed, so the world must be. . . .'[1] By February, 1945, he was a physical wreck, an old man with grey skin, shuffling walk, trembling down the left side, totally exhausted and yet ready to scream with rage when even momentarily opposed. This was the Hitler so well described by Trevor-Roper:[2]

> So Hitler ordered; but his orders bore no relation now to any reality. He was moving imaginary battalions, making academic plans, disposing non-existent formations. The Steiner attack was the last, most symbolic instance of Hitler's personal strategy; it never took place.

This cloud-cuckoo-land operation took its imaginary course in April, 1945. Berlin was by then partly in Russian hands. Hitler shrieked at Gottlieb Berger 'Everyone has deceived me! no one has told me the truth! the armed forces have lied to me!' All this was strictly accurate. Night was Falling on the Gods. There was no alternative to suicide and Hitler duly shot himself on 30th April. He was already senile although only just fifty-six years old. His forces surrendered on May 4th and Alan Bullock remarks that 'The Third Reich outlasted its founder by just one week'.[3]

This story of rapid decay is, of course, complicated by circumstances unconnected with Hitler's moral and physical collapse. But it is tolerably certain that the Third Reich would in any case have died with him. We know, however, that Hitler at one time (in 1942) visualised having a regular successor, an elected chief with absolute authority, chosen by a Senate meeting in secret conclave.

> Although a State founded on such principles can lay no claim to eternity, it might last for eight to nine centuries. The thousand-year-old organization of the Church is a proof of this—and yet this entire organization is founded on nonsense. What I have said should *a fortiori* be true of an organization founded on reason.[4]

This suggested period of eight or nine centuries proved to be an overestimate. It did not last eight or nine days. Nor, in more favourable circumstances, could it have lasted very much longer. There was no possible successor, as Hitler himself had realised:

[1] Bullock. *op. cit.* p. 701.
[2] *The Last Days of Hitler.* H. R. Trevor-Roper. London, 1952. p. 123.
[3] Bullock. *op. cit.* p. 732.
[4] *Hitler's Table Talk.* H. R. Trevor-Roper. London, 1953. p. 389.

. . . If anything happens to me Germany will be left without a leader. I have no successor. The first, Hess, is mad; the second, Goering, has lost the sympathy of the people, and the third, Himmler, would be rejected by the Party.[1]

The historian, while accepting Hitler's verdict on these three, must be more impressed with the fact that they would have been hopeless in supreme power even if acceptable to the rest. Goering had run to seed. Himmler—'Faithful Heinrich'—was a stupid, insignificant, pedantic ex-Sergeant-Major, naive enough to believe the Nazi mythology. Joseph Goebbels, ablest of the Party, was no leader. In Albert Speer and Hjalmar Schacht, Hitler had two technicians of genius but they never aspired to more than expert knowledge and Schacht ended in prison. Ribbentrop, Rosenberg and Robert Ley were nonentities, fit members of what Trevor-Roper calls 'a set of flatulent clowns'. As for the soldiers, those of any ability were eliminated—Halder (too outspoken) being told to commit suicide in 1944. Those that remained—Keitel, Jodl, Burgdorf and the rest— were mainly remarkable for their subservience to Hitler, who rejected them all (in his last days) in making Doenitz his successor. The fact that Hitler ended with a circle of second-rate sycophants about him was, of course, no coincidence but the logical consequence of dictatorship. A Leader who wishes to appear supreme and unrivalled in policy, strategy, tactics, finance, architecture, planning and ideas, cannot afford to employ assistants who rise above mediocrity, least of all as generals. But what success can the forces achieve if all the best commanders are systematically murdered or dismissed? Dictatorship decays by the laws which govern its very nature. It could not last for more than a lifetime in any case. In practice it may not last as long. The dictator believes in his own genius—how otherwise could he have seized power?—so he resents opposition. He believes in his own vision of the State—so he will listen to no advice. He believes in the need for centralised authority—so he will delegate no power to others. The natural results are that he is surrounded by flattering nonentities; that he is never told the truth; and that he is driven mad by overwork. He is apt to end as a physical wreck, unable even to make the decisions which no one else is allowed to make for him.

[1] Bullock. *op. cit.* p. 705.

CHAPTER XXIV

Bonapartism

THE Collapse of dictatorship owing to the disability, defeat or death of the dictator is unlikely to prelude a more than momentary return to democracy or oligarchy. Much depends, it is true, upon the length of time which has elapsed since the dictator first came to power. Ordinarily speaking, however, the tendency will be for the people to have forgotten how to govern themselves. Democratic politicians, often elderly men, may well die off—even in the course of nature—during a dictatorship, leaving no one available with any experience of power. The dictator's own followers, should they survive, will usually turn out to be nonentities. Members of any previous aristocracy will have nothing left but vague pretensions and hatreds. Even the middle-class may have lost, during previous revolutions, any claim to leadership it could ever boast. The dictator's fall will leave a vacancy which might seem, at first sight, ready for the next dictator to fill. But that solution often proves impracticable, at any rate in the first instance. For the previous dictator will normally have seen to it that he should have no obvious successor. He will have killed all possible rivals. If there is to be another dictatorship it will be the result of further bloodshed; for it is only in the course of fighting that a new leader is likely to emerge. As against this, the fall of the inspired Leader does not always leave the people in the mood for war. Of war they have, not infrequently, had enough.

So the end of a period of dictatorship may often predispose a people towards monarchy; which is indeed, probably, the form of rule appropriate for them. Kingship may offer them stability without demanding from them the civic virtues which they simply do not possess. Kingship is the natural aftermath to a Caesar, a Cromwell or a Napoleon. But much depends upon the circumstances. When there is a recent tradition of monarchy, the throne is there to fill. When, however, the tradition has been broken, there may be a tendency to give royal honours to the dictator's heir. It is this rather odd preference which accounts, in part, for the restoration of Napoleon III and even for the brief rule of Richard Cromwell. Bonapartism is thus the name given in France to the cult of those who demand the restoration of the empire, not in the name of De Gaulle but for the benefit of Napoleon's collateral descendants. One would have thought that believers in the principle of inspired leadership would have sought to instal a soldier (if one could be found) of comparable talent. One would have thought that believers in hereditary succession would have demanded, as some indeed do, the restoration of the ancient kingship. It is an odd confusion of ideas which can favour an hereditary line of inspired leaders; although no more odd perhaps than the British trust in hereditary champions of egalitarian democracy. This, however, is the basis of Bonapartism; a term we may use to define the attempt made to restore monarchy after a period of dictatorship but without reinstating the previous royal house. It involves founding an entirely new dynasty.

The history of China provides us with many good examples of this development. Chinese dynasties lasted for about two and a half centuries each, on an average, their period of decline representing a phase of oligarchy or democracy, half concealed by the observance of kingly ritual. The dictators who secured imperial office were of varied origin. Liu Chi (or Pang), who became emperor in 202 B.C. was a commoner of officer rank. Wu-ti was succeeded by the nephew of the late Empress. From the disorder which followed the socialistic experiments of Wang Mang there emerged, as supreme, a distant cousin of the former Han Emperor. Li, founder of the T'ang dynasty, who succeeded after the murder of Yang Kuang, was of a ducal family. Chao K'wang-Yin, regent in A.D. 959 and emperor in 960, was of similarly respectable origin. Chu Yüanchang, on the other hand, who captured Nanking and made himself emperor in 1368, was a monk of humble origin. The problem for the Chinese political theorist was therefore to find justification for the revolt which brought the current dynasty into power. He had to do so, moreover, without lending any general sanction to future revolts designed to expel it. This problem was solved by teaching that the bad emperor was not emperor at all and that the current emperor was a model of the virtues which his predecessor had lacked.

This process is well exemplified in the revolution which established Chu Yüanchang as first emperor of the Ming dynasty. Revolt in this instance was directed against the Mongols and Chu Yüanchang was able to enlist nationalist feelings on his side, expressing his views in a manifesto which has survived and which reads:—

> We Chinese have regarded the ruler as the father of the people, the court as the center of the nation, and moral principles as principles of government. The conduct of the Mongol monarchs violates the Chinese sense of morality and cannot be exemplary. The Mongol ministers are dictatorial, the Mongol censors arbitrary, and the Mongol judges prejudiced. . . . It is said that 'no barbarians ever reign for a century'. This saying must come true, now that we have

started a nation-wide revolution to overthrow the Mongol regime.[1]

The revolution succeeded and had the effect of installing as dictator one of the most ignorant, suspicious and brutal characters ever recorded in Chinese history. Chu Yüanchang followed good dictatorial practice in executing all the ministers and generals who had assisted his rise to power. He ruled directly, combining the offices of emperor, premier and commander-in-chief. He founded a new dynasty, nevertheless, one which lasted until 1644. There followed a period of disorder, during which Li Tse-Cheng tried to make himself emperor; a period which ended with the establishment of the Ch'ing dynasty in about 1659. The Ch'ing or Manchu emperors then held sway until 1911, using Chinese terminology to justify an alien rule.

> It sounds very Confucian and Chinese when one reads the Manchu proclamation that the 'wheel of the world' had turned, the decline of one dynasty had made room for another, the Ming had lost the heavenly mandate. 'Through heaven's favor and the new emperor's blessing' the Manchus had conquered Peking.[2]

It is this phrase 'the mandate of heaven' which is of particular significance.

The doctrine of the mandate of heaven was a feature of Chinese political thought from an early period. It was adopted by Tung Chung-shu (*circa* 179-104 B.C.) adviser to the emperor Wu Ti, who was first responsible for making Confucian ethics the basis of official teaching and the key to public office. The Confucian ideal, none too precise in the first instance and afterwards blended with concepts derived in fact from other thinkers, could be made an invaluable ally of those actually in power. Many Confucian ideas have no immediate and practical application but some, as interpreted by Mencius (and Tung Chung-shu) could be very usefully emphasised. 'God creates the people' said Mencius, 'and appoints for them emperors and teachers'.[3] 'The Master said:— "The people may be made to follow a course, but not to understand the reason why".'[4] There was no nonsense in Confucian theory about equality. People differed from each other in position, wealth, age, wisdom and ability. Some were fitted to rule and others fit only to obey. But neither was fitness to rule a matter of noble descent. How could it be in a land where the ruling dynasty had gained power in a revolution which some might remember and of which all would have heard? No doctrine will do

[1] *Men and Ideas. An Informal History of Chinese Political Thought.* Lin Mousheng. New York, 1942. p. 131.
[2] *The Origin of Manchu rule in China. Frontier and Bureaucracy as Interacting Forces in the Chinese Empire.* Franz Michael. Baltimore, 1942. p. 116.
[3] *History of Chinese Political Thought during the early Tsin Period.* Liang Chi-Chao. Trans. by L. T. Chen. London, 1930. p. 50. Liang Chi-Chao was a pupil of K'ang Yuwei, last of the Confucians.
[4] *Hsüntze, Moulder of Confucianism.* H. H. Dubs. London, 1927.

which fails to show that the *last* revolution was in accordance with
the order of Heaven and in response to the wishes of men. The
previous dynasty must have lost the heavenly mandate. On this point
Mencius is explicit.

> . . . 'In order to be a king one must fulfil the functions of a king.
> When a king fails to do that, he loses his claim to be the ruler of the
> people'. On this point the following conversation is illuminating:
> "King Hsuan of Chi asked, 'Is it authentic that Tong put the Emperor
> Chieh in exile, and that King Wu led the expedition against the
> Emperor Chow?' Mencius replied 'It is so recorded in the book'.
> 'Is it permissible then for a minister to put to death his sovereign?'
> 'One who outrages the virtue 'Jen' is a robber; one who outrages
> propriety is a ruffian. A ruffian or a robber is a mere commoner. I have
> heard that a man named Chow was decapitated; but I have never heard
> that a sovereign was put to death".'[1]

Political advisers clearly had their anxious moments. They had
somehow to combine their approval of past revolution with an
assurance of loyalty in the event of any future revolt. They were like
early Hanoverian divines preaching the doctrine of divine right—
those who gained their bishopric had earned it. But the Confucian
doctrine of Names evades the difficulty rather neatly. The king who is
not saintly and benevolent is not king at all. He has deposed himself.
He has virtually abdicated. It was the usefulness of this, among
other doctrines, which induced Tung Chung-shu to advise Wu Ti to
adopt Confucianism as the official doctrine.

> Your humble servant proposes that all doctrines that deviate from
> the arts and classics of Confucius be suppressed completely. Once
> subversive and pernicious doctrines are quelled, the unity of the
> Empire may be maintained and laws and rules may be so clearly stated
> that the people will know what to follow.[2]

Confucianism provides, or can be distorted to provide, a valuable
support for monarchy. It does not, however, justify a despotic rule.
For the emperor could retain the mandate of heaven only by display-
ing, or seeming to display, the virtues which such a mandate would
seem to imply. The ruler was considerably fettered by the etiquette
and conventions which surrounded his office. It was no part of the
accepted legend that the emperor was (as in Japan and elsewhere) a
descendant of the gods. Instead, it was the convention to assume that
the emperor owed his position to his superior virtue. The story was
told of the emperor Yao (2356 B.C.) who offered to abdicate in

---

[1] Liang Chi-Chao. *op. cit.* p. 62. The virtue 'Jen' is, roughly speaking, the practice of
doing for others what you think they should do for you.
[2] *Men and Ideas, An Informal History of Chinese Political Thought.* Lin Mousheng.
New York, 1942. p. 148. See also *In Quest of Civilisation.* R. Latham. London, 1946.
p. 136 *et seq.*

favour of the hermit, Hsu Yu. It was held that only saintly kings and virtuous officers could guide the people by their character and example. Monarchical government is best but only through the ruler's display of benevolence, righteousness, propriety and knowledge. Confucius perceived, incidentally, that a useful test of efficiency is that of time. He held that a kingdom ruled by an aristocracy would be lost within ten generations and one ruled by the many would be lost in three.[1] Only virtuous kings could rule indefinitely, governing so quietly that the people might not realise that they were governing at all.

> The more restrictions and prohibitions are in the Empire, the poorer grow the people. The more weapons the people have, the more troubled is the state. The more there is cunning and skill, the more startling events happen. The more mandates and laws are enacted the more there will be thieves and robbers. (Lao Tzu).[2]

The moral pressure brought to bear upon the emperor by a widespread reliance upon his virtue must have been considerable. There were bad rulers but fewer perhaps than there might have been had no conventional virtue been attributed to them. There were tyrants but less oppressive perhaps than they would have been if not continually reminded of the good example they were supposed to set. In at least one important respect, moreover, the conventional virtue coincided with the most everyday prudence. For the good king had to listen to the remonstrances of his ministers and the complaints of his people. 'If an emperor has seven outspoken ministers' said Confucius, 'he cannot lose his empire'. As for public relations, 'to gag the voice of the people is more dangerous than to dam the flow of a river. . . . The wise ruler encourages men to speak out freely'.[3] More than that, the system of censorship and the appointment of official chroniclers used to provide the ruler with official critics, some to remonstrate and some to record his faults.

> . . . while Chinese government in form lends itself to despotism, it is so surrounded by theories of virtue and good actions that in practice despotism is not only checked but to a great extent actually done away with. The teachings of the philosophers with their restraining influences and the almost universal acceptance of propriety as a basis of action have led to a condition where the ruler is constantly reminded of what is right, what is proper, what ought to be done, and how one should act.[4]

[1] *Chinese Political Thought.* E. D. Thomas. London, 1928. p. 154.
[2] *Ibid.* p. 159. For the Chinese detestation of economic restrictions see *The Economic Principles of Confucius and his school.* Chen Huan-Chang. 2 vols. New York, 1911. Later Confucians would not even *discuss* economics.
[3] *Government and Politics of China.* Ch'ien Tuang Sheng. Harvard, 1950. See pp. 22-23.
[4] Thomas. *op. cit.* p. 184.

This was hardly compatible with despotism; nor even (one might add) with progress.

The emperor who was thus expected to keep in close touch with public opinion and well within the bounds of established custom, had the further general duty of being successful. The mandate of heaven, like the Calvinist proof of being one of the elect, implied a visible token of divine favour. Military defeat was not normally attributed to tactical error but rather to the withdrawal of heaven's mandate. After a reverse, the emperor had to examine his conscience, to discover how he could have offended heaven. The Chinese had no love of lost causes. They were more inclined to join the winning side. There was therefore a tendency in public bulletins to pass lightly over the less encouraging items of news, bringing into warfare that atmosphere of unreality which was never wholly absent from politics. Fictions are useful but not perhaps beyond the point at which fact becomes totally obscured.

The ever-victorious emperor had the further responsibility of making the rain fall. The more inconvenient manifestations of nature were clearly attributable to his shortcomings. The drought of 1832 brought the emperor to his knees before a public altar, complaining to heaven that no rain had fallen all the summer. The prayer with which he memorialised heaven included the following words:

> . . . I, the minister of Heaven, am placed over mankind, and am responsible for keeping the world in order and tranquilising the people. Although it is now impossible for me to sleep or eat with composure, although I am scorched with grief and tremble with anxiety, still, after all, no genial and copious showers have been obtained. . . . Looking up, I consider that Heaven's heart is benevolence and love. The sole cause is the daily deeper atrocity of my sins; but little sincerity and little devotion. Hence I have been unable to move Heaven's heart, and bring down abundant blessings. . . .
>
> . . . I feel impelled, by ten thousand considerations, to . . . assail Heaven, examine myself, and consider my errors; looking up and hoping that I may obtain pardon. . . .
>
> Prostrate I beg imperial Heaven [Hwang Tien] to pardon my ignorance and stupidity, and to grant me self-renovation; for myriads of innocent people are involved by me, the One man. My sins are so numerous it is difficult to escape from them. Summer is past and autumn arrived; to wait longer will really be impossible. Knocking head, I pray imperial deliverance—a speedy and divinely beneficial rain, to save the people's lives and in some degree redeem my iniquities. Oh, alas! imperial Heaven, observe these things. Oh, alas! imperial Heaven, be gracious to them. I am inexpressibly grieved, alarmed, and frightened. Reverently this memorial is presented.[1]

This prayer was, of course, a ritual form of words; not the

[1] Thomas. *op. cit.* p. 160.

spontaneous petition of a man whose throne is in actual danger. The Han dynasty was overthrown by plague but the Manchus were not seriously endangered by drought. There is on the other hand much that is significant in the self-examination which forms the central theme of the memorial. The emperor asks himself whether he has neglected to sacrifice, whether he has been proud and extravagant, whether he has regularly attended to the affairs of government, whether he has been just, whether he has overspent on mausolea and gardens, whether he has appointed the right men to office, whether he has listened to the appeals of the oppressed, whether there has been needless slaughter in war, whether relief has been properly distributed and whether revolts have been humanely suppressed? These were evidently the sort of sins of which emperors were sometimes accused, and the list reveals an acute sense of responsibility, not only to Heaven but to the public.

To the Chinese system of attributing the mandate of Heaven to whatever ruler has grasped and retained the supreme power, the nearest parallel is to be found in Islam. Muhammad (born *c.* A.D. 570) left no definite scheme of government apart from his religious teaching and example. Nor did the attempt to provide him with successors in office last for more than a few years. He did, however, enjoin obedience to rulers.

> . . . Obey your rulers whatever may hap, for if they bid you do any-thing different to what I have taught you, they shall be rewarded for it and you will be rewarded for your obedience. . . .'
>
> The political theory thus enunciated appears to imply that all earthly authority is by divine appointment, the duty of the subjects is to obey, whether the ruler is just or unjust. . . . Such a doctrine seems also to be implied in the following Tradition in which the Prophet says: 'When God wishes good for a people, He sets over them the forbearing and wise, and places their goods in the hands of generous rulers; but when God wishes evil for a people, He sets over them the witless and base. . . .'[1]

In point of fact, the various territories occupied by the followers of Islam speedily fell apart, each under a separate ruler, many of these rulers eventually aspiring to the title of Sultan. Provided he is a Muslim, the ruler of a predominantly Muslim State is entitled to obedience, by whatever means he has come to power. He is 'the shadow of Allah upon earth'. Islamic law and custom would permit a series of non-hereditary rulers. Their power would fall short, how-ever, of dictatorship. For the Muslim ruler is subject to Muslim Law, which he cannot amend, repeal or even interpret. His duties are

[1] *The Caliphate.* Sir Thomas W. Arnold. Oxford, 1924. See pp. 48-50. See also *Muhammad 'A Mercy to all the Nations'.* Al-Haji Qassim Ali Jairazbhoy. London, 1934. p. 239. and *The Law of War and Peace in Islam.* Majid Khadduri. London, 1940.

theoretically restricted to judgment, taxation, the Friday worship and the Holy War.[1] As compared, however, with the Chinese monarch, the Muslim ruler was less responsible to the people. Misfortunes in China might be attributed to the sins of the emperor. Similar events among Muslim peoples would be attributed rather to the sins of the people themselves. This left them with no religious sanction for deposing the ruler. Neither, however, did it restrain them from offering obedience to his successor, should the government chance to be overturned.

While Chinese and Islamic custom both used thus to offer a ready means of converting a dictator into a regularly appointed and even hereditary monarch, the same cannot be said of countries in which the idea of kingship has actually died out. We have seen that South American Republics have seldom managed to turn dictatorship into monarchy. The tradition has not been alive and there has always been the definite opposition of those with liberal or republican views. It cannot be supposed that the escape from dictatorship in such states can ever be easy, and historical examples would seem to suggest that it is impossible without foreign intervention and the virtual annexation of the territory by another and more efficiently organised power. Fortunate, in that case, are the states like Spain and Italy in which monarchy might easily revive. Granted, however, that such a revival were possible and granted, moreover, that all or most of the dictatorial states of the twentieth century could be transformed somehow into monarchies of a more or less stable kind, this would be no final solution to the political problem. We have no reason to suppose that the monarchies thus restored would prove much more permanent than any other form of government. There would seem to be cyclic fashions and an inherent law of change. Were we to accept the teaching of history we should conclude that the political units we now describe as nations are likely to repeat the political sequence through which most of them have passed. Some, it is true, are too small to experience all these changes; and two, perhaps, of a federal pattern, may prove too large. For the rest we might be tempted to predict a continuance of the treadmill round, ending only with the end of civilisation itself; a finish not necessarily very remote. Such a prediction would, however, be unjustified. For, while the course of history may reveal a trend, it does not prove that the trend is inevitable. There are instances of a danger being avoided, provided only that the danger has been perceived.

[1] See Development of Muslim Theology, Jurisprudence and Constitutional Theory. D. B. Macdonald. London, 1903. See also Mohammad Theories of Finance. Nicolas P. Aghanides. New York, 1915; An Introduction to the Sociology of Islam. R. Levy. 2 vols. London, c. 1931; Muslim Institutions. Maurice Gaudefroy Demombynes, London, 1950; and The Legacy of Islam. Ed. by Sir Thomas Arnold. Oxford, 1931.

EPILOGUE

IT is no part of the historian's business to deal with the future. In so far, therefore, as this book is an academic study, its conclusions have already been reached. The story has been told of how monarchy arises, to be superseded by aristocracy, which is replaced by democracy, which ends in dictatorship, which may well be the prelude to monarchy again. The sequence is by no means invariable but it can be shown, with some plausibility, that the tendency exists. The attempt has been made to indicate, in outline, some of the merits and defects of each form of rule. Some description has been attempted of the works in which political theorists have sought to define, assess, praise and decry the various patterns which government has assumed. The historian can do no more than that, unless it be to point out that the assumption of a finality reached seems to be the illusion common to almost every age. But while the historian, as such, can go no further than we have gone—and may be thought rash to have gone as far—the author of a book may justly shrink from leaving unanswered the questions which an intelligent reader must feel bound to ask. He may perhaps be forgiven for attempting to answer beforehand the questions which might otherwise reach him by post. He may even be allowed, in doing so, to express what is merely opinion and quit, for the time being, the realms of fact.

Several questions may have occurred to the reader who can claim to be still in the hunt, but the first will certainly be this: 'Which form of rule is best?' There must, after all, be something unfinished about a book which does no more than define, describe and collate. In this instance, the inconclusive finish would be emphasised by the fact that no single form of rule has been singled out for commendation. The author may seem rather to have concentrated upon the defects which cause impermanence, leaving the reader to conclude with the psalmist that all is vanity. But that is not the message that the author wishes to convey. To the reader's question he must reply, it is true, that he sees no great merit in any of the forms of rule he has had to describe. They represent phases of human experience from which some wisdom may be gained, but no one of them would represent finality even if finality were to be reached at all. No one, in fact, represents any marked improvement upon any other. They reveal, taken together, an almost startling lack of progress. The fact, however, that progress so far has been slight does not mean that progress is impossible; and the object of this epilogue is to assert the author's belief that progress may yet be made.

Our starting point is the contrast between the progress made in science and the stagnation in political thought since 1900; or indeed since 1850. During the last century we have had a series of industrial, technical and scientific revolutions affecting the whole of human life. During the last fifty years we have had the revolutionary changes brought about by the car, the film, the radio, the aircraft and the submarine. We have seen startling progress in chemistry, physics, biology and medicine. We have heard almost monthly of scientific developments ranging from penicillin to jet propulsion, from nuclear fission to radar. Life has been technically transformed in twenty different ways. During the same period, political progress has been nil. Theory has been at a stand-still and practice shows perceptible retrogression. No one is more acutely aware of this contrast than the modern traveller by air. The organisation of the Air Line is relatively efficient, modern, smooth and stream-lined. The aircraft is a technical achievement which would have been impossible ten years ago and which will certainly be obsolete ten years hence. The crew are highly trained technicians handling costly equipment. The passage is, by all previous standards, unbelievably swift and safe. But the traveller, on landing anywhere, finds himself confronted by a political organization which is practically medieval. The passport and visa formalities are of a kind which our Victorian ancestors regarded as belonging to a remote and barbarous antiquity. The customs shed reminds us at once of the gifts formerly lavished by traders on the chiefs of savage peoples. The currency regulations date from some period before Adam Smith. The fuss about alcohol seems to be based on the ideas of the more remote Arab tribes. Books are liable to be confiscated and burnt by darkly brooding inquisitors. The forms to be filled in have been apparently devised in the nursery by children so backward as to be almost imbecile. The contrast, in short, between skilled pilots and more or less illiterate officials is very painful indeed.

Why have the physical sciences advanced and why has political science stood still? Before we attempt to answer that question we must remind ourselves that progress and improvement are not identical. Confronted by the contrast between the old and the new, Mahatma Gandhi came to the conclusion that modern industry is itself sinful and that moral progress must involve a return to the simplicities. He certainly pointed the way to a method (and perhaps the only method) by which democracy could be made to work. His views will certainly repay the closest study. It may be doubted, however, whether a world-wide return to the simplicities is even possible.

The simple village life is subject, under primitive conditions, to famine, drought, epidemic, flood, storm and pest. Can we now ask the peasant to discard the help of the railway, road, pipe-line, electric-cable, clinic, dam, injection and spray? With no modern equipment the world could not support its present population in comfort—still less the population of the future. We could not feed, clothe, maintain or even restrict the present numbers without the aid of industry and science. While the reversal of the present trend might seem attractive, it will be assumed here that it is impracticable. It might well be shown that Gandhi's condemnation of western medicine is justified and that religious meditation is better than any drug. Even so it would seem unlikely that people will now discard all they have been taught to value. We must assume, however reluctantly, that scientific progress is not to be reversed and that the problem is to discover why there has been no comparable progress in politics.

The solution of this problem depends upon a clear understanding of what scientific method is. We cannot help but suspect that the methods of science, if applied to political problems, would produce the sort of progress that we have observed in physics. What methods are these which produce such remarkable results? Basic, we suppose, to all scientific method is the desire to find out. Real progress begins at the point at which the scientist admits his ignorance. And this point, as a matter of historic fact, comes fairly late in the history of science. The main handicap of the medieval scientist lay not in his ignorance but in the fact that he knew it all already. He had read Aristotle and St. Augustine, Hippocrates and Galen. He was primed with the eternal principles of his art, approved by his Faculty and memorised by his pupils. No real progress was possible until they had been stuffed in the waste paper basket. What were these dogma?

Physicians believed, following Hippocrates, that everything is founded on a united confluence of all the humours. They considered that phlebotomy or blood-letting is useful but only if governed by the movements of the stars. They knew that a drink made from mistletoe will at once make women fertile and prevent poisoning. They were impressed with the obvious danger of eating pork unaccompanied by wine. To avoid catching the plague the correct thing—as is well known—is to purge oneself with pills of aloes. As for syphilis (when it appeared in the later middle ages) there could be no doubt that it was due to a corruption of the air. When in doubt, medieval or sixteenth century physicians might turn to specialists in zoology, chemistry and astrology. Nor would they turn in vain. Experts were at hand to assure them that the unicorn or monoceros is guilty of excessive pride, that the salamander lives in fire and that parrots are taught to speak by being beaten with an iron rod (for they feel nothing else). Other experts were eager to affirm that cinnibar, well known to pharmacists, is formed from the blood of the dragon and elephant, mingled in their mortal combat. The quintessence of the elements, they would remark, is full of the virtues celestial. Others were fully aware of the doubled or trebled dangers resulting from the conjunction of the dragon's tail with the evil planets.

Roger Bacon was perhaps the first European to point out—following his Arabic teachers—that these and similar axioms were an obstacle to progress.

> . . . If I had my way I should burn all the books of Aristotle, for the study of them can only lead to a loss of time, produce error, and increase ignorance. . . .[1]

Some centuries were to pass before Roger Bacon's advice was even approximately followed. But it can be asserted with some confidence that progress began when the scientists ceased to look at books and began to look at things. Their first task, and the start of all that was to follow, was to make a bonfire of all that had been written. Once they had done that, scrapped all they knew and admitted their complete ignorance, they were able to go straight ahead, assembling facts and checking them by experiment. Facts henceforth were to come first and eternal principles were to come (if at all) long afterwards.

In the field of politics we have not yet reached the point at which scientific progress began. We are still (literally) at the stage of reading Aristotle. What is worse, we are still telling each other the eternal principles of political theory. One theorist will say 'The history of all known society . . . has been the history of class struggles'. Another will reply as firmly that representative government is 'the ideal type of the most perfect polity'. A third will cry that the general will is always right, and a fourth will assert that the dictatorship of the proletariat is bound to come. A fifth will intone his conviction that all men are born equal, only to be shouted down by a sixth who will have it that men are everywhere in chains. Government, we are assured by a seventh, is instituted to secure for men their right to life, liberty and the pursuit of happiness. At all times, shouts the eighth, the principles of democracy have brought people to ruin. The place of the hero, growls the ninth, is with the stars of heaven. As soon as the people are brought to silence, concludes the tenth (hopefully) their voice is most distinctly heard. In the course of this book we have had occasions to notice a score of these eternal principles, founded for the most part on nothing. They are valuable to the historian as

[1] See *The Legacy of the Middle Ages*. Ed. C. G. Cramp and E. F. Jacob. Oxford, 1932. p. 270.

illustrations of popular or unpopular emotion. They may be valuable to the politician as a fund of slogans upon which to draw in a time of mental blackout. To the constructive political thinker they are mere claptrap; rubbish to be removed from the site before the building can begin. They are all, and without exception, drivel.

If the first stage in scientific thought (the stage we have not even reached) is to rid ourselves of all the eternal verities, the second stage is to learn how to progress step by step, and only one step at a time. The reader who has restrained his impatience until now may feel tempted to repeat his question. 'Well, at the end of it all, what form of rule *is* best?' To that the student of politics must reply 'How should I know? My researches have scarcely begun. Nor do I understand your question—what do you mean by "best"; and "best", anyway, for whom?' To try to answer that sort of question is to assume that we are somewhere near the top of the ladder, whereas we are scarcely on the bottom rung. Your true scientist is content with one step at a time. He does not claim to produce a medicine which will cure every known disease. He tries instead to isolate and identify a single bacillus which may (or may not) be associated, in a majority of cases, with the symptoms of one particular illness. Or he may be intent on investigating a problem of fatigue in a certain metal when used in a certain way. In just the same manner a student of politics will try to establish some facts before proclaiming his discovery of universally applicable rules of nature. Of the facts needed scarcely a fraction have been ascertained. And if past experience is any guide, the facts are needed before the theory, if only to prevent the theory from distorting the facts.

What facts do we need? We need first to assemble and collate the political experience embodied in history. This experience includes the relative success of different forms of rule among different peoples, on different continents, in different circumstances and in different centuries. It will be obvious, in collecting this information, that the problems of ruling China and the problems of ruling Cocos Keeling Island are not identical. It will also be obvious that many questions can never be answered. Jeremy Bentham judged governments by his yardstick of the greatest happiness of the greatest number. Were we to do the same, we should have no means of discovering whether people of past centuries were happy or not. Were the Egyptians happy under Rameses II? Were the Chinese happy under Wu Ti? We cannot tell and will waste our time if we seek to discover. If we cannot measure happiness among people still living; still less can we measure the happiness of people who lived and died centuries ago. Governments of a remote period may be judged a little on their material achievement and a little by the arts.

Often, however, we know little more about them than their period of survival. That fact, if known for certain, is seldom, however, without significance. The virtue of stability is at least measurable, which so many other criteria are not. Of governments more recent we know far more and of those still in existence we know more again—except, indeed, about their capacity for survival.

Next we need to know something about political theories of the past. We have found that these theories are usually a more or less faithful reflection of current practice. We have also found that the theories are mostly, to a scientific thinker, unhelpful. Theories based on Divine Right, Original Contract, the Rights of Man and Human Equality are likely to seem invalid or meaningless. We must dismiss at the outset the idea that a perfect form of rule can be discovered, set up and maintained for ever. The whole concept is pre-Darwinian. Nothing human is likely to be perfect, and if it were (here and to-day) it would no longer be perfect a century hence nor perfect now in another place. It is in that sense that Karl Marx is still ahead of some other thinkers. He had at least an idea that things evolve. Nowadays, while fully alive to the laws of change, we lack his Victorian certainty that change is for the better. We are even familiar, as patrons of the cinema, with the change that leads us back to the starting point. But while we may cheerfully discard most of the old theories, we might do well to trace among them the growth of one important idea; the idea that government is to be judged by results. To the semi-theological theorist who says that good government is of the people, by the people and for the people there have always been a few, here and there, ready to retort that good government is that which governs well.

Such a one was Benedict Spinoza (1634-1677) whose training (significantly) had been not in theology but in optics. In his unfinished political treatise[1] he expresses no definite conclusion about the forms of rule. He applies, instead, this test of excellence: 'that dominion is the best where men pass their lives in unity and the laws are kept unbroken'. That is the beginnings of a scientific approach, and one worthy of a contemporary of Descartes. There is some faint echo of this idea in the text of Hobbes' *Leviathan* (See p. 84 above). Descartes, in his *Discourse on Method* pointed the way to a science of experiment and deplored 'the speculative philosophy taught in the schools'. In politics it is just such philosophy that is still being taught; a teaching in which Spinoza detected the fallacy nearly three hundred years ago. The truth seen by Spinoza had been at least glimpsed, as we have noted, by Confucius, who applied to governments the test of duration. It was seen again, and more clearly, by Rousseau. He

[1] *Writings in political philosophy*. Benedict de Spinoza. Ed. A. G. A. Balz. New York, 1937.

refused to decide upon the relative merits of the different forms of rule. He maintained, however, that one can decide, as a question of fact, whether a given people is well or badly governed; a question never settled 'because every one wishes to decide it in his own way'. Let us repeat what he says once more:

> ... What is the object of political association? It is the preservation and prosperity of its members. And what is the surest sign that they are preserved and prosperous? It is their number and population. Do not, then, go and seek elsewhere for this sign so much discussed. All other things being equal, the government under which, without external aids, without naturalization, and without colonies, the citizens increase and multiply most, is infallibly the best. That under which a people diminishes and decays is the worst. Statisticians, it is now your business; reckon, measure, compare.[1]

These words deserve to be remembered when the Social Contract has ceased to be read. Among the pages of nonsense that have passed so far as political philosophy we can discern, here and there, the first faint glimmerings of scientific thought.

All this runs counter to the main current of British and American sentiment. To many of these the test of good government is not concerned with unity or duration, nor with the laws being kept nor with the increase of population but simply with the question of what is or is not democratic. There have thus in the past been patriots who have cried 'My country, right or wrong!' There have been authors eager to proclaim that the will of the people is sacred. It is not, they say, the duty of government to make the wisest decision: government must do what the people wish. If it be urged that the majority may be wrong, they reply that it is through making mistakes that people learn. It may be doubted, however, for two reasons, whether this point of view is any longer tenable. In the first place we have seen that the will of the people in the modern world is the synthetic result of mass-suggestion; created by schools, press, films and radio. In the second place, there are some suicidal mistakes that can only be made once. A people cannot, save through ignorance, will their own destruction by famine, disease or war. There can be nothing particularly sacred about ignorance. And yet it is easy for intelligent and energetic people to destroy the fertility of the soil upon which they live. It has been done repeatedly. It is easy for a people to oppose, on religious grounds, the sanitary measures which alone can save them from the most fatal epidemics. It is happening daily. It is easy for a people to neglect their armed forces, quarrel with every possible ally and declare war upon a stronger power, thereafter suffering complete disaster and obliteration. It may happen at any time. No such process

[1] *Social Contract.* J. J. Rousseau. Chap. IX. Book III.

can be justified, surely, by any statistics of how the majority voted at recent elections. We know, without any such research, that they cannot have wanted what actually happened to them. The final test is that of survival. The path which leads to destruction may be democratic but it cannot, in any useful sense, be right.

Having learnt something of history and something of past political theory, the students of politics must next turn for their facts to the allied fields of knowledge. We must learn from the anthropologist that human beings have some deep instincts which we cannot ignore. We must learn from the psychologist that man is less rational than some thinkers have chosen to assume. Democracy must be studied in terms of crowd-psychology, dictatorship in terms of megalomania. We must learn from the expert in social medicine, who may tell us at what age the human being reaches his peak of efficiency and at what age he should retire. We must learn from the social investigator the extent to which ability is inherited and the extent to which it is acquired. What other qualities are heritable, and how? From what sort of background does genius usually derive? We must learn from experts in mass observation, who can tell us what public opinion really means. We must learn from advertising agents, who know the extent to which people can be influenced and by what means and at what cost. We must learn from physiologists, who will tell us in what ways the decisions of a committee may be affected by such factors as the hour, the temperature and the ventilation. We must learn from physicians who have studied the whole question of human fatigue. We must learn from a score of specialists before we venture to attempt the solution of a single minor problem. By the standards of modern scientific method the amount of work devoted by Tom Paine to the whole field of politics would not suffice to decide the optimum number for a standing committee's membership.

Our next source of information concerns the states existing at the present day. We must study their vital statistics; the increase of population, the size of family, the tendency to emigrate, the tendency to commit suicide. We must collect and study all data relating to health; the statistics of height, weight, sickness and insanity. We must assemble the results of intelligence tests. We must discover the number of road accidents in proportion to the number of vehicles. Then we shall need facts and figures about crime, hooliganism and juvenile delinquency. When all that information has been collected, we can begin to approach the more difficult problems. First of these might be the question of the economy of effort. How many public servants are employed to administer a certain city at a given period: how many clerks, how many police, how many firemen, how many dustmen—all representing what total of expenditure? We must then measure the time it takes, under a certain regime, to arrest and execute a murderer; to pass an Act of the Legislature; to finish a Public Inquiry; to pass the plans for a building; to announce the results of an election; and to receive an intelligent reply from a government department on any subject. The next stage might be to estimate the public spirit shown by those living under the given regime. How many of them do ambulance work, how many serve as auxiliary police, how many belong to charitable organisations? We might go on to inquire into standards of punctuality as affecting railways, aircraft, 'buses and public meetings. These are only a few of the headings under which we might group all the factors which together represent efficiency.

But efficiency, the reader may object, is not all. That is true enough. The social scientist must move, however, step by step. To measure the efficiency of different states does not show us which political system is best. The results are merely a few facts to be considered alongside many other facts still to be ascertained. Nor would the conclusions reached necessarily concern the exact form of rule. It might well prove more possible to discover, in the first instance, what size of state is to be preferred; or, rather, perhaps, what size of state tends to produce the highest level of efficiency. It would seem probable that an optimum could be found and even a rough idea gained of the decline in efficiency observable after population exceeds a certain total.

The danger, of course, in this sort of measurement is that it applies only to what is easily measurable. One may picture (one may even know) a well-proportioned community of healthy and contented people, clean, hygienic, sensible and prosperous (if possibly a trifle smug), producing nothing except another generation of similar people, equally contented, healthy, clean and prosperous (and perhaps a shade more smug than their parents). This picture of pointless repetition should compel us, from the start, to pursue other lines of investigation. In what sort of state and in what circumstances have people produced the noblest achievements in art, architecture, sculpture, literature and music? Which peoples have been most appreciative of the arts? Among what sort of peoples do we find the greatest scientists, explorers, physicians, inventors and mountain-climbers? We might discover that disorderly, criminal and diseased people produce great works of art, and that healthy, smug, law-abiding people produce nothing. We are not compelled, however, to decide which is preferable until we know that the contrast exists. Healthy children and good orchestral music may, after all, prove compatible.

Even when all the facts from past history and present experience have been assembled and compared, the political scientist can base upon them only the most tentative conclusions. For theories, even when based upon facts, have still to be tested by experiment. In countries organised on federal lines nothing could be simpler than to nationalise the health service in one State or District and measure the results (in health and cost) in comparison with the States still unreformed. Would mines produce more if co-operatively owned by the miners? The fact can be ascertained only by experiment. Ought there to be secret voting in the legislature? Should half the members of the Cabinet be women? Ought we to compel ministers to retire at the age of fifty—or eighty? These are not subjects for discussion but for experiment and observation.

The difficulty in solving these problems by the scientific method is that people in general, and politicians in particular, are little influenced by scientific thought. They demand, instead, religion, inspiration, poetry, clamour, strife and hatred. People who want colour, drama, action and conflict will never be satisfied with the cold facts of dispassionate investigation. And this suggests the need for research in another direction—the study of how to satisfy the political demands of ordinary people while simultaneously providing for their actual needs. There are, beyond question, people well qualified to investigate such problems as these. It may, however, be doubted whether any western democracy is so constituted as to be capable either of experiment or of self-reform. For progress in the science or art of politics we should look perhaps, first and foremost, to India; and eventually to China. It is hardly probable that the subtle brains of China will for very long be satisfied with the crude doctrines of Karl Marx. In any case, a reaction is due against the present tendency to make all political dispute a matter of economics; and people may yet turn with relief to a programme of purely political reform. Mounting and obvious dangers—especially of population increase and famine—not to mention war—may compel peoples to resort to scientific method in the end.

When, if ever, research leads to definite conclusions; when, if ever, States prove sufficiently enlightened to accept advice based on patient investigation rather than on crude emotion and selfish interest, mankind may break away from the treadmill which seems to lead from kingship to democracy, from democracy to kingship. There would seem to be no fundamental reason why there should not be as fresh a departure in politics as there has been in physics—provided always that we can take the first essential step of discarding all that we think we know. That step, if taken in Russia, would mean relegating the works of Karl Marx to the history section of the library. It would mean discarding the belief that communism has any special sanctity. It would imply that communist theocracy should be judged by results not by the criteria contained in holy writ. The same step, if taken in the United States, would mean relegating the works of Jefferson to the history section of the library. It would mean discarding the belief that democracy has any special sanctity. It would imply that universal suffrage should be judged by results not by the criteria contained in holy writ. It cannot be sufficiently emphasised that a research hampered from the outset by unproved assumptions can lead nowhere. The starting point of any real investigation is not the assertion of a passionate (if ill-defined) belief but the frank admission of ignorance coupled with a genuine desire to find out.

This emphatic warning is more especially needed among the believers in democracy, who are less conscious than the communists of all that they have tended to assume. Theirs is not normally, for one thing, the religion of the single sacred volume. They are more inclined to base their arguments on a vague knowledge of history. 'Monarchy and Aristocracy have failed', they say, 'it remains to try Democracy'. The more enlightened will then agree to discuss the ways and means. But the unproved assumption is still there. For in asserting that Monarchy and Oligarchy have failed they have omitted to explain in what the alleged failure consists. What have these forms of rule failed to accomplish? They have failed (we are told) but in *what*? When that failure comes to be analysed we find ourselves driven to the further conclusion that Democracy has also failed. Once that is admitted, we can discuss the merits and defects of each system. Without that admission, the discussion will lead nowhere.

In any fair discussion of political theory and practice it will be absurd to deny that there is any merit in monarchy or oligarchy. There are manifest advantages in both, quite comparable with the advantages of democracy. Arithmetical arguments for democracy must be balanced against all the biological objections to it. Improvements in the speed of horses have been brought about by careful breeding, by the early training of a few thus bred and by the subsequent care of those few. Many notable men and women have also been the result of careful breeding, of early training and subsequent guidance. The care which can be given to a few would be physically impossible for the many (whether men or horses). One might add that the promotion of someone to a position of responsibility at the age of twenty has the possible merit of producing, later on, a man aged thirty-five with fifteen years' experience; a person conceivably more useful than another aged sixty with only ten years' experience. This is no final argument for monarchy or aristocracy but it is the sort of argument which must at least be considered.

It would be absurd to predict now what the result would be of a vast project of research which has scarcely begun. One might, however, be excused for making a guess at what it will not produce. If the analogy of the physical sciences can be taken as a guide, we should not expect the result of this investigation to be either universal or final. The problems of administering areas of different size, shape, population and character are too diverse (one would imagine) to admit of the same answer being applicable to all. Nor should one expect to find an answer which would remain valid for more than twenty years. The error of the Utopians has been to imagine a final solution to a problem of which the factors are almost bound to change. The conclusions reached in the biological sciences (to which politics would seem most nearly comparable) seldom have any such petrified permanence. Not only do the facts change but other facts are brought to light by further study. On the one hand, a further and rapid change in the expectation of human life might affect all our conclusions concerning the age at which an officer of high rank should retire. On the other hand, a new treatise by a brilliant psychologist might show that our previous beliefs on that subject had, in any case, been completely wrong. When political science takes its place among the other sciences its progress should presumably resemble theirs.

Wrote Thomas Hobbes on this subject:—

> The skill of making and maintaining Commonwealths, consisteth in certain Rules, as doth Arithmetique and Geometry; not (as Tennis-play) on Practise onely: which Rules, neither poor men have the leisure, nor men that have had the leisure, have hitherto had the curiosity, or the method to find out.[1]

Hobbes was enough of a scientist to be able to indicate the two essentials to progress: curiosity and method. We may hardly suppose that the results of further research will reveal rules as precise as those of arithmetique or geometry. We may no longer believe that the rules, when found, will be as immutable as those mathematical rules in which Hobbes believed. But we may still be assured that the principles we seek, which we know to be neither universal nor eternal, will never be discovered except by scientific means. When found, our rules will have only a restricted validity. But without curiosity, without method, they will never be found at all.

[1] Hobbes. *op. cit.* p. 110.

INDEX

320.9
P   Parkinson, Cyril

The evolution of political
thought